THE CECIL KING DIARY
1970-1974

by the same author

WITH MALICE TOWARD NONE

STRICTLY PERSONAL

WITHOUT FEAR OR FAVOUR

THE CECIL KING DIARY 1965–1970

THE
CECIL KING
DIARY

1970-1974

JONATHAN CAPE
THIRTY BEDFORD SQUARE LONDON

FIRST PUBLISHED 1975
© 1975 BY CECIL KING

JONATHAN CAPE LTD
30 BEDFORD SQUARE, LONDON WCI

ISBN 0 224 01166 9

920
C34928
20·10·75

PRINTED AND BOUND IN GREAT BRITAIN
BY COX & WYMAN LTD, LONDON, FAKENHAM AND READING

CONTENTS

ACKNOWLEDGMENT

I should like to thank the publisher's researcher for providing background notes to each year and the footnotes.

INTRODUCTION

In my last diary a few entries were left out, but only one sentence was altered. This was the very last one in the book: 'I hope Heath will be a success and I have no idea what will happen if he fails.' Actually I had written 'when he fails', but I thought it unkind to a friend to be quite so discouraging so early in his Ministry.

Edward Heath is a friend whom I regard with affection and respect. I have never found him the cold, unresponsive fish described in the newspapers. He is able, intelligent, honourable and immensely hard-working. His misfortune is that he has taken up a career for which he is entirely unfitted. His opponents and some senior civil servants have told me that he would make a great civil servant. As Prime Minister he has two fatal defects—he has no political antennae, and he likes to be surrounded in his Cabinet by his friends rather than by the ablest members of his Party. The result was a very weak Cabinet and a Prime Minister out of touch with the voter and even with the members of his own Parliamentary Party. The obvious comment on this judgment is why, then, did he become the Tory Party Leader and eventually Prime Minister? The answer lies in the House of Commons, which in this century has promoted to 10 Downing St a motley assortment of politicians, few of them with any talent for national leadership. Presumably they performed in the House in a way acceptable to M.P.s, if not to anyone else.

And of course politicians commenting on elections tend to take the view that they won an election, which gave their Party a mandate to carry out the policy laid down in its manifesto. This is a flattering view which does not coincide with reality. Mr Wilson did not win the election of 1964 nor did Mr Heath win that of 1970. The result of 1964 reflected a rejection of the Tories who had enjoyed thirteen years of lack-lustre rule. The election of 1970 marked the rejection of Mr Wilson. The two elections of 1974 were rejections of Mr Heath. Had he realized this, Mr Heath would have resigned the leadership in February last year. Even if you give him the benefit of that doubt, he should certainly have resigned in October. His closest political friends urged him to do so. I wrote to him myself to the

9

same effect. I had a friendly reply but he stayed on, only to be rejected in February—and in the outcome not only was he rejected, but his closest colleagues, Jim Prior and Willie Whitelaw, were rejected too. We now have Mrs Thatcher, who has been chosen because, when no one else would stand against Mr Heath, she had the courage to do so. As Leader of the Tory Party she is a wholly unknown quantity, but she has intelligence and courage and is a much nicer person than the political commentators make out.

During the years covered by this book I was particularly concerned with Northern Irish affairs. In the nature of things much of my experience in this field has had to be omitted, but my acquaintance with all the principal parties involved has convinced me that a peaceful outcome from all the miseries of the past six years will only be possible when the solution is left to Irishmen without the ill-informed meddling of politicians in London. Dr Paisley is not a devil in human form; the I.R.A. are not just a band of murderous thugs; and a policy built on Mr Brian Faulkner and the S.D.L.P. never had a chance of getting off the ground.

1970

On Thursday, June 18th, 1970—three days before this volume of Cecil King's diary opens—a Conservative Government under Edward Heath was returned to power in Britain, after nearly six years of Labour rule and in defiance of the forecasts of most opinion polls. The internal difficulties which beset Britain were not altered by the change in administration, however. Inflation and industrial relations continued to dominate the domestic scene, while clashes between Protestants and Catholics continued in Northern Ireland—a mild foretaste of the violence that would eventually grip the Province. The new Prime Minister's attempts to grapple with these problems while changing the structure and style of Government were the main internal preoccupations of the latter half of 1970 and the beginning of 1971. Cecil King became 70 in February 1971. No longer holding any public position either as chairman of the International Publishing Corporation or as a director of the Bank of England, he observed these attempts without enthusiasm. In spite of his disenchantment with Harold Wilson and the previous Labour Government, he was not unduly impressed by either the composition or the apparent competence of the new Cabinet.

Externally, apart from widespread violence—wars in Vietnam and the Middle East, dramatic hijackings of commercial aircraft, tidal waves, floods and earthquakes from Pakistan to Peru--the most important development was the commencement of negotiations at the end of June 1970 for the enlargement of the European Economic Community by the additon of Britain, Denmark, Ireland and Norway. General de Gaulle, a leading opponent of British entry, who had retired from office a year before, died in November.

These negotiations concerning entry to the E.E.C.—the Common Market—provided a main theme of internal British politics during the whole of 1971, and culminated in Parliamentary acceptance of the proposed terms of entry in October and the signing of the Treaty of Accession in January 1972. The twin problems of inflation and unemployment continued throughout 1971, and the strife in Northern Ireland escalated to near civil war.

In the wider world the main events of 1971, though they impinged hardly at all on Britain's domestic affairs, were the vote in the United Nations to admit the People's Republic of China, the changing relationship between the United States and the Republic of China (dramatically symbolized by President Nixon's announcement of his intention to visit China in 1972), drifts and delays which brought the Middle East chaos no nearer to solution, and the final victory of India in a briefly-renewed Indo-Pakistan war.

Sunday, June 21st, 1970

The members of Heath's Cabinet were announced last night. The appointments have filled me with alarm and despondency. The membership suggests that Heath is mainly concerned, (a) with entering the Common Market, and (b) with containing Powell. But his most important and immediate problem is labour relations and the trades unions. If this view is accepted, then Carr at the Ministry of Labour, Maudling at the Home Office, and Carrington at Defence are a hopelessly weak team. Maudling is both idle and weak and appears to be a gesture to show that Powell does not represent Tory policy. I think Iain Macleod at the Treasury is all right if his health will stand it. A.B. [a senior civil servant] when he lunched with me last, said Macleod would not last more than two months at the Treasury before his health gave way. He is obviously a sick man, but one can recall the prophecies on L.B.J. and on George Brown, to both of whom office seemed to act as a kind of occupational therapy.

Wednesday, June 24th, 1970

Yesterday I called on Denis Hamilton, as Thomson has been telling all and sundry he is going to close down *The Times* if present losses continue. I am certain to be asked by Gavin Astor what I think of it all, so I thought I had better say my piece to Denis first. He spoke of nothing but cuts in expenditure, increased cover price, higher advertisement revenue. I, on the other hand, had come to say how bad the paper is, and particularly the Business Section. It was a very friendly meeting but I don't think my points really sank in. One of his difficulties is that the finding of the Monopolies Commission, which allowed the Thomson takeover, was that the editors of *The Times* and *Sunday Times* must have complete editorial independence. This apparently means that the two editorial staffs must be kept independent, which necessarily means duplication and unnecessary expense.

He had recently had Barnes, Ministry of Labour, to lunch who said there would be a full-scale dock strike a fortnight from now, and that the Transport and General Workers Union were hoping to shut down Heathrow at the same time. If this is what happens, it means the big unions are declaring open war on the new Government, while Heath is pursuing a feeble policy of appeasement. I dare say the strike would have been called against the Labour Government if Wilson had won, but mid-July gives Heath no chance of organizing his forces, even if he had shown signs of wanting to do so. The Labour Government would have just had to give in.

A lot of new appointments were announced last night—one good one, David Eccles as Minister responsible for the Arts. The others seem bad whether of people one knows or of unknown characters who have so far made no mark. Lady Tweedsmuir is fished out of obscurity for the second job at the Scottish Office: Amery, a nasty little man, and a very bad former Minister of Aviation, is in charge of Buildings and Works; Balniel, a pleasant nonentity, will answer for Defence in the House of Commons; the two Ministers of State in the Home Office are Sharples, a former Junior Minister, and Lord Windlesham from the Conservative Party organization. This seems like very feeble backing for the weak Maudling.

In the past Whitelaw assured me that it had been definitely decided that outsiders would be brought into the Government. I understood this to mean that two or three non-politicians would be brought into the Cabinet. It now seems that all that is to happen is that a dozen or so men from industry are to be lent to the Civil Service for three years!

Saturday, June 27th, 1970

On Thursday I had lunch with Noel Annan at University College. As Eccles is to be a Minister he can no longer be chairman of the British Museum Trustees. I asked who would succeed. Noel said probably Humphrey Trevelyan, or possibly Lennox-Boyd. He is a Trustee himself but does not regard himself as in the running, and also thinks it unlikely he will be kept on as chairman of the new inquiry into television and broadcasting generally. Noel said he found Eccles one of the ablest men he had met. I agreed and asked why the Tories so constantly denigrated him. Noel gave various reasons: (1) he is outstandingly able, (2) he knows it and is inclined to boast, and (3) he bullies his subordinates. The latter is why when I spoke up for Eccles to Wolfenden (the director of the Museum) Wolfenden was very obviously in disagreement.

In the evening Peter McLachlan came to supper. He has a temporary job at the Conservative Party Central Office to keep an eye on Ulster, whence he comes. He thought Bernadette Devlin had won in a very high poll because at the last moment the Catholic authorities decided she should be supported in spite of her anti-Catholic bias.* He said both sides are very heavily armed, and that if the British troops were withdrawn the whole of Ulster would explode. He found it difficult to get his Tory employers to take Paisley seriously. Peter himself thought Paisley a brilliant politician and a most dangerous element in the political world of Northern Ireland. He thought Chichester-Clark had improved as Prime Minister. He is very isolated and may well not be able to keep his job, but he is making a better attempt than seemed likely when he first took over.† There is no solution of the present situation: all that can be attempted is an endeavour to keep the temperature as low as circumstances permit.

Sunday, June 28th, 1970

Dinner last night with the Maurice Parsons—both so very nice. Maurice had little news: expressed his respect for Roy Jenkins but lack of same for Jim Callaghan; does not know Macleod at all. He plans to ask for an interview with him, or Heath, or Maudling, to try and bring home to the Government that the wage explosion will damage our balance of payments position; that to devalue again might destroy sterling as a trading currency, and that we are in no position to trade in any other currency.

One of the other guests was Creswell, former Ambassador to the Argentine. He was very bitter indeed about the damage done to the country's standing abroad, and to the morale of the service, by the impossible behaviour of George Brown.

The news from Belfast this morning is the worst yet—at least three killed in the shooting. The Ulster problem seems insoluble at the moment. The time when something might have been done was just frittered away. Now there is no time, no good-will and no personality to act as an acceptable mediator.

* Miss Bernadette Devlin had originally been elected to Parliament at a by-election in April 1969, standing as an independent candidate while a 21-year-old student. She was re-elected in 1970. She was in favour of left-wing and republican solutions to the Irish problem.

† Major Chichester-Clark, the Ulster Premier, was committed only to a modest programme of reform which was to prove insufficient and ineffective.

Monday, June 29th, 1970

Lunch with Rupert Murdoch. He had no political news, but was full of gossip about Fleet Street and the recent strike. Robens was approached to take over the chairmanship of the N.P.A.* The terms he required were £25,000 a year for five years, a flat in town, a chauffeur-driven car and generous pension provision—total cost to the N.P.A. about £40,000 a year. However, it was not the cost that scuppered the deal: at the last moment, Esmond Rothermere and Michael Berry discovered it was wrong to have a socialist politician in the N.P.A. chair so they now have Goodman, who of recent years has been far closer to Labour than Robens. Don Ryder, having kept aloof from N.P.A. affairs until the last hours of the strike, is now trying to run the N.P.A. as well as everything else. I.P.C.† is apparently short of cash as it is planning to lay out £5 or £6 million in redundancy payments, but hopes to rid itself of the London printing plants and the *Mirror* coloured supplement. Ryder is trying to sell almost anything except the *Mirror*, and perhaps the trade and technical papers, to raise the money. The *Express* is short of money and so, apparently, is Thomson; but Rupert does not see how the *Telegraph* can be short. The recent strike was engineered by Briginshaw, general secretary of NATSOPA,‡ to out-bid his militants, but the agreement is not a generous one by current standards, is not likely to be endorsed by the ballot at present being conducted, and Briginshaw's future is uncertain.

The news from Ulster is bad, and it looks as if Lynch in Dublin and Chichester-Clark in Stormont will find their position untenable. More troops are being poured into Ulster, but they cannot solve anything. It now appears that the I.R.A. is active, which was not true in the riots a year ago.

There has been some talk of Barbara Castle standing for the deputy leadership of the P.L.P.§ Wilson assured Rupert that if she did so, she would not get more than twenty votes.

Thursday, July 2nd, 1970

The Weinstocks to dinner last night. He told me that Les Cannon, reputedly the ablest of all the union leaders, has had a lung removed

* Newspaper Publishers' Association.
† International Publishing Corporation.
‡ National Society of Operative Printers and Assistants.
§ Parliamentary Labour Party.

for cancer. This is likely to mean before long a battle for succession at the E.T.U., with the Communists making a determined bid.*

Maudling has been in Ulster, and on his departure made soothing noises and declared Government policy to be the same as Labour's— no alteration in the constitution unless the majority wish. Weinstock was very clear that no forthright measures against strikers or others is to be expected from the present Government, or anything like it. Meanwhile both Scanlon and Jack Jones have made statements warning the Government against taking any steps to weaken the power of the unions. Weinstock regards Jack Jones as a respectable revolutionary: Clive Jenkins as a man with no respect from the trades union movement.

Tuesday, July 7th, 1970

Lunch yesterday with Eric Roll—just back from Paris and off to Vienna. He is a keen European and was interested in the latest developments on the Common Market. Did Wilson deliberately omit to instruct the public on the subject? I thought probably not. It would never occur to him to do anything so constructive. The argument has been used that the Six must be helpful to us, otherwise Her Majesty's Government would be unable to carry the British public with them. This argument will do for Greeks or Portuguese but is not one we have had to descend to so far. Eric thought the strongest argument in our favour would be to show how strong we are and how much we have to offer.

Wednesday, July 8th, 1970

Yesterday I paid a call on Rees-Mogg to see if he was still interested in contributions from me. It seems he is. From that we went on to other matters. I don't know what it is about these Establishment figures; it seems impossible to get through to them. We talked about Ireland, and particularly about labour relations and the wage explosion. One cannot get beyond a feeling that they think it will all come right on the night. He applauded the appointment of Maudling as Home Secretary—conciliatory, shrewd, good judgment, good experience. But in the actual situation in Belfast, and with the possibility of a general strike, is he the man to be in charge of the police? The

* The Electrical Trades Union had a long history of communist infiltration; at one time it had been the subject of an inquiry, following suspicions of left-wing election-rigging.

answer to this is that we must not yet give up hope that conciliation will work. On the subject of *The Times* itself, he was far more optimistic than Denis Hamilton. He took completely seriously the plan of the *Guardian* to print only in London, and assumed that that would be its end. In talking about this possibility, he suggested that *The Times* had greater scope in policy whilst the *Guardian* is in being. If the *Guardian* went, *The Times*, like the B.B.C., would have to give both sides of every issue. This was to me an entirely new idea on newspaper politics—and quite absurd.

Friday, July 10th, 1970

Lunch with John Stevens, just back from the U.S. He said Leslie O'Brien told the Court* yesterday that Macleod had told him our financial position was worse than he had expected. For various reasons—notably the strength of the deutschmark—money has been pouring out of the country in some quantity. Imports are up—mainly because of restocking rather than rising consumption: exports are tending to fall off. At the moment higher wages are not leading to greater spending. Short-term money is pretty plentiful, with interest rates tending to fall; long-term interest rates are high and rising and investors, even at current figures, are holding off. The Pilkingtons† want a public quote but it would be impossible to get an issue underwritten. It was expected too that prices would rise sharply after June and the balance of payments would deteriorate, causing anxiety in the second quarter of next year, but this is all happening rather sooner. The general shape of things would seem to indicate a world slump next year. No one knows what to do in a world of booming wages, rising unemployment, low profits and a grave lack of liquidity. A partial answer, it seems to me, would be to get some order into wage rates with no increases except with Government consent.

Outside New York and Washington, Stevens said the opinion among the people he met is that Nixon is doing well in South-East Asia, and that he will get them out of Vietnam with honour. If he

* The Board of Directors of the Bank of England is known as the Court. Cecil King had been a member of the Court until May 1968, when he resigned before publishing a leading article in his newspaper, the *Daily Mirror*, attacking the Labour Administration and commenting on the state of Bank of England reserves.

† Pilkington Brothers Limited was a large international enterprise, mainly concerned with the manufacture of glass and allied products. It was founded in 1894, but did not become a public company until November 1970.

can do this—and they think he can—then he should also be able to handle the Middle East and inflation. I must say I incline to the view in *Newsweek* this week that he has only succeeded in extending the war into Cambodia, Laos and probably Thailand; that in Hanoi he was opposed by the Russians but in Cambodia, particularly, he is up against the Chinese. While the Russians might be prepared to talk peace at the present time, the Chinese certainly are not.

Roy Jenkins had asked O'Brien to stay on another two years after the end of his term of office (next year). This surely must mean that Roy was utterly certain of a continuation of the Labour Government. This offer would not bind Macleod, and I should think it unlikely he would want O'Brien to continue. Meanwhile Macleod has had an emergency operation for alleged appendicitis. This seems to confirm what A.B. said to me.

Tuesday, July 14th, 1970

Lunch for William Whitelaw, now Lord President of the Council. I asked him if he had thought his Party would win. He said that up to the Saturday, five days before the election, he was certain the Conservatives would lose—perhaps by a big majority. In his own constituency he knew his majority would be up and that the Liberals would be down and out, but that this might be exceptional and for his area only. But on the Monday, with the publication of the trade figures, he became more optimistic, and from then on thought his Party had a chance. He said Ted Heath was magnificent throughout, giving an appearance of confidence which he by no means felt.

I said that I thought the Cabinet appointments indicated that Ted regarded Europe as his first priority, and the containment of Powell as his second. Against the opposition of Powell and Wilson I doubted the Government's ability to get into Europe; and I thought that Powell could not be contained—except by events. Whitelaw said the opposition of Michael Foot to the Common Market would be serious in Parliamentary terms. I said the wise course was not to make too much of the approach to the Common Market, so that it could be called off without too much damage. He wondered what line Wilson would take. I said that, inevitably, he would be in favour in principle while condemning any possible terms. Whitelaw said that if Wilson did that, he could certainly block any possible agreement.

I said I thought Paisley a formidable factor in the Irish situation.

He is not the provincial clown he appears to be to some people. Ted's idea that he will be worn down by the House is quite unrealistic. He will only turn up when it suits his own purposes. Whitelaw said how true this was. He had bellowed his maiden speech to a startled House. The speech had no kind of relevance to the debate, and was probably identical with the speech he made the week before in Ballybunion (if there is such a place). Nevertheless, reported in the Ulster papers, it will be very relevant. Having made his speech Paisley walked straight out of the chamber, hailed a taxi, and was off to London Airport and a plane back to Belfast. He had no intention of waiting to hear the rest of the debate. I gathered the Government has no more idea than I have of what to do about Ulster. They cannot keep the troops there indefinitely, and feel committed by every P.M. since the War, who all said the border is inviolable.

The threatened dock strike was called off last night with a big climb down by Jack Jones. If the strike had happened, the Government were prepared to call for emergency powers this morning and to fight it out. They realize that their biggest problem is inflation, wage explosion and all that, and that any legislation on the subject must be passed in their first twelve months. I expressed doubts whether (if you were prepared to go to a general strike and beyond) Carr at Labour, Maudling at the Home Office and Carrington at Defence, were the best trio to cope. Whitelaw's argument was that Carr is better than I was told; that Carrington is a brave man and probably could be tough; and that anyway isn't it wise to start by being conciliatory and toughen up later if it proves necessary?

I said the Labour leaders regard Mrs Thatcher as the ablest woman in the House. He expressed some surprise and mild disagreement. Whitelaw says she is able, and good in the House, but in her dealings with people she is apt to lecture and to bulldoze her way, when more conciliatory methods would be more successful. In this connection he did not think much of her opening moves with the N.U.T.*

Like the Labour leaders in their day, the Tories are obviously primarily pleased to be in office—the quite appalling problems confronting this country and the world have really made little impact. Ted has acquired self-confidence; is a much abler manager

* National Union of Teachers.

than Wilson; and all will be well. I don't think the team is strong enough, and the Tory honeymoon will be short. They will be up to their necks in trouble by this time next year.

Two further points—the monthly trade balance is the worst for sixteen months, £51 million down. Whitelaw commented on the fact that the Stormont Ministers were inflexible in their determination to maintain the status quo without modification.

Whitelaw said that Wilson's appointment of Greenwood as the new chairman of the Commonwealth Development Corporation on the same day as he announced the election, could only have been from the certain knowledge that he would win the election. The fuss now being made by Labour M.P.s over the cancellation of the appointment is quite ridiculous. Wilson appears to have resented the fact that Heath is not taking over his Principal Private Secretary. So much so, that the man in question has issued a statement protesting that there is nothing abnormal in the new arrangements. Trevor Lloyd-Hughes was made an Under-Secretary at £8,500 a year in charge of the co-ordination of information services. In fact he and his staff had little to do and the whole department has been abolished. Trevor Lloyd-Hughes was the worst Downing Street Press Officer that I've known of, but apparently his flattery was necessary to Wilson.

Wednesday, July 15th, 1970
Lunch for Hugh Fraser—not very informative. He said the new name for Eccles is 'Arty-boots'. It used to be 'Smarty-boots' but now he is the Minister responsible for the Arts! To begin with, Fraser said the situation in the Middle East reminded him of 1914; the labour situation here, of 1926; and the financial situation in America, of 1929. And yet he criticized me for being gloomy! This has been a frequent experience of mine in the course of my life, but events have generally showed that I was being too optimistic, not the reverse. Fraser thought well of Ted's team, and took the typical House of Commons' view that Ted had won a notable electoral victory, and had a Cabinet almost entirely composed of his men, so he was in a very strong position. As a contrast he also thought that a real trial of strength with the trade unions could only be undertaken by a national government. The strength of a Prime Minister ultimately depends on his success in tackling the problems of his day—not in having many stooges in his Cabinet. The more

23

numerous the stooges the less effective the Government and, over a period, the weaker the Prime Minister.

The dock strike, having been arrested by Jack Jones inviting his men to accept the employers' offer and go back to work, has been decided on by the delegates from the ports. The majority was substantial but not very large and we shall now see what the Government's determination amounts to.

Thursday, July 16th, 1970

Lunch with Paul Hamlyn. Very recently he had dinner with Rupert Murdoch—other guests were Lord Sainsbury, George Wigg and Harold Wilson. It was a long dinner ending at 2.30 a.m., at which Wilson drank a lot, mainly brandy. Wigg also had a few and attacked the Prime Minister for mistiming the election. Wilson apparently was rather subdued, but held forth at length about his old father who, like Wilson himself, has a marvellous memory. Wilson told Paul that he could always drop off to sleep at will, and that during his time as P.M., even at the height of the Rhodesian crisis, he had not missed any sleep. He had only had recourse to sleeping pills since the election. It was interesting that he should refer to the Rhodesian negotiations as the most testing period of his Prime Ministership.

Paul thought Don Ryder had been planning the Reed take-over of I.P.C. for some months. Frank Rogers had had visions of himself as a great newspaper operator, and Hugh Cudlipp as chairman had been merely futile, unable to come to a decision on anything. Paul thought Ryder would sell the book division and some magazines, as well as the freeholds and the trade investments. All decisions are made by Ryder personally and appointments to see him are subject to a delay of six weeks! Obviously this set-up will not work. Rogers was a disappointment. He is now actively seeking a job.

Wilson, on losing office, is not very flush and cannot employ a chauffeur so he is relearning to drive—as he told Paul.

Tuesday, July 21st, 1970

A real shock this morning—the death of Iain Macleod. So the prophecy of A.B., when he lunched with me last, that Macleod's health was so poor he would not last more than two months at the Exchequer, is borne out. Though in my opinion not a great administrator, he was a wonderful debater, a clear speaker, and an intelligent man in a Government of mediocrities. He will be sadly missed as a member of the Government. As Chancellor, I suppose he will be succeeded by either Maudling or Rippon, preferably the latter.

Lunch for Edwin Plowden (chairman of Tube Investments Ltd). In good form but no particular news. He had lunch alone with Heath in January but finds, as others do, that you do not get any nearer the essential Heath. He thinks him an honest man, brave and able, but with no gift for swaying the populace. He knows Carr rather well and hears on all hands that he has done well so far. Vic Feather, who loathes Barbara Castle, is relieved by the change.

Plowden does not think there are any preparations in existence for a general strike—arrangements for the distribution of food for instance. Such a challenge would have to be met with authoritarian measures, and it does not seem that these are being contemplated at the present time. Plowden says we are moving towards an authoritarian regime, presumably of the Right. In the recent past people moved away if he propounded this opinion. Now they agree. He did not think we should succeed in joining the Common Market, unless the Americans pulled out of Europe and we were called in to take part in Europe's defence.

He had called in his personnel people to have lunch with Carr, and to explain that the Tory plan for reformation of the trade unions would not work. Carr's response was that other people had told him differently. Plowden thought that it was Alec Douglas-Home who had so precipitately taken up the question of arms for South Africa. It was surely an unnecessary row to start at the present time. Evidently the hullabaloo has caused the Government to have second thoughts, as the statement by Home yesterday was far more tentative than had been expected.

I have just come upon a note of some slogans from our trip to Nigeria in January—a bus labelled 'Jesus Only'; a bus that had run off the road and into a wall had 'God is our leader' as its motto; '"God is able" cushions and covers here'; 'Slow and steady', another bus motto; 'Jesus no tumble': Eatem Poultry Farm!

Friday, July 24th, 1970

The Tvarohs to dinner last night. He has been Washington correspondent of *Rude Pravo* and has been recalled. He assumes he will lose his job and his party ticket as he was a Dubček man. He surprised me by saying that neither he nor any of the Dubček faction thought a Russian invasion conceivable. They realized they would not be allowed to leave the Warsaw Pact and had no intention of doing so. It seems that even intelligent Communists like Tvaroh believed all the Communist nonsense about concern for the welfare of the toiling masses, and disregarded the evidence of common or garden imperialism when it was Russian.

Monday, July 27th, 1970

Dick Marsh for lunch. He was in a rather bloody-minded mood. He has evidently not recovered from his expulsion from office. Anyway, he can see no good in the political scene, but also sees no reason why it should change. Of current political figures he thought Carr might be a success; Barber, the new Chancellor, he considers is nothing but a nice chap; Heath, he thinks the most colourless figure ever to rise to the top in British politics.

He was talking within the last week to two trades union figures, one of them prominent on the docks side of the Transport and General Workers Union. He said that like other trades union leaders, they have little idea of what they are doing to the country's economy. Their attitude is weak towards their members and irresponsible towards the country. Marsh thinks the trades unions are even more powerful than the Government, but does not see what any Government can do about it. We shall have to wait until the big unions throw up two or three powerful responsible leaders.

Six weeks ago Marsh was in Israel on a sponsored visit. He had two long talks with the top officials of the Foreign Ministry. They clearly could only see a real settlement if the two Great Powers were prepared to dictate one. Of this at present there is no sign. So what they are hoping to develop is a confrontation, with clearly understood but unwritten rules, that will prevent them from being in action against Russian personnel. On this they want guidance from their Western friends—guidance which they are not getting. It was explained to Marsh that he could pass on what he had been told, and that if he wished to pursue any matter further, Israeli civil servants would be available. But he must realize that any meetings might have to be repudiated by the Israeli Government.

On getting home he wrote a seven-page letter to one Tripp, head of the Middle-Eastern section of the Foreign Office, whom he had seen before setting out. In this letter he recounted what had been said, by whom, when and where. The letter was sent round by hand, but has not so far elicited even an acknowledgment.

Evidently Alec Home had no idea his plan of arms for South Africa would cause such a furore—including severe letters from Trudeau of Canada, and Mrs Gandhi. He has had to defer any decision, but meanwhile has lost much face with his colleagues and with the officials at the Foreign Office.

Wednesday, July 29th, 1970

Lunch yesterday for Geoffrey Rippon. It appeared during the lunch, and was officially announced later, that he is to take Barber's place as Common Market negotiator. I told him I thought this was to misuse his talents: Heath had only two first-class men—himself and Whitelaw; that they were not being deployed to the best advantage; and that anyway, in the teeth of opposition from Wilson, Powell and Michael Foot, it would almost certainly prove impossible to get in. Rippon said if we don't succeed this time we shall never join. I don't agree on this, as I think the logic of events is bound to bring us together in the end, however remote that end may be. Rippon is growing in weight and authority, but is no politician. He is the best administrator the Tories have at the top, and Technology is just up his street—if he could be spared from some more important post. I said I thought the Ministry of Technology far too big a job for any one man. Rippon said, not really, as he delegated. For instance he made over Fuel and Power to John Eden, one of his Ministers of State. Eden is nephew of Anthony, and has been an M.P. since 1954, during which period he has made no impact on anyone. The idea of giving him any responsibility for Fuel and Power is quite frightening. Rippon's other Minister of State is Eric Bessborough, who presumably also has an important sphere of interest. He was a director of A.T.V.,* so I knew him quite well at that time—a pleasant nonentity.

One cannot expect a Minister to criticize the P.M.—particularly so soon after a successful election. But Rippon was not particularly ready to defend Heath and made no attempt to defend the appointment of Barber to the Treasury. Rippon's attitude in general was the usual one among politicians. Everything will remain as it is for ever and ever, amen. I got the impression that the new Ministers

* Associated Television Corporation.

27

feel they were left a worse mess than they realized, and Rippon said he wondered what on earth Wilson would have done if he had won.

He is M.P. for Hexham, and they have a Bishop who was formerly Bishop of the Gilbert and Ellice Islands, and treats his parishioners, including Rippon, as if they were Gilbert Islanders. He is apt to read out the number of a hymn and say, 'Now don't mumble; but there is no necessity to shout'!

In the evening it was announced that John Davies, formerly head of the C.B.I.,* is to be the new Minister of Technology. I should guess that this is the outcome of the agitation to bring in people from outside. There is this to be said about Davies, that he is familiar with industry because he was managing director of Shell-B.P. On the other side, I would say that M.P.s will resent his leaping into the Cabinet after only six weeks as an M.P.; that industrialists will think he has been promoted well above his ceiling; and that the Left will regard this as proof that the Government is in the hands of the employers. Outside the House he will make a better impression than the Barbers, Walkers, Carrs, etc.: inside the House he will be much worse, and anyway he is a sad come-down from Rippon, transferred to what looks to me like a dead end.

Lunch today for my son Colin. He told me that he had lunched yesterday at Reeds. Their guest was Campbell Adamson, director-general of the C.B.I., who told them that Rippon had refused the job of negotiating our way into Europe. John Davies was to get the Technology job, but only after a year's apprenticeship. This is not how things turned out but is probably an accurate account of the situation a few days ago.

Friday, July 31st, 1970

I was giving lunch to Douglas Houghton at Claridge's. While waiting for him to arrive I had some talk with Norman Collins. He said, in the course of our conversation, that Crossman's mention of George Brown's peerage in today's *New Statesman* was done out of malice—in the hope that the premature disclosure would at least postpone the honour. Crossman is doubtless capable of such a manoeuvre but I wonder if his dislike of George Brown would carry him to such lengths. Norman's second item, on which he spoke with authority as if he knew it as a fact, was that Heath had wanted to

* The Confederation of British Industry, the leading British management organization; almost the 'management' equivalent of the Trades Union Congress (T.U.C.).

take on the Exchequer as well as the Prime Ministership. He was not allowed by his colleagues to do this, so he put in Barber as a sort of P.A. to bear the title, while he ran the department. This is of course a nonsense. Both jobs are at least full-time. To try and do both means that neither is done adequately.

Douglas in excellent form—thinks that Labour's defeat did no harm unless Heath is a failure. This would call in question the future of Parliamentary Government. He won his seat by a narrow margin—about 450 votes—and at one time thought he was losing, so he was up all night before taking the train from Wakefield to London. When he reached London he had an urgent call to 10 Downing St. They had all had a bad night, but even so Wilson wanted to discuss the election of Leader of the Parliamentary Labour Party with Douglas. He was most anxious to head off the nomination of any rival. He only had with him Mary and Marcia. Actually, it was unlikely any rival would be named, but Wilson wanted to be sure.

Douglas referred to Alec Home's speech about arms for South Africa. It was apparently a disaster: (a) he had obviously given the whole matter inadequate thought; (b) he clearly had no idea he was stirring up an international political hornet's nest; and (c) he twice referred to Wilson as the Prime Minister. As a result of this performance everyone now knows that the Tories were right to discard Alec in favour of Ted. He also thought Alec now to be expendable.

He was glad Jennie Lee had lost her seat. This was partly because the character of the constituency had changed, but partly—or mainly—because her regal manner had put so many backs up.

Douglas is a convinced European, and does not think the Europeans in the P.L.P. and the Shadow Cabinet will allow Wilson to take a purely opportunist line. The trouble is that the agricultural policy of the Six is to bolster up French agriculture which is so grossly inefficient.

He thinks Carr did relatively well over the dock strike. The dockers seem to have got much less than they asked for, but they established a £20-a-week minimum. This will obviously be regarded as a goal throughout industry and will be seriously inflationary. Douglas, like everyone else, regards the Tory proposals for trades union reform as quite unworkable. He made a point that was new to me—that the tradition of conciliation in all its forms makes it difficult to challenge any strikers in a direct confrontation. For instance, the dockers are numerous and unpopular and their claim seemed a good one to stand on, but the Government is in no position to instruct the employers, who are not subject to Government orders. He regards wage explosion as a serious menace to the economy, though he said some people think it will just level out. This I regard as the merest wishful thinking.

Today I heard my old office building at Holborn Circus described as the Glass Menagerie!

Douglas is a member of the Royal Commission on the Constitution. Last week they had Terence O'Neill and MacDermott (Northern Ireland Chief Justice) to give evidence. O'Neill was very gloomy: MacDermott blamed the whole trouble on pressing ahead with liberal reforms too fast.

Douglas, like so many others, expresses a high opinion of Whitelaw.

Wednesday, August 5th, 1970

Lunch for Stonehouse, recently Postmaster-General and later Minister for Posts and Telecommunications. He says he is greatly relieved to be out of office, and is now occupying himself as an export consultant. He is just back from Toronto, where he was concerned with piping for oil and gas, and with computers.

He thinks Ted will play along with the unions for two and a half years, and then have an election which he will win. He does not think Wilson will ever again be Prime Minister, but he sees a political future for himself in eight years time. He has known Wilson for twelve years and says he has changed visibly for the worse in that time. He is now an arrogant man surrounded by a small clique, who only tell him what he wants to hear.

When he arrived at the Post Office he found that Benn had committed him to the Giro, to the two-tier postal system and to turning the Post Office into a Corporation. The Giro has lost a lot of money but might break even, or even make a profit on the present basis of accounting. But if the Giro had charged against it the net cost of the postal services on which it depends, then it could never possibly make a profit! There was never a ministerial discussion on this service, which was decided on by Benn and concurred in by Wilson. The two-tier postal system would have been a good idea if the upper tier were guaranteed delivery next day. This would have meant a charge of a shilling and all other letters would have taken their chance. The present two-tier system makes no sense. On the Corporation, he was urged by Wilson and Jenkins to appoint one of a number of party hacks whose names were submitted to him. In spite of some refusals he did find a good man, but this appointment was vetoed by Wilson as too Tory. The result is Lord Hall, regarded by Stonehouse as one of his mistakes.

I mentioned arms for South Africa and Alec Home's poor performance in the House. He said Alec was misled by the officials at the Foreign Office, who told him there would be no fuss. But Alec is supposed to be the politician, keeping his officials straight on the political aspects of policy. Stonehouse says the arms for South Africa negotiations will now have to be dropped, which will be a considerable rebuff for the Government in its very early days.

He thought the election was lost in the last few days, influenced by Enoch Powell, by the trade figures and by the doubts expressed late in the day by Heath on the strength of our balance of payments position.

He was very contemptuous of Parliamentary procedure. He said Ministers in practice have not got to bother about Parliamentary opinion, and that in no sense now is the House of Commons a watchdog keeping its eye on the Executive. Parliamentary question and answer he described as a farce.

Friday, August 7th, 1970

Lunch yesterday for Ralph Harris of the Institute of Economic Affairs. I asked him what ought to be done in our present economic plight? He said the Government should have acted quickly on taking office—something dramatic was necessary to create a new mood. He would raise the bank rate to 12 per cent, which at the present rate of inflation does not represent an unduly generous rate of interest. He was horrified recently at a lunch to hear Campbell Adamson and Don Ryder maintain the view that it was the Government's duty to bail out any substantial firm in difficulties. Harris thought the opposite—that it would have a salutary effect on employers and trades unions if some substantial firms were left to go bankrupt. He did not think Carr tough enough for the Ministry of Labour, and thought Davies at Technology would prove weak and inadequate—satisfactory to neither labour nor big industry. He had recently seen something of Lincoln Evans, now dead. Evans thought the trades unions would give way to any resolute Government. This may be true, but only after a trial of strength in which the unions clearly come off second best.

Ruth hears from her medical friends that Macleod died of cancer. He was operated on for suspected acute appendicitis, but proved to have cancer in an advanced state—his spine was already affected. Some work was done to ease his pain, but it was too late for any effective surgery and he was sewn up. He had no idea of his condition.

Saturday, August 8th, 1970

Last night we had to dinner Mr and Mrs Rohan. He is a Czech Jew, formerly head of Czech Television, but now doing a little journalistic work and some monitoring for the B.B.C. I asked him why Dubĉek had let liberalization go ahead to the point where it led to intervention by Russian troops. He said Dubĉek was no leader, and the liberalization in Prague got out of hand. He thought the Russians were less afraid of the Czechs defecting to the West than of the liberalization spreading to Moscow. He thought the Russians are really frightened of China.

Meanwhile, there is a cease-fire in the Middle East, and an anti-aggression pact between Germany and Russia. Rohan interpreted this to reflect a change in Russian policy—perhaps feeling that with Hanoi, Cairo and Eastern Europe they had too much on their plate. The German–Russian pact may mean very little or, on the other hand, might come to have sinister implications. The cease-fire in the Middle East, repudiated by the Palestinians, is, I should have thought, bound to break down.

Thursday, August 13th, 1970

Lunch yesterday with Kenneth Rose (Albany in the *Sunday Telegraph*). He had no great stock of news. He said he had recently had lunch with Harold Macmillan at Birch Grove as he is writing a book about the Cecil family, children of the Prime Minister, Lord Salisbury, and Macmillan knew some of them.* He said Macmillan was in crashing form and threw aside his normal pose of great age. Macmillan said the Cecils were really cockneys, and hated the countryside. Conversation at their dinner-table was highly intellectual, as it might have been at the table of the Medicis. The Devonshires were quite different. His father-in-law, the Duke, if asked a question at meals might well not answer but continue rinsing out his false teeth in his finger-bowl!

Rose is insinuating, and knows a great many people and would hear a vast amount of gossip. He said the present Government is a weak one: he was surprised at David Eccles' appointment. He said Macmillan would have made Eccles Chancellor of the Exchequer (a job Eccles dearly wanted) if it hadn't been for Eccles' appalling manner—conceited, arrogant and rude. This is not what I have experienced with Eccles, but I know he is violently unpopular in some quarters. Rose also said Gardiner was the worst Lord Chancellor for a long time—ineffective and partisan.

Wednesday, August 19th, 1970

Lunch for Fforde of the Bank. He is a shy, highly intelligent Irishman. He has been Chief Cashier and is now an executive director. I had had no proper talk with him for a long time. He confirmed that Heath had wanted to be Chancellor as well as P.M., and thought this would have been a better solution than the present one. Barber's name was not mentioned, so evidently he is not rated very high. Fforde had hoped for Keith Joseph. He said Roy Jenkins was a strong Chancellor. While he was at the Treasury everyone knew who was in charge. I said he was highly intelligent and charming, but surely weak. Fforde would only agree with this to the extent of saying that he was very cautious—far more concerned to make no mistakes than to do the right thing. Fforde thought Douglas Allen more intelligent than William Armstrong, and with a better grasp of national finance, but had no means of judging his quality in other fields. To me, to meet Allen does not lack intelligence but does lack personality and authority. He did not think well of John Davies's appointment, and gave me the impression that he is not alone in the official circle with this view.

Perhaps he was being cagey, but he offered no opinion on what should be done about the current wage inflation. He did not think it would level off and did think it would bring us back into balance of payments trouble by the middle of next year. The pound is at its lowest against the dollar for over a year, but this is not due to any significant amount of selling. Gilt-edged have been up and are now down—big swings within a very short time. Fforde said it was

33

agreed about two years ago that the Bank would not support the pound in the way it had been doing, but would let the interest rate find its own level. But this left the day-to-day position a bit indeterminate; and though the Bank made a market, it sometimes did not know in which direction the trend lay—hence the wide fluctuations.

I think he thought that inflation would accelerate and eventually make investors shy of buying long-term bonds even if the interest rate is very high. At the moment the confidence in fixed-interest-bearing securities is not what it was, but it has by no means disappeared.

On the general subject of wage inflation he had no particular views. He thought Carr's recent exhortations carried one back to the late 'fifties and are likely to have even less success. I thought it was clear from the way he spoke that the Government is not at the moment planning a blitz on the trades unions. Even if they were, Fforde thought it would be hard to find a clear issue that would have the support of the general public.

Beeching came to lunch yesterday. He had no news, but mourned that things get steadily worse. He felt that they could not go on like this much longer without a crisis, but then he had been thinking that for years!

To return to Fforde. I said, surely the pressure by *The Times* and others for an easing of the credit restrictions was misconceived. Such action could only lead to further inflation. Fforde said the effect of relaxation would be higher output and higher productivity. For the first six months it would probably not add significantly to the inflationary pressure. If one thinks, as some do, that inflation will level off of its own accord, then relaxation makes sense. If you think, as I do, that inflation will accelerate unless something is done about it, then any relaxation could only make matters worse.

Friday, August 21st, 1970

Lunch for Peter Carrington. He is the nicest man, and very shrewd in a quiet way. I asked him how Denis Healey looked in retrospect as Minister of Defence. He said that the service chiefs had lost their respect for him, and that he had altogether crushed Dunnett, the Permanent Under-Secretary. The Chiefs of Staff attended Defence Committee meetings but were not expected by Wilson to speak unless spoken to. They were never invited to give their opinions.

The service chiefs lost their respect when Healey reversed himself on the policy to be pursued East of Suez—this apparently within twenty-four hours. Doubtless the change of policy was imposed by the Cabinet, but at the Ministry he was the Cabinet's voice. It was interesting to hear from this very different source the same accusation of arrogance.

Evidently on Ireland there are no bright ideas, but Carrington is well aware that the troops' patience will soon be exhausted and they will become increasingly bloody-minded.

He had had lunch a few days ago with Dick Crossman, who told him that Harold Lever and Roy Jenkins would both rat on the Common Market. He thought Rippon a dull man, no negotiator, but an able administrator who would do the groundwork for the Common Market negotiations well.

I spoke about the wage inflation and the trades unions. He has certainly thought of a confrontation ending in a general strike. He says Carr is much tougher than he seems and he thinks will be a success as Minister of Labour. I got the impression that there were no plans, but that they realized how important it was to choose the right issue.

He put up no defence for Walker; thought Barber would make more impression inside the Treasury than outside; thought well of Balniel; but said the Government needed more 'fifteen-inch guns'. It was in this fact that lay the real loss of Macleod. They knew his health was bad but thought he would last a year. Carrington said he had been urging the inclusion of Soames in the Government, but they doubt if he would find a seat. He is arrogant and tactless, and they would look silly if they put him in the Cabinet and then couldn't find him a seat. We spoke of Ted and his lack of self-confidence. Carrington was confident (as I am not) that the Prime Ministership will cure this weakness. I spoke warmly of Whitelaw but got no response. He frankly admitted that Alec Home had made a boob over arms for South Africa.

Carrington is a fellow of Eton, so I asked him why Chenevix-Trench left. He said Trench was very good academically but that as headmaster he has to deal with twenty-five housemasters, 'mini-Napoleons' he called them; some of them very nasty people, he said. He failed to establish his authority over them, and by the end different houses were varying in their rules from rigid discipline to extreme permissiveness. His departure was necessary to prevent an explosion. Carrington thought he would do much better at Fettes, a much smaller school, to which he has gone.

Apparently at the *Daily Telegraph* dinner-party on election night, before we arrived, all the talk was of the constitution of the new Labour Government—who was going where!

During the election Carrington spoke only in marginal constituencies. In most cases they reported that the Conservatives were doing well and might indeed capture the seat. But Carrington, confident that Labour would win, had put this down to wishful thinking!

Tuesday, August 25th, 1970

Lunch yesterday with Alf Robens at the Coal Board. About the Bank of England he said only that it is more and more being run by the Treasury. Harry Pilkington is completely bewildered by events at Pilkington's, which he had supposed was one big happy family. Maurice Laing very unhappy about a bribery case in south London, in which his firm had done the bribing. He was so upset he made a personal statement to the court, though no one could suppose he is personally involved. The P.I.B.* has recommended that the Coal Board should centralize their organization. This seems to the Coal Board at Hobart House to be mere nonsense and a complete reversal of their policy for some years. The dockers have recently secured a £20-a-week minimum for not working, so naturally the miners are asking for a £20 minimum for working. Alf sees no way of contesting this claim. And this admission of comparability has spread up the social scale, so that heads of nationalized industries look to the salaries paid to the chairmen of big companies, and the Permanent Under-Secretaries look to both. Robens referred to the recent gaffe when the heads of nationalized industries got their second rise in a year in the very same week that the Government laid it down no one was to get two rises in the same year, and in any case this rise was brought forward from next April for no obvious purpose. The real reason was that the senior civil servants wanted their rise from January 1st because it helped their pension rights, and it was thought best to announce the nationalized industry chairmen's salaries at the same time and to operate from the same date.

I asked him what he thought of Carr—he said he seemed to be

* The Prices and Incomes Board, established by the Labour Government in the mid-1960s.

trying to follow in the footsteps of Ernie Bevin who, as Minister of Labour, sought to be the honest broker between the employers and the trades unions. He did not think the Government had got anywhere with its plans for trades union reform. In his opinion, the essential change would be to take away all legal privileges from unofficial strikers and to do something about the Government subsidies to strikers. At present the trades unions are being led from the rear, and responsible officials are forced to put forward wage claims they know are irresponsible.

He thinks Heath is a nice man and 'straight as a die' but that he lacks any outstanding gifts. He thinks Heath should have announced that his Ministers would not take holidays this year. Instead of this, the Government will have been at a standstill for the whole of August, with Heath spending a fortnight on his boat. He thinks the Home Office—with Labour—a key ministry and one in weak and easy-going hands.

I asked him if he meant to accept another term as chairman of the Coal Board. He said almost certainly not, but he would not say so until later, because immediately it was known he was leaving his authority would go. This is one of the reasons for not taking another five years. It would be obvious from the start that this was his last five years, and half-way through his authority would go and the industry would be looking to his successor.

Robens said Wilson's idea of bliss was to leave the chamber of the House of Commons with the cheers of his supporters ringing in his ears. For him that is what politics are all about.

Robens said John Davies is a good office man and would make a good Permanent Under-Secretary for the Ministry of Technology, but as Minister he would be a total failure in the House. Robens agreed with me that he has no authority with the big industrialists and is regarded by Labour as the stooge of the employers.

Thursday, August 27th, 1970
Lunch for A.B. [a senior civil servant]. He was more forthcoming than usual. He said that at the memorial service for Iain Macleod, the civil servants and ambassadors were on one side of the aisle and the politicians were on the other, so he had half an hour or so to study the faces of the Cabinet set out in a row opposite. He was not impressed. In particular, he said, John Davies looked completely out of his element—as if he had never before sat in a cathedral stall.

A.B. said the Government lacked weight—hence the importance in his eyes of bringing back Soames, who, with whatever faults, has real weight.

I asked him about the country's economic policy. What should we be doing? He said no one anywhere knows how to maintain steady economic growth. When politicians say this is their Party's policy, the statement is meaningless. He thought that to ease up on the present restrictive policy would merely speed up the present rate of inflation—lowering taxation would have the same effect. To maintain the present policy would lead to an increasing degree of unemployment, which is, however, negligible except in certain areas, He said the Government at the moment is making no plans for a blitz on the trades unions. Have they even the determination to maintain the present rate of unemployment?

I said I didn't think economic growth was a very glamorous idea. A.B. said that in October 1964 he was sitting up late alone with Wilson preparing the White Paper that included the import surcharge. The document included some reference to 'economic growth'. Wilson said he didn't like the word growth—people died of growths! Incidentally, A.B. said he did not go all the way with me in my jaundiced view of Wilson's integrity.

He did not seem to have heard that Heath's intent had been to be both P.M. and Chancellor on Macleod's death. He doubted if Barber would prove to be a mere stand-in. I said I thought Whitelaw was wasted as Leader of the House. A.B. disagreed, saying that in that job he was never far from Heath and had already exercised useful influence on him. He obviously thought very highly of Whitelaw. He thought nothing of Maurice Macmillan and did not believe we should get into the Common Market for some ten years.

A.B. commented on the fact that Jarratt, the youngest Under-Secretary is going to I.P.C. as managing director. He didn't try and dissuade Jarratt but doubted if he would be a success—hardly any civil servants in industry have made good. The sole exception, he thought, is Wilson-Smith, whom I knew at the Bank. He has no fire in his belly. A very drab performer, I should have thought.

A.B. thought our politics were clearly moving to the Right but he thought this move was slower than I appeared to think. Much, however, would depend on events in other countries.

I said I had been told by Tory leaders that Alec Home's gaffe over arms for South Africa was due to bad advice from his officials.

A.B. said, quite rightly, that officials are not there to give political advice. He said the matter arose from an unwise answer to a loaded question at a press conference. His opinion of Alec as a foreign affairs expert seemed to be a low one.

Wednesday, September 2nd, 1970

C.D. [a senior civil servant] for lunch—very friendly, and more communicative than sometimes. He asked how I thought the new Government was doing. I said, 'Disastrously.' He asked why I thought this was so. I said, Ted is neither a leader nor a politician, though an able man. C.D. agreed on the ability and evidently likes him. I said that, at a time like this and so soon after taking office, to leave the country without government for five weeks was a quite extraordinary error. How do you afterwards convince the public that our plight is a serious one? C.D. said Heath was extremely anxious to get away from the Wilsonian idea of instant government. I said it was surely a mistake to guide one's behaviour by taking the opposite course to one's predecessor. Wilson's '100 days' may have been a lot of nonsense; nevertheless, the first three months of a new regime are ones in which its prestige is at its highest, and Heath has frittered his 100 days away.

I told him that I had told Whitelaw in the spring that I thought the Conservatives would win the election, and that Heath would be a failure. In such an event would it not be a good idea to have an alternative leader, other than Enoch Powell? What about Whitelaw himself? C.D. (1) agreed in Whitelaw's ability, (2) seemed to think a reserve leader other than Enoch was a good idea, but (3) said that in such an event Reggie Maudling would regard the succession as his right. He thought well of Soames's ability and evidently felt that a return by Soames would strengthen the Cabinet. He spoke very highly of Peter Carrington, and said that behind his 'throwaway manner' he is shrewd and able. He asked my opinion of Walker. I said I had had him to lunch at the *Mirror*, and he only stuck in my memory because I disliked his aggressive manner.

He spoke of the Labour Government—said Roy Jenkins was 'so cold'. He agreed that Roy did want to be P.M.; Denis Healey probably genuinely did not. He doubted if Wilson would have another turn as P.M. Coming events were unlikely to be helpful to him. He thought Dick Marsh confident and able in his handling of people and situations. He knew what he wanted and how to achieve it. His departure he put down to an inclination to speak his mind when it would have been better for his career to dissemble. Stonehouse he thought a man of similar abilities, but not so confident nor so adroit.

We spoke about the wage explosion. He agreed that inflation as an international problem was worse than if we were the only victims. We had suffered from inflation since the War; and though no doubt it had led to some injustices, it was on the whole beneficial to the public and not yet intolerable to any group. Could we not just go on as we are? I said if the inflation and inflationary wage demands were kept to the 2 or 3 per cent of some years ago, this might be possible. But our own experience, and that of other countries, was that inflation proceeded at an accelerating rate getting more and more out of control. In the long run we either have to stop the wage explosion, or let it run and take the consequences of an uncontrollable inflation. He said any government's successful attempt to control wages must end in a control of all wages. I said this was indeed true, but would not be implemented in one move. Quite apart from the inflationary aspect of the wages explosion, society will not remain stable and coherent if unskilled labourers are allowed to earn more than the highly skilled professionals. Such an over-all control of incomes would only come as the result of an authoritative regime of some kind. But then we are moving in that direction anyway.

C.D. said I seemed to be looking for a quite different kind of politician than the ones we have. I said surely the attributes of statesmanship are foresight, political skill and administrative ability. Without these qualities a man was a mere politician with no claim to be a statesman. C.D. thought this was expecting Ministers to have far more foresight than they have. They are usually preoccupied with the immediate. How would one set about recruiting a different kind of politician? Obviously one would have to reform the procedure of the House of Commons so that really able people would wish to take part. Perhaps you would need two bodies, one on which to try things out—a representative body that would act as a kind of litmus paper to advise on what could be pursued and what could not; and another set of people who would be concerned with the actual government. Surely, I said, something must be done. The last really able Prime Minister was Gladstone—more than seventy years ago.

We talked about arms for South Africa. I asked if the matter could not be swept back under the rug, from which it should not have been allowed to emerge. He thought this impossible. If we go ahead, the Commonwealth will break up, but at issue is the naval defence of the Indian Ocean against the Russian navy. I said I thought the Commonwealth was an idea with no reality. There is a bond with the old English-speaking Dominions, but not really with the others. At the same time to break up the Commonwealth on the issue of arms for South Africa seems a most unfortunate way of setting about things.

Thursday, September 3rd, 1970

At the Russian Embassy this morning to meet the Kirov dancers. I had some talk with Canon Collins. He said that in December 1964 he was talking to Wilson, who said it was important to remove Alec Home from the leadership of the Tory Party. Collins asked him who he would like to see in Alec's place. Oh, Heath, because I can run rings round him!

Collins also said that in a recent debate Alec Home three times mentioned Tanganyika when he meant Tanzania. The third time Michael Stewart said in a loud aside, 'He means German East Africa.' Collins is no admirer of Stewart, but thought this a good crack.

I afterwards had some talk with one Pronin, Second Secretary at the Russian Embassy, who is charged with the job of keeping an eye on British politics. His main interest was to know the reaction of the recent German–Russian pact. I said I thought in principle it was a good idea for the West Germans to establish closer links with the U.S.S.R. and Eastern Europe generally, but people here do not trust the Germans, and there is always the possibility that they would desert their Western allies and join with Russia in return for some degree of re-unification. It is a natural suspicion even if there is nothing in it. Pronin seemed surprised when I described Nixon as a weak President.

Friday, September 4th, 1970

Lunch for Ray Gunter. He sweated a lot and seemed rather confused in his thinking. But roughly speaking, this is what he said: (1) he did not think any available terms for joining the Common Market would get through the House of Commons; (2) Carr is not a good House of Commons man, but he thought might be a very good Minister of Labour; (3) he thought Ted, in composing his Government, made use of what talent was available in his Party in the House of Commons; (4) he thought the Labour Party was in a bad way, and only superhuman blunders on Ted's part could win the next election for Labour; (5) he thought the big issue before the country was wage inflation, labour relations and all that. So far so good, but peering into the future he expressed various contradictory opinions. On the one hand he thought a clash with the trades union movement would merely lead to chaos unless the Industrial Relations Commission were reconstituted with legal powers. On the other hand, he thought any trades-union legislation could not become law before Easter, and that the clash with the local government employees would come this month or next. He didn't seem to suggest buying off trouble until Easter. He also said that something would have to be done about the motor industry soon. He blamed the employers a good deal, but saw clearly that the present situation was beyond their powers and could only be handled by the Government.

Towards the end he volunteered the fact that 'in his darker moments' he did not see how a dictatorship could be avoided—or at least a national government—but had no idea how we could get to such a result from where we are.

He said that Roy Jenkins told him he anticipated balance of payments trouble by the end of this year. His reassurances on the subject during the election were apparently mere electioneering. He did not think Wilson had much of a part to play in the stormy times in front of us.

Thursday, September 10th, 1970

The main news these last two days has been of the hijacking of four aeroplanes—three of them down in the desert in northern Jordan, and one jumbo blown up after being diverted to Cairo. This is the appalling consequence of the weakness shown to earlier kidnappers and hijackers. The planes are to be allowed to go if guerrilla prisoners are released in Switzerland, Germany, here, and perhaps Israel. The Germans and Swiss wanted to give way at once: the British were more cautious but essentially willing to give in. Weak governments have been giving the green light to disruptive forces for some time and the full consequences have yet to be seen.

Last night we were invited to dine with Heath at Chequers. It was to be a musical party, with the Stern Trio giving a Beethoven concert. Owing to the hijacking Heath remained at No. 10. Though it was disappointing not catching a glimpse of Ted, I was enormously interested to see what sort of occasion his first big party as P.M. would prove to be.

I only had a brief talk with Whitelaw. I said I thought we should have let the law take its course over the girl hijacker detained here. He said the trouble was that we didn't know if any offence had been committed over British territory, and that extradition proceedings to Israel might take weeks. Meanwhile the guerrillas were threatening to shoot all the hostages—nearly 300 of them.

For me the main interest of the evening was a long conversation with Robert Carr, the Minister of Labour. He greeted me as if we had met before, but I could not remember doing so. Though he is fifty-four and has been in the House since 1950 I had never heard of him until he became Shadow Minister of Labour under Heath. He is a very nice man—the whole Cabinet seems to consist of outstandingly pleasant people! I had got the impression that he is a conciliatory chap with no fire in his belly; though his colleagues have told me he can be tough when need be. But in conversation my worst fears were confirmed. He thinks that by wise legislation and Government influence the trades union movement can be steered into more responsible policies. The trades union legislation cannot be law before next summer, and in the meanwhile the Government will urge employers of all kinds to resist unreasonable wage demands. He said at one point that perhaps results could only be expected in a historical rather than a political setting, so there was no feeling of urgency. He did not seem to be very clear in his mind—was rather woolly in fact. There are certainly no preparations for a head-on clash with the unions. The inflationary effects of the wage explosion did not seem to bother him.

Also at the party was Harold Hutchinson, formerly industrial correspondent for the *Mirror*, later a very good political correspondent for the *Herald*, and now holding the same job for the *Sunday Mirror*. His first words were, 'So your revolution is coming nearer!' I asked him what he meant, and he said he thought the Conservatives would run away from a real clash with the unions, and he foresaw the eventual outcome as a dictatorship of the Right. This feeling is evidently gaining ground in all sorts of unexpected quarters.

Saturday, September 12th, 1970
Lunch with my son Mike at Lockeridge. Drogheda and Gordon

Newton of the *Financial Times* lunched in the C.B.I. office the other day. They said they were expecting balance of payments trouble in December. The *Financial Times* is usually unduly optimistic—anyway in what it prints—but this is a more definite and gloomy view than I have heard so far.

Also this last week—since I saw him on Wednesday evening—Carr addressed about eighty leading industrialists at the C.B.I. He urged them to resist inflationary wage claims and said the Government would support them. The industrialists were apparently impressed—it is difficult to see why. The Government will presumably be firmer in its own sphere, but settlements will be inflationary unless the Government is prepared for a real clash, and this does not appear to be so. In any case the ability of the industrialists to be firm is extremely limited while the strikers are in one way or another so heavily subsidized by the State.

Mike says that after the election Roy Jenkins and Denis Healey were ready to move out of their official residences; Wilson was not. The reason was that Wilson never thought he could be defeated, and Roy was to move to the Foreign Office, and Denis to the Treasury.

Tuesday, September 15th, 1970

Last night a dinner at the House of Commons given by the Institute of Economic Affairs. The guest of honour was Professor Friedman, the currency expert, a most brilliant and provocative speaker. His theme was that by their efforts to control legislation special interests do themselves and everyone else more harm than good. Ruth sat next to Peyton, the new Minister of Transport. He ran true to the form of this administration—terribly nice.

I sat opposite Douglas Houghton, who said he had spoken to Wilson at the T.U.C. Conference, and had said to him, 'Never was so much forgiven by so many so soon!'

Wednesday, September 30th, 1970

Lunch today for Kenneth Keith. His judgment does not seem to me to be outstandingly good, but he moves about a lot and meets a lot of people. He had recently had a drink with Heath at six o'clock. These evening occasions have been arranged for a number of people. Kenneth was reticent about Heath's remarks, but said that he had told the Prime Minister that in due course the trades union leaders would give him an opening and he could then go to the country asking the voters whether they wished to be governed by Whitehall or Transport House. If an election campaign were waged on such an issue, he was sure the Conservatives would win a massive majority. Kenneth seemed to imply that this was Heath's view too.

Kenneth's own worries seemed to be more in the industrial field. Managers of large businesses did not seem to realize the damage that inflation would do in raising costs, lowering investment and reducing liquidity. I said I thought a prominent feature of the present scene was the lack of any sense of urgency or crisis. Kenneth did not follow up this thought.

On *The Times*, he said the paper is now to lose £2 million in the current year—a short while ago, as the result of economies, it was to have been £1 million. The management told the board that a recovery in advertising would soon see them in the black. Ken Thomson, Kenneth said, was entirely ineffective. At the Board meeting on Monday Kenneth had held forth on the shortcomings of *The Times* as a newspaper, but had got nowhere. Kenneth thought nothing would be done even if Roy Thomson were to die.

When saying goodbye, I said to Kenneth what nice men the present Ministers are. He said he thought them more straight-forward than the last lot, but that Ted was 50-per-cent abler than any of them. He will no doubt make a big speech at the Conservative Party Conference, but so far he has allowed the prestige of his election victory to evaporate, and his administration has now no initiative or impetus. These can, perhaps, be recovered but it would have been far easier not to have lost them in the first place.

Kenneth said the industrial world was watching very carefully the progress of the General Motors strike in the U.S. It is believed here that G.M. really mean to beat the union this time, and any success they may have will have its effect here.

Thursday, October 8th, 1970

Lunch with Norman Collins of Associated Television. It was his invitation, rather urgent and at rather short notice; the reason is not obvious. He is off to the Conservative Party Conference at Blackpool tomorrow morning, mainly to preside over an I.T.N.* dinner for Heath in the evening. Norman had little news and seemed fairly pleased with the Government's performance so far. He said that,

* Independent Television News.

45

like all Prime Ministers, Ted is less accessible to information or ideas now he is in office. He described Ted as dangerously 'inflexible', and said he tends to take decisions over the heads of his ministers. For instance over Leila Khaled, the Arab hijacker, he made some of the decisions without even informing Alec Home. He expressed doubts over the appointments of Barber to the Exchequer and John Davies to Technology. He thought very well of Carrington and quite well of Carr. He said one of the Government's problems had been the unexpected lack of Tory talent in the House of Lords. Eric Bessborough had got his job because of diligent work in the Lords in Opposition. He admittedly has no brains. Norman thought, or hoped—it was not clear which—that Whitelaw was making contingency plans for a big strike. The only one in the offing is the miners' and that would not be a popular issue to fight on. The Government is handling the dustmen's strike with kid gloves. It has not yet been suggested by anyone that increased wages will have to come out of the pockets of the general public in increased rates or rent.

The Government's proposals for dealing with the trades unions have been published, and promoted by a speech from Carr at the Party Conference. They seem to me (a) to be unworkable, and (b) to presuppose that in this matter almost unlimited time is available. Some of the proposals are unimportant but would be rejected by any trades unionist. So far there are no proposals to abolish the subsidization of strikes out of public money. I expect the whole policy to fail, thus wasting valuable time and good-will and leading to a further aggravation of inflation. It is in this area that I expect Ted to meet his Waterloo. From all accounts he has rejected any tendency to move to the Right and thinks he is holding the middle ground. But politics are moving to the Right—all over the world.

Norman said he thought Enoch Powell's destiny is the wilderness. Like Duncan Sandys he gets over well to a crowd, but cannot establish a satisfactory relationship with those working most closely with him.

Saturday, October 10th, 1970
Took part yesterday in a radio programme, 'Speak Easy', to be broadcast this evening. It was interesting as the other guest on the programme was Hugh Scanlon of the A.E.W.,* whom I had not

* Amalgamated Union of Engineering and Foundry Workers.

previously met. He is a nicer and more intelligent man than I expected. His wife too seemed a nice, sensible woman. Whatever he may be on other occasions, there was no sign of the irresponsible fire-brand last night.

The chairman was Jimmy Savile—an unprepossessing figure with long, bleached-white hair, a necklace of painted shells, gym shoes, white socks and a *very* shabby corduroy suit. But, ignoring the trimmings and looking into his face, you could see that here was an absolutely genuine human being. He gets a lot of money from the B.B.C. and from a column in the *People*, lives in a mini-bus or a caravan (sometimes one, sometimes the other), and devotes his life to good works—particularly at Broadmoor and Rampton. Here is indeed a latter-day saint, dressed up in clothes that render him acceptable to the young multitude. He has great psychological insight. I was saying I wondered why people are uninterested in the old, though they will all be old some day. He said it was 'conscience': the old remind them of their old relatives, who they neglect. He said one of the B.B.C. higher-ups has a mother in Leeds he has not seen for several years. He also said people don't want good health. He recently broke a finger wrestling and still wears a finger-splint when he wants attention and sympathy, though this must not be overdone. People don't want to have to cope with someone really ill, but like sympathizing with someone wearing a finger-splint. With all his fun he devotes his life to the drearier kinds of good works.

Wednesday, October 14th, 1970

Lunch with Mike. He has known Alec Home rather well for many years. I said he did not seem to be doing very well. Mike said that it is his age—he is a very old sixty-seven. Of Adamson, his boss, he said he is a very nice man and a very intelligent one, but an academic rather than a businessman and with nothing like Davies's ability. The Government's proposed trades-union legislation is seen at the C.B.I. as an active policy. Whether it will work or not is another matter, but it is something rather than nothing. They regard enforceable contracts as an unworkable proposal, and have told the Government so repeatedly. The attitude to Heath at the C.B.I. seems to be that Heath is trying to turn his back on the Tory past with a new team and a new policy. I cannot believe this will work as the team is weak and Heath is no politician.

Friday, October 16th, 1970

Yesterday the Government came out with a White Paper on its plans for Government reorganization. John Davies is to be Minister for Industry, which will include Fuel and Power, Technology, the Board of Trade, etc., etc. His Ministers of State are to be Noble for Trade, and Eden for Industry. Peter Walker is to be Minister of Housing and Local Government, Buildings and Works—and Transport. I don't believe that any man, however able, can effectively cover such immense areas of the economy. To delegate Industry to Sir John Eden, who has never been anything more than vice-chairman of some Tory committee, is pure farce. Davies is able, but not that able. Walker has made a lot of money, but is neither liked nor admired. Lord Drumalbyn (né Macpherson), a pleasant fool, is resurrected to be Minister without Portfolio to deal with the new Labour Relations Bill in the Lords. A small group at No. 10 is to be formed to keep the P.M. better informed on what goes on. This last idea is sound in principle, but may be used as a means of concentrating more power in Heath's hands.

This arrangement will mean that some Cabinet Ministers—e.g. the Secretary for Wales—will have little or nothing to do, whilst the Chancellor, the Foreign Secretary and the Defence Minister are fully stretched and the two new Ministers will be overwhelmed.

The more I see of Ted's Government the less I like the prospect. I don't see how his ideas can work and the consequences of his failure will be unpredictable and unpleasant.

Monday, October 19th, 1970

Lunch for Dick Marsh. He is in good heart running a sort of executives employment bureau, and he is an active director of National Carbonising Company. He was deputy secretary of the dustmen's union, whose strike is now in its third week. He says Fisher, the secretary, was eager to accept the employer's offer of 14 per cent but was voted down by his executive who wanted more and look like getting it. He thinks Ted's trades-union legislation quite unworkable. It will be passed into law and the Attorney-General will then be kept busy—as happened with the Labour Government—advising the Government on how not to operate the legislation it has just passed. Clive Jenkins apparently defied the Government to arrest him when he broke the Prices and Incomes law and the Government were at great pains to avoid doing so.

Marsh thought the Labour Party would be impotent for another year.

I said Roy Jenkins did not look very buoyant these days. He said Roy enjoyed the power and prestige of office; was in great doubt whether to stand for Deputy Leader and now faces a long period in Opposition waiting for Wilson to go. He doesn't like the idea, but does not know what else to do. He is no hatchet man and will certainly do nothing to hasten Wilson's departure.

I asked Marsh about Denis Healey. Why is he said to be so arrogant? Marsh said he is perfectly at home in a four-ale bar, but at a Party meeting, or in the House, he expects to be met on his own high intellectual level. The world is then divided into those that agree with him—and fools. He has lost a good deal of prestige lately because he has all along been enthusiastically in favour of arms for South Africa. Within three weeks of vacating office, however, he was denouncing the very idea. This volte-face was to ensure his election to the National Executive, which indeed he achieved. Arrogant though he is in public, he is not so in private.

Marsh said it was quite impossible for Davies or Walker to cover the ground assigned to them. He thought nothing of Peyton, but said he, like others, was appointed on the basis of personal liking by Ted.

Marsh thought that by normal democratic methods it was quite impossible for the Government to control the unions. This Government would have no more success than Labour. Draconian methods no doubt would work but are out of the question with these people. The leadership of the trades unions is so weak that there is no chance of them disciplining themselves either. The answer to this equation is runaway inflation, but I didn't think Marsh let his mind dwell on the consequences of serious inflation. He seems to assume that the present Parliamentary game will continue unchanged no matter what stresses or strains it will be subjected to.

Peter McLachlan has been acting as a sort of liaison between the Tory Party and Northern Ireland, and recently he and his little group had an interview with Ted. They got nowhere. Ted evidently knew no Irish history and was not interested in their judgment on Irish public opinion. He had laid down the policy to be pursued and that was that.

More recently Heath gave a dinner to Kaunda and the Zambians. Kaunda is a nice man and sensible, within the limits allowed by political pressures at home. He lectured Kaunda (who had come to put the case against arms for South Africa) on the fact that Great Britain was an independent country with its national interests to serve. Heath was said to have been repetitive and arrogant, leaving Kaunda badly ruffled and convinced that Heath will go ahead with arms to South Africa, come what may. Heath and Home's argument is that we need a base at Simonstown to defend our trade routes in the Indian Ocean against the Russian navy, which is building up there. It is inconceivable to me that a few frigates at Simonstown would have any relevance in a war between Russia and the Western Powers.

Friday, October 30th, 1970

Lunch with Don Ryder. Don is not a politician and so his views may be of interest as reflecting opinions he hears from other chairmen. (1) Barber as Chancellor is regarded as a bad joke. (2) The trades-union legislation is universally considered to be unworkable. (3) Heath is considered already to have shown himself inflexible and obstinate. (4) He is more prone to appoint his friends to office than even his predecessors. (5) If the unions try and block his trades-union legislation by means of a general strike, he will fight. (6) He does not, however, appear to realize that a head-on collision with the unions is at some point unavoidable. (7) Events are shifting the political centre of gravity to the Right.

I had Melvin Lasky, editor of *Encounter*, to lunch on Tuesday. He told me his sister in the United States had given advice to her daughters. When consulting a doctor or lawyer look up his credentials. If he was in training between 1963 and 1971 avoid him—he won't know his stuff. This is anyway one woman's view of the effect of campus unrest.

Monday, November 2nd, 1970

Sir John Stevens to lunch—recently back from Hungary and soon off to Russia. His main theme was the fuel shortage, which is worldwide and must mean steeply higher power prices. A lot of apparently unrelated events have conspired to bring this about: (1) the closing of the Suez Canal; (2) the closing by Syria of the pipe-line from Saudi Arabia; (3) the restriction on exports by the Libyan Government; (4) the Russians are short of oil and have instructed the satellites to buy in the open market. So much for oil. But the United

States is short of natural gas; we are short of coal; the demand for power is unexpectedly high; and there have been a number of mishaps to big tankers, of which there is a shortage anyway. Higher prices for power will affect all other prices here and elsewhere.

The balance of payments is not as good as was expected earlier in the year but will be all right to the end of the year. Stevens expects trouble in the second quarter of next year. The inflation in other countries is helping our balance of payments—if nothing else.

There has been a certain lack of harmony between the Treasury and the Bank, and the Bank has not done too well—bank loans have been expanding much too fast and the recent call for special deposits looks merely silly. The banks sold £100 million of gilt-edged, with which they paid the special-deposit call. As it was the Bank that bought the gilt-edged the net result was nil, or very nearly so. From the independent line taken by O'Brien at the bankers' dinner (calling for an incomes policy) and from casual remarks let drop ('The Prime Minister is so headstrong'), the impression is that O'Brien knows he will not be re-appointed in June. The suggestions current have been around for some time: Gordon Richardson, John Stevens or Cromer —but then Cromer is tipped for Washington as Ambassador.

Stevens said he has been conducting a lot of good banking business with Communist countries (he is chairman of the East European Export Council or some such body). One of his friends is a Hungarian banker who was formerly a convinced Communist and a member of the Red Army. He told Stevens they all hated the system: they knew it wouldn't work, but kept it going to protect their position. Stevens said the situation under a glittering exterior is pretty grim and even the Russians are having severe economic troubles.

The urgent immediate business confronting the Government is what to do about Rolls-Royce and B.A.C.* They are desperately in need of cash and the Government has said it will not bail out firms who get into trouble—they will have to go broke. However, they can hardly let these two firms go to the wall.

Tuesday, November 3rd, 1970

Forty-five minutes with O'Brien this morning. He was very polite and saw me off right down to the Bullion Yard. He had no sensational news to impart. He said Ted takes a larger and stronger part in economic affairs than any P.M. of recent years. He is apt to give

* British Aircraft Corporation.

51

off-the-cuff opinions on subjects which he has not sufficiently studied—how could he find the time to do so? He thought an incomes policy, under whatever name, is inescapable; but Heath is very headstrong and when he has stated his decision tends to press on regardless.

The balance of payments position is not so favourable as seemed likely earlier in the year, but is quite good—storm clouds are not expected until next year. Interest rates here will tend to rise: the gold price suddenly shot up to $39 but now is back under $38. He thought the long-term outlook is for an increase. He thought Macleod a great loss to the Government. Without him the intellectual level is low—lower than in the last Government. I said that in view of the problems ahead it was surprising how happy Heath looked. He said he supposed this was natural—look at the way Wilson was enjoying himself in spite of the mess on every hand. Barber was not mentioned once. O'Brien said he hoped the Government would not press on with their sales of arms to South Africa. The consequences would be serious and far outweigh any benefits.

And so to Claridge's to meet Reggie Maudling over lunch. He had come from a Cabinet meeting and said he was exhausted, but perked up over a roast grouse and some good claret. He had little news of Ireland. He supposed things might continue much as at present, though there was always the danger that the troops might get fed up and go on the rampage. He had no apparent confidence in the proposed trades-union legislation. He has been trying to convince his colleagues that rising unemployment will not stop unreasonable wage demands from those able to extort them. He thought a show-down with the unions might become necessary, but clearly none was being contemplated at the moment. On the whole I got a disappointing impression. He is the Deputy Leader of his Party, in a key ministerial post, and, allowing for ministerial discretion, no one could have concluded from his manner and his matter that here is a national figure clearly on top of his job as a departmental chief and senior Cabinet Minister. He was doubtful about the Common Market and fully understood the weight of opposition that could be put up by Powell and Wilson. He also thought that as France became less antagonistic to our membership, so the German opposition would grow.

To return to Leslie O'Brien. He had recently had dinner at the invitation of the 'Round Table'. All sorts of people were present, but he named only politicians—of both Parties. The main point of the dinner seemed to be Alec Home justifying arms to South Africa to the assembled company. O'Brien thought his case a weak one and Alec, anyway, a spent force.

He commented at the end of our interview on the fact that in Barber's important speech as Chancellor he twice referred to Wilson as the P.M. This is really inexcusable, as Ted has been in office for more than four months and Barber is his closest associate.

Wednesday, November 4th, 1970

Lunch for George Bolton. Though seventy he could pass for fifty, and is a far more effective character than most of that age. His main theme was that Vietnam and the Middle East are really side issues. The big developments are signs that the Japanese are moving out of the American orbit into that of China. The other big development is that the Russians are so confident of dominating all Europe that they are not bothering to come to terms with the U.S., and have inflicted much humiliation on Brandt while conceding nothing at all. The Russians may be underestimating the Americans, who are both ruthless and unpredictable. They may seem to have immobilized themselves but that might well prove to be an illusion. Their foreign policy is absurd—they have now landed themselves with one real ally—Israel of all people.

World trade, he thought, was turning down—the price of nearly all metals had dropped. Consumption was off in all countries except Japan—and Japan might follow. George is a friend and admirer of Charles Court, Premier of Western Australia, and he says the Australians are worried over being so dependent on Japanese trade. For this reason George is trying to develop an Anglo-German venture to import iron in pellet form from Western Australia. The German partner is willing to do business now; but the British end would require the separation from the British Steel Corporation of two of the electric-furnace mills, formerly of United Steel. Would the Government sanction this and how soon? We have not the electric-power output to develop electric-steel furnaces on a modern scale—anyway our steel industry is overmanned, out of date, and losing money. He had less than no opinion of Melchett.

On the Bank, he said Barber had taken over Jenkins's monetary policy, and that that was more suitable for the 'eighties of the last century. It made no allowance for the inflationary world in which we now live, and which cannot be changed so long as we preserve our democratic form of Government. He said what remained to O'Brien of his prestige had vanished with his clumsy attempts to raise money for Rolls-Royce. He said there is nobody now at the Bank who is taken seriously in the City, and the Bank itself no longer speaks for the City or any part of it. He was particularly contemptuous of Fforde. I said I suspected from O'Brien's public and other statements that he did not expect to be appointed for another term. He said this is so. The names under discussion have been Gordon Richardson (vetoed by Cromer for health reasons) and John Stevens (doing very well at Morgan Grenfell), who might only take the job on certain terms. Incidentally, when he came to lunch the other day I thought he was clearly a candidate. Also Toby Aldington, who thinks he has the reversion to the job. This sounds an unhappy choice. I like him personally but don't think he would be effective at the Bank. In any case, his would be a purely political appointment and this would be a bad precedent to set.

George did not know many Ministers but has a high opinion of Keith Joseph, and thinks Rippon will go to the Home Office before too long. He thought Alec Home clearly past it. He pointed out how short of leadership we are in every field. In the industrial world he spoke highly of Weinstock, Strath, and Woodroofe (new chairman of Unilever). He thought Reay Geddes had done much better than was expected.

Friday, November 6th, 1970

Lunch for Campbell Adamson, director-general of the C.B.I. He is a very nice man, and a very intelligent one, whom I had not met before. He said he was very gloomy about the general industrial outlook. He had formed a favourable opinion of Carr and thought he might prove a great success. He saw John Davies, his predecessor, yesterday and said he looked positively haggard due, he thought, to the double strain of a huge department and being roughed up in the House. He saw Heath very recently, who said he was 'shocked' to find the extent to which inflation had taken hold. This is surprising as there has been no manner of concealment about inflation. I said I thought there would have to be a head-on clash with the unions at some time. The moment may not yet have come, but were the necessary arrangements being made? We both thought not. An inflationary settlement has been reached for the dustmen's strike;

another is likely with the miners, but Adamson seemed to think a stand might be made over the men in the electric supply and generating industries. He was afraid that some of Heath's reputation for being 'headstrong' might spring from a weak man trying to appear strong. He thought the Government's trades-union legislation was really designed to be put on the statute book to take serious effect after the present effervescence in the industrial world had died down. I said I thought a clash with the trades union movement would build up into something like a mild civil war and would have to be fought with the Government's gloves off—no unemployment pay, no out-relief for families, freezing of union funds, etc., etc., including censorship. Adamson went along with the rest but not with censorship. But I have been coming round more and more to the view that it is impossible to conduct a modern state without a degree of censorship. In the past, in the newspapers, there was a kind of unwritten code, but this has never been true of the much more powerful medium of television. Modifying and largely abolishing the libel laws would make censorship a lot more acceptable.

Adamson deplored the low standard of management and of solidarity among employers in industry, and thought our education might be largely to blame. He knows Sir John Eden well, the so-called Minister for Industry. I told him that Peter Carrington had said the Cabinet lacked fifteen-inch guns: Adamson said on this scale Eden is a one-inch gun. He thought little of Barber—'a lightweight'.

Incidentally George Bolton, earlier in the week, spoke highly of Peter Carrington and said that when he took over the chairmanship of the Australia and New Zealand Bank he became without question the boss, organizing the enterprise and its merger with the English, Scottish and Australian Bank as he thought fit.

Monday, November 9th, 1970

Hugh Fraser to lunch. He seemed to think the Government was in something of a mess. The inflationary settlement of the dustmen's strike is pushing the Government towards an incomes policy, but so far they are standing out against it. Fraser thinks Barber clever and nice but that he lacks weight and leaves the big decisions to Heath. Alec Home has made another mistimed speech about Israel and is rapidly becoming a liability. Fraser thought Walker an able man and the only real find of the Heath team. Davies he thought more of than I do, but agreed that his ministry covers far too much ground. John Eden he knows and likes, but has a very low opinion of him as a Minister. He said the in-group around Heath is thought to consist of Barber, Whitelaw, Carr and Quintin Hogg—and perhaps Walker (I am not sure if he was included). Fraser was pro-Common Market, and is now mildly anti. He does not think we shall get in as a result of this round of negotiations. Heath's team are people loyal to Heath rather than the most competent available. This is because Heath is very suspicious, and has good reason to doubt the loyalty of many senior members of his Party. They thought, some of them, that he was going to lose the election and were sharpening their knives in anticipation. Fraser thought Cromer's appointment to Washington, announced this morning, a good one. He had not heard that Lord Aldington is tipped for the Bank. He thinks the report is probably true, as he is a considerable friend of Heath. If Heath has Barber at the Treasury and Aldington at the Bank he will be in a very powerful position in that area of state activity. He will be able to dictate his policy—even if a mistaken one.

Fraser had seen recently a very senior member of the armed forces in Ulster (unnamed) who told him that trouble is now simmering, but that if it boiled up they would need twenty battalions instead of the present ten. This military figure also told Fraser that he didn't think we could go on like this and that we must negotiate.

Fraser said our approach to the Common Market bedevils our policy in other parts of the world. The chairman of Lonrho* told him that a deal of his in the Congo was frustrated by H.M.G. because it was thought the deal would annoy the Union Minière and so the Belgians!

Tuesday, November 10th, 1970

Heath appeared on 'Panorama'† last night. He was in my opinion quite ineffective—he was evasive on inflation, but once more reiterated his refusal to do anything about controlling incomes.

Today I had Vic Feather to lunch—after a long interval. He was very friendly and chatted away quite freely. He has a self-indulgent face but a shrewd eye, and is, by any standard, a vast improvement

* Lonrho Limited, an international conglomerate with large mining interests, especially in Africa.

† A popular B.B.C. public affairs television programme, noted for its searching interrogations of public figures.

on George Woodcock. He expressed nothing but contempt for this Government—said it must be the weakest ever, with Ministers chosen for their loyalty to Ted and for no other reason. In particular he scorned Barber and Peyton. He thought a lot of the country's economic troubles were due to weak employers, and dismissed any idea that strikes are subsidized by the State. He thinks that Ted will shortly have to set up a wage freeze with a tripartite body to vet increases—say $7\frac{1}{2}$ per cent per annum for those with less than £25 per week, 5 per cent for those with £25–£40, and nothing for those over. It would be about 70 per cent effective and might last as long as a year. In any case he expected a devaluation in about a year's time. He saw no future for Ted and thought that within two to three years he would be succeeded by Enoch Powell—by that time the slump might be more considerable, and if so there would be a strong demand to send the blacks home. He thought fascism in this country would wear a bowler hat and carry a briefcase, and he thought Powell an ideal leader of such a movement. The idea that the Government should seriously take on the trades union movement was an idea that had clearly not been presented to him (nor was it presented by me). He is gloomy about the future and has a greater sense of crisis than I find among politicians. His loathing of Barbara Castle is really quite something. He said she should really be a commissar. She has told her friends that in future Wilson is on his own—she is not going to bolster him up any longer. Feather expressed total contempt for Wilson's intimates at No. 10— Marcia, Kaufman, Trevor Lloyd-Hughes and Wigg.

Finally, Feather thought that Barber's mini-Budget had lost the Government a lot of support. He surmised that the Tories would not now win an election.

Wednesday, November 11th, 1970

Peter McLachlan to dinner. He is on the Conservative Party staff and acts as Party liaison with Northern Ireland. He says General Freeland has no more to contribute and is going. Young, the Chief of Police, was a disaster and is going. There is a civil servant called Burroughes who lives in a hotel in Belfast distributing generous hospitality. His role is not clear. Peter thinks that at the moment the moderates are doing better—both Lynch in Dublin and Chichester-Clark at Stormont are stronger now than they were. The whole situation is very precarious. I quoted Fraser's story about the general who thought this to be the time for negotiation. Peter said a mere rumour of negotiation would bring the Protestants out on the streets in open civil war. The distaste of Ulstermen for the Catholic hierarchy is as strong as ever.

Last night there was a special documentary on TV about Enoch Powell. It was a rather scrappy film but lasted the best part of an hour and gave a good impression of the man. A nice man in many ways, a loner, highly intelligent—with a possible sadistic streak. As a gadfly on the outskirts of the Tory Party he seems to me to have a valuable role to play, but as a possible future Prime Minister he fills me with misgiving. In the film last night he said that Heath seems to be afraid of him—and of course this is true, though a public statement of the fact is hardly likely to sweeten their relations. It was quite clear last night that he has 10 Downing St in his sights.

Thursday, November 12th, 1970

Dinner last night with the Advertising Association. The president is now Lord Cole, former chairman of Unilever and appointed chairman of Rolls-Royce by the Government yesterday in a big upheaval. He is not a small man and may be a strong one, but neither at the United Africa Company nor later has he seemed to me to be a man of any ability, personality or flair. I was amazed when he was moved from being a very undistinguished managing director of U.A.C. to being vice-chairman of the whole group—and my amazement continues.

Talking to the advertising types at the dinner it was clear that advertising is in the doldrums, where it will remain till next September. This is bad news for the newspapers who are anyway desperately short of cash. Ruth sat next Gordon Brunton, managing director of the Thomson Organization. Brunton said Ryder is hugely ambitious and sees himself and Wilson playing a major political part in the future!

I had quite a long talk with Robens, who is coping with striking miners at the moment. He thinks John Davies brilliant, but that he will fall flat on his face in the House of Commons. He had a long talk with Carr who said the Government is quite prepared to adopt an incomes policy if they can hear of one that will work. This seems extraordinary as they have been exceedingly definite in repudiating the whole idea. Robens himself thinks the labour situation is getting quite out of hand, and that the Government can only regain control by defeating a major strike. The more this is considered the clearer it is seen that this can only be done by the adoption of totalitarian methods, which are distasteful to all of us. But the alternative seems to be chaos.

Friday, November 13th, 1970

Lunch yesterday for Baylis of the Stationery Office—a civil servant, I should have thought, with a great future. He made one point which I thought interesting. A friend of his was one Hall, Wilson's Principal Private Secretary, who died recently at an early age. Hall told Baylis that you could not have a nicer boss to work for than Wilson. Baylis said that Hall was very appreciative of his position as the Prime Minister's Principal Private Secretary, but even allowing for that fact, he was loud in Wilson's praises as a most considerate chief.

Saturday, November 14th, 1970

Lunch for Val Duncan of Rio Tinto Zinc—very friendly, very charming, with no particular news. He is very interested in a deal he is negotiating with the Russians for developing and working a big copper mine for them in Siberia. A smaller deal would be a nickel mine in the Southern Urals. He wants to arrange a continuing association, perhaps with a contract to act as their agent in marketing their metals outside the Iron Curtain. Owing to the slow development of atomic power, the world has a huge surplus of uranium. His company is protected by long-term contracts, but it will take a number of years to work off the surplus. He does not think the falling price of metals has any sinister implication of a world slump.

On home politics he expressed great admiration for John Davies, and something like contempt for Sir John Eden. He thinks a much stronger line should be taken with violent demonstrators, whether strikers, students or others. To this end the police should be largely reinforced, and more amply rewarded, to prevent the wastage of police recruits in their early years. He thinks Maudling much too soft and lazy to be Home Secretary.

At 5.30 p.m. I repaired to 10 Downing St. On October 31st Heath rang me up at home and asked me to come and see him—his secretary would ring on the Monday to fix a date. On the Monday, as it is sometimes difficult to get through to us on the telephone, Ruth rang up the girl on the Treasury exchange to explain this. She was merely rude and advised Ruth to have elocution lessons. On Wednesday, nothing having been heard, Ruth rang the appointments secretary, who knew nothing. Finally she rang some more senior secretary on the Thursday and a date was fixed. Of all the people Ruth contacts on the telephone, Heath seems to be worst served.

When I arrived I was expected and ushered in to the waiting-room. Very shortly afterwards I was taken up to Heath's study—an attractive small room I had not been in before. Heath has tried to make it all more homey and I think the atmosphere was a much pleasanter one all round than under Wilson. Heath himself seemed well, relaxed and most friendly. When leaving he saw me downstairs and almost to the door.

He had been in Paris the day before for General de Gaulle's funeral, and I said I thought there was a remarkable turn-out for a man who was a petty, spiteful and bitter enemy of this country, and of America. He said the French, by having the funeral so quickly, hoped for a quiet village burial and a memorial service in Notre Dame for Ambassadors. But Nixon announced that he was going to attend, so everyone else felt they had to do so too. (1) The President should not leave Washington on such an occasion; and (2) Nixon should not have paid such an extravagant honour to such an enemy of his country. However, I quite see that once Nixon announced his attendance our people had to go along. In the plane to and from Paris Wilson was correcting proofs of his book, for which Heath said he believed Wilson was getting £250,000 from *The Times*. Heath said he was surprised *The Times* should pay so much, as the Macmillan memoirs that have been appearing in *The Times* just recently have been an expensive failure. He had himself glanced at the first instalment of Macmillan and hadn't bothered further. I asked how Wilson could get that sort of money without really spilling the beans, and how could he spill the beans and remain Leader of his Party? Heath said, 'Quite so,' but that Wilson had told him quite three times on the Paris trip that he did indeed intend to tell all.

Our interview lasted just under an hour. Heath had asked me to call as a friendly gesture, not with any purpose. The conversation tended to flag if I did not keep it going. As I felt it unwise to utter any criticisms, however oblique, I asked questions which he very readily answered. He expatiated at length on the dustmen's strike, which he thought had been appallingly badly handled by the local authorities. Heath said they were winning, but then they put in an improved offer, the Scamp Committee of Inquiry was appointed, and they committed themselves to accept its report even though the unions did not. Then Scamp came out with a report that conceded the unions almost everything they had asked for, to which he added some irresponsible and inflationary *obiter dicta*.

Another theme was Rolls-Royce, which the Government is rescuing on very onerous terms.* Apparently the directors did not know the cost of development of their new engine and were out by £70 million, and their fixed-price contract with Lockheed binds them to a trading loss of £40 million. The chairman of Rolls that I knew was Kindersley, who was clearly useless, but his successors seem to have been no better.

Heath clearly intends to oppose unreasonable wage demands and to continue a squeeze that will cause rising unemployment and many bankruptcies. It is not much use saying private firms must be strong and stand up to unreasonable wage claims. They are so short of cash they have no money to do so. Heath realizes that a major strike in the public sector will have to be fought. It might end in a general strike or its equivalent, though he does not think so. Val Duncan had said earlier in the day that the trouble with the power stations is that they all feed into the grid, and that this will only work if 85 per cent of the stations are in operation. Heath said they could probably carry on, even with a power-station strike, by restricting supplies to people with priority claims, and after all the Scottish hydro-electric stations would be working! These last are tiny affairs; I doubt if they supply 1 per cent of the total electricity output. It was clear from this part of the conversation that there had been no real study of the problems involved in a real clash with the unions. Both he and Duncan said that most British working men are decent chaps, which of course they are. But they have to be shown by the result of a clash that the Government is stronger and more effective than the militant shop stewards. Until then the decent chaps will take what seems to be the line of least resistance.

* Rolls-Royce Ltd, the famous British automobile and aircraft-engine manufacturers, had been forced into liquidation by the escalating costs of development of an advanced-technology jet engine (the RB-211) for use in a Lockheed aircraft, the L-1011. A Government rescue operation was mounted, partly to enable Rolls-Royce to fulfil its contracts for this engine, partly to safeguard the company's defence commitments and partly to safeguard employment. Such rescue operations represented of course a change of policy for the Conservative Government.

I asked Heath how Wilson was doing. He said he is lying very low and his big speech in the recent debate was frivolous and ineffective. I said I thought that in the cold and rough weather ahead Wilson's clever footwork would seem increasingly irrelevant. Heath agreed, not only about Wilson, but also about the troubled times ahead. Nevertheless, I don't think he realizes how rough it will be, nor how weak his team is. His contingency planning, if any, is obviously inadequate.

As I came away I could not help feeling that Heath has no idea of the problems ahead. He is living in a world that probably never existed, but if it did, certainly passed away long ago. It seems to me that his confidence is based on a complete mis-assessment of the situation. From all accounts his dream will be rudely shattered before the end of next year. But then what? Nobody knows.

Monday, November 16th, 1970

Lunch for Pronin, from the Russian Embassy. He has been two years in Canberra and three years here, but his English is not very good. He appears to derive his knowledge of our politics from reading and looking at television—also attending Party Conferences. He does not seem to know personally anyone in politics. He had read about me in Moscow and is anxious that we should meet again. He had nothing to say of interest about Russian affairs except that Soldatov, formerly the Ambassador here, is now Ambassador to Cuba. This seems to show what a high importance they attach to their link with Castro.

Wednesday, November 18th, 1970

Lunch yesterday for Douglas Houghton—such a nice man, and, under the new arrangement, chairman of the Parliamentary Labour Party. He said there is nothing presidential now about Wilson—he consults his Shadow Cabinet on everything. I asked about Wilson's memoirs. Houghton said he thought Wilson was not to get as much as £250,000. He had been warned by his colleagues that any 'rough stuff' would be answered in kind—and that there were more of them than of him. Houghton is under the impression that he will not jeopardize his position as Leader of his Party by anything he may say; that the memoirs are to be in three volumes; that he thinks the contract is for life so that the indiscretions, and much of the money, can come later. He is told that Crossman's memoirs are to be published after his death. One wonders if, by then, anyone will be interested.

Houghton does not think the Government's labour relations bill will work. There may well be a serious strike in the coming months and this may lead to sporadic unofficial strikes of all sorts. He does not think a general strike at all likely. He mentioned in passing that the constant changes in the grouping of ministries means continual moves—not only of staffs but of files—all of which militates against efficiency.

In the evening I dined with Maurice Allen at his house in Chelsea. I had not seen him for months as he has been abroad, and has been ill with jaundice. He was, if possible, gloomier than anyone I have spoken to. The liquidity problem is widespread: the difficulties of Rolls-Royce and Fleet Street are duplicated over all industry. This problem is likely to get worse. The effect of inflation plus the money squeeze is to leave everyone short of cash, but this will not halt the wage explosion unless it is carried to a point where unemployment creates a revolutionary situation. As Maurice said, the unions are now taking the equity in the case of successful businesses. The result can only be a cessation of enterprise and of new investment. There is talk (e.g. from Feather and Robens) of a further devaluation in the latter half of next year. Maurice does not think this is likely, but it depends on the industrial situation here. He would not expect a devaluation anyway, but a collapse in the exchange rate of sterling in 1972. The immediate fly in the ointment is that there are liquid funds invested in London which could be moved out in large amounts at any time. The owners take short views, and they think all is well as of now, but they could change their minds at very short notice. Maurice showed me a letter by the great economist Marshall who, at the end of the last century, was complaining of the damage done to our economy by the unions at that time. Marshall's point was that their low productivity, 'laziness at work', raised unnecessarily the price of houses, and at the same time destroyed the workers' ability to enjoy leisure.

Meanwhile, Ted, in the House of Commons, was in great form trouncing Jenkins & Co. This is all good fun but I can find no one who believes the Government's policy will or can work. At best Ted is living in a past age when his remedies might have been effective. His constant reiteration of his belief in our 'free society' leaves me with the impression that he is living in a dream world. He speaks now with such confidence that people think there must be something in what he says. I think it is more likely that he clings to the belief that he can make a new omelette without breaking any eggs. The alternative is too horrible for him to contemplate. Nevertheless, reality will one day break through, and then what?

Thursday, November 19th, 1970

I attended the annual dinner of the Printers' Pension Fund. The principal speakers were Heath, Redcliffe-Maud, Hartwell and Goodman. I asked Goodman how he was getting on in my old chair at the N.P.A. He said he must have been out of his mind to accept such a job! Heath made a quite good impromptu speech and was enthusiastically received. He looked confident and spoke confidently in stark contrast to the various printing and publishing tycoons present. They are all becoming alarmed—particularly over the general shortage of cash. The newspapers this morning are showing signs of apprehension which are long overdue, but a change for the better. There was more talk last night of Heath's intransigence. In Opposition, it was said he was obstinate, and now he is both arrogant and obstinate. I don't find anyone with a bright idea on what to do in our present troubles, but Heath's idea of a return to laissez-faire is accepted by no one outside his immediate circle.

I had a long talk with Briginshaw, for long general secretary of NATSOPA. He has not been a reliable man, at times is unattractively vain, and has had little or no education, but he is a man of ability in a field where ability is in extremely short supply. He started by wishing I were twenty years younger, and went on to speak about the future as he sees it. He thinks we are moving towards something like national socialism. He thinks some kind of autocracy is inevitable, but if brought about from the Left—or at least including a leftward ingredient—it would be more generally acceptable. In other words, in an autocratic regime he thinks he would be useful. We are to meet over lunch before long. William Barnetson, chairman of Reuters and of United Newspapers, was very gloomy about I.P.C. The mistakes being made were due to the belief that financial gimmicks—e.g. sale and lease-back of properties—are any substitute for excellence in the content of the publications.

Wednesday, November 25th, 1970

Dinner last night at the Griersons; not a particularly interesting evening but for one story. The London correspondent of the *Corriere della Sera* was there. He is one of the eight correspondents of Continental newspapers who have a private briefing from the P.M. every month. At one of these the Dutch member of the party asked Wilson if he identified himself with any recent British Premiers. He said he saw himself as a *mélange* (his word) of Gladstone, Lloyd George, and Churchill!

At the Kuwait Embassy this evening I had some talk with Maurice Parsons, who spent an hour with Ted recently, and also with John Stevens, who has been seeing William Whitelaw. Stevens gave his opinion on what should be done—and Whitelaw said he fully agreed! Parsons told Ted what he thought of the situation and the prospects, and left him a paper prescribing what should be done. Ted took it well apparently and Maurice may see him again soon. I gather Maurice and Stevens both said something *must* be done about inflation and the wage explosion or we face disaster on a grand scale.

Thursday, November 26th, 1970

There is a tremendous hoo-ha this morning because Lord Hall has been dismissed as chairman of the Post Office. He appeared on TV last night saying it was a case of rape! He put up a bad performance, but there have been stoppages all over the country as it is thought that his dismissal is due to political malice. I met Stonehouse at the Kuwait party last night, who has taken no part in all the fuss—he said to me months ago that Hall's appointment was a bad mistake. Last night he was again quite frank about it.

Lunch for Jo Grimond. He seemed older and less interested in what is going on. He didn't see how Alec Home could remain as Foreign Secretary much longer: he seems completely out of touch. Jo thought the Government's housing policy was better than Labour's. He thought little of the capacity of these Ministers, but perhaps they were better than their predecessors—the Labour Junior Ministers were so bad. He thought Ted was in an unjustifiably euphoric mood. He had dined last night with Vic Feather and Jack Peel of the T.U.C., but does not seem to have come away with any definite impressions. He says present tendencies are sending small businesses in the north of Scotland to the wall. The unemployment rate is nominally high but there is in fact an acute shortage of labour. Men read of 'low-paid workers' in Coventry taking home what seems to them a generous pay-packet, so they demand big increases, or leave for the South. The small enterprises themselves cannot pay for higher wages out of increased productivity—there is no scope for expansion. Meanwhile Government policy imposes on his islands ever more, and unnecessary, overheads. He likes Carr but cannot believe we have the years in which to make his labour relations Bill work (if it ever would). He had heard of another devaluation, perhaps next year, but to him it was no more than a rumour—he had no information.

Monday, November 30th, 1970

Lunch for A.B. [a senior civil servant], who said he is coming round to my pessimistic point of view. He said Ministers on both sides are having arguments about conditions on the sun-deck, confident that all is well in the engine-room and that the great ship is well and truly on course. But this is not so—there *is* something grievously wrong in the engine-room and precious time is being wasted. He does not see this Government fighting a strike to the bitter end—and certainly not in the next big wage claim, which is coming from the power-station men. He sees a further tightening of the money squeeze; large numbers of bankruptcies, some of them important; mounting unemployment; and the show-down with the unions coming over a march of the unemployed on Whitehall—or some such event. But the Government is making no contingency plans for such an emergency. He thought that a big crisis would be met by emergency regulations which would be continued—perhaps indefinitely. He thought a snap election on the theme of Government by Whitehall or by the T.U.C. would get us nowhere. It might impress M.P.s, but the principal result would be to waste two to three months of valuable time. He is puzzled by the vociferous support of Lord Hall by the trades unions. He was a complete failure and would have had to go under any regime. My friend is always discreet, but he left me with the clear impression that he thinks Barber a weak Chancellor, and that Whitelaw is the ablest member of Ted's team.

Before, he had argued that the Ministry of Technology was not too large. Now he is saying that chunks of both Davies's and Walker's empires are to be chopped off.

A.B. said when he first joined the Civil Service it was impressed on him that no legislative or other measures should be imposed that were unenforceable. Now this argument is brushed aside by Ministers who attach no importance to it. In consequence there is an increasing bulk of regulations which cannot be implemented.

Dinner with the Industrial Educational and Research Foundation to hear Robens give the Earle Memorial Lecture. I sat between Sir John Reiss, chairman of the Blue Circle group, and Sir Donald Macdougall, Chief Economic Adviser to the Treasury. Macdougall is a dim little man—a stage civil servant: Reiss is an attractive big man with a stutter, larger on charm than on ability one would think. Robens spelled out in some detail his belief that the Government legislation on trades unions would not work, and otherwise seemed to suppose that his experiences at the Coal Board are generally applicable throughout industry—a view I do not share.

Wednesday, December 2nd, 1970

A hilarious lunch with George Bolton and the directors of BOLSA.* The others were teasing George and saying it is too easy just now to be gloomy. What he needs now is some good news to test his pessimistic mettle!

He spoke first of what he called disaster areas in the U.S. The air-travel industry is in real trouble, and this combined with cut-backs in the aero-space industry means that the most advanced technological concerns are in real trouble. I understood him to say that Boeing, who employed 130,000 workers quite recently, will be down to 13,000 by March. Their customers are cutting back on their contracts and Boeing may well go broke. Lockheed should scrape by with orders from the Pentagon and cheap engines from Rolls-Royce.

He thought that in spite of brave words nothing much would be done about inflation. He did not think we should follow the path of the Germans, whose inflation after the First World War was largely introduced to defeat the purposes of the Versailles Treaty. He thought that, as in South America, inflation would destroy our political institutions and leave us with an autocratic regime with the tacit (or not so tacit) support of the armed forces. I asked him what should be done, but like others, he has no clear idea, though obviously a clash with the unions must be part of any measures to bring inflation to a halt.

I asked him if Toby Aldington was to be the new Governor of

* Bank of London and South America.

the Bank. He thought he probably would get it. Cromer was the front runner, but is not regarded by Ted as a friend, and so is sent off to Washington. Gordon Richardson is actively canvassing for the job and may still get it. Stevens he thought a very outside chance because: (a) he is lazy; (b) Morgan Grenfell is in a mess having lost a lot of money financing films; (c) it is held against him that he accepted the Treasury job in Washington from the Wilson Government.

BOLSA do a lot of financing of British Leyland exports and know Donald Stokes well. George spoke of him as a disaster and hoped, or had hoped, that Robens would take over the company. Stokes is a salesman and no more. George thought Chrysler might well close down in this country, which could be supplied from their plants in France or Germany.

On the international plane he thought attempts were being made in this country to build up the reputation of Willi Brandt, who, they said, has little influence in Germany. The huge industrial expansion in Japan will be unable to trade on the required scale with the U.S. or Europe and is bound to turn to China. On previous occasions he has confidently foretold civil war in Italy. Now he says it will not break out as long as Carli (of the Central Bank) is in control.

He thought our financial affairs had been badly conducted with a huge Budget deficit under Maudling and a huge surplus under Roy Jenkins. On the whole he expected a financial crisis next autumn.

Had a brief word with C.D. at our film party last night. I got the impression he was disappointed that I had not handed out a few home truths to Ted about his leadership and his team. I explained that I had been given no opening. He said that Ted shows his hand to no one, and so it is quite impossible to guess what he really thinks of the situation.

Friday, December 4th, 1970
Lunch for Rupert Murdoch. He had some Fleet Street gossip. The *Mirror* circulation figures are down 680,000 on the year; *Express*, down 280,000; *Mail*, 180,000; *Sketch*, 120,000; *Times*, 76,000; *Guardian* and *Telegraph* a bit up, and of course the *Sun*. Esmond Rothermere is apparently very gloomy—even the *Evening News* is losing money, and the *Sketch* is expected to be closed any day now. The journalists are in a very militant mood. In part they want parity with their brethren in the mechanical departments, but there is a

minority that is seeking workers' control. Neither Rupert nor anyone else has any idea where this will all end, but a sharp reduction in the number of London newspapers seems inevitable. Rupert did not seem to be politically well-informed, but supposed that the Government will not seriously fight a major strike and that inflation will continue until there is some kind of collapse. The seriousness of the situation is increasingly seen by the newspapers and by other political observers, but so far no sign of anxiety by ministers.

Sunday, December 6th, 1970

Dinner last night for Peyton and his wife. She is attractive and very suitable, but he is more interesting. Preliminary accounts were that he is a nice man with a head of solid bone. He has been in the House for a number of years and is now Minister of Transport, deputy to Walker (Environment). He is no intellectual and has a thick, slow speech which gives an impression of stupidity. But this is quite wrong: he is a sort of Whitelaw, an admirable, warm human being with excellent intuitive judgment. Ruth's comment at the end was that perhaps Whitelaw, Carrington, Peyton and some others in the Government have a spiritual link (hence their niceness) which will enable them to achieve results that their executive abilities would not.

Peyton was quite clear that we are in for a very rough time—widespread bankruptcies and unemployment. At some point there would be a major clash between the Government and the unions. The outcome of the present situation is bound to be a humiliated Britain depressed to a point where there will be no feather-bed for anyone. At present adversity meant stepping out of the sitting-room on to the balcony. There will come a time when it will mean a drop from the fourth floor on to solid concrete. He could envisage a time when the number of unemployed would make it impossible to pay out present levels of unemployment pay.

Though Peyton clearly anticipates a crunch of the most drastic and painful kind, I didn't get the impression that appropriate precautions were being taken.

An interesting point he made was that now all water is pumped by electricity, as is sewage. At one time power was supplied by all sorts of independent engines, but now it is all electric and all off the grid. This makes the whole community desperately vulnerable to an electricity stoppage—though no decision on the subject was ever made. It was just allowed to happen. Finally his description of Wilson—'anaesthetist rampant'.

Two last-minute recollections of our talk. Peyton said: (1) no real national recovery is possible until we have been deeply humiliated; and (2) what a nice man Jack Jones is!

Tuesday, December 8th, 1970

Lunch for C.D. [a senior civil servant]—very friendly and less discreet than usual. He agreed with Ruth's point that Whitelaw, Peyton and Carrington, with perhaps one or two of the others, including Ray Gunter, may not have brilliant academic brains, may not have great administrative ability, but do have an intuitive judgment of men and their ways that may prove to be what is most wanted. He obviously has a very high opinion of Whitelaw, and evidently thinks that if Ted fails to make the grade, Whitelaw should and would be the successor. He doubted Enoch's ability to cope with the practical problems of government and wondered if he has someone more dangerous behind him. He certainly hasn't, as far as I know. He agreed that the Ministries of Walker and Davies are far too large. He said Ted, in his own eyes, is a man with a mission, but I got the impression that he is not convinced that Ted will pull it off. He thinks the attempt to get into the Common Market will now have to go forward. It has acquired a momentum of its own. Whether, when the time comes, we shall be unable to proceed because of lack of agreement here, or because of our financial difficulties, remains to be seen. He thought the situation would be very different a month from now, as by then we should either have given in to the power-station men's go-slow or we should still be fighting— and either way the consequences would be apparent.

Wednesday, December 9th, 1970

Lunch for Richard Briginshaw of NATSOPA*—he is trying to get out of his partnership with the paper workers that constituted SOGAT. I asked him, 'Why the divorce?' He said the Central London Branch of the paper workers has always been militant, not to say subversive; and this branch, though largely autonomous, has succeeded in dominating some of the regional branches with a view to furthering the objectives of the International Socialists. When

* National Society of Operative Printers, Graphical and Media Personnel. Formerly, National Society of Operative Printers and Assistants.

Briginshaw tried to bring any discussion back to the interests of members he was always out-voted. I asked about the International Socialists, but he was very vague. They were Marxists, but they were not orthodox Communists (Chinese or Russian), nor were they Trotsky-ite, and they seemed to be well supplied with money. It is because of the political dominance of this group that Briginshaw wants his divorce.

Briginshaw's main theme was that we are moving towards an autocracy of the national socialist kind. It is hard to see how it could work without mass backing similar to Mussolini and his Black Shirts, or Hitler and his Brown Shirts. At the moment there is no such body in existence and it would take at least a year to get one going. It is interesting that a member of the T.U.C. General Council should so frankly regard existing parties and institutions as at the very end of their useful life. The lunch was at his request and he looks forward to a further meeting some time in the future.

Thursday, December 10th, 1970

The power go-slow continues. The most serious news is from Belfast where all power to industry has been stopped, and 200,000 men are without work this morning. Carr saw the union leaders last night and they refused an offer of arbitration. Carr said publicly he saw no occasion for emergency regulations. It is difficult to see what the Government is hoping to achieve. Perhaps they believe that the weight of public opinion will cause the unions to give in. This they will certainly not do.

Dinner last night with the Keswicks—John and Claire. He thinks this is the beginning of the real crunch; that this time it will not be patched up, and the men will not be bought off. Humphrey Trevelyan was the other guest—intelligent and charming as ever. He didn't seem to have any definite views; perhaps he was being discreet.

Monday, December 14th, 1970

Lunch for Barnetson of Reuters and United Newspapers. He is a Scot and has known Alec Home for a long time—anyway since before the War. He thinks him a nice man and an absolutely honest one but with nothing there, propelled into prominence by his wife. She did not like him renouncing his peerage, but fully enjoyed No. 10. Barnetson said Alec believed the Tories would lose the election last June. In that case Ted was to be replaced—by Alec, or so Alec believed! Barnetson thinks the present Government policy with the unions—resistance to unreasonable wage claims but otherwise patience and forbearance—won't work. This will become increasingly obvious and Ted's term of office will not exceed another eighteen months. Barnetson believes that this does not give Whitelaw enough time to establish himself as the next Leader and so it will be back to Alec.

For reasons which did not appear, Barnetson is becoming involved in the affairs of *The Times*. He is shortly to have a meeting with Ken Thomson, Gavin Astor and Kenneth Keith. This will be unknown to Roy Thomson or Denis Hamilton. These last two are on indifferent terms with each other. Ken is not very interested in *The Times*, and at his father's death intends to return to Canada. He is not ready to finance large losses indefinitely.

Reuter is doing very well—turn-over up from £8 million to £15 million, and a rising profit in spite of huge wage increases. This is due to their very profitable commodity service, and increasing profits in the U.S.

Monday, December 21st, 1970

The news is of the upheaval in Poland and the resignation of Gomulka. The Russians can hardly be happy about this, following on trouble in Czechoslovakia and, earlier on, in Hungary and East Germany. However, the Russians are not the people to ease up, though it might make them more cautious over the Middle East and escalating armaments.

Lunch for Eric Roll—in great form as usual, though expressing doubts about our financial future in the spring. He had little news but had recently seen Ted for an hour. He worked with Ted for two years over the Common Market and knows him well and likes him. His interview, like mine, seems to have been almost entirely a relaxed gossip. However, Eric went so far as to tell Ted that he thought Ted's policy of influencing the trades unions to moderate their demands to acceptable limits had no better than a 50–50 chance of success. This caused no reaction. Ted was apparently most emotional about the Rolls-Royce rescue in which he had played an active part.

Eric had no particular information about the Governorship of the Bank. He thought of the three contestants, Gordon Richardson wanted it most. He doubted if Stevens could be spared from Morgan

Grenfell, so perhaps it would lie between Richardson and Aldington. Eric did not think Leslie O'Brien was quite out of the reckoning.

Before the election he and three other ex-Permanent Under-Secretaries had been advising Ted on the structure of Government, and particularly the organization at No. 10. At the end they came to the conclusion Ted was just the man for the top Civil Service job at No. 10! And of course it has been standard comment on Ted by members of the Parliamentary Labour Party that he is essentially a civil servant not a politician and Minister.

1971

Monday, January 4th, 1971

Lunch for Alex Jarratt. He had been in the Cabinet Office, then with Aubrey Jones at the P.I.B. and now is the new managing director of I.P.C. He has been described to me as intelligent but cold. He is obviously highly intelligent and a man of stature—certainly the most impressive addition to the higher echelons of Fleet Street for a very long time.

He said the story that Wilson had put an end to the electricians' go-slow was true. The *Sunday Telegraph* certainly printed it as if they knew it for a fact, but Jarratt said he knew it was so from 'other than newspaper sources'. He thought Carr's experiences in this affair had made him much more steely and that he might yet prove to be a tough Minister of Labour. He thought Walker and Keith Joseph adequate run-of-the-mill Ministers, and Whitelaw the 'dark horse' of the Government. Davies, he thought, was a good general manager but no more. Maudling as Home Secretary he thought a joke. He thought Barber's mini-Budget a mistake both politically and economically. He thought nothing was being done about inflation and that Whitelaw was the obvious successor if Ted came unstuck.

He thought the present regime in this country prevented the emergence of 'powerful eccentrics', so we have the inadequate leaders in all spheres that we see.

Ministers live in a vacuum, cut off from life as it is. When in the Cabinet Office, he used to feel as he walked out into Whitehall that he was moving back into reality.

As we left Claridge's dining-room, Soames ran after me. He was very friendly and seemed to think that, despite Wilson and Powell, we should be in the Common Market in nine months.

Jarratt said his friends (apparently in the Treasury) told him how immovably obstinate the P.M. is; also that the Treasury is even more against an expansionary policy than the Bank.

Tuesday, January 5th, 1971

Lunch with Edwin Plowden at Bridgewater House, the Tube

Investments headquarters. He returned on Saturday from a six-week trip round the world. He seems to have been mainly impressed by the huge population explosion in Malaya and Mexico.

Having been away for so long he has no news. He thought a tight deflationary policy, or a direct clash with the unions, or runaway inflation, would all create a revolutionary situation which could only be handled by totalitarian methods. He had thought this for two years and saw no escape. The danger of inflation was not basically because it effects the destruction of our society. All Western societies are affected by the disease which will destroy society as we know it.

Plowden thought Carr such a nice man—so patient and so reasonable that he may prove a success, though it is still uncertain how he would behave in a crisis. He has a low opinion of John Davies, and was annoyed by his promotion to the Cabinet. He was told by Douglas Houghton that Wilson will not lead the Labour Party into the next election. I wonder what led to this prediction. Douglas is anti-Wilson, but he must have some other grounds for this assertion. Perhaps he is thinking of Wilson's book. Plowden did not think he would be succeeded by Roy Jenkins, whom he regards as too dilettante.

Saturday, January 9th, 1971

Have just returned from the Annual Conference of the Psychologists Association at York. Last night at dinner I sat next one Wallis, psychologist at the Ministry of Labour, now D.E.P.* He said he and his colleagues were in great difficulties over the labour relations Bill.† They knew it would not work, but Ministers insisted on pressing on with it. I asked was this the opinion of all the officials at the D.E.P.? He said, no, because administrative-grade officials in a political matter like this can have no opinions. As principal psychologist he is a professional adviser and apparently not bound by the same rules.

---

* Department of Employment and Productivity.

† The labour relations or Industrial Relations Bill, which later became law, was to be a constant source of political strife in Britain until its repeal by the Labour Government in 1974. In oversimplified terms, the Act endeavoured to curb some trade-union powers by requiring unions to 'register' (many unions did not register and thus lost some financial and other privileges), by lessening their ability to enforce 'closed shops' and by restrictions on picketing.

Wednesday, January 13th, 1971

The political climate seems to be warming up. Yesterday evening in the Albert Hall there was a great rally of trades unionists to protest against the Government's Industrial Relations Bill. Wilson was constantly heckled and interrupted by cries of 'Judas' and 'hypocrite': Vic Feather was not allowed to finish his speech. Then, later in the evening, two bombs went off at Robert Carr's house near Barnet. Much damage was done and the back of the house seems to have been blown down. Presumably this is the work of trades-union militants on the extreme Left.

I had lunch at Whites with Hugh Fraser. One of the few men there that I knew was Neill Cooper-Key, formerly M.P. for Hastings. Hugh said he was only fitted to be a motor-car salesman!

Fraser is still preoccupied with two cases—one, official secrets, and the other, Biafra. But he presumably reflects the opinion of some section of his Party. He thinks nothing of Barber and considers he may have to go after the Budget; Alec Home is a spent force and may be succeeded by Carrington; Davies he regards as an unfortunate appointment.

Whether out of Party loyalty or conviction, he seemed to think Ted is doing quite well—the test will come over his success with inflation and he should not be judged on this until April. The Industrial Relations Bill, he thinks, might be useful if Ted is given time, which he regards as doubtful.

I said I thought nothing useful could be done about inflation and labour relations until the Government has met the unions in a head-on clash and beaten them. To make sure of winning, the Government would have to be very, very tough. Fraser said measures as tough as that would never get through the present House of Commons. If this is so, we shall have to wait for anarchy to supervene—and with it the end of Parliamentary government.

He said he is being guarded as there is some threat of his being kidnapped! He was not clear about who would do the kidnapping but he reported a conversation he had had with the Chief Constable of Stafford, who told him he could always call on police protection—and the name of McVicar was mentioned. If this is why he is being guarded, it obviously is feared that McVicar would have him kidnapped with a view to his own release.

Monday, January 18th, 1971

One item of news is interesting since my last entry. Leslie O'Brien has been appointed for a further term of five years! From his attitude as described in the papers, he was as surprised as I was. It is a bad appointment and the reasons are not obvious.

Lunch today for William Whitelaw—very friendly, very frank exchange of views. Firstly Enoch Powell. He came out on Saturday saying inflation was due to Government policy; that the unions were more sinned against than sinning; and that the wage explosion was an inevitable consequence of Government liberality with the money supply. He has also been speaking against the Common Market. Whitelaw has had a long conversation with Enoch recently, and says it is clear that when all else has failed Enoch expects to be called in. Enoch was very impressed when the dockers marched on his behalf on the House of Commons after his first big speech on immigration. He thinks this shows that it is his task to unite Right and Left—hence his speeches about the wage explosion and about the Common Market.

Whitelaw had come from a Cabinet meeting on Ireland. Chichester-Clark, after saying that all was now so quiet that the regulations on marches could be relaxed, a day later said that the situation had so deteriorated that sterner measures were necessary. Evidently the Government here is unhappy but has no policy. I told Whitelaw that I had published a piece in *Hibernia* saying that the Government's policy over Ireland was limited to a wish that Ireland and the Irish should go away and get lost. Whitelaw said, 'Exactly.'

Arms for South Africa has become the central issue at the Prime Ministers' Conference in Singapore. The controversy has no real substance at all. The arms will come from France if not from us. The whole issue was raised by an unwise answer by Alec Home to a question at a press conference; the matter was not discussed by the Cabinet until it was more or less out of control. Now the most they can hope for is to scramble out of the affair without loss.

We talked about Ted—to whom Whitelaw is entirely loyal. He said, unlike Wilson, Ted is deeply interested in governing the country. At times he sees too clearly what has to be done and is reluctant to listen to people who point out the difficulties that will have to be surmounted. As for the obstinacy, he cannot be deflected from an unwise move by direct opposition. It has to be a steering process. I pointed out that governing the country is such a big job it has to be done by a team, and Ted's team is a weak one. Whitelaw agreed. He also said Ted has 'his silences'. He sends for people and they leave him without knowing why they were summoned. I said both Eric Roll and I had had that experience.

Whitelaw thought that terms for our entry into the Common Market would be arrived at, but the crucial point would be the majority the Government secures in the House. He thought seventy would be all right, but thirty would be too little for such a major undertaking. Would fifty do? He said there is no means of judging at this stage what the number would be.

I said I thought the question of our entry should be deferred until after the inevitable show-down with the unions. So we turned to that. I said I thought at some point the Government has to take on the trades union movement and win. It can choose the moment and the issue, but must then win. A clash of this magnitude must leave the economy in tatters, and it is then that serious attempts can successfully be made to put labour relations on a sensible footing. It is only after such a clash that we can see our way clear to joining the Common Market. Whitelaw said he was inclined to agree that a series of minor successes would not add up to a major victory. One difficulty, he said, was to convince anyone that the Government really meant what it said. It was clear that no preparations had been made for a major clash. He said the emergency regulations urgently needed attention. They sounded as if they fell within his province, and that in their present form they would not be adequate. The legislation I always believed was sufficiently comprehensive, but the orders under the Act have perhaps not been adequately thought through.

Wednesday, January 27th, 1971

Lunch with Hartley Shawcross. Though he has a number of directorships he seems to me to have largely retired—anyway in his attitude. He said that the candidates considered for the Governorship of the Bank were Richardson, Stevens, Aldington—and David Montagu! Cromer, he did not think was seriously contemplated. To mention Montagu—a conspicuous Jew—in view of the vast amounts of Arabian money in London, seems quite cracked. Hartley thought the final decision was that none of the alternatives were obviously better than Leslie O'Brien. Hartley thought a clash with the trades unions was inevitable—would this lead to a coalition? I said not under Wilson or Heath but perhaps Healey or Whitelaw? He said

Whitelaw did not carry enough authority, and Healey was too devious—look how he had campaigned for arms for South Africa in Cabinet but ran a moral campaign against the arms in public. He said he had to say with regret he thought the Labour administration better than this one. In an emergency he thought it possible that Robens might play a leading part. Meanwhile the emergency seems to be coming nearer. In the House, the obstruction by Labour over the quite innocuous labour relations Bill is being carried to unprecedented lengths. The engineering union says it will refuse to register when the Bill becomes law and other unions are urging a national strike. In any case we now have a suspended strike of power-station and other electricians, and an actual strike of the Post Office and British European Airways. Barber claims the Government's anti-inflation policy is working, but this appears to be the merest wishful thinking.

I was lunching at Warburg's one day when *The Times* in its business section had confused Hoesch and Hoechst, two of the largest firms in Europe; one steel, the other chemicals. My daughter Scilla says that recently *The Times* had spelt Landseer, the painter, Lancia, and *Rosenkavalier*, Rose and Cavalier. This is her husbands home ground so the story may well be right.

At dinner yesterday at the Shell Centre the conversation turned on John Davies, the Minister for Technology. He was well known to those present from his days at Shell-B.P. They said he was much liked at Shell, at the C.B.I. and at his present ministry, but he was not highly regarded as an executive at Shell-B.P.

Thursday, January 28th, 1971

Lunch with Denis Hamilton and Hussey at *The Times*. Both very friendly and it was nearly three o'clock before I got away from Ken Thomson and the others.

First, Fleet Street. Denis had done his best with the *Guardian* but they insist on maintaining their independence, in spite of now moving into the red on both papers together. The obvious move is for *The Times* in London, the *Guardian* in Manchester and the *Scotsman* to co-operate with news and other services; but Richard Scott, the chairman of trustees (and Washington correspondent!) of the *Guardian* will have none of this. It is thought the *Sketch* will fold in the next few weeks. It has been making a small contribution to overheads but is doing so no longer. Esmond and Max Aitken have been discussing for months a merger between the *Mail* and the *Express*, but now Esmond has run away to South Africa, and it is thought Vere Harmsworth (egged on by Mrs Vere) will attempt to soldier on alone. Murdoch is threatening to start a new evening paper if the *News* and the *Standard* merge. It would a be a sort of evening *News of the World*. The *Sunday Telegraph* is losing a lot of money, and the *Observer* is in serious financial trouble. The *Mirror* has lost all character and has become an imitation *Sun*. The unions continue as militant, short-sighted and irresponsible as ever. I have been told recently by both John Bonfield, general secretary of the N.G.A.,* and Briginshaw that the Central Branch of the paper workers is politically dominated by a group called the International Socialists. Vic Feather told Denis this, and said these Socialists get money from China via Ceylon and that this is well known to the Special Branch. *The Times* has done quite well out of its increase in price to 1s. and its losses are now manageable.

The *Sunday Times* has bought Wilson's book on his six years in office. He is receiving £260,000 and the book will be out about May. Denis thinks he is going to tell all (why not make sure—for that money?) and he certainly goes to town on George Brown. *The Times* has bought Rab Butler's memoirs. According to Denis he was very dependent on his first wife for decision and courage, but had a built-in sense of timing and a feel for politics all his own.

Over the book, Denis had seen Wilson recently who told him he had done his best with Frank Chapple to get the electricians back to work. He is afraid, as I supposed, that too direct a challenge to the Parliamentary majority would lead to an election and a majority of 200 for the Tories. Denis thinks people before Christmas were fed up with strikes and unions, but now rising prices was the principal worry. If this is so, an election now would be counter-productive as they say. Wilson thinks the Tories will be in a horrible mess some time next year and that is when there will be an election and his own return to office.

Hussey seemed clear that some time there will have to be a fight to a finish between the Government and the unions—Denis seemed less sure, though he supposed the recruiting of territorials was a straw to show which way the Governmental mind was working.

Denis said it was remarkable that Conservative Party headquarters had ceased trying to recruit talent for the Tory benches. Three

* National Graphical Association.

members of the Thomson Organization got in last June—all three of them men of no distinction or talent.

One of the printing unions had threatened the employers that they would on no account permit the employers to implement the Industrial Relations Bill when it becomes law.

Saturday, January 30th, 1971
Dinner last night alone with the Peytons. We like them both very much.

Peyton said Wilson had apparently lost all grip. In the House he was boring and long-winded and showed no sign of his former skill. Ted he described as a very active P.M.—chasing up his Ministers and at times very impatient. Peyton thinks the Government is moving to the Right and that events will force them to continue to do so. He could not see the country turning to Enoch Powell under any circumstances. Like all Ministers today he is optimistic: thinks Ted is in No. 10 for a very long time and described the trades union movement as in its death-throes!

Monday, February 1st, 1971
Lunch at the Heinz headquarters at Hayes. It is evidently exceedingly well run, in an American style, but until recently there were no Americans on the staff: now there are two, on the selling side. They came to the lunch-table from a board meeting at which they had discussed the probable outcome of the present situation as a qualified national strike. The managing director is a very impressive young Irishman in his late thirties.

In their own sphere they have little competition—their worry is the supermarkets. In the U.S. any discount to any one retailer must be given to all, however small. Here there are no limits, and as a result Tesco and Fine Fare are squeezing the food manufacturers dry. They thought Cadbury had made a mistake to go in with Schweppes, and Imperial Tobacco would much like to get back out of food. Campbell's Soup's incursion into the British market had so far been a catastrophe—£7½ million loss, plus the absence of any interest on the initial loan from the parent company.

Wednesday, February 3rd, 1971
Lunch at the *Punch* office. The other guest was Arnold Goodman—the host, Barnetson, as United Newspapers are now the owners.

Davis, the editor, said that the official biography of Prince Philip has just been completed. The *Observer* bid £1,500 for the serial rights but the *Sunday Telegraph* got them for 26,000 guineas!

Barnetson said that Roy Thomson was completely disillusioned about the reassurances he had had about *The Times* but had agreed to continue to finance it till the end of 1972. The talk is still that Rees-Mogg will be replaced by Louis Heren as editor.

Saturday, February 6th, 1971
The unexpected collapse of Rolls-Royce, the squeeze put on Western countries by the oil-rich countries, and serious riots in Belfast and Rome, leave one wondering whether the balloon is now beginning to go up. There is an official strike of all Ford workers; the postal workers' strike continues; and we have yet to hear the ruling on the electricians' strike by the Wilberforce Tribunal.

Tuesday, February 23rd, 1971
At my seventieth birthday party last night I had some talk with Ted Heath and others, but nothing much emerged. It was a social occasion and everyone was enjoying himself. Ted seemed to me unduly optimistic; and Douglas Houghton alarmed by the militant attitude of some unions and the irresponsible support they received from Vic Feather among others. Whitelaw seemed to me to have dwindled in personality.

Ruth had more confidential talk with Ted than I had. He said his greatest problem just now is the subversive fifth column 'reaching right up to the top'. He also said he had not yet got to the bottom of the part played by Wilson in my expulsion from the *Mirror*.

Thursday, February 25th, 1971
Dinner in Paris last night with the Lazareffs—the principal other guests were the Couve de Murvilles and Mike Cowles, now 23-per-cent proprietor of the *New York Times*. It is clear from all the contacts I have made so far in Paris that there is some anxiety here about our willingness to join the Common Market. The public opinion polls in Britain have shown a large popular majority against, but then the issue has never really been explained to the great British public, and has often been discussed in terms of the price of butter.

The Couve de Murvilles have recently returned from China, and

Madame told Ruth that it was essential that we should come in for the sake of Europe and the world. This point of view had been pressed on her by the Chinese, who expressed great hostility to both Russia and the U.S. The Chinese view was that without us Europe was too weak and that world civilization depended on the health and strength of Europe.

Mike Cowles had been seeing something of Nixon, who said that come-what the American army would have to be out of Vietnam by November 1972. There might be a residue of 50,000 professionals to supply air cover or logistical support. In the meantime the important Vietnamese attack on Laos seems to be going badly.

Cowles had recently entertained to lunch in the South of France Humphrey and Dewey. The former is not a very probable candidate for the Presidency next year: the latter was a candidate against Truman, but is apparently now much consulted by Nixon. Nixon has announced a budget with a deficit of $11 billion to stimulate the economy. Dewey was asked what the actual deficit would prove to be and guessed $30 billion. Humphrey, a very different man, put the figure at nearer $40 than $30 billion. If these figures are realized there will be roaring inflation in the U.S. leading, Cowles thinks, to a depression in 1973 of major dimensions. If this is all done to ensure Nixon's re-election in 1972 he will be buying four years of what Hoover had to endure from 1929–32.

Cowles thought that both in the U.S. and the U.K. there would have to be a major clash with the unions.

In conversation with Ruth at my birthday party, someone from the Russian embassy said to her that the Russian problem was too many bottles and too few corks!

Friday, February 26th, 1971
Lunch yesterday with Soames to hear Schumann speak on the Common Market—and dinner with Mosley. No particular news from either source. Soames says we shall be offered reasonable terms for entry into the Common Market—doubts of success are due to lack of interest by the British public. Mosley—as last time— gives the impression of good contacts in Europe and America and a busy life, though the nature of the busy life can only be guessed at.

I had a talk with Charles Gombault, who said everything in France is quiet but the situation is unstable and almost anything might happen at any moment. The Algerians have nationalized the French oil companies in Algeria. Pompidou is blamed for his handling of the matter. In his attempt to have a different style from de Gaulle he hesitates to act and prefers to react, which often means moving too late.

The most striking aspect of our visit to Paris was our usual pilgrimage to Notre Dame. I am not susceptible to atmosphere but even so, even to me, this great church has gone dead. It has been cleaned up and is better lighted, but the side chapels are no longer used for worship; the altar has been moved down to the centre of the church, and the whole place is now just a great architectural monument. It is astonishing that this could have happened in the short period—less than two years—since we were last there.

Friday, March 5th, 1971

Lunch yesterday with Dick Beeching. He is now chairman of Redland Ltd* and seemed less interested in public affairs. He is still very gloomy about the outlook but says he is tired of crying 'Wolf, wolf'. He is more favourably impressed by the labour relations Bill than anyone I have spoken to outside the Government. He doesn't think it will achieve much but it is a very necessary beginning. His one interesting story was to recall that Macmillan had said to him that he was surprised by the Tories' selection of Ted as their leader: that he was no political leader but an excellent staff officer.

Saturday, March 6th, 1971

Ted Heath to tea yesterday to plant the tree he gave me for my seventieth birthday. He had little news but was most friendly. He had had a talk with the Italian head of the Common Market Commission from which it emerged that they had not really thought through the various problems. When asked to say precisely what he meant by various generalities, he was unable to do so. Other impressions were, that he disliked Enoch Powell more than somewhat, and that he had never considered a comprehensive solution of the Irish problem. Ruth thinks Ted is fond of me; I think he is fond of her and finds the friendship of an intelligent and musical woman, with no possible axe to grind, very welcome.

* Redland Limited is a well-known firm with interests in construction materials, quarrying, concrete, engineering and related fields.

Monday, March 8th, 1971

Lunch for Dick Marsh. He has come on a lot, both when Minister of Transport, and since. He says Wilson does not seem yet to have accepted the fact that he lost the election. In November he was telling Marsh that this Government would not last eighteen months. He takes little part in the business of the House, but embarrasses new members by recounting the brilliant speeches he made years ago.

Marsh spoke at length of the air of unreality that pervades the House of Commons: Barbara Castle, in almost hysterical terms, is denouncing the policy she advocated less than a year ago; other ex-Ministers are denouncing 20 per cent wage increases as inadequate, when a year ago they were denouncing a 5 per cent increase as excessive. The whole life of the House is centred on the chamber and on debating successes there. The impact on the outside world is lost sight of. Marsh says the politics of the Parliamentary Labour Party are determined by the Tribune Group, a tiny minority.

As he was formerly a trades union official, many of his friends are trades union officials, and they regard with amusement the pretensions of the P.L.P. to represent their interests—they are quite capable of dealing direct with any government.

Marsh regards the Industrial Relations Bill as unworkable—if anything it will make matters worse. Both with the Pilkington strike and the miners it would have prolonged the strikes, and in the case of the postmen and the dustmen it would have made no difference.

He said the Government seems to have started out with various doctrinaire ideas, found them unworkable and then stalled. Important decisions have been pending for years on both the ports and the Electricity Council, to the great detriment of the people involved. There was a proposal to merge the C.E.G.B.* and the Electricity Council (the manufacturers and the retailers, so to speak, of electricity). No one, not even the Permanent Under-Secretary, knows whether this plan is to go forward or not. The Labour Party ports Bill was scrapped but nothing has been put in its place. Marsh said Sir John Eden is a nice man, quite wet and with no discernible ability.

Marsh is alarmed by the growing strength of the militants and subversives generally. The success of excessive wage demands has

* The Central Electricity Generating Board, the nationalized organization responsible for the generation of all electric power in Britain.

88

added to their influence. Jackson of the Post Office workers and Fisher of the dustmen both advised against a strike. It remains to be seen how far Jackson was right when we hear the result of the Court of Inquiry. The proposal for a one-day general strike is now supported by the engineering and the transport workers' unions and it only needs one other big union—say the miners—for the plan to be adopted. I asked Marsh how he saw the future. He said he saw no likely change from the present decline—we could become the 'slum of northern Europe' or 'a more sophisticated Spain'. He regarded the present Government as a disaster, but saw no salvation in a Labour one. He thought the sabotage by the militant trades unionists might lead to a fascist autocracy, but that the Communists would regard this as a useful step in the break-up of our society.

Tuesday, March 9th, 1971
Lunch with Mike—he had two interesting items. Recently he and Libby had dinner at the Chinese Embassy. The party was uninteresting, but the Chinese made it quite clear that their policy vis-à-vis the United States was based on the belief that the U.S. was sliding inexorably into chaos.

Gary Weston told Mike that some time ago he was looking for a new managing director for Associated British Foods and Adamson, then at the D.E.A.,* was looking for a better job. Gary saw him among other applicants and concluded he lacked administrative ability and that his future should be at a university. However, he is now Mike's boss at the C.B.I.

Thursday, March 11th, 1971
Lunch for Stonehouse, who now has a job which keeps him busy and has brought him on. He is lying low for the present but intends to make his voice heard in a year or so. Incompetent as he thought the Labour Government, this one he thinks even worse. He finds politics rather nauseating, with Denis Healey (on South African arms) and Barbara Castle (on wages) denouncing policies they favoured only a few months ago. He said it is widely believed in the P.L.P. that Wilson cannot win another election. He is tired and may drop out, but is hard to push—particularly in the absence of a declared alternative. Stonehouse is particularly hostile to Dick Crossman—a shameless liar, he calls him. When President of the

* Department of Economic Affairs.

Council he habitually arrived five minutes late for Council meetings to keep the Queen waiting.

Stonehouse thinks the Industrial Relations Bill was cooked up by intellectuals in the D.E.P. He regards it as unworkable. He has a low opinion of Vic Feather and thinks he has lost stature since he became T.U.C. Secretary. Of Ministers he was particularly critical of Corfield (Aviation Minister), who handled the Rolls-Royce affair exceedingly badly in the House.

Stonehouse thinks Ted will not last to fight the next election though this is not quite certain yet. If he goes, he will be replaced by Enoch Powell. Enoch will have no support from the P.L.P. or the unions, but will pick up many votes from the Labour rank and file. Of the Ministers, he thought John Davies would learn to put up an adequate performance in the House; he thought Whitelaw had gained most in reputation but would need a spell in a department before he could aspire to the leadership.

Ruth called on Iain Paisley this morning to urge him to see his future in an all-Ireland setting. Surprisingly, she found him a warm and humble man of prayer, borne down by the burden of responsibility that he felt was laid on him by events.

P.S. Stonehouse thought that the Tory Party led by Enoch could win the next election.

Monday, March 15th, 1971

John Peyton to lunch. He is not very bright intellectually, but a terribly nice human being with good judgment. He has seen something of Jack Jones. If ever there was a man riding a tiger, Peyton thought this was he—a nice man, very different from Scanlon whom Peyton regards as a dangerous subversive. Jones was reported to him as saying he thought that by the end of the year wage increases would be down to 5 per cent. Peyton has a high opinion of Marsh and a low one of Barbara Castle, two of his predecessors at the Transport Ministry. He thinks the attitude of the engineers may well end up in a general strike, or something equivalent. He thought this Government would fight it out, however rough the going was. He seemed surprised when I said that Reggie Maudling is lazy and does not do his homework. He gave John Davies a B-plus though it was not clear if he meant this to reflect his present standing, or what he enjoyed in the industrial world. He did not evidently attach any probability to Enoch's succeeding Heath as P.M. under any circumstances. He thought Ted had improved in his capacity to get across to the British public but evidently did not rate his demagogic skill at all high.

Tuesday, March 16th, 1971

Lunch for Jo Grimond. He seems to have contracted out of any active part in politics; regards the labour relations Bill as largely irrelevant; perhaps Ted may pull round the trades-union attitude. He criticized the Government and the press for the very small efforts made to inform the public—neither the Common Market nor inflation had really been explained. As a hundred Labour M.P.s were subsidized by trades unions they played no useful part in discussing trades-union matters—they just shouted remarks they thought would please their masters.

While I was waiting for Jo, Sophie Brown appeared. She seemed doubtful of the greeting she would get from me and was very grateful for a few kind words. Evidently she regards the publication of George's book with apprehension and distaste. Later George came up. Last time I had seen him he had cut me dead. This time he was very polite. I gathered I get a sweet-sour reference in his book, to appear on March 29th. He said he had been kind to Wilson, though I have heard Wilson is in no way kind to George in *his* new book.

Thursday, March 18th, 1971

Another one-day strike by engineers and others. Carr made some severe remarks yesterday, but so far there is really no Government reaction.

Forty-five minutes with Leslie O'Brien yesterday. He could not have been more friendly. He was reticent. Was this due to caution or a lack of anything to impart? He evidently was very apprehensive about the future and was surprised that Heath was so chirpy. He did not anticipate any trouble in the near future—a good surplus for this year in spite of everything. His biggest worry—again not for this year—was the American deficit in their balance of payments. The Germans have dollar reserves equal to 85 per cent of the American gold reserve. If these were turned into gold there would be an immediate crisis, but this will not happen—anyway not now. The huge sums in dollars in the hands of various foreigners means the Americans will almost certainly have to devalue—a difficult operation in their case—but this excess of dollars helps us as our liabilities are in dollars.

Lunch for Ray Gunter—a terribly nice little man. I asked him about Wilson. Gunter said he has not yet recovered from his defeat in the election and does not show much inclination to wait for the job again. But he is quite determined not to relinquish the Leadership of the Party until he has made sure that Jim Callaghan will not get the job. His nominee is Denis Healey—and a new book about Denis to be published shortly would seem to indicate a bid for the top job. Gunter said it was strange that neither Denis nor Roy Jenkins did anything to ingratiate themselves with the back-benchers on whom their elevation would depend. Jim is treasurer of the Party and is likely to give an indication to the Conference in the autumn that he will be resigning. His idea, according to Gunter, is to get his friends in the trades union movement to change the rules so that the secretary of the Party can be an M.P. Harry Nicholas retires from the secretaryship soon and Jim would try and get elected as his successor. His position as secretary, in charge of the machine, and as a member of the Shadow Cabinet, would put him in a strong position to bid for the leadership. Meanwhile Arthur Skeffington has died—he was more or less an ex-officio member of the N.E.C.* representing the Co-op movement.† Roy has done a lot for the Co-ops and it would strengthen his position to be their official spokesman at the N.E.C.

So far Gunter was on his home ground—well-informed and convincing. On the subject of national politics and the Conservatives he was far less so. He knew full well that the Industrial Relations Bill would become law. He thought the Act would be fought by trades unions over a period of a year of two, and if Heath were then prepared to modify the less workable parts of the Act, it would come to be accepted. He said some unions, e.g. the miners, would never accept the provision barring the closed shop. Carr knows this but is unable to convince his colleagues. I said I thought that if the unions are to be put in their place we shall have to have a clash amounting to a general strike. Gunter said 'No', there would be no general strike, or its equivalent, beyond possibly a one-day stoppage.

* The Labour Party National Executive Council.

† The Co-operative Movement is a traditional part of the British Labour Party. It was mainly symbolized by its chain of small departmental stores which return a percentage of profits to customers in the form of 'divis', or dividends.

The militants did not form more than 10 per cent of the shop stewards, and with rising unemployment their power would fade. At the same time he said you cannot expect men to forgo a rise in wages equal to the rise in prices. This is a formula for runaway inflation. In general, the problem of inflation, which underlies everything else, did not really seem to have been thought through.

He described Heath as inflexible, and said Maudling would have been a better Party leader, because he was more of a father figure. He expressed affection and respect for Whitelaw, dismissed Powell as without a future, and was utterly comtemptuous of Peyton.

Tuesday, March 23rd, 1971

The two big stories: Laos, where the American invasion, in spite of Nixon's frequent assertions of victory, seems to have been a disaster: and Northern Ireland—Chichester-Clark has gone and in his place we are to have Brian Faulkner. The new P.M. will have to pursue the same policy, as laid down in Westminster, and seems to have far less support in Ulster than either Craig or Paisley. Peyton last night gave Faulkner three weeks! On TV it was interesting seeing the pictures of Chichester-Clark two years ago and now. In the earlier pictures one saw a man delighted to become P.M.: in the later pictures an aged ghost of his former self. What a bashing he must have had!

Friday, March 26th, 1971

Dinner last night with the Eccleses—not a great success as a party, but we picked up two or three crumbs of information. Though David Eccles is not in the Cabinet he attended the first few Cabinet meetings of the Heath administration. They had been working for two years on their plans, but when they took office they found the plans had little relation to the problems. They thought Government expenditure was the problem, when in fact it was inflation. Eccles said it took three months for the Cabinet to readjust its ideas.

On the general political situation he found it surprising that the unemployment figures created so little feeling. Counting in Northern Ireland, it is now 800,000, the largest figure for a very long time. I suggested the reason was that only a part of this number were really seeking work. He had just returned from Scotland, where the proportion is much higher than in London, and would have none of my contention. Actually the real unemployment figure is very low—

except in certain areas—and anyway the dole, with children's allowances and out-relief, leave the unemployed man far more comfortable than he used to be.

On Enoch Powell David was contemptuous—a weathercock and opportunist. Peregrine Worsthorne, one of the guests, is pro-Powell in a general way. He thought Powell's stock-in-trade was to be tough. At the moment Ted was being even tougher, so Powell was deprived at present of his *raison d'être*. I have no exaggerated opinion of Enoch's abilities, but in the present state of political bankruptcy I think the professionals are writing him off too readily.

Lunch today for Vic Feather—a complete contrast with last night. In a long and rambling conversation, the following points emerged. The unions think they can turn the Industrial Relations Bill to their own advantage. They will register and accept everything favourable in the Bill. Heath tells them the employers will be more generous in the case of an enforceable contract than with a non-enforceable one—possibly by as much as 4 per cent. They will agree on an enforceable contract and then break it. They do not think the employers can refuse an enforceable contract or that it will be possible to enforce it. They think that by September or October the Government will be in such a mess it will come to the T.U.C. to rescue them—which will be done, at a price. Vic's expression was that they have the Government by the balls and intend to make full use of their advantage.

I asked where the bill came from—certainly not from the employers or the unions. He said it was cooked up by Dunnett when he was Permanent Under-Secretary at the D.E.P. It is the product of lawyers and civil servants, not of politicians.

Of the politicians, he said Heath was impossibly stubborn and obstinate. His support among senior Ministers was declining—Vic mentioned Carr, Maudling and Whitelaw. He thought the knives were being readied though still sheathed. While Eccles saw a right-wing government as the only alternative to this one, Vic visualized a general election next year in which the Tories would be massacred. He thought little of the Opposition and said the real opposition was the trades union movement, which was now our only protection against a totalitarian regime. If Heath was deposed, he thought it would be by a friend not an enemy, by Whitelaw not by Powell—as he said, 'Your enemies never get near enough to cut your throat!'

On the general subject of inflation his ideas seemed to be very naïve—reflate and all would be well. At present high wage-claims were all that was keeping the economy from a real recession. He seemed to think that in the rough-and-tumble after the labour relations Bill became law it would be a case of Gresham's Law—bad trades union practice driving out the good. He thought Carr impossibly suave and controlled, surely there must be some fire somewhere!

Vic said the Government was now reduced to lying. The electricians' increase was somewhere between 15 and 21 per cent, it was certainly not 10·9 per cent as claimed by the Government. The gas workers were said to have got £2 per week when it was actually £3.

Wednesday, March 31st, 1971
Lunch with Don Ryder at Reed's. I do not think he is politically well-informed or that his judgment is particularly valuable, but he meets people and would tend to repeat their views. He says Carr's attitude to the N.P.A. is to advise them to fight a rearguard action with the unions—any direct clash would be discouraged, and they are not even going to sue the engineers for damages for their one-day political strikes. He does not see how the Government can contemplate a head-on collision with the unions, and seems to expect a continuing surrender to their demands.

The Budget has received an almost hysterical welcome. It is hard to see why. There is a little to please everybody but the effect of the whole package is inflationary. Don's information is that the unions mean to register under the new Act and to insist that every agreement is unenforceable—defeating the purposes of the legislation. I think Vic gave me a truer picture of their present thinking.

Thursday, April 1st, 1971
Lunch for Campbell Adamson—a nice man but rather diminished, I thought, since our last meeting. He had no particular news, but of course has been in the limelight a lot recently. Wilson had been boasting to him about the unique quality of his forthcoming book and had also pointed out that even if Heath had a run of nine years, Wilson would still be younger than Macmillan was when he first became P.M.

Adamson's information is that the unions will register and insist on all contracts being unenforceable. He thinks the Bill was dreamt up mainly by Carr and Geoffrey Howe (the Solicitor-General). He thinks the Bill may not effect much in itself, but its existence will impinge on his many members and bring labour relations and all that forcibly to their notice. He thought the Budget passable. The concessions made in the Budget were largely neutralized by the increased health charges announced next day. The drop in the Bank Rate and the sum total of all the measures will be a mild degree of reflation and will tend to prevent unemployment going higher. I should have thought the main problems facing us all are: (1) inflation, which has been given a modest push; and (2) investment by industry, which has been far too low and has now been given a very little help; (3) and the fact that the welfare state already does too much for the inadequate of different sorts and is now to do more.

The figures Adamson found most significant are the growth in incomes as compared with the growth in profits. I understood him to say that, at constant prices, between 1965 and 1970 incomes were up 45 per cent, profits up 4 per cent, and if adequate provision were made for replacement of plant at current prices the 4 per cent would be converted into a loss.

Monday, April 5th, 1971

Lunch for A.B. [a senior civil servant]. In the course of a lively lunch he said he thought the Industrial Relations Bill largely irrelevant. Our entry into the Common Market he still thought a distant prospect—1979 or so. He thought the Government propaganda on the subject deliberately muted, but did not understand why. He said Walker was well thought of by the civil servants in his ministry. Sir John Eden he thought an acknowledged failure suggested by Whitelaw and the Whips, but he would be removed at the earliest opportunity, presumably in the summer recess. He said there was no one at the Treasury who really understood money—certainly no one comparable with Harold Lever (who, however, has moved on— into industry!). He thought the outlook for inflation and for our balance of payments is pretty gloomy and may be seriously worsened by American inflation.

I said the Cabinet was weak and I wondered why an effort had not been made to include Soames. A.B. said Soames had been playing hard to get, and anyway, at an earlier stage, when he thought Ted would lose the election, saw himself as a possible successor to Ted as the leader of the Party. Another name that came to my mind was du Cann. He said du Cann was a money man, but that he could see him in no other role—and anyway even at that he was not in the Harold Lever class. Another good money man, he thought, was David Eccles. A.B. thought he would have made an excellent Chancellor of the Exchequer. I said it was surprising that he had got no further in spite of his great ability. A.B. said it was not the efforts of his competitors that had frustrated him, but his own shortcomings. He was so able he did not seem to think it was necessary for him to try really hard.

Subsequently I met Hugh Fraser to talk about Ireland, whence he has just returned. He said the two salient facts in his view (this was his first real visit) are: (1) that the political power of the hierarchy in Dublin has been reduced, and will have to be broken by Lynch in Dublin. Lynch is a devout Catholic, receiving Mass every day, but he cannot any longer get away with the Church policy on the Pill; meanwhile, (2) in the North the Protestant ascendancy is clearly on its last legs, partly because of the declining prosperity of Ulster industry, which is in Protestant hands. Thus the two great obstacles to a united Ireland are both declining in importance. But at the moment the Dublin Government does not seem to be urgently interested in unification, and the Catholics in the North are more interested in welfare benefits on the English scale than in a united Ireland. Fraser did not see Paisley, whom he seemed to think a demagogue and prisoner of his own oratory. While his speeches in the House of Commons here are mild enough, not so what he says to his working-class followers in Belfast. Fraser had seen the Cardinal in Armagh and the military commanders. The most Cardinal Conway could hope for was the maintenance of peace for the present; he could see no long-term solution, though a united Ireland must come in the end. In Fraser's talk with the Governor, Lord Grey had stressed the need for more police, but they can only come from here; and both Lord Grey and Fraser agreed that growing disorder would lead to a need for more police in the U.K. I asked why the Government is against internment of known trouble-makers. He says the number would be a thousand and would take two battalions to guard. I had thought of a figure nearer thirty!

Fraser said the I.R.A. is a very ill-defined body. It includes Communist elements and large numbers of young people whose membership is purely nominal. Most of them are not really trouble-makers, unless some event raises their anger—as would direct rule from Westminster. The paramilitary forces of Unionism are better

97

armed and disciplined than the Republicans and would be a formidable element in a civil war.

Father Murphy—a well-known parish priest in one of the most troubled areas of Belfast—told Fraser that they had had a clandestine radio preaching subversion. So he found out where the radio was and sent for the operators, who turned out to be two Englishmen, a Frenchman, and a tart of uncertain nationality. He told them he didn't want them around and they were to go. They said they had achieved their purpose in Belfast, had heard of trouble in Marseilles, and were thinking of moving on there. Could they borrow a car? 'No,' said Murphy, 'you came on your feet and can go out the same way.'

Tuesday, April 6th, 1971

Lunch for Norman Collins. He meets a lot of leading Tories and had recently dined with Peter Carrington. He had no special news, but regards the Industrial Relations Bill as necessarily the precursor of a general strike. I asked if appropriate precautions and plans are in hand. He didn't know, but said both Whitelaw and Carrington were expecting a general strike and were ready to fight one to the bitter end. He had no specific news about Ted's attitude, but thought that on this he would be as obstinate and inflexible as he is on other matters—if not more so.

Thursday, April 8th, 1971

Lunch at the Turf Club with Peter Carrington. He was in good form, so nice and so friendly. We started by talking about the absurd preoccupation of M.P.s with the details of events in the House. Peter said in the Shadow Cabinet almost all the discussion was of Parliamentary tactics and not on policy to interest the outside world.

He then asked me how I thought the Government was doing. I said, 'Not well: in fact badly'—because nothing had been done about inflation: the Budget did a very little to help investment but otherwise would increase consumption which was already too high. I got the impression that he is not too happy about the inflation/ labour relations front, but was not himself much involved. I said there would surely one day have to be a clash with the trades union movement and it was only after that battle had been won that we could see where the country stood. Peter was rather inclined to repeat that in such a situation one must have public opinion behind one. I said, 'Yes, indeed,' and if at present the idea is to build up an impression of reason and conciliatory behaviour by the Government, contrasted with the intransigence of the trades unions, the long delay in tackling the issue might be justified. But is this really the policy—to bide one's time and wait for the moment to strike with maximum effect? Listening to Carrington, I thought it was clear this was not the present policy and that he was doubtful if a favourable climate of opinion for such drastic action could be created. I said then that if nothing is done, the pound will become worthless and we shall be in a revolutionary situation anyway. Enoch's idea of acting on the money supply would create the revolutionary mood by massive unemployment. Taking the long view there is no soft option.

And so to Ireland, which he does not know, but which he has very recently visited. He is appalled by the bigotry, drunkenness and stupidity of the Unionist Party in Ulster, and is in general very gloomy. When Chichester-Clark resigned it took Carrington two hours to persuade him not to blame his resignation on the Government, though he could point to no specific act by H.M.G. to which he took exception. Faulkner is a real politician, flexible, ambitious and unscrupulous. He is the only man, in Carrington's opinion, who stands between them and direct rule from Westminster, which the Government would only implement under dire compulsion. The Government will do its best to prop Faulkner up, but is well aware that if an election took place not one moderate Stormont Unionist would be returned, and that almost certainly Paisley would take over. He regards Paisley as a man of such extreme views that no dickerings with him are possible. If there is an election and he does win, the Government will be in an acute dilemma. It feels it could hardly accept Paisley but equally could hardly throw over a recently elected Government.

I asked him why no internment? He said the number of I.R.A. in Northern Ireland is about two thousand, of whom eight hundred are in Belfast. They have the names and addresses of less than half, and think that any attempt to round up the men they do know would be only 50-per-cent successful. He seemed to think that an internment policy that was only about 25-per-cent successful would be worse than nothing.

I said Reggie Maudling was just the sort of Englishman to drive Irishmen up the wall—Peter said that was precisely what he did. It is clear there is no one on the job who has any understanding of

Irishmen or Irish politics. They feel Ireland will have to be united in the end, but that it would not be possible now. The outlook in Ministers' opinion is a gloomy prospect of more of the same into the indefinite future.

Friday, April 16th, 1971

Lunch with Edwin Plowden at Bridgewater House. He was in good form but even more pessimistic than before about the outlook. He regards Carrington, Whitelaw and Carr as the successes of this Government. He doesn't suppose the Industrial Relations Bill will work, but thinks that it is a first step in the right direction, and no doubt will have to be drastically revised in the light of experience. He thinks democratic government is clearly on its way out, here as elsewhere. It does not work and will be replaced by an autocracy of the Right or of the Left—he didn't think it would make much difference which. He thought the speed of change would be determined by the degree of arrogance shown by the trades unions.

He was invited by Marsh to be the chairman of the Steel Board, but declined.

John Davies's appointment as Minister of Trade and Industry, he thought quite grotesque. The Ministry is far too big—some things can be delegated, but not the job of representing your department in the Cabinet. To be a convincing advocate you must really know what you are talking about and this is impossible over the area covered by this department, and also that of Environment.

He thought the Rolls-Royce business had been badly mishandled, and that in the end the Government will decide to go ahead with the RB-211 and will find itself putting down *more* money than if it had not bankrupted the firm but had continued to feed it with loans. He thought the Concorde project a fantastic waste of limited resources.

He saw no future for Enoch Powell except, just possibly, as a front man for others. He thought Nixon had run away from his deflationary policy as soon as it began to have an effect. It is difficult for the U.S. to devalue as we are in fact on a dollar standard. The U.S. will do nothing about its inflation and the deficit on its balance of payments, and other countries will have to revalue their currencies in terms of the dollar if they are to do anything about it. He was in Australia just before Christmas, and says the Australians have economically sold themselves to the Japanese: the Australian economy is now entirely dependent on the Japanese purchases of iron ore, bauxite and wool.

Other comments—he thinks the incompetence and dishonesty of the Wilson administration have done the country immeasurable harm. He does not think we look like getting into the Common Market now, or perhaps ever. He was saying to Douglas Allen, of the Treasury, this morning that we should have done better without Marshall Aid. We should have had to pull ourselves up by our own boot-straps.

Later. He dwelt at length on the folly of the Government in financing three aluminium smelters. The one in the Tube Investment group is to cost £37 million, and the attendant power station is to cost £31 million. They are being built at Invergordon and will provide under 550 jobs. It is good business for British Aluminium as so much of the cost is a free gift from the Government, but the whole policy is quite uneconomic and was embarked on by Wilson to provide some meat for an important speech.

Monday, April 19th, 1971

Lunch for Tony Keswick. We had a rather discursive conversation, but he made it clear that Leslie O'Brien's renewal of his contract was only nominally for five years. Jenkins offered him only two and this may be the private arrangement.

He is a director of B.P., and said the increased price for crude would cost the country much more than any price so far made public. He said the increased price for Libyan oil would give the Libyans an income they would have grave difficulty in spending. In the negotiations with Arab countries the European consuming countries made it plain that they had to have the oil, never mind the price. They were very weak—particularly the Germans—which naturally governed the attitude of the actual negotiators—the big oil companies.

Tuesday, April 20th, 1971

William Whitelaw to lunch. He did not impart much, but gave me a more attentive hearing than I have had before. He agreed with me that Peyton is doing well at Transport and that Eden will have to be moved. He seemed surprised that I would only give Davies a B-plus. Evidently Carrington's reputation inside the Government is very high—and rightly. Willy has been resting in the South of France and saw Soames on his way through Paris. Soames thinks the French will remain very tough bargainers, that they will come to terms, but only when Pompidou intervenes. Pompidou needs a success and this is to be it.

I talked mostly about inflation, labour relations and all that, stressing that until the trades union movement has been brought to heel all other aspects of Government policy will be in suspense. It is only after such a confrontation that one can seriously get down to planning for the future, whether in Europe or elsewhere. At least Whitelaw expressed no disagreement with this line of thought.

I said I did not see how Government can be conducted without a censorship. When I was young there was no censorship, but there was a general agreement on what should and what should not be printed. Now every proposal was objected to: irresponsible people could get publicity for the most absurd opinions—such as objections to the census. In a democracy it had always been hard to get action, but it is rapidly becoming impossible. We are moving towards a more autocratic form of society because the present permissiveness won't work. I should guess that he fully realized all the difficulties faced by a government in this sphere, but had not yet come round to the view that in time very drastic steps will have to be taken.

He said he thought the Wilson of 1964 had gone for good, and that if he had another term of office it would be as the front man for some far-left group.

Governments abroad always think the B.B.C. is the voice of the Government, which is often the opposite of the case. Recently the B.B.C. staged a feature on Lynch and the Pill, which was acutely embarrassing to him. I said I knew this is the belief of foreign governments, but one day it will surely have to be true.

Wednesday, April 21st, 1971

Lunch for Arnold Weinstock. He is growing in self-confidence and authority all the time. The Government made him a director of the new Rolls-Royce company. He thinks the company was grossly mismanaged and the matter has been badly handled by the Government. It is now in the hands of Peter Carrington, of whom Arnold has a high opinion. He also thinks well of Heath and Whitelaw; but does not think Alec Home has the intelligence to be good at anything; and sees no useful role for Maudling. In connection with

Rolls-Royce he has had to deal with Peter Rawlinson, the Attorney-General, who he said is so stupid it is hard to see how he passed his Bar final. George Cole, now the chairman of Rolls, he thinks weak and ineffective. His attitude to the Industrial Relations Bill is that it is a gain to have something on the statute book. No doubt it will be radically revised, but with all its faults it is a start. He thinks all the talk of a free society is now obsolete. Circumstances are compelling us to have an authoritarian state, though there is as yet no indication how we get there. He put Enoch's chances higher than I do.

Saturday, April 24th, 1971

Lunch for Douglas Houghton on Thursday, and Barbara Ward yesterday. Douglas said his greatest trial was having to see Wilson four days a week while Parliament is sitting. He said Wilson has no inspiration or enthusiasm to impart, dwells on the glories of the recent past, and has no vision of the future. Douglas talked at length about the Industrial Relations Bill, to which he attached more importance than did anyone else to whom I have spoken. He said the Government could get no serious discussion of the Bill in the Commons so all the modifications were to be introduced in the Lords. The Labour peers have all sorts of plans for obstructing the course of the Bill and may have an unexpected degree of success. William Whitelaw, earlier in the week, said that the whole of our democratic procedures were designed to cause delay. I imagine Douglas would agree with others that though the Industrial Relations Bill won't work it will prove to be a first step.

Barbara is very ill indeed, but was full of chat. She says that Heenan has never fully recovered from his illness and is thinking more of retirement than of extending his influence among religious people generally. Her view on public affairs is that all over the world we have taught people to look for more and more—and to demand from industry and the state an ever greater degree of affluence. This attitude has led us into our present troubles and in the long term is not sustainable anyway. The young are looking for something more plausible without knowing what. Which brings me back to Douglas, who said, 'This nation has lost its soul and there is no one around who can give it back to us.'

Douglas spoke with contempt of Wilson's closest associates, notably Wigg and Kaufman.

Wednesday, April 28th, 1971

A hilarious lunch with George Bolton. He retired from the chairman-ship of BOLSA and was succeeded by Maurice Parsons, who com-pletely lost his memory and had to retire almost at once. He was succeeded by one Taylor—very able and energetic, but who has now succumbed to a coronary, so I gather George is still holding the fort. Taylor is—or was—the Vatican's financial man in London and one of the reasons why BOLSA has been so well informed.

I said George had prophesied civil war in Italy. It still looks like it but nothing overt has happened. Carli is still in charge of Italian finances; Vatican influence is declining week by week; and leap-frogging demands for wage increases are being granted, in the public sector, to an extent which cannot be indefinitely continued.

His man in Paris sees Couve de Murville every week and Couve tells him that the future of France will be settled in the streets. He agreed with what Charles Gombault told me in Paris recently that, while all is quiet in France at the moment, almost anything can happen from one day to the next.

He said much is made of the risk of the Dutch Catholics seceding from Rome. He thinks they will maintain their own opinions on some subjects, but that the real risk of secession is in South America.

On America, George thought that the Americans are dangerously demoralized and seem quite unwilling to assume their responsibili-ties for the dollar as a world currency. He doubts whether the American troops in Europe serve any purpose. He says Nixon, faced by any unpleasant fact, either ignores the fact or denies its unpleasantness.

On this country, George says so much has changed in the financial sphere since 1945; but the changes, being beneath the surface, have passed unnoticed. He has had dealings with Sir John Eden over his plans to take over a segment of the steel industry. He first said he had been too busy to study the subject, and eventu-ally said the whole question would have to be left over till September. George's opinion of him could not be lower. He said he imagined Ted had a poor opinion of Davies as he had turned over the question of Lockheed, Rolls-Royce and the RB-211 engine to Carrington. George cannot make out why Ted keeps Alec Home or Reggie Maudling, both of whom he thinks quite useless. George has a very high opinion of Enoch Powell's intelligence and obviously thinks he might one day lead a right-wing government. He does not think balance-of-payments problems are likely to be crucial here. Financially we shall be dragged along wherever the U.S. chooses to take us. Clearly some day the trades unions will have to be fought and until then the Government's writ only runs over a limited area. In time we shall have an autocracy of the Right but he does not see how or when this will come about.

He is against our joining the Common Market as it is such a flabby, amorphous body; there is so little for us to join. Douglas Jay has made a careful study of Parliamentary opinion and believes there is only a majority of ten for joining.

In Brazil you enter politics to make money. One Barrios was governor of the State of São Paulo for a time and took so much money he established a whole university—the Barrios University—at his personal expense.

Sunday, May 9th, 1971

Lunch for Geoffrey Rippon on Friday, and with Harry Walston on Thursday. Harry had no news of any interest, but Rippon was interesting. He was in great form and thought the basic decision to enter the Market would be taken by the end of June. Before then they would really know whether the French were determined to keep us out, or whether they were merely playing hard to get. He thought there would be a debate to report progress which might—or might not—end in a division. In October the terms would be known in detail and if the French had agreed to let us in, then Rippon thought there would be a majority of eighty in favour. Many more Labour M.P.s would vote in favour than Conservative M.P.s would vote against. He thought, too, that many of the pro-Market M.P.s were important (Houghton, Jenkins, Shirley Williams, Harold Lever) and that it would not be possible for Labour to put on the Whips against joining the Market.

Rippon is a moderate man in general so he surprised me by saying that Enoch Powell is the biggest hypocrite in politics; and that Couve de Murville is the nastiest man in public life—rigid, bloody-minded and violently anti-British.

I asked whether the currency crisis of this weekend would operate against his negotiations. He said he thought not—that even the French would have to see that this is an issue where all Europeans (including Britain) should act together.

Looking further ahead he said he thought Portugal and Spain

would follow us into the Market and that this would only leave two neutral countries (Switzerland and Sweden) and two countries dominated by Russia (Finland and Austria) outside. He did not seem to know—what I am told by Alfred Evenson—that Sweden is to stay out at the insistence of the Russians.

Rippon does not look far ahead in national affairs—he is too preoccupied with his job. He entirely agreed that a show-down with the unions would have to come, that until then the Government is not really in control. He said this must happen within eighteen months, but it was not clear whether he meant eighteen months from now or from last June.

Monday, May 10th, 1971

Lunch with Eric Roll at Warburg's. As we finished, Sigmund Warburg came in, and this is the general trend of what they said about the financial crisis and all that. The announcement in Bonn that the mark will be allowed to float by not more than $2\frac{1}{2}$ per cent, and will in some months' time be allowed to settle back to last week's par, is clearly nonsense: it will almost certainly appreciate by more than $2\frac{1}{2}$ per cent and will not return to last week's par. Sigmund thought the newspaper comments fairly poor stuff. No paper pointed out that by up-valuing the Swiss franc by 7 per cent they were lowering the value of gold in terms of Swiss francs. This might be important and is anyway interesting. The long-term effects of the crisis may well prove inflationary here—and hence detrimental. Its immediate effect, however, is favourable to our balance of trade and should help us into the Common Market. What no one has pointed out—either in Warburg's or elsewhere—is that here is a serious international financial crisis in which we play no part and have no influence. This must be the first such occasion. Sigmund had heard Barber at some meeting recently and thought him very, very shallow. He understood that the Ministry of Trade and Industry is to be re-organized and that Eden and Corfield will go. He had some talk at the beginning of the Rolls affair with some member of the Government and urged them not to take the course of bankruptcy. The reply was that to continue supporting Rolls would have cost £100 million. Sigmund said even if it cost twice that, it would be a preferable course to adopt. He and Eric said that it will now cost more than £200 million. No one thinks the present financial measures will solve anything. They may act as palliatives for a few weeks or months. Sigmund would like to see a Marshall Aid plan for the U.S., to help them out of their troubles caused by overseas aid and the Vietnam war. I am not surprised that this idea has not caught on.

Afterwards, some talk with Eric about *The Times*, of which he is a director. He missed a board meeting but got the papers when he returned from America last week. They were evidently very bad—unexpectedly so. He is a friend of Denis Hamilton but thinks Rees-Mogg has obviously failed as editor. He still sees some hope of retrieving the position; I see none. Sigmund said he does not now bother to read any paper. He listens to the seven o'clock news. The newspaper comments are not worth reading—even the *Financial Times*, though it is better than the other papers.

Eric thought Denis Hamilton quite mad to have paid £260,000 for Wilson's memoirs. The book rights fetched £30,000 and were thought dear at the price. The book is dull and so far, as serialized in the *Sunday Times*, guilty of serious inaccuracies.

What was curious about the conversation over lunch and afterwards was that there was no reference to any political upheavals. I said I thought the political situation here, in Italy and in France was such that trouble might break out at any time. This failed to produce any response. The financial problems were expected to be worked out under political conditions of a flat calm.

Wednesday, May 12th, 1971
Lunch for Brian Walden. It went exceedingly well. He is lively, intelligent and well-informed. Though now on the Opposition front bench covering the Army, he has an independent mind.

He thinks Maudling has one of the six best brains in the House, but he is bone lazy. It was all too evident in the Immigration Bill that he had not read his brief. He thinks very highly of Carr, though not of the Industrial Relations Bill. He gathers that its less practical clauses were imposed on Carr by the Cabinet, and in particular by the P.M. John Davies has been a disaster. This is partly Ted's fault, who should have buttressed such a novice with really good Junior Ministers. Barber he regarded as a totally inadequate Chancellor of the Exchequer. It is not known why Boyd-Carpenter is not in. On any view he is one of the six best debaters in the House (some think the best). Walden made no attempt to conceal his opinion of Wilson —devious and self-centred.

Walden's constituency is All Saints, which is on the west side of Birmingham with 40 per cent of the voters and 50 per cent of the population coloured, mainly Sikhs. The Sikh children are the brightest—brighter than the English—and are kept in order and made to work by their parents. The West Indians have a disorganized family life and are much duller. Walden's supporters make it a safe seat, but after Walden they favour Enoch Powell. Walden thinks that in a referendum, Powell would be elected P.M. by a handsome majority. Walden takes the possibility of Powell at No. 10 a lot more seriously than anyone else I have met. It could only come about as the result of a serious crisis, and so, like de Gaulle, he is hoping for a break-down in the political status quo and will do anything he can to bring it about. Walden thinks that if Heath has to be replaced the most likely successor would be William Whitelaw. Though more detached than most, Walden thinks of politics in terms of House of Commons business and personalities, so the effects of the exchange crisis does not come into his conversation.

Incidentally, he thought that on Macleod's death the obvious candidate for Chancellor was Keith Joseph.

Friday, May 14th, 1971

The big news today is the landslide Labour victory in the local elections yesterday. The Conservatives did so well three years ago that a reaction was inevitable—but not one of this size. For instance, Manchester was Conservative controlled, but after redistricting, which was supposed to help the Conservatives, the Tories have only kept 15 seats out of 99. In London the Conservatives controlled 28 out of 32 boroughs: they now control 10. It is too early to say what the effect will be on Heath and his Ministers, but it won't help, even though his bid to enter the Common Market looks as if it may come off.

Had lunch today with John Stevens, who was in unusually good form. He says McMahon and O'Brien at the Bank are very pessimistic, more than they have ever been. On the other hand Stevens is quite cheerful—at least for the time being. He thinks the balance of payments will be favourable, at least for the rest of this year; invisible earnings are rising; the terms of trade are still moving in our favour. Stevens takes a favourable view of Barber, on the grounds that he really has the ear of the P.M., so that when the Bank secures Barber's approval they know that the decision has been cleared at No. 10. Stevens is on the board of the Suez Finance Company and has a daughter working in Paris. He hears from these sources, and from his bank, that the situation in France is very precarious—exactly what Gombault told us when we were in Paris. He thinks that both here and in America our attitudes are becoming more restrictive and that we may well restrict ourselves into a serious slump. The American Senate is discussing a proposal to halve the number of American troops in Europe, and a reduction of some sort seems inevitable. Stevens talked about Enoch Powell, but said he will not make any real progress unless or until he gets some real financial backing. Stevens said the Junior Ministers in the Department of Trade and Industry were hopeless—not only Ridley, Eden and Noble, but a Junior Minister called Grant that he has to deal with. Davies he has found business-like but hopelessly over-worked. He knows du Cann quite well, but does not consider his absence from the Government important. So many of my friends take the situation as it is and do not try to look as far as next week. Stevens occupies an intermediate position—he is looking ahead six to nine months but not more, and thinks in financial not political terms. Even so he takes Enoch Powell more seriously than most politicians.

Monday, May 17th, 1971

Val Duncan to lunch—a very nice and very able man—perhaps less impressive this time than on previous meetings. He is always interesting about his mining ventures—the big reef of copper ore in Persia had been the big job for the future, but the Persians wanted 88 per cent of the profit so the project has been dropped. The tough line taken by the oil sheikhs has caused more thought to be given to atomic power—and Rio Tinto Zinc are very big uranium producers. They are investigating the economics of a gas diffusion plant at Churchill Falls for enriching uranium. The plant has to be in Canada, as it is only there that electricity is available cheap enough, and in an area of political stability. It was Duncan who persuaded the Government to agree to a special price for electricity for aluminium smelting—in his case in Anglesey. Duncan wants the same policy extended to other products, notably steel. New electric furnaces should supersede blast furnaces. He is told that the Steel Corporation should be investing £400 million per annum. In any case there should be a national policy for energy, which there is not.

On politics he spoke warmly of Davies and Leslie O'Brien, and it was this that rather shook my faith in his judgment. He said the local elections tend to go against the party in power. He thought Wilson so discredited he could never again be P.M. and might prove to be Heath's secret weapon. He thought inflation not such a bad thing as it brings about a massive redistribution of wealth. He thought commercial and industrial property would prove a good investment. He thought Heath's policy on the unions and labour relations might work over a period of eight years, though not over four.

Wednesday, May 19th, 1971

Lunch yesterday at the Czech Embassy; and Peter McLachlan for supper. The embassy lunch was a social occasion at which there was little serious discussion, but the Ambassador did express surprise that Heath is propounding a laissez-faire philosophy which is just not on in this day and age.

Peter commutes back and forth to Ireland. He thinks the situation very dangerous with no sign of any improvement. Faulkner is a clever tactician and unscrupulous. He is at present moving to the right. In any case, the Catholics have no confidence whatever in his good faith. He thinks Bernadette Devlin has now no political importance. The old Protestant ascendancy has gone, but the Protestant working-class underworld remains as bigoted and intransigent as ever. It looks as if Paisley is moving over to a more responsible attitude, but can he take his people with him?

Tuesday, May 25th, 1971

Lunch for Rupert Murdoch to hear the Fleet Street news. The combined scale of the *Sketch* and *Mail*, when they merged, was 2,400,000 copies. The new *Mail* now sells under 2 million. The paper is generally condemned and no one thinks it has a future. The *Sun* is doing 2,400,000, the *Mirror* about 4,250,000, the *Express* 3,600,000. The *Express* has kept its sale in Scotland but has been dropping elsewhere. *The Times* is down from 450,000 to 320,000 and is now below the *Guardian*. Rupert thought Denis Hamilton was now on his way out. He did not think Rees-Mogg knew what was going on among his staff: the paper just gets itself out. The *Sunday Express* is fully booked for ads and doing well. The *Evening News* should now be making money: the *Standard* is still losing.

The best serious paper, Rupert thinks, is the *Financial Times*. *The Economist* is not now worth even a glance.

Wednesday, May 26th, 1971

The du Canns to dinner—a nice man and intelligent. He made his money out of unit trusts, and his main interests appear to be the chairmanship of Keyser Ullman, a merchant bank, and his director-ship of Barclays Bank, of which he is tipped as the future chairman. He is deeply disappointed at not being offered office in the present Government. He and Ted are apparently temperamentally incom-patible. Here is a summary of his views. Ted will successfully lead his Party into the Common Market. He will force this through come what may. Ted seems to think success over the Common Market will disguise his failure over rising prices, but du Cann thinks it is inflation which is the real problem. Back-benchers took the long night sittings over the Industrial Relations Bill in a good spirit, but have been badly shaken by the losses in the local elections. If by-elections go the same way it will not be long before Ted is in desperate trouble. Du Cann thought Enoch a declining influence in both the House and the country. He thought Whitelaw tired and not as effective a no. 2 as he had hoped. He does not think he wants to be P.M. Du Cann did not seem to have given any thought to a possible successor to Ted. Evidently Walker is considered a success in the House, though very unattractive on television. The con-sequences—or lack of them—from the Industrial Relations Bill did not seem to loom large in du Cann's eyes.

Faulkner has addressed back-benchers on Northern Ireland on Monday. It was a relief to have to deal with a professional politician, but his optimism seemed quite misplaced.

Lunch with Gladwyn Jebb and Norman Collins—both full of the Common Market. They said no propaganda had been done yet as the Government was not sure it would be possible to get in. Serious political trouble in Italy and France was belittled, as was also the by-election prospects—two of which take place tomorrow.

Tuesday, June 1st, 1971

The big news last week was the victory of the Labour man at the Bromsgrove by-election. A Tory majority of 10,000 was turned into a Labour one of 1,800. The other two by-elections were for safe Labour seats, but even there the Labour candidates did well.

According to du Cann there are an average of twelve by-elections a year—four Conservative, four Labour and four marginal—but then Bromsgrove was not considered marginal. Ted's majority is twenty-six, so he cannot lose many by-elections before he is in desperate trouble.

Vic Feather made a speech at a union conference saying that the T.U.C. would fight any attempt to impose the Value Added Tax* on children's clothes, food, etc. This is a direct challenge to the authority of the House of Commons, but nothing will be done.

Had some talk with Rees-Mogg at lunch today at the Garrick. He thinks Ted has the skids under him, but that he will linger on into 1973 when he will be out in a landslide. He thinks the Labour Party will waffle over the Common Market and that Ted will get us in. In this event Labour will accept the position. If Labour decides to oppose entry as a Party decision then we might well be stuck half in and half out. He hopes that the Common Market will give us a new interest to take the place of Empire. If it does, then perhaps the present position may be seen as the bottom of the trough from which we shall saucer out. I said a new Labour Government under Wilson would in fact be dominated by Scanlon and Jack Jones, two very dangerous men. Rees-Mogg said he thought the Parliamentary Party after a landslide would be dominated by right-wing M.P.s who would not accept dictation at the hands of the union chiefs. But are Labour M.P.s in any position to challenge the union leaders? Rees-Mogg thought that anyway from 1966 onwards Labour had made a better job of controlling the unions than this lot.

Thursday, June 3rd, 1971

Lunch for Barnetson. He has been consulted on *The Times*'s affairs by Ken Thomson and others. It is losing about £2 million a year. Denis Hamilton thinks this—with luck—can be reduced to a loss of £850,000 next year. Neither Barnetson nor I think this is possible. The *Financial Times* are repelled by any idea of a deal, and Ken says when the old man goes his family will not be willing to sustain a

---

* Value Added Tax (V.A.T.) – a substitute for sales tax or purchase tax, in which each enterprise handling goods in the chain of production or marketing is charged tax only on the value it 'adds' to the goods. All elements in the chain (except of course the final consumer) can reclaim tax that has been paid by earlier elements. The introduction of V.A.T. (T.V.A. in many Continental countries) was necessary to ease the transition to Common Market taxation policies.

continuing loss of even £850,000. The new *Daily Mail* impresses no one, and some of the figures about its sales published in the trade press are untrue. The *Guardian* is losing more than the *Manchester Evening News* is making, and this may well continue.

Barnetson thinks the *Sun*'s success will continue and that it will, in due course, overtake the *Mirror*. Ryder keeps away from the publishing side of I.P.C. and leaves it nominally to Jarratt, but in fact to Hugh Cudlipp. In consequence the whole publishing enterprise is in trouble.

When Willi Brandt was here for the *Guardian* celebration, he asked Barnetson who would succeed Heath if he was deposed from his leadership of the Conservatives. Barnetson said Whitelaw. Barnetson thinks Lady Home will be busy pushing her husband if she sees any chance of his return to No. 10, but I cannot see this happening.

Barnetson said Ted had done nothing to put himself across in the last year. For instance, 'We,' said Barnetson (meaning who?), 'wanted him to be the principal figure at the cup final.' Heath said he could not make it as he was going sailing. So Wilson was invited and returned from the United States to be present.

Saturday, June 12th, 1971

Lunch with Sydney Bernstein on Tuesday—mostly concerned with the Conservative rigidity on the Industrial Relations Bill in the House of Lords. Apparently quite helpful suggestions have all been turned down flat. Godfrey Winn to supper on Wednesday—mostly social gossip.

John Peyton and his wife to dine last night. He is regarded in the House as densely stupid and a poor Minister, but I don't see this. He is no intellectual, but like Whitelaw seems to me to have good judgment and a very good understanding of human nature. He thinks this country will get nowhere without a conspicuous national humiliation. Our position has been sliding for a hundred years—at first slowly and more recently at increasing speed. He did not, of course, criticize the P.M. but I thought his endorsement of Heath was subject to serious qualifications. The only item of information was that in Yeovil (his constituency) there was a rally a few days ago for the Common Market—one speaker was Conservative, one Liberal and a third of unknown affiliation. Preparations were made for an attendance of two hundred, but only twenty-five turned up.

The papers today say that Ted wants the decisive vote in the House before the recess. This may not in any case be possible but even if it is, the rest of the Cabinet thinks the vote should be deferred to October. By then the voting would be quite open to doubt. The pro-Marketeers think that will give them time to mobilize public opinion. I should have thought it more likely that such a delay would give the anti-Marketeers a wonderful opportunity for fogging the whole issue.

Monday, June 14th, 1971

Lunch for Reay Geddes. He is a most charming man, and from all accounts a very adequate chief executive of Dunlop. He told me that Geddes is Norse for a pike (the fish) and that the family come from Hoy in the Orkneys. His Norse ancestors were a wide-ranging lot— some settled in the Canary Islands and others in Italy, where they are still to be found.

He had no very hard news but his general impressions were interesting. He thought his fellow-employers were surprisingly fickle—already denouncing Ted Heath for his lack of policy on prices and incomes—a policy which they denounced under Wilson. Geddes assumed Heath would get us into the Common Market in a way which would not be repudiated by Wilson in the next government—but this could not now be by general consent. He thought Heath very bad at getting his ideas across, but within his experience the penny was slowly dropping—unlimited money had to come from somewhere and we had each within his own sphere to accept some responsibility for our behaviour. He thought that by 1973 or '74 the Industrial Relations Bill might be having a good effect, though he did not believe there would be any large recourse by employers to the courts. In his own company wage demands were more modest and negotiators seem to understand that to bankrupt the company is no help. He thought also that in the Transport and General Workers Union and the Engineering Union, the militants were having it less their own way. However, Cooper of the Municipal and General Workers (the most Conservative of the union leaders) was increasingly ineffective.

Geddes thought a measure of reflation was now inevitable, whatever its ultimate effect on the price level might be. But of course in the present stagnation of trade it would take time for the reflation to be effective, and private enterprise would not launch out just because money was more readily available. They would want to see some prospect of longer-term stability.

Geddes thought Wilson's public behaviour was deplorably weak. He had no great admiration for the Heath administration either and criticized in passing, on various grounds, Barber, Hailsham, Maudling and Carrington.

Wednesday, June 16th, 1971

Lunch with George Bolton, to meet Max Aitken. Why this was arranged did not appear—perhaps it will later. Max had no news and no views of any interest. George was personally very cheerful, but his outlook was gloomier than ever. They thought the Upper Clyde Shipbuilders debacle was merely a beginning, and that unemployment in Scotland and the North would continue to rise at least until the end of the year. He said opinion in the City was turning against the Common Market, but then George was always anti-Market, for reasons that do not clearly appear. I think he thinks the Continental powers would treat us ungenerously once we are in, and that anyway the long-term political stability of any of them is open to grave doubt. The local elections in Italy have shown a swing to the far Right, and George says that Pompidou's political activities are constrained by right-wing Gaullists who are becoming more militant. He thinks the financial policies here and in the U.S. are increasingly irrelevant to twentieth-century problems. In particular he considers we should float the pound.

It seems to me that our main problem is inflation and the trades unions, but this was hardly touched on. Instead, George and Max both thought Ted would bash his way forward, very possibly destroying the Tory Party in the process of trying to get into the Common Market. They seemed to think a left-wing leader, other than Wilson, would take over but had no names to suggest. George is alarmed by the falling off in industrial investment—low in the U.S. and almost zero here. He thought it increasingly evident that there would be a rapprochement between Japan and China.

George said the largest—or one of the largest—oil pools in the world has been found under the Mekong Delta, but this has not been reported in the British press though it is front-page news in America. The oil companies seeking concessions in Washington have been referred to Saigon, which they consider unhelpful!

Roy Thomson told Max that the *Sunday Times* is now losing money.

Friday, June 18th, 1971

Lunch for J. S. Fforde, director of the Bank. He is a nice man, very intelligent and very shy. He has been concerned in putting over the alleged revolution at the Bank. The revolution is in two parts: (1) the Bank will not support the gilt-edged market; and (2) they are now encouraging a greater degree of competition between the clearing banks. The former change in policy will lead to sharper fluctuations in the price of Government stocks, but presumably the Bank would have to step in as a buyer in a crisis. The latter should mean higher interest rates for deposits and lower rates for loans, though Fforde did not seem to think the difference would be perceptible.

Fforde has been putting over these changes in the City, which has kept him busy and interested. But for this occupation, he said, he would be in the blackest depression. Like everyone else he assumes our balance of payments will go sour next year—the month will depend on the mark and the dollar. Any postponement of trouble would be detrimental in the long run. He thought the Government would be driven to reflation by political pressure, whatever it thought of the wisdom of such a move.

Labour kept Hayes and Harlington this morning with a swing of more than 16 per cent. Any reflation now could not have a visible effect on the economy by the time of the Common Market debate in the autumn—in fact the lack of confidence all round is so great that any reflation might be very slow-acting indeed.

Ruth had some talk with Mrs Healey on the telephone, who seemed to think Labour would be back by Christmas. Though I think this is quite out of the question, Heath is in deeper trouble than he and his Party seem yet to realize. Talking to Tories one gets the impression that Whitelaw is not coming to the fore as he was some months ago. Peter Carrington is highly spoken of by everyone, but he is not a great personality, is in the Lords, and cannot renounce his title.

Tuesday, June 22nd, 1971

Lunch for C.D. [a senior civil servant]—more expansive than usual. He was evidently involved in Government concern over Prince

Philip's speech at Edinburgh. It was a highly political speech on a very sensitive subject. I have not seen a full text, but no doubt we shall hear more.

The more significant part of our talk was about Ireland. C.D. expressed surprise that I thought Faulkner is water over the dam. He agreed that at the beginning of Wilson's ministry Dublin would have paid a stiff price for a united Ireland. Now Lynch would be taking Ulster off our hands and would want compensation. He agreed that unless something is done soon Lynch's position will weaken and we might be left with some pro-I.R.A. successor.

Throughout the conversation C.D. made no mention of Heath. I got the impression that he is disappointed in Ted. He said the twin pillars of the administration are Carrington and Whitelaw—they are not self-seeking and play up to each other very well. He sympathized with John Davies and his over-large department, and the poor quality of his Junior Ministers. He wondered how Whitelaw would do on television. He hadn't seen him (nor have I).

I said I thought no sense could be made of wage inflation, labour relations and the rest without a confrontation with the unions. This had to be done in the first year, and now Ted has not the popular support to pull it off. I told him Mrs Healey had told Ruth last week that they expected to be back in office by Christmas. This is absurdly optimistic (from their point of view), but C.D. spoke as if this Government expects to be around until 1975!

I told C.D. I did not believe the Industrial Relations Bill would work. He said the Government view is that bit by bit the unions can be got to see sense. But (a) this supposes their leaders want to see sense, and (b) that enough time is available, and neither of these conditions applies.

C.D. had had lunch with George Bolton last week, and there he had been told by a Frenchman of the political and social instability of France at the present time. This was news to him.

He wondered what Feather was up to and I told him what Vic had told me at our last meeting—that they had the Government where they wanted it.

He said Wilson's surrender to the unions in 1969 was an unmitigated disaster, the consequences of which would be important in any future Wilson government. He evidently hoped that a future Labour administration would be led not by Wilson—preferably by Jenkins.

Wednesday, June 23rd, 1971

Lunch with the Association of British Chambers of Commerce. Outside London, I was told, this body is more representative of business firms than the C.B.I. I attended the lunch to listen to Anthony Barber, the Chancellor of the Exchequer. I have met him once and seen him on television, but have never heard him speak. It was not likely to be an interesting speech nor an important one, but I wanted to get an impression of the man in action. He has been described in public as a boy doing a man's job. This is almost flattery. If you were told there was a bright young man behind the counter of the local Boots, who might make the grade as a manager one day, you would feel Barber about fitted the bill. He is quite nice and quite intelligent but has no weight, no authority, dignity or personality of any kind. Like all Government figures he was optimistic. My neighbours at table, one from Manchester and one from Birmingham were also optimistic—on the general grounds that somehow it would all come right on the night.

I was rather put out when leaving to be greeted by an unknown who, when I looked blank, revealed himself as Sir Douglas Allen, head of the Treasury! He has had lunch with me. I have met him on other occasions, but in a crowd he looks like everyone else.

The Common Market negotiations are complete and as favourable as anyone could have expected, but already the Labour Party and the anti-Marketeers are preparing to sabotage the whole idea.

Sir Donald Macdougall, Economic Adviser to the Government, was at my table at lunch. He has an intelligent face but, like so many eminent civil servants, no personality at all.

Friday, June 25th, 1971

Dinner last night with the Weinstocks—other guests being the Margadales and the Pooles. Margadale I had not met before; as Morrison he was the very influential chairman of the 1922 Committee. A nice man—no great brain but good instinctive judgment, like so many of the present generation of Tory leaders. Oliver Poole was most friendly, greeted me as Cecil, and twice said how others tended to laugh at our blunders and failures but I had always been inclined to grieve and deplore. However, the main interest of the evening for me was that Weinstock held forth on the failure of our present Parliamentary democracy and the need to replace it with something else. This arose from his description of the fantastic mishandling of the Rolls-Royce business by the Government. He is a Government director of the new company and trumpets abroad his contempt for George Cole, the Government-appointed chairman. One might have expected a protest from those present, but not so. I should say their attitude was one of complete agreement about the failure of our political set-up, though no one knows what to do about it. Weinstock also said that equal pay for women, to which both this Government and the last were pledged, would cost his company £25 million per annum. He thought the logical argument unanswerable, but the only practical solution was to pay the men the same as the women! Weinstock also said the new Industrial Relations Bill, in a totally unsuccessful effort to placate the unions, has some clauses—for instance on the disclosure of profits—which will make life much more difficult for employers.

At dinner on Tuesday Eccles-Williams, chairman of the Associated Chambers of Commerce, told me that they and the C.B.I. want a report on their future role, their relations with each other and the Government, and so on, and decided to invite Lord Devlin to do the job. They reckoned it would take a day a week for eighteen months and suggested a fee of twenty-five thousand guineas. Not so, said Devlin, my figure is forty thousand guineas!

Tuesday, June 29th, 1971
Lunch for Shawcross yesterday. He had no news—like others he thinks the world is in such a mess that we may be witnessing the end of Western society. Like others, too, he regards Whitelaw and Carrington as the two outstanding successes of this Government. Like others, further, he thinks Wilson, weak as his Government was, fielded a better team than Heath. As chairman of Thames Television he gets numerous complaints from Enoch Powell about the coverage Enoch gets. They are mostly so trivial that Shawcross has difficulty answering the complaints in appropriately polite terms.

Friday, July 2nd, 1971
Lunch for Gordon Richardson on June 29th. He had no specific news. We talked about the success of London as a financial centre in recent years. He said it was remarkable and had drawn to London very numerous branches of foreign banks, all anxious to make money. The Jewish element in all this is surprisingly very low. The competition is very severe. Compared with twelve years ago,

Gordon says, he has to keep his eye constantly on the ball—could not, for instance, possibly spare the time for a trip to New York by sea. He says prices on the Stock Exchange obstinately refuse to go down. He assumes the Government will be compelled to reflate—and soon—whatever their misgivings and whatever the consequences. Gordon shares my high opinion of Arnold Weinstock.

Tuesday, July 6th, 1971

Lunch yesterday for Hugh Fraser. He was mainly concerned with the Common Market—he is an anti for reasons that do not clearly appear. He thinks the feeling against joining is too strong, both in the country and in the House, and that in fact the terms will be rejected—or accepted with a majority so small that it will be clear the Government will not succeed in carrying the consequent legislation. This of course throws into question Ted's position as P.M. He thinks Whitelaw is becoming increasingly worried, and that Carrington and Whitelaw are not enough to keep a weak Government going. He thinks Carrington has much common sense, but has little ministerial expertise, and is in the Lords anyway. Fraser has no regard for Enoch Powell, and realizes that a few old sweats like himself and Boyd-Carpenter will have to decide for the Conservatives where they go from there. If Ted does get into trouble, Fraser would like to think of a national government, but has no idea how you get from here to there.

He seemed to have given the Industrial Relations Bill little thought except for thinking it much too complicated. I said I thought rising prices, unemployment and labour sabotage of the Industrial Relations Bill would continue to show the Government in such a poor light that by the spring something would have to be done—otherwise the Conservatives could lose enough by-elections to be out by the end of next year. Fraser thought that the crisis would come in November. He dismissed the present Government as a lot of Ted's yes-men. He seemed inclined to praise Maudling, but we were interrupted at the point when he was going to hold forth. I think he was a supporter of Maudling, not Heath, for the leadership.

In a nervous period both here and in the U.S. people are saving money, but as inflation takes hold they are bound to move out of cash into goods; but so far, thinks Fraser, this has only happened with houses, whose prices recently have shown a very sharp increase.

Wednesday, July 7th, 1971

The Healeys to dinner last night. I had not seen him since the election. We last had lunch with him at his flat in the Admiralty. I thought he looked older, and his wife said he was in a rather nervous state and working on one thing and another harder than when he was in office.

I think my main general impression was of his optimism. Our Parliamentary system has been fixed for all time; blunders and failures don't really matter; our affairs will continue to be conducted exactly as they are now, in spite of inflation, Communist trades-union leaders or anything else.

In particular matters, he thinks Whitelaw the best of the Tory Ministers, though he is not emerging. Carrington he thinks shrewd and able, but a light-weight who has been overridden on several matters affecting his department in Cabinet. Healey thinks Heath will get a majority of twenty or so for the Common Market and will accept this as sufficient. His difficulties will come later with the consequent legislation. Healey thought the Industrial Relations Bill will be regarded as largely irrelevant and will be ignored. With rising prices it is hard to see how Heath and his Government can pick up any popularity, but they are unlikely to lose more than two by-elections a year and so can remain in office for another three to four years. This is a typically Parliamentary view, ignoring the force of public opinion.

I think it was clear that in the election last year the verdict was against Wilson. If there were an election today, the verdict would be against Heath. Healey, on the other hand, thought Labour lost the election because so many Labour voters felt poorer and stayed at home, and now so many Tory middle-class voters feel poorer under Ted—and are staying at home.

Wilson made a very cryptic speech at a Labour rally in Wales. I asked Healey what it was all about. He said he thought Wilson is afraid of Callaghan as an anti-Market candidate for the leadership. So Wilson will come down against the Market; but he does not wish to appear, in doing so, to be heading off Jim, but rather Roy who is strongly pro-Market but no menace to Wilson's leadership. It all sounds like Wilson being too clever by half.

Saturday, July 10th, 1971

Jo Grimond and Bethell (of the Staff College) to dine on

Thursday—yesterday lunch with Malcolm Muggeridge at Roberts-bridge. Grimond seemed older: had no news or special views. Muggeridge is busy with his autobiography. He thinks all the evidence points to the dissolution of our society. At all levels the competent are, if possible, excluded; the Wilsons and Heaths are obviously unfit to govern anyone; Communist and other subversion is rife, particularly in the media. In America it is now said Teddy Kennedy may be the candidate to run against Nixon—neither man either competent or qualified in point of character to lead a boy scout troop. Muggeridge thinks, as do others, that Enoch is a spent force; but if they think the present regime cannot last, then who or what will take its place? On this I have heard no single, plausible suggestion. Muggeridge thinks the media are at a very low ebb. He is disgusted with the permissive policy of the *Guardian* and never now glances at it, though it should be his paper. *The Times* he thinks a mere mess. He is so familiar with the tricks of television that he cannot bear to look in, and depends for news on the radio.

Wednesday, July 14th, 1971

Mike to dinner last night. We had been surprised some time ago to be rung up by 10 Downing St and asked for his telephone number. It appears that Ted wanted him to prepare the precis of the White Paper on Europe, to be distributed free at Post Offices. Mike's value as a journalist lies in his contacts—he is no hand with his pen. However, he says they were very happy with the result and Ted sent him a magnum of champagne!

On Thursday the C.B.I. are to come out with an offer to freeze prices for a year, signed by two hundred of the largest enterprises in the country, and next week Barber is to issue his plans for refla-tion; meanwhile, the balance of trade for June is surprisingly favourable. I wonder if the unions will co-operate. Won't they think this offer a sign of weakness? Anyway, what is needed by business is more profit, a higher cash flow and more investment, and these objectives will not be helped by a price freeze. I think the main argument is that businesses feel compelled to do something (as does the Government) and this is all they can think up.

This Government has come out with many silly schemes for extending the welfare state and squandering still more public money, but their new rent scheme announced yesterday sounds sensible. Proper rents will be charged to those who can afford them, and the others will be subsidized.

Friday, July 16th, 1971

Last night attended a party given by Whitelaw at the Privy Council Office—brief talks with Blakenham (John Hare), Robert Carr, Whitelaw, etc., and quite a long talk with Peter Walker. Walker is obviously able and equally obviously feels on top of his job. To me he lacks political antennae. He spoke as if it was now assured that we should get into the Common Market with a sufficient majority—and live happily afterwards. John Burgess—of the *Cumberland News* —was sure that once the Industrial Relations Bill became law the unions would dutifully co-operate. This optimism is ludicrous but widespread.

A.B. [a senior civil servant] and I were discussing the C.B.I. suggestions, published this morning. He thinks very strongly that the idea of a price freeze (limited to 5 per cent) by the C.B.I. will not really help. He also has no confidence in the Government's economic policy. It is now believed that a measure of reflation will be announced by Barber on Monday. A report this week by the Common Market economists does not expect the rate of unemployment to fall this year, but does expect our economy to show the greatest degree of inflation of any major country.

Saturday, July 17th, 1971

At a reception at the Iraqi Embassy last night had some talk with the Russian Ambassador, Smirnovsky. He is always very friendly and I wanted to hear what he would say about Nixon's sudden announcement that he is going to Peking some time before next May. Smirnovsky was cagey about this, but did say a bit about the recent revelations about Vietnam in the *New York Times*. He said he was Ambassador there at the period covered by the Pentagon documents, and that nothing in them came as any surprise. He had warned the Americans how easy it would be to get into a war, and how difficult to get out. He seemed to be implying, in part of the conversation, that the documents had been leaked to direct attention away from other material that would damage the leakers, that—in his words—there is a double plot.

Tuesday, July 20th, 1971

Lunch for Rees-Mogg. He had been at an American Bar dinner last night and remarked on the excellent speech made by Rawlinson, the Attorney-General. I said that Arnold Weinstock, said the other day, in connection with Rolls-Royce, that Rawlinson was so stupid it was hard to understand how he passed his Bar exam. Rees-Mogg said that that is the usual impression he makes, but last night 'with his actor's voice' he put over a very charming and difficult social speech.

Rees-Mogg said the *Sunday Times* has lost ten pages of Situations Vacant and is losing money, though with the colour supplement they are together in the black. He said *The Times*'s loss was £450,000 less than last year for the half-year and was now less than the *Guardian*'s.

He thought that on the Common Market the Government was O.K. They have a normal majority of 34; this will be plus 30 Labour, but minus 15 Conservatives—a gain of 15. But they count 30 on a division, so the present calculation is for a majority of 64. I said Ministers seem, in general, unduly optimistic. He said, 'Why not? They will soon have to their credit the biggest achievement of any British Government since 1945.'

The papers are full of Barber's reflationary package announced yesterday. When the Tories took office last year the problem was inflation. Since then we have had three Budgets—all inflationary. The argument is that if the unions moderate their demands, and if the employers keep down prices, then the extra production will be possible without inflation. This is a version of Maudling's dash for freedom in 1963, and is likely to be as disastrous, but perhaps in the short run it will help Heath's opinion polls and ease the passage into the Common Market. The announcement was well received though it belies so much that was said at Budget-time. I should expect the result to ease unemployment, but bring forward the day when we are in trouble with our balance of payments, and lead to a surge forward in inflation.

Jenkins, Michael Stewart, Harold Lever and George Thomson have all come out with uncompromising declarations in favour of the Common Market. Wilson has said the agreed terms would have been unacceptable to Labour. But the ablest of his Ministers say that the Cabinet would have been glad to accept them.

Monday, July 26th, 1971

Lunch at Lazard's with Oliver Poole and Mark Norman—Poole rather exhausted after a long and tiresome meeting (on Lawleys, I gathered). Poole agreed with me that a fascist dictatorship in Italy is their only course. He said when the middle classes are frightened you get a fascist take-over, and in Italy today the middle classes are indeed frightened. On France, he said we have by no means heard the last of 1968-type riots, and that Lazard Frères are nervous and apprehensive, but the situation is not so advanced or clear-cut as in Italy.

Mark Norman had been at the C.B.I. meeting at which it was decided to offer the Government a price freeze with a maximum increase of 5 per cent in the coming year if an increase was inevitable. He said no one was very hopeful of the success of the undertaking, but felt that they had to make some move, and what else? Poole thought the latest mini-Budget would give a boost to the economy just when it was getting one anyway from the April Budget. The motive was to get a better wind for the Common Market, and perhaps provide enough boom for a successful general election next year. He thought the result would be unduly inflationary. I mentioned the row at Trust Houses with Crowther on one side and Forte on the other—ostensibly over one Packard who has been severely criticized by a Board of Trade inquiry. Poole said Crowther was a very difficult man to work with—at *The Economist* he insisted on remaining chairman while refusing to do the work, and he has the votes to remain immovable. He thought the merger between Trust Houses and Forte had been a mistake; the two men, Crowther and Forte, were at odds and had been for months. He assumed that Crowther would be eased out.

Tuesday, July 27th, 1971

The Mosleys to dine last night. He now thinks any real political crisis is some distance off and his own participation impossible. His judgment of the situation seems to be built more on his experiences in the '20s and '30s than on the situation as it now is.

Wilson's book was on sale yesterday. The reviews are all unfavourable and the general feeling is that this orgy of self-justification has done him a lot of harm. His handling of the Common Market issue has divided his Party and is discreditable to him personally. Unfortunately, he is so discredited already this won't make much difference.

Wednesday, July 28th, 1971

Mosley appeared on an A.T.V. programme last night. It was well done, but he made it clear that he is hoping for some role in the future. I see this morning that this long and, on the whole, flattering interview on television is given a very favourable puff in the *Telegraph*. I must say I am surprised, but then we are so bankrupt of political talent that circumstances might come about in which Mosley did have a role.

Thursday, July 29th, 1971

Lunch for Douglas Houghton. He is a terribly nice little man. He opened the political part of our conversation by asking what he should do about his Leader—a most unhappy man. I said it would be in the interest of the country and of his Party if he were ditched. However, as I well realized, that is not too easy. His book has won him no bouquets and his stand against the Common Market leaves him in a contemptible light. To change the leadership might well split the Party: on the other hand his handling of the Common Market affair may split the Party anyway. Denis Healey has emerged from the whole episode without credit—so it seemed to me, and so it apparently seems to Douglas. Roy, on the other hand, has shown courage far beyond what had been expected of him and has earned general respect, if not support, within his Party.

Douglas seemed to think the Industrial Relations Bill would not cause any major upset. I think they have been so obsessed with the Common Market they have forgotten this very explosive material so near at hand.

Douglas evidently thought Wilson had had about all the criticism he could take. I think Wilson, if allowed, will put up with any amount of humiliation if he still has some chance of returning to No. 10.

In the afternoon I called on Leslie O'Brien. He is a nice little man and in good heart. He has done better than expected, but his rewards seem totally out of proportion—£27,000 a year, G.B.E. and Privy Councillorship for no particular achievement.

He was discreet, of course, as usual. Straws in the wind of conversation were: (1) no reference of any kind to Barber; (2) Heath was described as 'unapproachable'. In general terms it became clear that he thought the latest Budget had no economic justification but was forced on the Government by political necessity. Opinion polls have shown the Government in so unfavourable a light that something had to be done, and this was also necessary to get the Common Market off to a good start. The huge deficit on the American balance of payments and the revaluation in Germany, Switzerland, Holland and Austria have helped sterling, and are likely to look after our balance of payments well into next year. In the short term, American excesses are helping us; in the long term, the reverse. If Japan revalues, that will also help us.

O'Brien said the C.B.I. price freeze was not universally supported by their Council, but was eventually accepted as the only gesture anyone could think of. Government reflation and C.B.I. price freeze are all these two bodies can offer. What will the T.U.C. offer? Can it deliver anything anyway? The whole programme, I gather, involves a large component of hope but little real confidence.

Peter McLachlan to lunch. He travels to and from Northern Ireland on behalf of the Tory Party Central Office. He spent one and a half hours this week with Tuzo, the G.O.C. Maudling has publicly declared an all-out war on the I.R.A. Tuzo says the effectiveness of this declaration depends on their information, which he thinks inadequate. Peter thinks Faulkner is finished, and probably so is Stormont. The I.R.A. no longer consists of Catholic nationalists, but includes more and more extreme left-wing elements. Paisley has not been much in evidence these last few days and recent statements by him seem particularly extreme. Lynch is having increasing trouble with his extremists and may not last long. The prospect is more and more for civil war in Northern Ireland, with an unforeseeable outcome. Protestant paramilitary groups are in course of being formed and reprisals against the Catholics are more than likely. Meanwhile, Ted is more concerned with his chances of winning the Admiral's Cup.

Lady Mosley said the other night that she had friends who had owned a house on the Lansdowne property in Kerry. The buyer, an English businessman, is now trying to sell it, but a large part of the value of the property consists of salmon netting rights. When the property was to be auctioned in Dublin the I.R.A. announced that they would not permit the salmon-netting rights, belonging to the Irish people, to be sold to foreign investors. So there were no bids for the property. This sounds more like Bernadette Devlin and her socialist friends than the traditional I.R.A.

Friday, July 30th, 1971

Lunch with Hugh Fraser. He thinks the Common Market will pass with a majority of 40–60: the Tory vote against being 15–20. He thinks that the real difficulty lies later on with Ireland. Labour relations and higher prices will cause trouble when the time comes to pass the legislation consequential on joining the Common Market. In particular, eight Ulster M.P.s show signs of causing trouble if Reggie does not toughen his policy in Ulster. The *Financial Times* this morning says that Faulkner is now doing better, but Hugh's information—and Peter's yesterday—is that the situation is deteriorating and that it looks more and more like civil war. Meanwhile Ted seems particularly absorbed in the Admiral's Cup, for which he captains the British team.

Tuesday, August 3rd, 1971

Ruth had a talk with Paisley at the House of Commons—at his request. His main theme was the need to establish law and order in the Six Counties. He had been to see one Johnson, senior civil servant at the Ministry of Defence, who had been quite frank about the inability of the British Army to re-establish order. For this reason Paisley wants to rearm the R.U.C.* and to re-establish the B.-Specials. Ruth asked him about the possibility of a deal between him and Lynch. Paisley says this is not possible at this stage. Order in Ulster will have to be established first. He said the Catholics in the North have been completely terrified by the Provisional I.R.A., much of whose violence has not been reported. Catholic priests and two bishops have come to him to say they have lost control of their people and can he do something? The Provisional I.R.A. are financed from abroad and are playing a more and more important part in the Republic. At least in Belfast the authorities are backed by the British Army, but in Dublin Lynch has no equivalent, hence his request to see Heath—the meeting is to take place towards the end of October. Paisley regards Faulkner as water over the dam, and Maudling as quite useless. He does not want to be a political leader, but is beginning to think this is now inevitable.

This represents a complete change from traditional Irish politics—and explains the continued prominence of Bernadette Devlin, in spite of her pregnancy. The old ruling class in the North, and the Catholic Church, have lost so much of their power, and Communists—

* Royal Ulster Constabulary.

particularly Marxists—seem to have moved into the power vacuum. What is hard to understand is that so far this Tory Government has done nothing—nor even said anything—against Communist influence here or elsewhere.

Wednesday, August 4th, 1971

Lunch for Peter Carrington—he could not have been more friendly though he had little news. Our talk was mainly of Ireland. He agrees in my assessment of Irish affairs—Lynch losing ground in Dublin; the old Catholic nationalism of the I.R.A. replaced by an extreme left-wing I.R.A. that is as much a menace in Dublin as in Belfast; declining influence of the old gentry in the North, and of the Catholic hierarchy in the South. He agrees that Faulkner is on his way out, but thinks he has a little more time. In contrast to Ruth, Carrington distrusts Paisley, dislikes him, thinks his religion a sham and his policy Protestant domination. He does not see how any British Government could agree to the re-arming of the R.U.C. and the re-engagement of the B.-Specials. I said I thought the alternative was a slide into civil war with consequences that might be of far wider import than anyone expected. It seemed to me that Paisley is the only card left. I told him he had had contacts with the clergy, but Carrington seemed to ignore this. I couldn't say where my information came from, and of course I have not met Paisley. I urged Carrington to meet him, but this is the crucial month with the Londonderry march on the 12th. He seemed to agree with Peter McLachlan that the secession of the Opposition M.P.s from Stormont was compulsory—forced on them at the point of an I.R.A. gun.

Sunday, August 15th, 1971

A call from Downing St yesterday morning—would we come to Chequers for lunch or dinner yesterday, today, or when? to talk about Ireland. So it was dinner last night—just the three of us. Ted was most friendly. He looks older than he is—could well pass for sixty-five.

When we started talking about Ireland, he asked me if I had any suggestions. I said that Maudling should be eliminated from the Irish scene. He asked why. I said, temperamentally, he and the Irish are not on the same wave-length. This is a widely-held view (held e.g. by Carrington) but seemed unfamiliar, or less familiar, to

Heath. I said Faulkner had no future. There was no comment on this and I thought Heath agreed. I said the only remaining card was Paisley. The reports he has had of Paisley have evidently been very unfavourable. However, he said he had had some talk with the Speaker (Selwyn Lloyd) who had met Paisley and thought he should not be written off as impossible. There will be an election in Northern Ireland next year, and under present circumstances Paisley would win. Though I got the impression that Faulkner is through, it did not appear that there has been any preparation for working with Paisley. I said if Paisley were P.M. it would be necessary, as a set-off, to make some gesture to the Catholics.

I said I did not think the Army could beat down the I.R.A. without the full support of the Protestants. Heath said they were very pleased with their swoop and had interned more than half of the leaders. Carrington, however, who had been at Chequers in the afternoon, was disturbed by the over-optimism of the Army spokesman. Heath seemed to think that with the policy of internment violence would die down, as it had in 1959–61, and we might have a quiet spell of ten years by which time the Common Market would have transformed the situation. He said the I.R.A. were already short of ammunition. I said, they have powerful friends, ammunition will not be a big problem: explosives can be made of chlorate of soda and sugar or nitrate of ammonia and fuel oil, the ingredients of which are readily obtainable anywhere. He didn't seem to know this.

This last week Lynch came out with a strong and unexpected attack on internment and on the Stormont regime. Heath said at four o'clock that afternoon he was talking to Lynch on the telephone, who told him he would be putting out a statement at five o'clock. It would be in general terms and create no difficulty. In fact it was violently controversial and was put out at ten o'clock. So evidently Lynch was subjected to very heavy and unexpected pressure.

I said the trouble over Ireland, Upper Clyde Shipbuilders, unreasonable wage claims, and even opposition to the Common Market, was initiated or aggravated by the Communists—particularly the Maoist wing. Why didn't the Government attack this evil in our midst? Heath was in full agreement about the evil but did not seem disposed to do anything about it. Perhaps he has no idea how to conduct this kind of campaign.

Ted said Vic Feather had come to see him at Chequers, and speaking of the Industrial Relations Act said he quite understood Heath had had to pass the Bill as a sop to the Monday Club. Ted was amazed that his four years' work on the Bill could be so regarded by anyone. At the same time Heath evidently had no idea how widely the Bill is regarded as unworkable—which is why Vic thought what he did.

Other items. Dick Crossman is writing his memoirs and wants access to the relevant Cabinet papers. This is normal, but Dick does not want to go through the papers himself—wishes to hand the job over to his staff. This is not allowed, so Dick appealed to Ted, who turned him down. But when he had gone, his staff told Ted that they were positive Dick had a tape-recorder hidden under his tie, recording the interview!

Wilson told Heath on the plane to de Gaulle's funeral that when he comes to write his memoirs, it is as well to remember that the Downing St staff keeps a record of what the P.M. does every hour of every day, and has a complete book of cuttings. This is all too evidently the source of Wilson's book.

Heath said Healey had completely discredited himself over his tergiversation on the Common Market. He had known Healey at Balliol; he was then a Communist.

Monday, August 16th, 1971

Lunch for A.B. [a senior civil servant]. He was in very good form. He thinks inflation will go roaring ahead and create really serious difficulties next year. He thinks that on Ireland and on labour relations the Government is far too optimistic.

Tuesday, August 17th, 1971

Lunch for Stonehouse—in good heart and looking very prosperous. About the leadership, he said Wilson could not be made to go against his determination to stay. His handling of the Common Market issue has been so incompetent that if it were continued it might split the Party and make his position impossible. If Wilson were to die this afternoon his successor would probably be Callaghan, but Roy Jenkins would have a chance (Stonehouse is a Roy man). He thought Tony Benn's activity—speaking here, there and everywhere—was damaging him in the eyes of the P.L.P. Stonehouse had dinner with Marsh a few days ago—both men indignant at the flagrant misreporting in Wilson's book of events in which they took part—notably of Marsh on Barbara Castle's labour relations Bill. I asked who in his view was responsible for the Tory labour relations Bill. He said both Bills were the work of a civil servant at the Ministry of Labour.

Wilson thought Stonehouse was anti-Market, when he is pro, and in an unguarded moment let out his hostility to the Market long ago—long before he was supposed to have begun shifting his position.

Stonehouse takes little interest in Ireland; regards the T.U.C. as wholly ineffective; and does not believe the leaders of the big unions have any control over their members. He does not believe the Tories can lose enough by-elections to shorten their four-year term (legally five).

Monday, August 23rd, 1971

Lunch for Dick Marsh, due to take over the chairmanship of British Rail in about three weeks time. I asked him about the C.B.I. idea of holding prices steady for a year, and anyway not increasing them by more than 5 per cent. He said the loss on British Rail for the coming year would be £15 million, but this price freeze would make it £60 million—so he had refused to co-operate. If the Government were prepared to give a special subvention for this purpose, O.K., but he was not prepared to borrow money he could see no chance of repaying. It then appeared that Partridge and Adamson of the C.B.I. had put the idea to Ted, who had adopted it enthusiastically. It had never been thought out in all its consequences: most C.B.I. members at best thought it a *pis aller* and this matter is not to be discussed at ministerial level till mid-September! The basic idea is that the C.B.I. and the Government are setting an example for the unions to follow. But with prices rising faster than 10 per cent, the unions will on no account accept a wage freeze that gives them less than this.

I asked about the Industrial Relations Act. The new chairman of the Commission on Industrial Relations is to be Neal of the Railways Board. He is a good man but very uncertain of the prospects at his new job. He and Marsh were interviewed by a man who is writing a book about the new Act and the way it will work. He asked if the Act would make any difference to the labour relations at the Railways Board. Both Marsh and Neal said 'No'. The interviewer then said he had interviewed so far twenty-four employers, who had all said the same thing. In fact the central provisions of the Act will be a dead letter. Marsh said it could only have a chance if the Government were prepared to be very tough indeed with the trades union movement and this they were evidently not prepared to be.

Marsh said union officials were beginning to take inflation seriously, but there was a limit to their control over their members.

He said Reid, one of the most active shop stewards of Upper Clyde Shipbuilders, had passed all the usual G.C.E. exams and had taken a job in a stockbrokers' office. He then joined the Communist Party and reappeared as a workman in a Clydeside shipbuilders. He had surely been planted there by the C.P. The recent Lucas strikes were led by a girl who had been to a university and got first-class honours in sociology. She then took a job at a bench at Lucas with a view to becoming what she is—the leading militant shop steward in the works.

We talked about Wilson's book and all that. Dick was particularly incensed over Wilson's description of the Cabinet meeting when Ministers were told of Wilson's agreement with the T.U.C., which was to take the place of his labour relations Bill. Wilson says the Cabinet were so relieved by this agreement that when they heard about it the entire Cabinet rose to their feet and cheered. As there were more than twenty people present Wilson can hardly hope to deceive others. He must have deceived himself. Actually the agreement, as I recorded in this diary at the time, was an empty formula devised by Douglas Houghton and Vic Feather to save Wilson's face. When the agreement was announced in Cabinet by Wilson, George Thomas said Wilson was marvellous, and Dick Crossman said he would now have to rewrite a chapter in his book on the power of the Prime Minister. No one else spoke!

Over Labour leaders and the Common Market he was utterly disgusted. Wilson had been a fanatical pro-Market man. At the Chequers weekend to discuss the matter, the only two voices against joining were Ross (Scottish Secretary) and Marsh. Even Peart and Crossman voted for—Crossman said he could safely do so as we should never get in! Crosland had been fanatically pro-Market for ten years, but is now stumping the country making anti-Market speeches. Healey was weakly anti, then came out with 100 Labour M.P.s in an advertisement in the *Guardian* in favour, but only a few weeks later turned his coat and is now actively propagandizing against. This is being done by both Crosland and Healey to ensure re-election to the National Executive. They feel the leadership may fall vacant, and if it does their candidature would have a much better chance of success if they were on the N.E.C.

Marsh was very severe on John Davies, saying he now had had a year to learn the job but apparently had no control of either Eden or Ridley. They apparently work quite independently of their ministerial boss.

Marsh had no news on Ireland, except to say that the British Rail boats were plying to and from Ireland every day. There was no means of ensuring that no bombs were aboard, and he feared that one day they would have a major disaster on their hands.

I said surely from a national point of view the cheapest way of moving people from Glasgow to London was by rail, but owing to the way the roads are paid for, it is cheapest to travel by bus, and a rival air service is actually subsidized. He said the trouble is that the road problems, the rail problems and the air problems are all considered in isolation. The Government is now agreeing to a proposal to turn ten million short-distance passengers in London off the railways and on to the roads. This is excellent from the railway point of view, but ignores the problems incurred on the roads—extra roadworks, added congestion, etc., etc.

The chairman of the Airports Authority, Masefield, had been to see him about the rail link to the new airport at Foulness.* Marsh had asked what number of passengers would be using the link. Masefield said he had no solid grounds for thinking there would be any. There is no means of making airlines use an airport they don't like—Foulness is nearly sixty miles out on the wrong side of London. Apparently the airlines and the Airports Authority both did their

* The British Airports Authority was a nationalized agency responsible for the development and management of most (though not all) the major airports in Britain. The alleged requirement for a 'third' London airport (to supplement Heathrow and Gatwick) was a continuing source of controversy. A number of prospective sites were opposed by environmentalists of various kinds, and by those who considered the present two airports seriously under-utilized by United States standards, especially if the fewer aircraft movements likely to be required by larger aircraft were taken into account. Foulness (on the Maplin Sands) at the mouth of the Thames was one such site; Stansted and Cublington were earlier suggestions.

best to deflect the Government from this decision, which may well switch air traffic to France. The correct location was either Stansted or Cublington.

Tuesday, August 31st, 1971

Lunch for John Peyton, Minister of Transport. He had no particular news but seems to have a far better idea of the scene than many politicians. He says the British are ineffective because they have not been frightened. Jules Thorn, a very mild little Jewish refugee, has been a huge commercial success because he has known fear. Peyton thinks it hard to take any drastic action these days because there is no solid ground on which to stand. Peyton thinks nothing of Scanlon, but wonders about Jack Jones. Is he, or is he not, a dangerous Communist? He has no good opinion of the Home Office and regards it as quite mad that it should be the department responsible for Northern Ireland. He spoke warmly of Carrington, loyally of Heath, but evidently has no great opinion of Maudling. His constituents tell him they want leadership: he tells them they wouldn't like it, it would be far too uncomfortable. He said there is now no stigma on failure—it has such a cosy side to it! He hated Anthony Eden, and has rather over-much respect for Alec Home.

He again strikes me as a man of no great brain, but good judgment. On television he looks like nothing, but has a good command of words. I should imagine his character developed when he was for long a prisoner in Germany.

Friday, September 3rd, 1971

Lunch with Alf Robens at Vickers—much talk of the problems of Vickers, of *The Times* and of the world in general. His item of news was that this week he went to see Kearton, chairman of Courtaulds, on business. Courtaulds have had three factories burnt down in Northern Ireland, and it is doubtful how long they will be able to keep operating there at all. Artificial fibre production has to be twenty-four hours a day, seven days a week. His people in Ulster do not like to be away from their families in these troubled times and it is increasingly difficult to keep things going. Alf assumes that this policy of bombing and general sabotage will spread to this country. He also seemed to assume there would be martial law in Northern Ireland, and wondered if events there might lead to some form of coalition, national government or whatever.

He has no opinion of Sir John Eden, and not much more of John Davies who, he thinks, lacks any political sense.

I asked him if Derek Ezra was his choice as the new chief of the Coal Board. He said, 'Yes.' Ezra would be very good at consolidation, which is what is now required. I said I thought Sheppard (the new deputy chairman) had more personality. He said, 'Shep has, but he makes favourites. His friends would be promoted.

Monday, September 6th, 1971

Barnetson, of United Newspapers and Reuters, gave me lunch. He says Roy Thomson is now diabetic and crippled—very bitter about the way he was misled over the prospects for *The Times*. However, he is likely to keep it on during his lifetime. Ken shows no interest in keeping the paper alive—nor indeed in staying in this country. The general opinion in Fleet Street, according to Barnetson, is that the *Sun* is on the up and up; the *Mirror* on the down and down; and there are no people or influences in sight to alter this.

Xenia Field yesterday said the talk is that Hailsham is not only a failure as Lord Chancellor but he does not like the job.

I see the *Süddeutsche Zeitung* has been commenting on British workmen in Germany, whose productivity is low and who set a bad example. The paper's comment is that we do not want these lice in our fur! Can contempt go further?

Tuesday, September 7th, 1971

Lunch for Kenneth Keith. He was in great form and we spoke of many things. Firstly *The Times*, of which he too is a director. He has criticized the quality of the product at board meetings, and privately, and has got nowhere. He says Roy has lost all grip of the business.

Keith said the economic set-up of our time seems rather like a house of cards that may collapse at any time, but has so far survived in spite of periods when it seemed the end was near. He thinks Nixon's latest moves will in fact operate to the advantage of this country, and that we can look for a good business year in 1972. He thought the domestic political picture for the next year or so looks fairly satisfactory—the Achilles heel (his expression) is Ireland.

Hill Samuel own, or have an interest in, Hayward Hill, the booksellers. They told Kenneth that politicians' memoirs, if they are popular, sell well. Wilson's book has had very poor sales.

Wednesday, September 15th, 1971

We had been going to see Paisley yesterday but he rang up on Monday to change the date and we spent two hours with him and Desmond Boal near Antrim. Boal is a successful lawyer and Stormont M.P. He resigned from his Party on Monday and is now an Independent Unionist.

Boal did most of the talking—an intelligent man, but apt to harp on minor legal or constitutional issues. Their view was that Faulkner's and Lynch's time is running out. Neither of them has a following and their importance is entirely due to their official position. They said Dublin could only speak for the Ulster Catholics to a very limited extent. Meanwhile the bombing, shooting and burning is continuing on an aggravated scale. The Unionists are getting dangerously restive and it is obvious that civil war may break out at any time.

It has to be remembered that Belfast is some years behind London —perhaps twenty years—so democracy in the Six Counties seems to be more real than it is here.

They disputed my assertion that the only solution of Ireland's problem is a united Ireland. They said that may well be the ultimate result, but it is quite unthinkable now.

I said I doubted whether Heath would call an Ulster general election, mainly because the idea of curtailing a Parliamentary term might be infectious, but also because it would be argued, as it was during the two wars, that you cannot have a general election at a time of national emergency. It was quite obvious throughout the discussion that Paisley has no channel of communication to anyone in the British Government.

Heath is recalling Parliament for a two-day debate next week. This may do harm, and can certainly do no good. There is to be a meeting on the 27th between Heath, Lynch and Faulkner which cannot possibly get anywhere: and Maudling is trying to organize a round-table discussion between all parties in London later on. This last will never get off the ground. Meanwhile, hourly we get nearer a civil war whose course and result is quite unforeseeable, and which may well spread to this country. There is still no fear and no sense of urgency in Government circles.

We drove into Belfast from the airport past one big factory building, still burning after being set alight the night before, and passed along a short stretch of the Crumlin Road with its burnt-out shops.

Ruth had met Paisley twice before so I was not surprised when meeting him. Whatever he may have said in his public speeches, he is no fascist thug. He is nearly as tall as I am, and seems to me to be bigger in his other dimensions. He is an honest man and a nice man. It is not clear to me why Tory Ministers regard him as a sort of pariah. He has a big personality, and as politician and orator knocks spots off any member of our present Cabinet.

Thursday, September 16th, 1971

Hugh Fraser last night to dine here. He is going over to Ireland tomorrow and hopes to see Paisley and generally check up before the debate next week, in which he intends to take part. He had no particular news, but we impressed on him that time was running out and that it was senseless to treat Paisley as a sort of outcast.

Today I called on C.D. [a senior civil servant] and said to him what I had said to Ted at Chequers —only with greater candour. The only question he asked was whether by any mischance I had given the impression that I represented the Government. I said I had specifically stated at the beginning of my talk with Paisley that I was no emissary and only represented myself. I said I found Paisley a good man, an honest man, and a big one. Doubtless in the course of his career he had said things he shouldn't, but what politician hasn't? most of all in Ireland. My two urgent suggestions were: a Minister for Northern Ireland, preferably usually resident there and detached from the Home Office; and that a channel of communication should be opened up between Paisley and the Government here. I said the summit meeting of the three Premiers, the recall of Parliament and Wilson's initiative were all likely to do some harm but no good. I said in my talks with Ted my ideas seemed to fall on stony ground, but C.D. said that quite often with Heath the penny does not seem to drop but it becomes apparent later that it has. He seemed fully aware that we might be on the brink of civil war.

Faulkner has signed 219 detention orders, which means he will be boycotted by all Catholics.

My friend asked who should be the Minister for Northern Ireland? I said Whitelaw would be very acceptable. He said, 'So he would— and everywhere else!'

In the afternoon I met a Professor Purcell, who is about to take up a post as Professor of English in Katmandu of all places. He has spent three years as a professor in Belfast, had written a book about ethnic politics in Cyprus, has a house in Donegal, and had been recommended by Tom Mosley. His idea of an Ulster settlement was to adjust the border in South Down, and to make over Londonderry, west of the Foyle, to the Republic. But the latter move would include the part which is the centre of Orange pride and traditional loyalty. However apart from his territorial ideas, he seems to have had a wide variety of contacts in Belfast. From them he got the strong impression that if there is civil war the Unionists will not stick to the Six Counties, but are likely to invade Donegal and Cavan, where there are considerable numbers of Protestants on the Republican side of the border. The Irish Army is neither large nor well-equipped and might not do too well. I personally cannot see this happening because the British Army would be involved. But I do think it illustrates the point, that if hostilities once began there is no knowing their course or the result.

Senator Kennedy dined with Fraser this week. He says that he is resisting all pressure to intervene on Irish affairs, but that if civil war breaks out he will have to speak up—naturally in the Catholic interest.

Saturday, September 18th, 1971

Ray Gunter to dinner here last night—a nice man, recently widowed, and rather lost. He didn't seem to expect to stand at the next election. He has a house in the Scilly Isles, so sees something of Wilson there—says he looks old and bent, a very different man from the old Wilson. According to Ray, Wilson is in two minds whether or no to retire—he certainly will if he thinks Labour will be defeated next time. According, again, to Ray, he would welcome Roy as his successor, though others say there is such ill-feeling between the two they cannot even sit next each other at a committee meeting. In any case Mary will exert all the influence she has in favour of retirement.

Ray thought the Industrial Relations Act might have a beneficial effect over a period of three to five years. He seemed to attach no particular significance to price increases, or to events in Ireland.

Watching Ted on television from Zürich, Ruth suddenly saw why Ted is so ineffective as a speaker. It is because he is thinking of his performance—not about the message he is trying to put across. I think this is the explanation.

The Times prints today an account of population movements in Belfast, mostly in the last month. They say the number of people involved is about 8,000, and the result is to push the Protestants out of Catholic areas and the Catholics out of Protestant areas. In many cases the Catholic areas are partly cut off from the rest of the city by stretches of waste ground. *The Times* article says this seems to be organized with sinister intent (i.e. on the assumption that civil war is pending) but, typical of *The Times*, it does not make it clear whether this sinister organizing is Protestant, Catholic or both. While time in Ireland is running out, the politicians here are pre-occupied with Party Conferences and the Common Market debate. They don't want to think of Ireland so they banish it from their minds.

Sunday, September 19th, 1971

A call from Hugh Fraser, just back from Northern Ireland. We had arranged for him to see Paisley, and he also saw Hume, a Catholic Stormont M.P.; Blakely, a Stormont Minister; Tuzo, the military commander; and others. He says the police are now sulking in their tents: intelligence was excellent under the B-Specials but was dispersed when they were disbanded by the Labour Government. In the meantime all authority in the Province is disintegrating. A Minister and an Under-Secretary of the Stormont Government have denounced Faulkner's policy on the Ulster Regiment and on internment, but they have not been dismissed. Fraser does not think anyone is contemplating civil war, but in the present state of near anarchy, almost any event might set it off. The civil power is in the hands of the Army, who do not know the local personalities, cannot understand their language and are there for only four months at a time anyway. Fraser is planning to take part in the debate in the coming week, and proposes to speak after Paisley, and to back him up. He has asked to see Ted and is to press him, (a) to open some channel of communication with Paisley, and (b) to have a Minister for Northern Ireland, detached from the Home Office. Fraser says the growing disorder in Ulster is leading to the revival of the anti-landlord agitation and much else from the last century.

Monday, September 20th, 1971

Fraser has seen the P.M. He said Ted seemed well-informed. Fraser made three points: (1) Maudling is 'over-worked'; (2) the necessity of establishing some contact with Paisley; and (3) that Ted should discourage all suggestion that Faulkner is the last chance. This plays into the hands of the I.R.A.

Lunching with Xenia and Debenham of the *Mirror* today, Xenia said she had been told by a banker that the big robbery at Lloyds in Baker Street was to get at the very large sums of money in safe-deposit boxes. This money came from proceeds of robberies, and from traders hiding their true profits from the tax collector.

Debenham said the *Sun* is selling about 2,750,000 and the *Mirror* about 4,400,000. He expected the latter figure to fall by 200,000 when the current strike is over. He thought the *Mail* is now selling less than 1,800,000. The figures when the *Mail* and *Sketch* merged were 1,800,000 and 800,000. Advertising is not too bad, but nothing like what it was three and four years ago. Advertisers are now spending huge sums of money 'below the line', i.e. on promotions of all kinds.

Thursday, September 30th, 1971

In Guernsey. Dinner last night at Government House—the Lieutenant-Governor is a retired admiral: his wife, Lady Mills, a very charming woman, was at the Royal Academy of Music with Ruth.* The only other guest was Lord Windlesham, Minister of State at the Home Office, in charge of immigration and the Channel Isles. Ruth had formed a poor opinion of him when she saw him recently at the Home Office to talk about illegal immigration, and to put forward suggestions made to her by a Sikh doctor in Southall. However, last night he seemed pleasant and intelligent and something of a politician, but hardly enough to stiffen a very weak team at the Home Office. He put the two crucial problems confronting Ted as rising prices and Ireland. This was interesting as Ministers have been inclined to skate over the question of rising prices.

The newspapers did not come out after the first day's debate on Ireland, and I wondered how Paisley's and Fraser's speeches had gone over—but it appears that they didn't speak. I wonder what this portends—perhaps it was connected with the announcement on the radio this morning that Paisley and Boal are forming a new Party. In spite of optimistic guff in the papers, it is evident that things in Northern Ireland are deteriorating fast.

* Dame Ruth Railton, Cecil King's wife, was the founder and director of the National Youth Orchestra of Great Britain and the National Junior Music School.

Tuesday, October 14th, 1971

In the last fortnight nothing new has happened. The situation in Ireland continues to deteriorate while the Government here remains complacent.

I had forty-five minutes this morning with Mulcahy, the editor of *Hibernia*, the intellectual Dublin fortnightly. I asked him how things looked from his neck of the woods. He said the change in the last three months was the increasing involvement of the South in the Ulster troubles. Three years ago opinion in the Republic was totally uninterested in what happened the other side of the border. Now opinion in the South—he mentioned Kerry and West Cork—was increasingly disturbed. He thought this would make it difficult for Lynch to hang on. He thought internment had been a gross error, and that it would be impossible to get even middle Catholic opinion to talk until the detainees were released. But if internment had to be brought in, a certain number of Protestant extremists should have been added.

Mulcahy thought it surprising that life went on as normally as it did in Belfast, but both at Stormont and here, no one knows how long the commercial and industrial life of the Province can continue.

At the Conservative Party Conference we have had wildly optimistic speeches by Barber and Maudling. The Conference voted with a large majority for the re-introduction of capital punishment. And there was much emphasis on the Common Market, the theme that dominated the Labour Party Conference the other day.

I see on looking back that I said Paisley and Fraser did not speak in the emergency Irish debate. They did speak, but their remarks were ignored by the papers which concentrated on Wilson's views, Maudling's views, Callaghan's views; none of which are relevant.

Saturday, October 23rd, 1971

I have had no particular news for some weeks. Lunch with Rupert Murdoch elicited nothing of great interest. The great debate on the Common Market began on Thursday and already yesterday was poorly attended. If M.P.s don't believe in their own institution, why should anyone else?

Having said repeatedly that there would be no free vote for the Conservatives, at the last moment before the debate Ted announced that after all there would be a free vote. The public opinion polls continue to show a substantial majority against. The reason for

Ted's sudden change of policy is not apparent. I suspect it is because he found the Conservative anti-Marketeers were more numerous than he had suspected. A free vote should secure the support of more pro-Market Labour men than would otherwise be available.

Meanwhile the situation in Ireland deteriorates while the Government does nothing. Government changes are expected after the Common Market vote, and if there are any we may have some clues to the way Ted's mind is moving on this and other matters. Government announcements are mainly devoted to wildly optimistic economic forecasts, with Irish affairs played down as much as is at all possible.

Monday, October 25th, 1971

A telephone call from Hugh Fraser this morning. He says the increasing violence in Ulster is bringing direct rule forward into the near future. He believes that both Heath and Maudling have been against a Minister for Northern Ireland. However, with direct rule this becomes inevitable. Ted seems to have offered the job— when they decide on direct rule—to Christopher Soames, who has turned it down. I should think that anyone who takes the job under such circumstances must be mad.

Tuesday, October 26th, 1971

Ruth had some talk with Paisley on the telephone yesterday. He is in despair over the situation in Northern Ireland and the inaction of the Government. He also had heard that the Government is becoming convinced that direct rule from Westminster is inevitable, and had offered the job of Minister in charge of Northern Ireland; but he did not say—perhaps did not know—to whom it had been offered.

Had lunch yesterday with Alf Robens. It was announced later that he had taken on yet another directorship, that of Trust Houses Forte.

His only item of hard news was that the Government's decision to have a three-line whip on the Common Market debate was Alec Home's. He said this was a Foreign Office matter and there must be a three-line whip. Others did not agree, but were willing to go along until they started counting heads seriously last week, when they found they would only get a whipped vote through on Labour votes. This would be ridiculous, so they announced a free vote. This would have been the best decision if made much earlier. As it is, it is an acute embarrassment to Roy Jenkins, and obviously a decision made from weakness. The spectacle as seen from abroad must be utterly contemptible.

Alf thinks politics are polarizing between Left and Right, with the Communists riding high (Reid, the left-wing militant leader of the Upper Clyde Shipbuilders shop stewards, has just been elected Rector of Glasgow University). Alf thinks Powell is now distrusted by both Right and Left. He sees a dictatorship coming, but whether of the Right or Left remains to be seen.

Thursday, October 28th, 1971
Lunch for Dr Paisley. He is a nice man—I am sure he is not the thug suggested by Ministers and others. The Government still has no contacts with him. His main reaction to Ministers is that they are in a state of bland unreality. We are on the edge of civil war which would spread, according to Paisley, not only to Glasgow and Liverpool but also to Islington. Paisley has heard that the Government is contemplating direct rule, but cannot believe this is so, as it would be violently resented by all Parties in Northern Ireland. I asked why, and he said, 'In Northern Ireland we feel we are far away in the outback, but Stormont is there to speak for us. Without Stormont we should be forgotten.'

The House is debating the Common Market. Paisley says it is a mistake to have six days—the same arguments are trotted out *ad nauseam*—and the result of spreading the debate over so long a period is to give time for bitter feeling to intensify. He says Ted's efforts to bring pressure on anti-Market Tories are unprecedented and much resented. The talk is that thirty-seven Tories will vote against the Government. When the matter was first being discussed the number was put at fifteen, and anyway not more than twenty. Months ago any difficulty over the consequential legislation was dismissed as out of the question. Now more and more the commentators are wondering if this legislation can be passed at all—and at best the impression left on the outside world must be deplorable.

Friday, October 29th, 1971
The great vote last night ended in a majority for the Government of 112—this is about 30 more than had been expected earlier. There is great jubilation around 10 Downing St, but will it be justified?

The result is produced by 69 Labour members voting with the Government and 18 abstaining, while 39 Tories voted against. Both figures are much higher than had originally been expected and will mean much bitterness in both Parties—particularly Labour. Earlier on, this had been represented as the crucial vote—the consequential legislation was said to be going to lead to no serious trouble. Now, opinion has changed and the comment is that the vote on principle is all very well, but what about the consequential legislation—can it be forced through? And of course, anti-Common Market attitudes will be reinforced by serious trouble in Ireland or on the trades union front, both of which are likely.

Monday, November 1st, 1971

Lunch for Edwin Plowden. He talked about the Industrial Relations Bill—he thought in the short term its effects would be harmful. In the long term, the fact that there is such an Act would be a good thing. Its central provision would be a dead letter and the Bill will have to be much altered, but a bad Act is better than none.

He said his machine-tool orders were down 45 per cent on last year—itself a bad year. He did not expect industrial investment to begin picking up until the latter half of next year. He expects the unemployment figure to be around 1,300,000 in February. Sales of consumer durables are good, but there is no sign of any pick-up in the ordinary retail trade.

Plowden thinks things have been going wrong since 1914, and have now reached a point where they cannot deteriorate much more without a catastrophe. He hopes he won't live to see it, but as his mother is ninety-nine he is afraid he may be around for the crash!

We spoke of the growing strength of the different brands of Communist—in the Labour Party and in the unions. Plowden has nothing but contempt for Tony Benn, whom he described as a ventriloquist's dummy, speaking for the far Left. He saw no similar movement on the Right, and thought Enoch Powell was becoming generally discredited.

In conversation with Mrs Roy Jenkins today, Ruth asked if it were possible that Roy would lead a pro-Market centre party. His wife said Roy believed we should get into the Market, the unions would accept the position, and in three years or so the present breach in the Party would be healed. This sounds to me like mere wishful thinking.

Tuesday, November 2nd, 1971

Lunch for George Bolton—in good heart personally, but very gloomy about affairs in general. The new chairman of what was BOLSA is a young man called Carroll, chairman of the family tobacco firm in Dublin. He has told George he is no longer welcome at the office because he has too much influence there. George thinks Carroll has little idea of the job he has undertaken.

As—of my recent guests—Paisley was mainly interested in Ireland, and Plowden with the engineering industry and unemployment, so George was mainly interested in international trade. He thought the boom since the War was the longest in recent history, and had been due to a monetary system set up after the War that had worked. This has now been broken up by the Americans, and there is nothing in its place—nor does he expect a new monetary system to be evolved for some years. He thinks world trade is grinding to a much slower pace, and certainly commodity markets are very weak just now.

He said the Japanese are planning to produce 180 million tons of steel per annum—more even than the 150 million I had heard about. They have contracted for all the raw materials they may need for fifteen years ahead. In Canada, British Columbia has built a new port in Vancouver Bay for the export of 15 million tons of coking coal per annum to Japan. It is the best coking coal to be had anywhere and will reach Japan at a price lower than that enjoyed by any other producer of steel—even the Canadians themselves! It is to be a continuous process with trains carrying 10,000 tons delivering to giant hoppers, or direct into bulk carriers of 150,000 tons.

George said the visit of Kosygin to Canada was for real business. The Canadians are indignant with the Americans' conduct of their affairs, and are turning more and more to the Russians and the Pacific. Unemployment in Canada is high; 14 per cent in the Province of Quebec, and the future lies more with Vancouver than with Montreal.

He recently had lunch with Barran, chairman of Shell, and asked him about Davies, who before the C.B.I. job was managing director of Shell-B.P. Barran said he had no complaints, so George asked if he was sorry Davies would not be returning to the Shell group. Barran said this was an unfair question, but he was not sorry.

George recently had a talk with van Straubenzee, Parliamentary Under-Secretary at the D.E.S. He said that raising the school-leaving age was not just a mistake, it would be a catastrophe. Already he could name thirty-four schools (in the London area) where the teachers had been terrorized by the children. Raising the school-leaving age would further intimidate the teachers at these schools and add many more schools to the list.

Friday, November 5th, 1971

Peter McLachlan rang Ruth up today. The Labour Party are talking about abandoning their bi-partisan approach to Northern Irish affairs and thinking up a formula for ending internment. This brought Faulkner over here hot-foot. It was announced that the visit had been arranged ten days ago, but Peter says this improbable story is quite untrue—the visit was arranged at exceedingly short notice, and the Government was only informed as he left Belfast. Peter says Faulkner is clinging to office by every available means, and that it is Lynch's position which is crumbling. He may be out next week. Paisley announced that direct rule from Westminster had been decided on and would take place shortly. Certainly the office of minister for Northern Ireland was offered to Soames. It seems likely that Paisley's disclosure was intended to make such a move more difficult. We continue to be told by Government spokes-men that the Army now has the measure of the gunmen. It seems even less true than it was. Meanwhile, Fraser has written a letter to *The Times* today advocating a general election at Stormont! Boal, at Stormont, apparently made an excellent speech ridiculing Faulkner's proposals for constitutional reform.

Monday, November 8th, 1971

Attended function in the morning at which Reggie Maudling opened the Field Wing of Bootle House in Whitechapel. Reggie looking relaxed and content. Peter Shore, the local M.P., was there looking a thought more mature than when I saw him last. Hugh Cudlipp told me that when Denis Healey signed the letter in the *Guardian* with 100 Labour M.P.s advocating our joining the Market, he asked Denis to write a piece for the *Mirror* on why he had changed his mind. Previously he had been mildly anti-Common Market. Denis duly wrote the article and received £250. Three weeks later he changed his mind back again.

On to have lunch with John Stevens at the Anglo-Swedish Club. He had just returned from a brief tour of the U.S. Nixon's popularity remains quite high in spite of multiple failures. It is not clear yet whether the U.S. is in for a serious recession. John Connally, the Treasury Secretary, may run as Vice-President with Nixon or may remain a Democrat and be the Democratic candidate. Agnew will be dumped, and anyway wants to get back into private life and make some money.

We spoke of the parallel pro-American, pro-Chinese policies pursued by the Japs. Stevens said they were also operating a third pro-Russian policy. It may be for the ultimate restoration of half Sakhalin or the Kuril Islands, but meanwhile gave them a lot of Russian trade.

Tuesday, November 9th, 1971

Lunch for C.D. [a senior civil servant]—it was a riotous occasion. We get on well, and I was in good form. With people in his position one has to listen for what is not said and may therefore jump to unwarranted conclusions. Little was said about Ted. I would judge that his opinion of Ted is not what it was. His opinion of Carrington remains high. His opinion of Whitelaw sky-high and rising. C.D. says Whitelaw is the only man who, when he speaks on something on which he feels strongly, has the personal authority to silence opposition. He and Carrington are apparently violently opposed to using Paisley. C.D. wants me to see them when I can and try to persuade them of my views. He thinks Balniel not a wet, but a young Carrington. This is the only word of praise for Balniel I have heard. He asked me what I thought of Mrs Thatcher—I said, very able, but surely calculated to put some backs up. I got the impression C.D. would not allow her even that much.

It appears that the Government opinion is that the Irish situation is gradually righting itself, and that the Industrial Relations Act will in due course transform labour relations. I don't think C.D. believed either proposition.

He saw something of Mrs Gandhi when she was here. Though she may not be in effective control of her vast country, C.D. thought she clearly had the measure of the politicians in her own Party and in the Opposition.

Barber was said to be doing better than some had expected. I got the impression C.D. thought little of him—but more than I did (I still think he would reach his ceiling as manager of the Kingston branch of Boots).

Thursday, November 11th, 1971

At a dinner of the Advertising Association last night I met Kearton and Goodman. The latter just off to Rhodesia for the fifth time this year. He is going with Alec Home. He does not think negotiations should be conducted by principals, and wonders whether they are going out for real negotiations, or to prove to the Tory back benches that nothing can be done. Politicians in recent years have surprised him by their liability to panic. Kearton said Courtaulds had very nearly made a bid for I.P.C. when Reed International did. He was sorry they hadn't, but David Eccles (a director of Courtaulds) had killed the idea at the time. Three of his factories in Northern Ireland have been burnt, but they are only rebuilding one. He is continuing to invest Courtauld money in Northern Ireland, and thinks the Army is slowly getting the upper hand of the I.R.A. This is current Government propaganda, but can it possibly be true?

Sunday, November 21st, 1971

The Peytons to lunch here. It was a very friendly occasion but nothing much emerged. The P.L.P. election for the Deputy-Leadership was nearly won outright by Roy on the first ballot—he missed by only two votes. However, on the second ballot he did not pick up one more vote and won by a mere fourteen. Peyton, I think rightly, attributed this to Callaghan's machinations in a 'stop Roy' manoeuvre. I was interested, after what C.D. said, that Peyton agreed that Balniel is one of the wettest M.P.s in the House. Peyton rather discounted the Government's flap over unemployment. He has had some talk in private with Jack Jones and does not believe he is a destructive force.

The Mosleys to dine on Friday night before they return to Paris after a month here. Mosley is evidently very active and equally evidently very discreet. Incidentally, both he and Peyton think Powell has practically written himself off.

Monday, November 22nd, 1971

William Whitelaw to lunch—such a very nice man. We spoke first about Ireland. He said he had suggested to Ted an approach to Paisley, but had got a dusty answer—to the effect that this idea was reaching him from many quarters. Whitelaw is going to return to the charge but thinks his seed will fall on stony ground, at any rate at present. He agrees that things cannot go on indefinitely as they are and that events may change Ted's mind before long. I told him what I told Ted at Chequers in August, and that I had suggested that Fraser be used. Whitelaw said Fraser's stock in the House is not high, owing to his activities on behalf of Biafra. I said that if Fraser wouldn't do, could anybody suggest anyone better?

He said the soldiers are under the impression that they are getting the better of the I.R.A. I said they seem indeed to be doing better, but that this is not the sort of war one wins—at best you can only hope for an intermission. Whitelaw said that if this is a lull, it should be a good time for a new initiative. He agreed that in the three years since the first outbreak in Londonderry, nothing constructive had been achieved by either Government—Lynch's position has obviously weakened; Stormont hardly exists, apart from the British Government; the Army is in an almost impossible position. Whitelaw said one difficulty about any suggestions is that Reggie would regard his removal from the Irish scene as a shattering personal defeat. I said surely this is irrelevant when one is faced with civil war. His remark on leaving Ulster, quoted in the *Sunday Times*, 'Bring me a stiff whisky and soda; God, what a dreadful country' (or words to that effect), will hardly help his usefulness in Northern Ireland.

I asked about Government changes. He asked where? I said most obviously in the Department of Trade and Industry. I gather he agreed, (a) that the Ministry was too big, and (b) that changes among the Junior Ministers were long overdue.

About Rhodesia, where negotiations are apparently in full swing, he said he did not see how agreement is possible. He thought the best course is to allow the sanctions gradually to be eroded—mainly by assorted foreigners—until there is in practical terms no sanctions policy left. I must say this is what has occurred to me as the only practical way out.

Whitelaw thinks there should be a boom or something like it next year, but does not expect unemployment to show any significant drop. He seemed to know little about the raising of the school-leaving age, and had no idea of the very adverse opinion held by senior people in the educational world. He said he was surprised that Mrs Thatcher managed to get herself represented as a granite-faced reactionary.

To me the most interesting aspect of the lunch was the impression that emerged that Ted is very much a presidential figure who shows little of his intentions to his colleagues—even to Whitelaw, who is said to be the Minister nearest to him.

Friday, November 26th, 1971

Last night at a charity performance of the London Symphony Orchestra we bumped into Reggie Maudling and Beryl. He looks as if he is going to seed. While we were talking to Reggie, up came Ted, who had conducted the overture. He asked me what I thought of the Rhodesian agreement, announced in the afternoon. I said it would cause a huge uproar. He said he thought there would be little more than rumbling except in Nigeria. I said I thought the uproar would be mostly verbal.

Saw Paisley this week. He attributes Faulkner's attacks to his weakness and desperation. Wilson had a very rough two hours with Paisley and Boal. He has now come out with a proposed settlement. This idea is a united Ireland, to be achieved over a period of fifteen years, ending with a Commonwealth Ireland under the Queen! The whole matter would be discussed in committees and commissions of all three Parliaments. The procedure wouldn't work, and the Queen is quite unacceptable to the Republic; but otherwise he is putting forward proposals which might have been achievable when he was first P.M. in 1964.

The Rhodesian proposals cannot be implemented until the middle of next year and are bound to run into a lot of heavy weather. Such a long delay may get the whole business bogged down in a morass of obstruction and frustration.

Wednesday, December 1st, 1971

Dinner last night with the Industrial Educational Trust. Sitting between Gerald Thompson, now chairman of Kleinwort Benson, and Sir Frank Figgures, now director-general of the N.E.D.C.* Figgures rather astonished me by saying it was curious how nobody had any power today: power had seeped away and none was now left. This was why it took so long to get anything done as so many consents were necessary. This is the same statement that Sir George Bolton made to me many months ago, 'There is now in England no power centre.' Even so it was surprising as coming from a man who, until very recently, was Second Secretary at the Treasury. Ray Gunter was there. I said to him his great Party seemed to be in a

* National Economic Development Council.

state of some disarray. He said that was the understatement of the year. His Party was in a sad state of disintegration not helped by 'that so-and-so Wilson'.

The principal speaker was Alastair Burnet, on the press. He was good, much better than you would expect from his editing of *The Economist*, which is undistinguished. I afterwards went on to a reception at St James's Palace and met Norman Collins, back from the U.S. Both he and Gerald Thompson held forth on the appalling gloom and demoralization in the U.S.—far worse than it was even a few months ago. Figgures said a world-wide slump was by no means inevitable but the danger was very present. He volunteered this opinion without any encouragement from me.

I said to Gerald Thompson that I thought, of all our institutions, the City was one that had done well since the War—finance and pure science were the only two fields in which we had shone. He said that in the state of roaring inflation in which we had lived for twenty years, industry—particularly heavy industry—had had a very rough time, whilst the very inflation created opportunities for dealing in money, i.e. for financial institutions such as merchant banks.

Friday, December 3rd, 1971

Lunch yesterday for Brian Walden. He is a very bright little man, though his health looks to me to be shaky. He had a bad time some months ago (haemorrhage from a lung?) but says he is all right now. He thinks this Government is doomed by the unemployment figures—in an election today Labour would win with a majority of 100 or more. He does not think Heath can reverse this and assumes that Wilson will be P.M. once again. Though Wilson is regarded widely with suspicion, Walden thinks there is only a slight chance of moving him. We talked about Ireland. He says Reggie Maudling is useless—or worse—as the Minister for Northern Ireland. He has the sharpest brain in his Party and thinks this excuses him from work. He is bone idle and has lost the respect of most of his former followers. Walden wants most to see the troops withdrawn as soon as possible from Ulster. He has been there recently and says they are (rather naturally) bitterly anti-Irish—and increasingly so. Left where they are, their morale will go steadily down. At the moment Ted is reiterating his determination to find a military solution, in spite of all evidence from the past that a purely military solution is not to be had. Walden said a senior Army officer (unnamed) told him in Ulster that the Army well knew a military solution was not on.

Walden's most contemptuous remarks were reserved for Barber. He says it is painful and embarrassing to see Barber cut to shreds time after time by Roy Jenkins. He is a mere puppet in the hands of Ted and his officials. The best Treasury Minister is said to be Higgins—nothing much to look at but a good brain.

Walden was at a Lobby lunch—I think on Wednesday—at which Ted spoke. Walden said his speech was quite amazing in its arrogance. Not an opportunity had been missed, not a foot had been put wrong. Ireland would soon be a peaceful province. Not only were his words confident but he exuded an entirely misplaced euphoria.

Walden thought the Industrial Relations Act would be largely a dead letter. Ted, in his speech, said how much of their success they owed to planning while in Opposition. The principal plan was this unworkable Act. Carr, in private conversation, revealed to Walden complete ignorance of some aspects of industrial relations.

Walden, I gathered, is now a front-bench spokesman on economics. When Wilson asked him to take this on, he asked Wilson why he had been selected as Wilson does not like him. Wilson admitted the dislike but said he had to balance his team with three more members with brains! Macintosh, Walden said, is one of the very brightest, but is too much disliked to be included.

According to Walden, it was Whitelaw who said, late at night at Brighton, that Eden and Ridley were going. Ted was furious and so, at any rate for the time being, they stay.

Paisley thought he had stopped direct rule for Ulster from Westminster by leaking the story early in November.

Walden thought there would be few changes in the Shadow Cabinet election, though he thought George Thomson might lose his place. In fact Thomson has gone up (so has Shirley Williams), while it is Barbara Castle who is replaced by Peter Shore.

The proposals for the Privy Purse are out and will be fought by the Labour Party.* Whatever you may think of the Queen's income, it is absurd to raise Princess Margaret's, the Duke of Gloucester's, and that of other minor and unimportant princelings.

* The Privy Purse is the name given to monies voted by Parliament to support various members of the British Monarchy. Such sums are quite separate from the Royal Family's private fortunes.

Saturday, December 4th, 1971

Lunch yesterday with John Peyton. I like him very much. He is a curious man—has obviously been badly hurt, but is now enjoying himself with the right wife and a real job. He is a doer, not a talker. I got the impression that he has no great opinion of Barber and realizes Maudling is not the man for Northern Ireland. He quoted Maudling as saying that the British had lost their pride but retained their conceit—an excellent aphorism.

Tuesday, December 7th, 1971

Lunch yesterday for Peter Carrington—such a very nice man. He was keen to talk about Ireland—said that in his view, and other politicians', Paisley was no longer untouchable, though still unacceptable. The reports he gets from the Army are optimistic—he suspects over-optimistic—but they are certainly doing better against the I.R.A. It was interesting that Wilson on television last night said that in his recent visit to Ireland the I.R.A. had sought an interview with him—an invitation which had (quite rightly) been declined. I said that C.D. had spoken in flattering terms of Lord Balniel, generally considered to be very wet, and suggested I should meet him. Carrington is to arrange this after Christmas. He said Balniel is 'willowy' and gives a bad impression sometimes. I noticed Carrington's references to his principal Junior Minister were far less flattering than my friend C.D.'s.

Carrington assumes the Indians will win in East Bengal pretty quickly and also that they will win the war.* I should think this is a bit optimistic. One can foresee a fairly quick win in East Bengal, but the fighting in the West may be so ferocious that a cease-fire would be hard to organize and the future integrity of West Pakistan must be open to considerable doubt. And if Pakistan breaks up, what about India, where Balkanization is always on the cards.

Saturday, December 11th, 1971

Sitting next Lady Plowden at our dinner-party on Thursday, I asked her what she thought of Mrs Thatcher. She said she thought Mrs Thatcher was intelligent and able, but so *silly*. She had antagonized so many people quite unnecessarily. Lady Plowden was another of those in the educational world who deplored the raising of the

* The Indians did in fact win the war. West and East Pakistan were permanently separated, with the former East Pakistan becoming the new state of Bangladesh.

school-leaving age. Like others, she thought it would win some easy applause, but do more harm than good.

At tea with Cardinal Heenan on Friday, he revealed that he had been summoned by Ted to advise on Ireland. This was towards the end of August, apparently later than our summons to Chequers. Heenan's advice did not amount to much except that he thought Paisley meant well, and that he thought a purely military solution out of the question.

Had some talk with Paisley on the telephone. He was summoned by Reggie to a private interview—very different to the one at Paisley's request some weeks ago. Apparently this time Paisley was treated as a V.I.P. and his views were listened to with respect. Reggie is going over to Ireland next week to collect opinions. Brigadier Bethell was at our party on Thursday and had had some talk with Tuzo on Wednesday. Tuzo is the G.O.C. in Northern Ireland, and expressed confidence (in my opinion quite misplaced) that he was getting the I.R.A. under control. Meanwhile, murders, shootings and bombings continue.

In the East it looks as if the Indians will have the whole of East Bengal by next week. Meanwhile, they seem to be successfully resisting the Pakistani efforts in Kashmir.

Monday, December 13th, 1971

Pam Berry writes to say that, at our party on Thursday, Professor Porter wrote off Victor Rothschild (head of Heath's 'think-tank') as 'quite useless'. It was not clear in what way he was useless, but evidently among Nobel Prizewinners his stock is not high.

Lunch for Fforde of the Bank of England. He said that at one time the Bank was afraid that, with inordinate wage-demands, we were in for a South American type of inflation. But this has not been so, and now inflation is on its way down from 10 per cent per annum to perhaps 5 per cent, though this may prove only to be a dip. The Government was taken completely by surprise by the rise in unemployment and does not really know what to do about it. Barber's inflationary measures may give us a boom with high unemployment and rapidly rising prices. Governments have for a long time sought a shake-out of excessive manning in industries. Now it has come, at a time and in a form that is not welcome. Fforde sees no reason why businessmen should spread their resources in industrial investment at the present time.

Tuesday, December 14th, 1971

Lunch with Reay Geddes at the Dunlop headquarters. He had one of his two managing directors with him—one Campbell Fraser, who is an economist and had been head of the Economist Intelligence Unit. Reay Geddes is the nicest man, but not a very tough commercial type one would imagine.

Fraser was very clear that there will be a slump—some people think soon; he did not expect it until 1973. Inflation, he thought, is an evil which has to be paid for. They said motor-cars are selling well, but the accessory manufacturers are not doing good business, so presumably more half-finished cars have been parked in fields than was generally supposed. They thought Europe provided us with a great opportunity for leadership, but where was the leader? The demand for Dunlop industrial products was poor—only golf balls were booming.

Rogaly in the *Financial Times* has what is to me a disgraceful piece saying that governments are not concerned with morals, and no one should be concerned with what adults do in private. Both Geddes and Fraser say they get the impression from their young relations that those who are now teenagers are much less in favour of permissiveness than their immediate elders.

Thursday, December 16th, 1971

We attended a carol party at No. 10 last night. Ted exuded optimism.

I had some talk with Watkinson, former Minister of Defence and now chairman of Cadbury-Schweppes. I said I was surprised how calmly Ministers took the very nasty situation in Ireland. Watkinson said the Ministers he knew were badly scared by the whole Irish situation. Like others, he assumes the Government will have their boom next year; and like others, he is certain the unemployment figures will remain high and the Government's situation will remain precarious.

Rees-Mogg was there speaking optimistically of the future of *The Times*, which seems to carry on regardless of its editor, though it may be losing less money.

Lunch for Vic Feather, whom I had not seen for some months—very friendly but not very informative. He says Carr is fed up with the Labour Ministry and would like to move to the Foreign Office! The Industrial Relations Bill Vic seems to regard as a dead letter.

Unions, representing about ten million workers, are pledged to make the Bill unworkable when it is law and will doubtless succeed. I seem to remember that last time we met binding agreements were to be entered into, then broken, and the Government was to be dared to do anything about it. This time such a course was repudiated with indignation. The idea seems to be to make no agreements legally binding. The employers seem to think it will be the smaller employers who will try and activate the Act. If the larger ones do, there will be a violent reaction from the T.U.C. But can the Government allow the nationalized industries to connive at making the Act a dead letter? Anyway, the T.U.C. is planning to react to moves by the employers—not to take the initiative.

Vic said Soames assumed the Tories would lose the election last year and that Ted would be knifed. In a speech at some function at which Vic was present, he apparently made it obvious that he was bidding for the succession. Under these circumstances how could Ted welcome Soames back to the House, let alone the Cabinet?

Vic supposes the unemployment figure will stay where it is, or rise slightly until March. It is now 970,000. Unless it comes down to 750,000 in July it will be higher this time next year than it is now. He realizes the Government is surprised and bewildered by the figure, and he professes to have the answer—steady and sustained growth for four years at 5 per cent per annum. He realizes that prices are on their way sharply up, but his remedy sounds to me like a lot of pie in the sky. The results he wants may be desirable, but how are they to be attained? He sees no reason why, with things as they are, industrialists should not invest more. But the fact that money is easier to borrow does not mean that the ordinary business will sink capital in expansion—the prospects of continued profit are far too uncertain.

Vic had a long story about the face-saving formula for Harold Wilson over his labour Relations Bill. Douglas Houghton made himself out as the hero of the episode, but Vic did not mention Douglas—it was all his own work. Wilson threatened Barbara's resignation and his own, but our Vic stood firm. The idea of threatening Barbara Castle's resignation is a big laugh, as Vic and his T.U.C. friends would have cheered if she had gone. Now she has lost her place on the Labour Shadow Cabinet (by trades-union M.P.s' votes) she no longer speaks on labour matters, which have been turned over to Callaghan.

Friday, December 17th, 1971

Lunch with Norman Collins. We talked about this and that—mainly Ireland. He commented on the fact that there are now no national figures of power and influence in their own person. He said of contemporary politicians, the only one who created any interest when he entered the Carlton Club was Rab Butler: Harold Macmillan caused no heads to turn!

Norman is just back from the United States—he says the situation in New York has deteriorated alarmingly in the last few months. He was staying at the Pierre, which, he says, is the equivalent of Claridge's. Under the glass on the dressing-table were the following instructions. 'If the buzzer goes at the entrance of the suite, only open the door on the chain; if the visitors claim to be workmen on a job, verify this with the main office before opening; never let it be known on the telephone that you are about to leave your room.' He said that on some wall—I understood visible from his bathroom —were a lot of hieroglyphics. He was told this was a code on what drugs could be got where.

Sunday, December 18th, 1971

Peter McLachlan on the telephone. He has recently seen Faulkner and is in close touch with affairs in Ulster. He says the British Army and the British Government believe that the I.R.A. are losing their guerrilla war. No one else believes this. The Army has been tougher recently and has been concentrating on Belfast, so the I.R.A. have been stepping up their activities on the border. There is no sign of their defeat.

Peter says Paisley may be losing some support as he is known to be dickering with some Catholics. Faulkner realizes his power is slipping and is believed to be contemplating a general election, and perhaps some sort of tie-up with Paisley. Apparently the Maudling/Paisley meeting completely foxed Maudling. He expected Paisley to be a self-seeking thug. When he showed no signs of being anything of the kind, Maudling did not alter his opinion—he was (and is) just mystified!

Wednesday, December 22nd, 1971

In conversation today, William Armstrong (of Sidgwick & Jackson) said that Michael Joseph and Weidenfeld bitterly regret having paid

£30,000 for the book rights of Wilson's memoirs. After much money spent on promotion they have sold only 22,000 copies. These are trade sales and it remains to be seen how many will be returned after Christmas.

Thursday, December 23rd, 1971
Lunch with Sir Frank Figgures. I had sat next him at a dinner, and this lunch was at his invitation. He gave me the impression that I should expect from a very clever civil servant. The conversation covered a lot of ground and nothing specific emerged. His general attitude was that though we had done worse than other countries in the last twenty-five years, we were enjoying a higher standard of living—a noticeably higher standard compared with only a few years ago. Trades unions were far from what one would like to see, but surely with patience our open society could be made to work—not only in the industrial but also in the financial sphere. I said I thought our society was in a very fragile state, and rather than tackle problems we brushed them under the carpet and hoped they would stay there. The reason perhaps was an instinctive feeling that a serious effort to solve any of our most important problems would bring on the deluge. Our national policy of recent years has been to postpone the deluge as long as possible. He said he is sometimes as pessimistic as I am, and quoted Dr Johnson as saying 'There is a lot of ruin in any nation.'

Thursday, December 30th, 1971
The Douglas Houghtons to dinner last night—a shrewd little man and so nice. He said the leadership of the Labour Party was not in question at the moment. The crucial year would be 1972. He ventured the opinion that Wilson would not again be Prime Minister. His book alone would make his position in foreign affairs impossible. Douglas thought that Denis Healey's turning of his coat (twice!) over the Common Market put him out of the running. He didn't say so, but left me with the impression that his choice would be Jenkins, and the only other serious candidate Callaghan. Jim now admits that he misjudged the Irish situation. He thought it was only a matter of civil rights, and now realizes the problem runs far deeper. The Labour Party is now trying to do something about Ireland. They are in touch with Paisley, and have to be in touch with the Northern Ireland Labour Party, though they are under no illusion

about its power or influence. They realize that any negotiations must be undertaken in strict secrecy. The trouble for everyone is to find some man or group who can speak for the Catholics. Fitt and Hume clearly can no longer do so, nor can the hierarchy. The Provisional I.R.A. remains, but no one seems to know who are its real leaders or what are its real aims.

Douglas thought the problem behind the Industrial Relations Act—at any rate for him and his colleagues—was to establish a constructive relationship between the trades unions and the Parliamentary Party. This has been brought to the fore by the demand of the T.U.C. for a straight repeal of the new Act. This is clearly impossible and Douglas wants to persuade the T.U.C. chiefs to abandon this negative stand and work out—with the Parliamentary Party—a constructive policy on inflation, price control, labour relations, etc. As it is, they are stuck with the same relationship between the Parliamentary Party and the T.U.C. as was established at the end of the last century, when all that was envisaged was a small Parliamentary group to put forward the T.U.C. point of view in the House. The possibility that this small group might one day be the Government with a Parliamentary majority never crossed anyone's mind.

Wilson is now said to be writing a full-scale autobiography and has a girl collecting cuttings. After the fiasco of his first book, he will find the terms very different!

Douglas said that Jim Callaghan had lost ground lately in the Parliamentary Party. His various manoeuvres had been too obviously self-seeking.

1972

The most important European event of 1972 was the enlargement of the European Economic Community (by a Treaty signed on January 1st, 1973) from six to nine members by the addition of Britain, Ireland and Denmark. The fourth prospective member, Norway, rejected the proposal for entry in a national referendum. Preparations for this entry played a large part in British domestic politics during the whole year.

The record of violence in Northern Ireland was the worst since the troubles began some four years earlier. 'Bloody Sunday' on January 30th, when thirteen civilians were killed by British troops attempting to restrain a crowd, was a day that has been incorporated in Irish mythology, and become a factor in the British Government's decision to suspend the Northern Ireland Parliament (Stormont) and to impose direct rule from Westminster.

Inflation and industrial unrest also continued in Britain, and some pragmatic solutions which conflicted with Conservative tenets had to be adopted. President Amin of Uganda decided to expel all Asians from his country, and the decision brought an influx of refugees to Britain, since many Ugandan Asians had nominal British citizenship.

Abroad, President Nixon visited China and Russia and these expeditions demonstrated the changing patterns of superpower relations. Japan hastened to establish its own relations with China. The Vietnam war continued, but the belief that its end was at least in sight was undoubtedly partly responsible for President Nixon's landslide victory in the November elections in the United States.

Wednesday, January 5th, 1972

Lunch for A.B. [a senior civil servant]. We talked—unexpectedly—a good deal about Ireland on which he wanted to have my views. He agreed with what I had to say, and said that Ted was well aware of the desirability of removing Reggie from responsibility for Northern Ireland, but so far had not found it possible. According to A.B., Prime Ministers were deeply impressed by Macmillan's Night of the Long Knives, when he sacked one-third of his Cabinet. This led to his own departure, and Prime Ministers ever since have been chary of making changes.

He finds it much more difficult in his present job dealing with the P.M. At the Treasury he often saw the Chancellor and knew where he stood. With the Prime Minister his relations are much less close. Wilson talked the entire time at their interviews, and A.B. found it difficult to make his point. Ted listens attentively and says nothing. It is impossible to guess whether he agrees or disagrees—and whether or not he intends to do anything about it.

On the economic front, he said neither Wilson nor Heath believes that 'economic growth' is a worthy goal for national policy, but Wilson really had no other. Heath is very eloquent in private on the possibilities of European union. It gives us a role instead of our Empire. The tragedy is that Ted cannot, but *cannot*, get his ideas on the subject across.

A.B. said we had hoped to maintain our exchange rate at its previous parity with the dollar. We have had to concede an up-value of 7 per cent, but that was not the original idea. It is assumed that agreed measures will reduce—though not eliminate—the American deficit. However, the deficit is so enormous that even a moderate improvement will affect seriously other nations' present surpluses.

He thought Government pronouncements unduly optimistic about the future of our economy. He sees no sign of the tide turning yet. The inflationary measures of the Government may take longer to take effect than they expect, and there will be an inevitable 'stop' after the 'go'.

I said that both Bolton and Figgures had commented to me on the lack of any power centre. A.B. said this was the one interesting point in Sampson's original *Anatomy of Britain*. He thought it was not a bad thing at the moment, as there is no national objective. Maybe it will be better to wait to assemble a power structure until there is something to use the power on.

Wednesday, January 12th, 1972

Lunch with Arnold Weinstock and some of the directors of the G.E.C.* Arnold was in great form, but had little specific information. He thinks ministerial talk of a reduction of unemployment to 500,000 quite unrealistic. He saw no reason why the present figure of about a million should decline. The consumer boom the Government is engineering will lead to more imports, not to more industrial investment. He thought the Post Office was even more inefficient now than it had been when it was part of the Civil Service. He seemed to have no clear idea of the likely impact of the Industrial Relations Act. He cannot envisage taking G.E.C. employees to court. He is much more impressed by the ability and dedicated ruthlessness of Jack Jones of the Transport and General Workers' Union.

The miners' strike has been on since Saturday. They seem bent not just on striking but on trying, by means of flying pickets, to prevent the movement and even the use of coal. If followed to its logical conclusion it could lead to a general strike, which neither the unions nor the Government seems to want. Meanwhile, the Government says and does nothing.

Thursday, January 13th, 1972

Dinner at home last night for Mrs Thatcher and others. She comes across in the newspapers and on television as an aggressive sort of woman, creating enemies wherever she goes. This is not at all the sort of impression she makes in the flesh. She is attractive, highly intelligent and very sensible. She says the so-called liberals (the left-wingers, the long-haired, and all that group) are determined to get her out of office and will doubtless succeed. She tried to help Surrey County Council to retain their four great grammar schools, but an overwhelmingly Conservative council was bullied into letting

---

* General Electric Company.

166

them go.* She told Ruth that the Americans are now beginning to realize what a disaster modern methods of education have proved to be. She had hoped we could learn from American experience and avoid the same mistakes. But this is not so; we are having to follow them down to our own disaster.

I said to her that we had been told by Dr Rhodes Boyson what a mistake it was to raise the school-leaving age. Mrs Thatcher said the same arguments had been used for not raising the age when she was ten. But there is more to it this time, as raising the age to sixteen fits in with A-levels, O-levels, and all the machinery for providing children with higher education. This does not really meet the point raised by Boyson, and the Manchester Council director of education, which was that more and more children are staying on voluntarily until sixteen anyway; that the proportion of truancy runs from 15 to 25 per cent and will certainly go up when the age is raised. Why compel unwilling children to stay at school. In so far as you can compel them, why not let the rising number of volunteers do the job?

Mark was also of the party, and said he was told by Elizabeth Home that Alec will retire when the Rhodesian settlement is through, which she thought would be in the autumn. That the settlement will be accepted by the Rhodesian Africans is not all that obvious, and without a green light from Lord Pearce's Commission, the deal is off.

Had lunch today with Don Ryder, very cheered over the financial prospects of Reed's. He said that there is a move to get Max Aitken out of the *Express*, and that with this in view he has been suggested as Governor-General of Canada (an idea killed by Trudeau), or High Commissioner in Salisbury when and if the Rhodesian settlement comes through. The idea is that there would then be a merger between the *Express* and Associated Newspapers†: the newspapers would be published from the *Express* plant and that would free the very valuable Associated Newspaper property for development. I said I understood Max had a tight control of the *Express* through the Beaverbrook Trust's three-fifths' holding in the voting ordinary

* State education policy was a continuing subject of acrimonious debate in Britain. Some (mainly conservatives) favoured the traditional system by which children in the state system were sent to either a grammar or secondary modern according to their success or otherwise in examinations. The Labour Party and Liberal supporters favoured the comprehensive system, whereby all children, whatever their academic abilities, were sent to the same school.

† Associated Newspaper Group Ltd, owners of the *Daily Mail* and London *Evening News*.

shares. Don says this control cannot now be as complete as that, as there has been consistent buying of *Express* shares, which has pushed them up to a p.e. rating of 30—far more than can be justified by their commercial prospects. Meanwhile, Vere Harmsworth sees himself as the master of the combined company, if and when the merger takes place.

Friday, January 21st, 1972

Conor Cruise O'Brien to lunch in Dublin today—a nice man I had not met before. He is an M.P. in the Dail and sits for a North Dublin constituency. He was exceedingly pessimistic and did not seem to think there was any likely way of avoiding a blood bath. He thought Stormont was finished, anyway; and he attached little importance to Paisley, though he did think Paisley's mood had changed for the better. He thought the only possible course was to install direct rule by Westminster, with a council representing Catholics and Protestants in the same proportions as that of the population. The chairman would be neutral, and it was to be hoped that such a council would succeed in lowering the political temperature. The I.R.A. chiefs changed so often that it could be said they had no central authority. There had been a difference between the Official and the Provisional wings of the I.R.A. up to a year ago, but now the distinction had largely disappeared. The gunmen were youths, or very young men, without political objectives, who had acquired a taste for violence, and this was a way of working it off without too much risk.

Next I had a long talk with Gageby, the editor of the *Irish Times*. He was born in Dublin, but his family comes from Belfast and he spends most weekends in the North. He said he has travelled thousands of miles in the North in the last couple of years and has only been stopped twice, in spite of his Dublin number-plates. This does not say much for the control of traffic by the troops.

He saw no advantage in altering the line of the border; he thought Faulkner's position in his own constituency a weak one; he saw no future for Stormont; he did not rate Paisley very high. Gageby thought Hume had as much influence as ever and had no reason to fear the I.R.A. (this is the opposite of what Hume told Hugh Fraser).

Neither of my informants thought a military solution of Northern Irish affairs was possible. Gageby struck me as more intelligent and better informed than O'Brien. He said that the I.R.A. had some irresponsible gunmen, but that in general they were well disciplined. He thought the only chance of an improvement would be if the British Government announced a decision to withdraw our troops from Northern Ireland and over a period to negotiate the unification of Ireland, under agreed safeguards. O'Brien thought this would encourage the gunmen and terrify the Protestants. Gageby said the problem is to convince the Protestant working man. The middle classes would now accept unification, but with high unemployment all over Ireland the proletariat would be much harder to convince. On the other hand this is the group that looks to Paisley, who is much the best demagogue in the business. Army searches are very thorough and necessarily involve tearing up the floorboards of houses they go into. In fact they partially wreck any house they search. This provokes violent hatred, not only among avowed nationalists and the working classes, but also to some degree from the better-off Catholics who were ready to put up with the O'Neill and earlier regimes.

Lastly, I had a long talk with Mulcahy, editor of *Hibernia*. He is an intelligent man, a nice man and a good editor, but not a politician, and not a very practical man outside his own field. He agreed that the Army is not getting on top of the I.R.A. and could not do so. He thought there was no initiative to be expected from anyone in Northern Ireland, it must come from London. Young Cudlipp (nephew of Hugh), now on *The Times*, is here telling people that Reggie is being moved from responsibility for Ireland, and is to be replaced by a rather Junior Minister, while the real responsibility will be assumed by Ted himself. Ted is already doing this with the Treasury, which must mean that the P.M.'s real work is mostly going by default.

The views of the three men I have met today differ on many points but agree on these: (1) that a military solution is not to be had; (2) that Stormont is finished; and (3) that any initiative must come from London. They all think that any course that is adopted, however successful in the long run, will cause a great deal of bitterness and disruption in the short run. They all seemed to think that much trouble is caused by the British Government's lack of a definite, consistent line of policy. They did not think Bernadette Devlin important, nor that there was any danger from the Communist, anarchist, Trotsky-ite, subversive element. Though the Catholic hierarchy has lost much power in Ireland, as elsewhere, and though Dr McQuaid, Archbishop of Dublin, has retired, there are more brave words by Lynch than deeds in such matters as birth control or divorce.

Saturday, January 22nd, 1972

We called on Dr Ryan, Archbishop-designate of Dublin. He is a lecturer at Dublin University, not a bishop, and is to be consecrated in Rome in about three weeks. He is a tall man in his forties, son of a respected medical doctor in Dundalk. He is intelligent, liberal and a most impressive and unexpected successor to the notorious Dr McQuaid. He seemed surprised that many of the Northern Protestants are terrified of being dominated by the Catholic hierarchy. They had indeed made a mistake over the matter of Dr Brown, way back in 1950 when he was Minister of Health, but even hierarchies learn from their mistakes.* Dr Ryan is not yet a member of the hierarchy and is not familiar with their views, but knows there will no opposition to an alteration of the constitution, abolishing the special position of the Catholic Church. He thinks the sale of birth-control materials will be legalized, and probably divorce also. Divorce and abortion are subjects on which strong views are held by the public, but they are not subjects on which the hierarchy is likely to insist—anyway for non-Catholics. He had heard that Paisley was a different character—much more liberal—and anyway he is obviously an Irishman operating in an Irish context.

Dr Ryan did not think Stormont could have a future. About the schools, he said the Church was now prepared to take a much more relaxed attitude. If Northern Ireland is to become an integrated community the children must be taught in the same schools. At present the Catholic authorities insist on Catholic children going to Catholic schools, and so you have Catholic communities springing up round Catholic schools—and these become the ghettos of which we hear so much. At present Catholic teachers are working in Protestant schools, and the authorities are prepared to countenance schools with an ecumenical complexion.

Newspaper contacts told me about the Provisional I.R.A. These were brave men with the interests of Ireland at heart—they were not just thugs. They said they could shoot Paisley any day, but saw in him a man doing his best for his constituents and his flock, and the

---

* Dr Brown resigned in 1951 as a result of opposition to his controversial proposed Mother and Child scheme.

new Paisley had nothing to fear from them. Their movement was well disciplined, they said, but any such movement attracts a sadistic or hooligan element. They knew which they were and had them under control. They thought a general election in Northern Ireland would be a help, as it would bring to the fore those who do now represent Northern opinion. They could guarantee a truce for the period of the election, if the Army could be kept out of sight for the same period. Any new initiative must come from London and, to have its full effect in Ireland, must take a dramatic form. New initiatives must succeed each other so that momentum is maintained. After the election perhaps a council of six could be set up—three from the South (? Catholics), three from the North (? Protestants), with a neutral chairman to run Northern Ireland and lead her by stages into a united Ireland. These men were confident they could keep up their campaign of violence indefinitely. It was possible, at the outside, that they might be compelled to order some kind of intermission if the going got really tough for them.

The idea of a council of non-politicians was also put forward by the priest with Dr Ryan, who said the one success in Northern Ireland since the troubles began had been the council running Londonderry, which had been installed instead of the corrupt elected council.

In the course of conversation with Mulcahy, he said the civil rights movement in the North presented Government with a new problem. How does one cope with a movement seeking to destroy the State yet subsisting on welfare funds from that State. I said the Government would put up with this form of subsidized sabotage for just so long. If it seemed to be endangering the stability of the State the welfare funds would be cut off and the rebels brought to heel. Mulcahy seemed to think that in a democratic regime this was impossible. If he is right then any considerable number of people in any area can set about disrupting and destroying the State, and can depend on getting away with it. Personally, I think the movement would fizzle out, or lead to repression on dictatorial lines. I don't agree with Mulcahy, but the civil disobedience movement in Northern Ireland does present a problem.

Sunday, January 23rd, 1972
Lunch with Major McDowell and his wife. He is managing director of the *Irish Times*, is a barrister, and has other business interests.

He asked us to talk about Irish affairs. He is a man with a very varied background—a Protestant father from the North, mother from the South, service in the British Army (Ulster Rifles), and has served on the Staff in Edinburgh, and in M.I.5. He had nothing specific to report or suggest, but the same pattern emerges: (1) any initiative can only come from Westminster; (2) a united Ireland is the only possible answer; (3) no good can come of Reggie Maudling; (4) surprised comment on the recent conciliatory attitude of Paisley.

McDowell seemed to think it uncertain that the Government would win its referendum on the Common Market. The same doubts seem to exist in Denmark, judging by the papers. In fact neither country has really any option. With all the talk of independence it surprises McDowell that the printing unions at any rate, are dominated by their London offices.

Meanwhile, I had a further briefing on the attitude of the Provos. It seems that while ready to accept a conciliatory gesture addressed to the Irish heart it is not easy to see what form it should take. An election is not thought practicable, but everyone thinks that Stormont is finished, so what emerges is a council established by the fiat of the British Government. The excellent and unpartisan work of Dr and Mrs Paisley in his two constituencies is widely appreciated. The idea of a truce is perfectly feasible, as no one enjoys shooting down British soldiers. They have no use for Wilson, whom they distrust—much more use for Callaghan.

The only successful development in Northern Ireland seems to be the council in Londonderry established to take over from the corrupt elected body. Therefore this is a model that might advantageously be followed.

Monday, January 24th, 1972

Lunch with a civil servant of the Irish Foreign Service. He is a highly intelligent man and obviously well informed. He had not met Dr Ryan, and was pleased that I thought such a convincing personality would do much to allay Protestant fears of the domination of the State by a bigoted hierarchy. My host was very critical of Faulkner and Taylor—regarded them as hard-liners determined to maintain their own and the Unionists' supremacy at all costs. Faulkner's recent speech is interpreted to mean that he will rouse a Protestant backlash if there is any serious talk of a United Ireland.

Stormont is now doomed—the minority will never accept it. Faulkner, he said, is planning a general election which he thinks he could win: Paisley would be out; the Catholics returned would be more extreme; and some Alliance candidates would be financed by the Unionists and returned. My host thought this whole idea a total miscalculation, but that anyway the problem of security in a general election probably removes any possibility of holding one. He said Bernadette Devlin has no following and no influence. For various reasons the I.R.A. distrust most of the Catholic M.P.s at Stormont—some are too volatile, and others are unreliable in other ways. The only one they trust is Hume. He did not say much about the I.R.A., or Paisley. The former, he thought, would fade out with the promise of unification; the latter was not denounced, as was Faulkner and all his works.

My host thought the first step must be the assumption by Westminster of control of the security forces, including both police and military; a speech must be made by Heath in Ireland saying that the long-term policy of H.M.G. was the unification of Ireland, and that the detainees will be released. Simultaneously, Lynch would announce his plans for a revised constitution. Other moves would have to be made step by step to keep up the momentum.

My host derided the idea that a military solution was possible, or that the troops were achieving one. At the moment the troops are on the offensive, so the I.R.A. are lying relatively low, with fifty of their best men in the Republic. These fifty will doubtless be sent back North when the moment seems opportune. New recruits more than make up for the loss by death and internment.

He said that at present Britain is giving Northern Ireland an annual subsidy of about £150 million. With unification, a sum of this magnitude could be paid over initially, diminishing gradually, and terminating after fifteen years.

He said British Ministers seem to be under the impression that if Lynch is forced out a more pliable man would succeed him. This is the opposite of the truth—a more extreme man would take Lynch's place.

My host had heard that Tuzo was very dissatisfied with the policy he was asked to carry out and had offered to resign. There were signs that the troops were beginning to be demoralized. On television yesterday not only were the police seen to be beating up the demonstrators in an anti-internment march, but officers were seen using their swagger-sticks on soldiers to stop them beating up the crowd.

Friday, January 28th, 1972

Lunch for Paisley on Wednesday. He had had a cold and was off-colour and depressed. He said the troops were becoming demoralized—a parishioner of his, a Protestant, came to see him in great distress. At 2.00 a.m. the troops kicked in his front door and three soldiers appeared at the foot of his bed. The man was hauled off protesting that he was not the man they thought he was; the wife's money was stolen. When the military authorities finally discovered he was the man he said he was, they sent him home charged with 'disorderly behaviour'!

Paisley is still keen on a Northern Ireland general election. He says the Faulkner regime is breaking up, but that Faulkner is quite capable of stirring up a Protestant backlash to stay in office.

Paisley asked me what I would do, and I said that from all I had gleaned lately there must be a United Ireland; that I thought Stormont was no longer viable, and responsibility must be assumed by Westminster. Paisley said he would attack such a policy—he could do no other. It would lead to the emigration of half the Protestant population of Northern Ireland—half a million people. I said I thought the spectre of Rome Rule was out of date, as the political ambitions and power of the Catholic hierarchy were not at all what they had been—in Ireland as elsewhere. It is increasingly clear to me that there is no generally acceptable solution to the Irish question and that the decision, which will have to be made in London, whatever it is, will cause fierce resentment in some important section of the population.

At a *Spectator* party last night I met various Fleet Street figures such as Drogheda, Bob Edwards, Larry Lamb, etc., also, notably, Derek Ezra, now chairman of the Coal Board, and Hugh Fraser.

Ezra is deeply worried by the coal strike, now nearly three weeks old. The maintenance men are not going down most mines, and permanent damage in some pits, and the destruction of much machinery, seems inevitable. The moderates thought they could get the Coal Board's offer accepted, but this proved not to be the case. Ezra is depressed as the price of oil is now much higher, and if the miners really worked with a will—the whole business is now so mechanized—the industry could be prosperous and the men too.

The strike will involve the Coal Board in immense losses and set the whole industry back. The Government, from Ezra's account, just does not want to know.

Fraser and I are to lunch on Monday, but he told me he had arranged a very secret meeting between Ted and Paisley. Meanwhile, Faulkner has arrived unexpectedly for a talk with Ted. It looks as if things are moving.

Tuesday, February 1st, 1972

Lunch with Peter Carrington to meet Balniel. He was said by some to be the wettest M.P. in the House, but others said I ought to meet him. Hence this lunch. He was certainly no wet, though no genius. He seemed to me a pleasant, intelligent, public-spirited Etonian—no more, no less. We talked mostly about Ireland, following on the shooting in Londonderry on Sunday in which thirteen civilians were killed by the paratroopers. There is to be the inevitable inquiry, which will operate to the disadvantage of the troops and the advantage of the I.R.A., by whom the march and the subsequent rioting was presumably organized. Carrington was well aware that the whole episode represents a big propaganda success for the I.R.A. He had little news, but said his choice for the Minister in charge of Northern Ireland affairs (if it came to that) would be Carr. I said he had been running away from the trades unions for eighteen months and the I.R.A. would regard him as easy meat. Carrington denied he had been running away. He also said that, as a man, he preferred Faulkner to Paisley. It was a hilarious lunch at the Ritz, and I hope I instilled in the pair my belief that a political initiative is necessary and urgent, and that it must envisage a united Ireland.

Next to see C.D. [a senior civil servant] in his office and tell him the story of our visit to Dublin. I like him very much and find him very easy to talk to, but of course he is the soul of discretion. Ted appears to feel it is rather unfair the way everything is going wrong at once—Ireland, Rhodesia, coal strike, Malta and unemployment. These are all problems that have been swept under the carpet in the past—though not by Ted—and are now emerging.

On Ireland, C.D. feels the most dangerous and disastrous course would be to do nothing. At the same time, any line of policy involves running great risks. I said I thought any policy must be concocted in secret and announced dramatically in Ireland—perhaps in Armagh, the religious capital of Ireland. It must include an acceptance in principle of a united Ireland. I got the impression that though, at last, the Government is in touch with Paisley, it is not in touch, however indirectly, with the I.R.A.; and they seemed to know nothing of Dr Ryan, who may well prove a key figure. I said I thought it a pity that the Government is so bad over its propaganda—it allowed the I.R.A. to win every round. C.D. groaned, as if this was a favourite theme of his. He asked if I had spoken to Whitelaw about this. I haven't, but I will.

Friday, February 4th, 1972
Ruth had thirty-five minutes with Heath yesterday. Ted plays with his cards very close to his chest, and anyway one wouldn't expect him to be expansive. He struck Ruth as essentially a religious man—more of a monk than a politician. He clearly has no understanding of, or acquaintance with, Ireland and the Irish. Ted was tired and depressed, and no wonder: Dublin is becoming openly hostile—the Irish Government did nothing to prevent the burning of the British Embassy in Merrion Square; the coal strike is dragging on; the outlook for unemployment remains bleak, etc., etc.

Sunday, February 6th, 1972
Hugh Fraser in for a drink last night. He had been in touch with Paisley, and said recent events had tended to make even the more reasonable Protestants more intransigent. The rumour in the House was that Ted is going to propose a re-drawing of the boundary between North and South. However, in a speech at Harrogate today he merely stood pat—no alteration in the present constitution without majority consent, and yet another plea that all parties should accept Reggie's invitation to a round-table conference. This seems to imply that Reggie remains in charge, though how anyone can suppose that Orangemen and the I.R.A. can helpfully sit at the same table defeats me.

Hugh was saying that no Government changes can be made until the Common Market legislation is through. It will be a close-run thing and Heath cannot afford to antagonize any existing Minister nor, for that matter, the eight Ulster Unionist M.P.s.

Monday, February 7th, 1972
Lunch for Dick Marsh. He has come on a lot since he left the House—a bigger, more confident man altogether.

He is now chairman of British Rail, and held forth on the problems of coping with the vagaries of the politicians. In June he was instituting economies, amounting to £8 million this year, and £15 million in a full year. In July he is informed he is to work with the C.B.I. and keep price increases to 5 per cent. This involves a loss of £37 million this year, which he was urged to borrow. He declined, and has received a grant of that amount, but obviously a further grant will be required for next year, and so on until they can get fare increases up to what they should have been. The Government had not thought of this. Then, in September, he is told to spend as much as possible, so he has to go back to the people who have been enforcing economies and ask them where they can spend more money not less. How you run any enterprise on these stop-go principles I have no idea. Added to which, the railwaymen are staging an unofficial strike on the Southern Railway, and are today refusing to handle oil for the power stations—in spite of efforts by the unions concerned. As he said, 'Anarchy is on the increase.'

I asked him about John Davies. He said his Ministry is impossibly big and he has completely failed to keep his Junior Ministers in line. John Eden is trying to run the steel industry on his own. Ridley is even worse. Marsh is impressed (to his surprise) by Peyton, who is decisive and seems to depend on hunch. The Industrial Relations Act has so far made no impact on anyone. Marsh says Carr does not believe in it. He also says Whitelaw is browned off. Being Leader of the House is a dull job and only important to M.P.s.

I asked him about the Labour Party leadership. He said when in Washington he had an evening at the Embassy with some politicians. They were well-informed about Wilson, and regarded him as untrustworthy, and his behaviour over the Common Market as contemptible. Nevertheless, Marsh did not think he could be shifted. While he is disliked and distrusted, the alternatives are Callaghan, who is distrusted, and Roy Jenkins who is disliked. Roy has never made the smallest effort to get to know his back-benchers, and there are senior ones he does not know by name even. The only alternative is Tony Benn, who is liked, but could only get the job as a result of a succession of unlikely events. He is energetic and ambitious but behaves like an immature schoolboy.

He thought Ezra had handled the coal strike badly, and in particular had made a disastrous showing on the Frost programme.

177

Tuesday, February 8th, 1972

Lunch with Frank Longford to talk about Ireland; and thirty-five minutes in the evening with William Whitelaw at the House, the latter most welcoming and very frank. Things cannot possibly be allowed to go on as they are; Stormont will have to be closed down; confidence in Faulkner has gone. They have looked at the possibility of incorporating Northern Ireland in the U.K. rule. They have also considered moving the border. To both policies there are insuperable objections. He did not say so, but the plain impression left was that they have decided on a united Ireland. It will cause much anger among the Northern Protestants, but there does not exist any agreed solution. A dark tunnel with light at the end is better than a dark tunnel with no light at the end. Whitelaw said that Paisley is no longer the untouchable. He made the outstanding speech in the North of Ireland debate last week. They believe he sees himself in a leading role in a united Ireland. To unite Ireland would require legislation, and in view of the strong feelings any decision will arouse, it will be necessary for the new Irish policy to be bi-partisan. Wilson has already come out in favour of a united Ireland, but he is so distrusted that a bi-partisan approach with him as partner is pretty daunting. I got the impression that he had not yet been sounded. Whitelaw quoted Lynch as saying that a transition period to a unified Ireland would be too long at fifteen years. This sounded as if he had been consulted. I said ten years was the maximum, but I was in favour of having no declared time limit. On the other hand, something must be happening month by month; otherwise the Government would be losing its initiative and its credibility.

Friday, February 11th, 1972

Forty minutes with Leslie O'Brien yesterday afternoon. He is a nice little man, doing better than had been expected, but not of a stature that would supply leadership to the City—or anywhere else. It was interesting that in our talk no mention was made of Barber. Leslie said how much he enjoyed working with Heath; he did not always agree with his objectives but he was clear and consistent—there was none of the self-absorption and gimmickry that was so tiresome with Wilson. Even the new appointment to the Court—Weir instead of Harry Pilkington—was Heath's work.

I tried out on him my theory that we are still living out the consequences of Roy Jenkins's essentially deflationary policy—high taxation, large Budget surplus, etc. This has checked the rate of inflation but has led to an unexpected degree of unemployment. Leslie would have none of this, and attributed the check to inflation to the policies of this Government. Anyway, he expects unemployment to be high until the second half of next year, when it may start going down. The Government's reflationary policy is already working, as can be seen in the record demand for houses, cars and consumer durables. There is so much unused capacity that there is no reason why increased demand should lead to higher prices, though it will lead to more imports.

We talked about international exchange rates, and I said I did not see the importance of America raising the price of gold from $35 to $38 if they were prepared neither to buy nor to sell at that price. I got the impression that Leslie did not really understand either. His 'explanation' did not explain. He said the Japanese had behaved well—wanting to be members of the international monetary club in good standing. I wonder. I should have thought they will long remember their recent treatment at the hands of John Connally of the U.S. Treasury.

Lunch yesterday for Jo Grimond, who produced one item of news. He had spoken to someone (perhaps from the *Guardian*) recently back from Rhodesia. This man said that Lord Pearce had made a deplorable impression—he did not seem to have any grasp of the situation. But the important result of this was that at his press conferences with the Africans they ran rings round him. This has given them much self-confidence. It seems likely that the Smith–Alec Home agreement will be rejected. Anyway, the Africans now know they are on their own and seem to think they will do better that way than relying on an impotent British Government.

The coal strike is really serious. The latest negotiations broke down with the miners demanding a 25 per cent increase in wages. Picketing is no longer peaceful and blatant intimidation goes unchecked. It is said that the strike will continue for at least three weeks, and from today we are to have a third of the country blacked out at any one time. It seems to me that the Government policy of appeasement can hardly be reversed at this late hour, but acceptance of the miners' demands would set 25 per cent instead of 8 per cent as the norm for wage increases.

Monday, February 14th, 1972

It seems that half industry is to close down this week because of the coal strike. The suddenness of the crisis has taken everyone by surprise—including apparently the Government. Picketing the power stations has been an important factor, but though intimidation of this kind is wholly illegal nothing has been done to discourage it. Presumably the court of inquiry will lead to a climb-down by the Government and an inflationary settlement, which will set the 'norm' for other claims. Neither Ezra nor the Government came out of this with any credit.

Meanwhile, the *Sunday Times* yesterday (and another Sunday paper which I did not see) have come out with what purports to be the Government plan for Northern Ireland—the Deputy Prime Minister and some Ministers to be Catholics; a referendum on joining the Republic or not every twelve years; release of the more harmless detainees, etc., etc. If this is really to be the Government's plan, it will be greeted with incredulity and laughed out of court. It bears no resemblance to the ideas emerging in my conversation with Whitelaw last week. Is it a kite sent up by Stormont? Or has Reggie persuaded Heath that these proposals might be accepted?

Wednesday, February 16th, 1972

Dinner with Mike yesterday. The information at the C.B.I. was that the Government was confident the offer made last Wednesday would be accepted. When it wasn't, they were utterly unprepared. The long-term consequences of the whole episode are likely to be very serious. We have had a mini-general strike in which the Government has been defeated; intimidation by pickets at power-stations and at the House of Commons, has been permitted; no reference has been made to the Communist influence in the whole business; and the settlement is bound to be inflationary and to set the level for other inflationary claims. Carr's conciliatory policy lies in ruins; Maudling's feebleness is given further publicity, but no changes are forecast. Simultaneously with Ireland and the coal strike, we have a crucial division on the Common Market tomorrow; the Rhodesian settlement seems to be a dead duck; and we are busy evacuating Malta.

Saturday, February 19th, 1972

So the coal strike is settled on terms that amount to total victory by the miners. Percentage figures always vary, but the percentage increase over the sixteen months of the agreement seems to be about 20 per cent per annum against the Government's 8 per cent ceiling. Much play is made with the miners' special case, which no trades union will accept.

The debate on the Common Market ended with a Conservative majority of eight. This is damaging in itself, but also means an interminable wrangle in Parliament.

Finally *The Times* this morning opines that the Government does not intend to take away security from Stormont, does not intend to separate Northern Ireland from the Home Office, and does not intend to do anything appreciable about internment. It is hardly credible that anyone—even this Government—could suppose such a negative attitude would be tenable.

Monday, February 21st, 1972

John Peyton to lunch yesterday. It was a friendly social occasion, and anyway you could not expect any indiscretions. He is well aware that after the miners it is the turn of the railwaymen, and that comes within his responsibility. He seemed rather shaken by the prospect. His gesture, when I asked when we are going to have some Government changes, seemed to indicate that he thought they were long overdue. He said he thought there should be one Minister responsible for all Northern Ireland affairs, but carefully abstained from saying that Ireland should be taken out of Maudling's hands.

Lunch today with Kenneth Keith, just back from the U.S. He said things are picking up there, and that should have a favourable influence on our economy here. He had little news, but was talking about Concorde, as he is a director of B.E.A. or B.O.A.C. (or both). He says the planes will cost £23 million each with spares; that there is no possibility of their earning a profit; and it is doubtful whether a number of countries will let them over-fly. So how will they get to Australia or South Africa—even New York is not certain. Keith also said it has never been made clear what B.E.A. is supposed to be doing. Its policy is in fact to be 'First in Europe', which means carrying a lot of passengers at a loss, notably on internal flights.

Monday, February 28th, 1972

Ted Heath, after much prior publicity, gave a ministerial broadcast yesterday evening. After the build-up I expected some definite pronouncement. But not so. It was an unimpeachable homily about the evils of inflation and of violence. Ruth, who is strongly pro-Ted, thought it sounded like a headmistress addressing a lot of girls in their low-teens. There may have been a hint on some fresh legislation on picketing. What is wanted is not fresh legislation, but the implementation of what we have.

This morning down-page on page two of *The Times* is the report of an interview given by Ted to the *New York Times*. It is by far the most important pronouncement on Ireland made by the P.M. for months. It is depressing stuff—no united Ireland—in fact no indication of a political initiative of any kind. We just soldier on. Ted's obstinacy on this, and on labour relations, will lead him to catastrophe. People still seem to think his obstinacy is a mark of strength, but of course it is just the opposite.

Monday, March 6th, 1972

In Paris. Spent part of the morning with Beuve-Méry, the former great editor of *Le Monde*. He had no particular information.

Peter Stephens says the drug traffickers and refiners are understood to be protected by a Cabinet Minister. There is a great deal of feeling over Chaban-Delmas, the current P.M., who quite legally pays no, or almost no, income tax. Peter says this fuss in the newspapers is due to the fact that Chaban-Delmas has made a great deal of money—said to be £3 million—out of politics.

The memory of de Gaulle has faded very fast. He is now hardly ever spoken of. Pompidou thinks Heath the best Prime Minister we have had since Churchill. Peter thinks Wilson is determined to bring Heath down, regardless of the effect on the Labour Party or on Parliament.

Tuesday, March 7th, 1972

An hour with Jean Monnet in the morning. He had no great news: thought that the referenda in Denmark and Norway might go against the Common Market, but that the English legislation and the Irish referendum would go through. These views seemed to me partly wishful thinking, and partly a much greater faith in Heath, which one notices here, than is usual at home. Monnet also thinks that once we are in the Market the Continental trades unions will have a restraining influence on our T.U.C. I myself do not see why English unions and their Communist leaders should be more moderate in their demands when we join the Market—a policy of which they disapprove.

Lunch with the Mosleys. He obviously thinks he has a role to play and is keeping in touch with all and sundry, particularly at the B.B.C. Events have moved more slowly than he had expected, but now the Heath Government is dead and a Wilson second innings could only be an interim affair.

Later called on David Weill at Lazard Frères—a very shrewd old boy. He thought American monetary behaviour quite irresponsible. They have recently pushed off on to other industrial countries the responsibility of dealing with their own deficit on their balance of payments. It was to be hoped that united action here would force the Americans to tackle their own problems. He thought the Japanese might well end up in the Chinese camp, but are at present forging closer links with the U.S.S.R. He, like others, expressed warm appreciation of Heath—the most courageous British P.M. since Churchill. He thought a world slump possible, but not probable, and considered the outlook in France to be for stability. The German Government is in trouble and may have an election, which they would probably lose.

Wednesday, March 8th, 1972

Lunch at the Embassy with the Soames. She is really a poppet. Christopher, I thought, would like to be back in politics but will make no strenuous effort in that direction.

Afterwards spent an hour with one Rougagnou on Pompidou's staff. Like everyone I have met here, he has a quite exaggerated idea of Heath's political strength. The conversation ranged far and wide, but the part that really evoked a response was about German politics. Brandt is down to a majority of one and has to ratify the treaty with the Russians by July. If he fails there will be an election, which he will lose, and then the Ost-Politik, and with it the Security Conference, will fall to the ground. Over our affairs, and the possible fate of the referenda in Ireland, Denmark and Norway, they are inclined to take things as they are and not to look too far ahead. When Pompidou comes to London in about ten days' time the subjects for discussion will be international monetary policy, and the future of Europe.

Soames had two good stories. (1) Churchill decided to sack Florence Horsbrugh from his Government. He hated sacking people

183

and asked the Chief Whip, Buchan-Hepburn, to do the job. However, he refused and said Churchill must do it himself. Churchill summoned Miss Horsbrugh, and said he was moving her to the House of Lords to make room for the promotion of younger members of the Party. Florence Horsbrugh burst into tears and sobbed and sobbed. Churchill could not stand against a woman's tears, and so said he had not realized she was so attached to her job, and by the time he had dried her tears she had been promoted Minister of Education! (2) When Alec Home resigned the leadership of the Tory Party, a Lobby correspondent (who told Soames) asked a Conservative back-bencher if Soames were in the running for the leadership. The Tory M.P. said, 'We are not going to get rid of a grouse merely to replace it with a pheasant.'!

Friday, March 10th, 1972

The last meeting before we left Paris was lunch yesterday with Charles Gombault, now of Regie Presse, and Relache, who is assistant editor of *France-Soir*—Lazareff is ill, perhaps with cancer of the lung. In any case, his day as editor must be over.

My hosts were not very informative, but the following opinions emerged. Pompidou is doing well and would be re-elected if there was an election now. Though this is true, his wish to drop two or three of his Ministers (including his Foreign Minister) came to nothing as he had not the political strength to do this. There will be a general election a year from now, in which the Gaullists will lose a lot of seats but not their majority. The changes that will take place will arise from a change of the balance of forces within the Party. In the meantime, the Communists are trying to give an impression of respectability to help them in a year's time, and are dismayed by the action of the Gauchistes who are increasingly militant. Gombault thought France was doing well at the moment, though there were signs of a business recession, but the whole set-up is very fragile. As when I saw him last, he thought anything in France may happen at any time.

The outlook in Germany is serious, as Brandt may not get a majority for his treaty with Russia. If this proves to be so then disarmament conferences and anything of the kind will all be out.

In France the principle problem would seem to be corruption at all levels of their affairs.

Tuesday, March 14th, 1972

Lunch yesterday for Paisley. He was pessimistic but personally in good heart. He is a big man and a good man and we both like him. He felt more free to talk about his interview with Ted, who frankly admitted that both internment and the ban on marches were Faulkner's work. Paisley gathered that Faulkner was not at all in favour. Whitelaw told Paisley that he had opposed the internment policy, and of all the ministerial decisions he had made he most regretted having been persuaded to agree to the policy.

The papers report that Ted had prepared a fairly forthright statement of policy on Ireland. But this failed to get through the Cabinet sub-committee or the Cabinet itself mainly, apparently, owing to Maudling's opposition. Maudling's attitude was confirmed at a meeting of Tory back-benchers, which was in effect pro-Unionist. Meanwhile, the Irish situation deteriorates. Paisley, who thought at one time that a united Ireland was a possibility and that in the meantime Stormont must be maintained, now says a united Ireland is postponed for a generation and Stormont is dead. He can see no alternative to integration of Northern Ireland with the U.K. This may be a necessary move in the right direction, as would be the appointment of a Minister for Northern Ireland, which is said to have been decided on. But the value of even that move depends on the quality of the man appointed.

Continued dithering by H.M.G. makes the whole Irish problem more and more confused and insoluble. It would seem to me that indecisive British Governments over the last three and a half years have (quite unwittingly) destroyed Stormont, and are in process of destroying Lynch in Dublin. Chaos may spread not only from the North to the South of Ireland, but also to parts of this country. But so far Ted is prepared to sacrifice everything to the Common Market.

Friday, March 17th, 1972

Lunch with Alf Robens at Vickers. We talked about the coal strike. He said the initial mistake was by Ezra, who was told to settle for an increase of $7\frac{1}{2}$ per cent. Alf had never accepted instructions of this kind. He learned what it was the Government wanted and then did his best to comply. Ezra thought he had secured agreement at 7·9 per cent, but this was because he listened to Joe Gormley (the president of the N.U.M.)* who did not know the attitude of his

* National Union of Mineworkers.

executive, instead of to Lawrence Daly, the secretary, who did. When the offer was rejected, it was withdrawn by order of the Government. This was a serious tactical error and, after this, events were bound to take the course they did. Before he left the Coal Board Robens had warned big coal consumers that a strike was coming and urged them to stock up, which most of them did. But the power stations omitted to carry adequate stocks of minor items— oil, hydrogen gas, etc. Maudling said that with very few exceptions the picketing was legal; Robens said that in fact none of it was, and now strikers knew they only had to picket the power stations and the Government would give in.

Robens thought there was no chance of dislodging Wilson before the next election. The P.L.P. distrusted Callaghan, and would not have Jenkins at any price—and there was no one else. If events continue on their present course, it might be that Wilson's ultimate successor would be someone from the Tribune Group.

On the Bank, he said it was obvious they were becoming more and more a department of the Treasury. The Bank can no longer seriously claim to voice City opinion.

Alf expressed the lowest opinion of Maudling, and not much more of Davies and his team of useless Junior Ministers. He was amused at the dismissal of Crossman as editor of the *New Statesman* —it obviously came to Crossman as a complete surprise.

Pompidou suddenly announced today that he is holding a referendum on whether we should join them in the Common Market. This can only seriously embarrass Heath, though presumably it is not intended to do so. Ireland, Norway and Denmark are to have referenda, but we are not—it would almost certainly go against the Government if we did, which is why we are not having one. Pompidou's move reminds everyone of this fact.

Lunch on Wednesday with Gordon Richardson and the directors of Schroder Wagg. They had no news and the main impression left in my mind was that they are entirely concerned with the day-to-day problems of their business. They do not seem to bother to be well-informed on the larger issues confronting the country.

Friday, March 24th, 1972

Lunch with Campbell Adamson—a nice man, though far from dynamic; he is an intelligent, civil-service type. I asked him about Anthony Barber, who seems to me little more than a messenger boy, and clearly had made little impact on Leslie O'Brien. Adamson says he sees a good deal of Douglas Allen (head of the Treasury) who expresses a very different opinion—that he is determined on reforms of his own devising, and will not be diverted. According to Adamson no one is very certain of what will happen, but with luck we shall have a boom next year with an election in the autumn; the unions see the danger of inflationary wage-settlements, like that of the miners, and in any case are anxious to get power back from the shop stewards to the centre.

He was very impressed by the statement that the Government will not cling to an inappropriate rate of exchange, but are ready to adapt it as required. He seemed to think that this removed an area of uncertainty for businessmen. But surely arbitrary alterations of the exchange rate, probably due to inflation, are just as defeating as clinging to an exchange rate that, owing to inflation, is no longer realistic. He could not make head or tail of Peyton, who behaved very oddly at meetings, but nevertheless ended with the right decisions. He assumed Carr would succeed Whitelaw as Leader of the House. He also assumed Geoffrey Howe (Solicitor-General) would be promoted.

Adamson had seen Heath just after the miners' strike settlement (at about 1.00 a.m.). He was very depressed. He had meant to fight the miners' claim but did not expect it to lead to power stations closing. Adamson thought both Carr and Ezra had erred from lack of experience.

After six weeks of discussion the Government's initiative on Ulster was put to Faulkner—and rejected. So we now have direct rule by Westminster, with Whitelaw as the new Secretary of State for Northern Ireland. This is the best possible appointment, but it has been linked with a repetition of the pledge that no change will be made in the constitutional status of Northern Ireland without majority consent. This is the old point that the border is not at issue, when it is *the* point at issue.

Tuesday, March 28th, 1972

Lunch with Willie Whitelaw. I had expected the lunch to be called off, but not so. I was treated with the greatest friendliness and confidence. The gist of what he had to say was that in the end the answer must be a united Ireland. With this in mind one must not say too often that the border is not in question. The delay in the announcement of the political initiative was due to the doubts of Alec Home and Quintin Hogg who, however, agreed that security must be taken over by Westminster. When Faulkner rejected this decision, the takeover could take place. Faulkner made a bad impression on the Cabinet—he said he had no idea he would be confronted with a demand for the transfer of security to Westminster. He did know, and they knew he knew. He put forward a woolly idea of a security committee with joint chairmen—one from Stormont, one from Westminster. He then left to consult his Cabinet. When he returned he said it had been unanimously endorsed by them, but in fact, as our Cabinet knew, it had been unanimously rejected. He brought with him his Deputy P.M., Senator Andrews—an old man who was at one time arguing the case against U.D.I. when the subject under discussion was direct rule from London!

I thought Whitelaw made a good appearance on television last night. His essential goodness and niceness came over so well.

Whitelaw's first visit was to the Governor, Lord Grey, at Hillsborough. I knew him in Nigeria where a great career was forecast for him, for no obvious reason. Whitelaw was naturally vague about the future. Some internees will have to be released. I understood Whitelaw to say that he saw Paisley as the future leader of Northern Ireland.

He said there were three grades of civil servants: the best were delighted at the takeover; the second best were pleased; the duds were shocked—they gave Willie the impression that they were political appointees. The police were very ready to co-operate, but were afraid they would be publicly blamed for past mistakes. On being told that internment was a political decision for which they would not be blamed, they were quite ready to welcome the new regime.

I said Tuzo was the one man I had not heard criticized in Northern Ireland affairs. Whitelaw thinks him excellent. I also said Ford, the second-in-command, looks a fool on television.

Whitelaw said he had chosen his Junior Ministers himself—Windlesham and Channon. I said the former was at least a Catholic with an Irish name, but the second was just wet. Whitelaw seemed surprised at this opinion, and says he is excellent at getting things through the House. This is a valid point, and takes one important chore off Whitelaw's shoulders. Whitelaw says he intends to have a kind of court at Hillsborough. He means to entertain widely and well and use the place as one means of bringing people together.

Good Friday, March 31st, 1972
Lunch yesterday with Rupert Murdoch at the *News of the World*, and on Wednesday with Val Duncan at the R.T.Z. office. The more I see of Duncan the more impressed I am. He has both charm and ability and is head of a first-class enterprise. The prevailing view today is that, with a rapidly growing world population and a rising standard of living, we shall be running out of basic raw materials by the end of the century. Duncan's view is the exact opposite— that all the raw materials we shall need are available in the earth's crust, and we shall develop ways of finding and working them. So we have to prepare for an enormous expansion in demand—particularly for energy. R.T.Z. is big in uranium, and Duncan is negotiating for the building of a gaseous diffusion plant in the province of Quebec. These plants are immensely expensive and consume vast quantities of electric power, but several new big ones will be needed by 1985. Duncan produced a sidelight on the coal strike which has not been reported—owing to the power cuts, all the pots at their Anglesey aluminium smelter were ruined and will have to be replaced at a cost of several million pounds. They were promised a supply of current from an atomic station come-what, but the promise was not honoured.

Lunch at the *News of the World* was not enlightening—mostly Fleet Street gossip. The *Daily Mail* is doing better; the *Express* worse; the *Sunday Express* better than ever. Why won't the abler provincial journalists come to London? Answer—because London pay is now not much better, and status much lower.

Rupert Murdoch's political information was that McMahon in Australia is doing disastrously badly, and cannot hope to win the next election. Nixon's inflationary policy should be taking effect by the time of the November election. Similar inflationary policies here and elsewhere should get world trade going in the coming months and so help the price of metals—as Duncan also believes.

Rupert said the pastoral people in Australia were doing unexpectedly well. They have sold their wheat to India and China. Last year wool was cheap with no buyers. This year the price is twice as high and buying is brisk—for no obvious reason.

Wednesday, April 5th, 1972

Lunch with Stonehouse. He sets his political ambitions high, but thinks it wise to lie low now. He has taken an active interest in Bangladesh, and is appalled by the indifference and incompetence of the United Nations. Of the two million tons of food needed, the Indians are providing 100,000 and no one else is delivering any. The Russians are clearing Khulna harbour, but it is assumed that in this they have ulterior motives.

Ruth was talking to Douglas Houghton yesterday. He said he was deeply troubled. Like Stonehouse, he said the P.L.P. is in sad disarray. Following on the French decision to have a referendum, the P.L.P. thinks to embarrass Heath by demanding one here. Wilson has frequently spoken out against any idea of a referendum in this country and in this, too, is to be made to eat his words.

Douglas was mainly bothered by the abandonment in this country of any idea of government by consent. Engineers at the moment are staging 'sit-ins' at factories employing hundreds of men. They could only be ousted by troops and this would lead to a general strike. In a general strike how reliable would be the troops and the police? Where can it all end? All this is increasingly heard among politicians, though not much in public, and is surprising coming from Douglas, a trades-union official of long standing and a man of great experience.

Friday, April 7th, 1972

Lunch yesterday for Dr O'Sullivan, the Irish Ambassador—a nice man and very friendly. I wanted to find out what is moving from the Dublin end, and see what help might be coming from that quarter for Whitelaw in Belfast. He was a bit cagey about the I.R.A. but not about anything else. He regarded the Official I.R.A. as Marxists bent on destroying society north and south of the border and therefore not people you could deal with. Of the Provisionals, he evidently regarded Sean MacStiopháin, the chief of staff, as (a) English, and (b) an undesirable. Rory O'Brady, the commander in chief, seemed to him much better material. He said the officials he meets in the Foreign Office regard Paisley still as untouchable. An idea the Irish Government has in mind is to appoint an economic committee of representatives of both parts of Ireland to consider the effects of joining the Common Market. These will be similar for both parts of Ireland, but not for Northern Ireland and the U.K.

Denis Hamilton came to lunch today. He has been twice to the

House of Commons recently. He says you may not think much of the senior members of the Government, but the Junior Ministers have to be seen to be believed. Denis has urged ministers to hold forth on the Communist menace, but for some reason the Government will not react. If they won't, it is hard, because of libel, for anyone else.

We were laughing over the Associated Newspapers oil well. Denis said not only has the *Daily Mail* got its oil well, but Roy Thomson has a 20 per cent interest in three important areas, in partnership with Paul Getty and Occidental Oil. If this comes good, Roy will more than double his fortune!

Denis was at a lunch last week at which Wilson was the speaker. He spoke for forty-five minutes, said nothing, and when he sat down there was not one clap! I have heard this before—that Wilson cannot stop talking and all his wit and sparkle have gone.

Monday, April 10th, 1972

Lunch for C.D.—I like him very much! He urged me three or four times to keep in touch with Whitelaw (which I shall do anyway), so I suppose he thinks I might help. He said he had done his bit to move things in the direction they have gone, but that Whitelaw was rather boxed in, and C.D. hoped I might help him to find a way out of the political straitjacket in which he found himself. I said there is no agreed solution of the Irish question—one will have to be imposed, and when that time comes Whitelaw will have to be very tough indeed. The Government has the money and the machine-guns, and will have to tell all and sundry they mean, if necessary, to use both. If such an attitude is convincing drastic action will probably not be necessary. C.D. said that he did not think Whitelaw yet realized that there is in fact no agreed solution to be found.

Of Government personalities he agreed with me on Peyton—thought still in many quarters to be a fool. Maurice Macmillan, the new Minister of Labour seems to me a ridiculous choice, and C.D. could only say he is intelligent. He gave me the impression that his assessment of Geoffrey Rippon is not as favourable as mine.

I argued that the Government, having run away from the miners, could not fight a big strike in this Parliament—and in the next only after a build-up. I rather gathered this essential fact had not soaked in to the P.M. Meanwhile, the dockers in Liverpool have defied the new Industrial Relations Court. Can the Government fail to back their new court? But if the unions fight it out, the Government is likely to lose. And the railways look like being strike-bound tomorrow unless they get more than the 11 per cent they have been offered (the 'norm' being supposedly 8 per cent).

Mark Norman yesterday said he had been talking to a prison governor just back from Holland, where there is little juvenile delinquency and a falling prison population. The prison governor came to the conclusion that the difference in their experience from ours is that in Holland mothers with small children do not go out to work. Public opinion there maintains very strongly that a mother must remain in the home until the children are twelve or more.

Wednesday, April 12th, 1972

The political news is all about the split in the Labour Party. Two days ago Roy Jenkins, Harold Lever and George Thomson resigned from the Shadow Cabinet, essentially over the Common Market. After Pompidou announced a referendum in France, the anti-Marketeers revived the idea of a referendum here, but did not carry the Shadow Cabinet. Then Heath spoke in favour of a plebiscite in Northern Ireland. There being no noticeable difference between a referendum and a plebiscite, the anti-Marketeers returned to the charge and got their way this time in the Shadow Cabinet. Wilson has always been strongly anti-referendum, but swallowed his pride and his policy and came out pro-referendum. Whereupon Jenkins resigned, unable to put up with any more somersaults by the Opposition. All this marks a triumph for Tony Benn, a most unconvincing political leader. Some comments are that Jenkins has resigned late and on the wrong issue, but that would probably have been said whatever he did. The whole episode is one more reflection on Wilson's leadership, strengthens Heath in the short run, but still further undermines Parliamentary government in the long run.

Lunch yesterday for Paisley. I like him and he seems to enjoy a meeting with us. Perhaps it gives him a bit of support when he doesn't get much from experienced people this side of the Irish Sea. He did not think the Labour Party would agree to eight additional Ulster M.P.s, to bring the proportion up to that prevailing in England. He thought a way of bringing Free Derry to heel would indeed be to cut off all welfare while they refused to admit troops or police. Whitelaw's public relations are first class. When Paisley lost his mother recently he received, by special delivery, a handwritten letter from Whitelaw. This is a gesture that will not be forgotten. I think Paisley, while agitating for integration of Northern Ireland with the U.K., knows that this is a non-runner, anyway long term, but that unification of Ireland would have to come after a period of years of good neighbourly relations. Paisley evidently does not realize how the Catholic Church has lost power and influence of recent years—not only in Ireland but over the whole Catholic world.

At the Foyles literary lunch I sat next Graham Sutherland. He says he painted only three portraits after mine and has now given up portraiture. He said the impression on him of Brian Faulkner's face was that of weakness; Wilson's never gave him the impression of any great potentiality; Heath struck him as having his first taste of power—and enjoying it.

Mike today said he has been trying to get the Government to give more information in industrial disputes. He made specific suggestions to Heath in one labour situation, got a charming letter back, but no action at all. Mike thinks the reluctance to invest by industrialists is due to the outlook on the labour front. However, even in this area, and even at this late date, important industrialists are still absurdly naïve. The chairman of the Midland employers group was delighted to find Jack Jones such a reasonable man to talk to—on a social occasion.

Mike was told by the *Daily Mail*, about a week in advance, of Macmillan's appointment to the Ministry of Labour. The appointment seemed so absurd that he refused to believe it!

Thursday, April 13th, 1972

Lunch for Vic Feather—very friendly, almost hilarious. The only reason he could give for Maurice Macmillan's appointment is that he must know something about the north as he sits for Halifax and his father sat for Stockton. In any case apparently the Tories have no industrialists in the House. Clearly Vic thought nothing of Carr, and did not think Macmillan could be any worse. He thought the miners' strike had been bungled from the start. 'The Ministry' had insisted on calling the moves and Ezra did not feel strong enough to do more than protest. 'The Ministry' might mean Carr's department or Davies's. He thought there would be a rail strike and a tribunal that would give the men what they want. He could not see how the Industrial Relations Act would work out. At present almost all unions have de-registered but, according to Vic, they plan to re-register at some point in the future to suit their purpose. The Transport and General Workers' Union will pay the £5,000 fine for contempt of court, but will protest they cannot force the dockers to cease 'blacking' containers.* If the court or the employers wish to pursue the matter they will have to proceed against individual dockers. If *this* is pursued, you will have real trouble. If and when the unions do register they will have a field day harassing small employers. Vic does not see how the Government can proceed with the Act, or how they can extricate themselves from it. He said he thought Peyton had a head of solid bone. I said that was not my impression. Nor, said Vic, was it the view of Jack Jones.

A few days ago Vic, Jack Jones and George Smith (of the Amalgamated Society of Woodworkers) were on a trip to Romania. Jack Jones lives in a council flat—the £10-a-week kind not one of the £3 jobs. He was set back to discover that the Communists don't believe in council flats—they favour 100-per-cent mortgages. They say people take greater care of their home if it is their own property. When the house belongs to the occupier he can leave it to his family —or sell it. This was regarded as realistic, but not very Marxist.

Friday, April 14th, 1972

Yesterday at 5.30 p.m. I was summoned to the Irish Office to talk to Whitelaw. He was friendly and expansive. He said the Augean stables were nothing to the mess he found at Stormont. Disproportionate ministerial salaries for Ministers; jobs for the Protestant boys; every power of the Government used to depress the Catholics. Whitelaw obviously thought the Catholics had far more to put up with than he had realized. I said he had not missed a trick so far but no decisive moves had yet been made. He said he knew there was no agreed solution to be found—it would have to be imposed. He wished the I.R.A. would pipe down so as to give him a chance to keep the troops more in the background, to step up the release of internees, and to take other similar steps that are difficult to take now, because without some response from the I.R.A., such moves would only infuriate the Protestants. Whitelaw did not think the present arrangement in Ireland could be completed in twelve months; he did not suppose for a moment that the old Stormont

* The dock workers were incensed that container traffic was often handled at installations far removed from the docks and by men who were not dockers. Employers maintained that productivity was considerably higher amongst non-dockers.

would be revived—a body with powers like the G.L.C. is as much as they could expect. Faulkner's stock is at zero both in London and in Northern Ireland.

At the end, I said, so much for Ireland, but the labour position here is very threatening and a grave crisis might well arise here that would push Irish problems to one side. As I had said before, in such a crisis he would be a key figure. He naturally brushed this aside. I am to see him again on my return from Ireland. I was not clear whether he was being discreet (as he had to be) or whether he thought I had spoken out of turn.

On television last night Barber was shown speaking to a Conservative body of some kind denouncing the irresponsibility of the railway unions in refusing arbitration. This was explicitly said to be at the request of the Cabinet. Presenting the Government point of view to the public in such matters is as it should be. But to start at this late stage and put the words in the mouth of a pip-squeak like Barber can only annoy the unions without impressing anyone.

Lunch for Arnold Weinstock—he was in a very militant mood. He recalled that I had often said we could not avoid a confrontation between the unions and the Government—now this was it. He was concerned not so much with the rail strike, as with the trouble with the engineers in Manchester, where a number of his factories are on strike. In Manchester the district committee of the A.E.U. is entirely Communist. They have rejected an offer of an 8-per-cent increase in wages as 'derisory'. Weinstock's business is in good shape and he is inclined to hold out—particularly as many of the striking engineers are in enterprises losing money. If the strike continues these factories will be closed down. The effect anyway, in an area of high unemployment, is bound to lead to a severe pruning of the labour force.

He exported, I understood him to say, £650 million of products last year. Exports are still high but there is a catastrophic drop in new orders. He was told by an official in the Export Credit Guarantee Board that their fees are down 50 per cent since last year. This means that exports—anyway of capital goods—will in due course be down by that amount.

Weinstock thought Carr such a failure at Labour that Macmillan could not be worse. The Industrial Relations Act was drawn up by people so ignorant of the real world that they thought they were restoring the balance of power between employers and unions. In fact they were weighting the balance still further in favour of the unions. He thought Heath—to his regret—could now be written off as a failure. Of his Ministers there were only Whitelaw, Carrington and Rippon. He doesn't know Peyton and has nothing but contempt for Davies, who recently spoke to Arnold of his (Davies's) successes.

The newspapers say the Government is determined to stand firm over the railway strike. After their defeat by the miners it is hard to see how they can effectively do so. If there is a stoppage of power stations can this Government send in the troops? If they shrink from that, will they call a snap election? This would be a logical step for M.P.s, but would it make any difference to militant trades-union officials? I don't believe a 'mandate', however overwhelming, would impress anyone outside Parliament. In the end would troops have to be used?

Monday, April 17th, 1972

Lunch for John Fforde. Once more one notices with these officials a certain lack of confidence about the future, but no alarm. He said he thought that as Wilson destroyed his Government by delaying too long over devaluation, so Heath seems likely to destroy his Government by delaying too long over a prices and incomes policy.

Saturday, April 22nd, 1972

In Belfast. At various social functions, and this morning in the *Belfast Telegraph* office, I have asked about the future of Northern Ireland. One fact emerges—that no one expects, or wants, Stormont to be resuscitated in its old form. All the Protestants now seek integration with the U.K. There would presumably be some local authority like the G.L.C. to cope with affairs in the Six Counties. Personally I don't agree with this idea.

An immediate problem confronting Whitelaw is what to do about the so-called no-go areas in which the Army cannot, or does not, penetrate. It is difficult to see how this situation can be maintained, but to storm the barricades would cause a lot of casualties. It has been suggested that welfare payments might be stopped until the barriers come down. So far the response here to this idea is unfavourable, as it is to the suggestion that these areas might have their water cut off, but no alternatives are suggested. It seems to me to be part of the softness of attitudes today. Let's have an omelette but *of course* we must break no eggs.

The Government took the rail unions to the new industrial court:

they have obeyed the court and called off the go-slow. The court has also fined the Transport and General Workers' Union a total of £55,000 for contempt. It now looks as if the unions will ostensibly urge their members to behave, whilst hoping and perhaps secretly urging them to carry on with their disruption. The Government seem at the moment to be on a collision course with the unions, but to have made no preparations for a general strike.

Sunday, April 23rd, 1972

Spent yesterday meeting more people—the *Belfast Telegraph* journalists, a school-teacher, a consulting engineer, a surgeon, a civil servant, etc., etc. I asked them all what they would do about Northern Ireland. They accepted—without regret—that Stormont would not be resuscitated in its old form. Beyond that they really had no ideas on what to do—or agreement on what the real situation is. They feel the no-go areas in Londonderry should be opened up, but wanted it done painlessly! Our host at dinner, a wine-and-spirit merchant, a Catholic and a very nice, quiet man, said under pressure that if he were Heath he would send for all parties concerned and tell them the British were pulling out in not more than ten years (say). We should help all we can in the meantime, but the date would be irrevocable. He thought that while the people here had the British Government to lean on there would be no agreement.

Yesterday I went to see Paisley's very fine new church, a short walking distance from his original church (now a tiny pentecostal mission) and then the first church he built (now his parish hall). The whole is an astonishing achievement for a man now only forty-six. Ruth had tea with Mrs Paisley, who had been visiting the maternity hospital. During the day three priests came in to see mothers with new-born babies, advising those with several children to go on the Pill. This caused much rejoicing.

The trades-union position in London is one of increasing complexity. The Government, through its Industrial Relations Court, seems to have declared war on the trades union movement without possessing the necessary weapons. The railways are back to normal today and we start a fourteen-day cooling-off period. What this will achieve is not clear. Meanwhile the engineering trouble in Manchester continues and the dockers at Liverpool continue to 'black' containers.

· · · · ·

Later. Lunch with A.B. [a senior civil servant]—more talkative than usual. He says the miners' strike brought home to Ministers for the first time that a clash with the unions would mean a general strike—and the defeat of the Government. The Industrial Relations Act is unworkable; the High Court is being drawn into politics and defied. What is the Government to do? A.B. thought it would take fifteen years to build up an adequate police force, and to rouse popular feeling against the Communist menace. The police force is below strength, and its establishment is too low; the territorials have been disbanded; the troops that can be spared are in Ireland. A general election on government by Transport House or by Whitehall might end by being devoted to something quite different—unemployment or rising prices. A.B. said Carr may be a nice little man to meet, but speaks out very forcibly in Cabinet. He seemed to assume that Eden and Macmillan were appointed because of their relationship to the previous Prime Ministers. No other explanation has come to light.

While Whitelaw is the best man for Ulster, his appointment does mean that he will wield less influence on the home front, which may become even more important.

We spoke about Geoffrey Crowther's recent death at Heathrow—due as we agreed, to worry over the Trust House Forte affair.* He said he had had dealings with Crowther, as chairman of the Commission on the Constitution, and that he clearly never had the kind of ability to make him a successful tycoon. Did he give up the editorship of *The Economist* when he realized he could not keep the paper up to its previous form after Barbara Ward left? Barbara did not believe she played an essential part, but I am strongly under the impression that she did.

Saturday, April 29th, 1972

Half an hour yesterday with William Whitelaw to report progress on Ireland. He was obviously very pressed and half an hour was not really long enough. However, the real purpose of my visit was to put to him the Belfast idea of presenting the leading figures in the public life of Northern Ireland with an offer—and a time limit. He thought this an interesting idea which justified more thought. He said he was insisting on the soldiers reducing their patrolling,

* Lord Crowther, the chairman of *The Economist*, had died suddenly at Heathrow Airport. He had been involved in complex commercial dealings following the merger between Trust Houses and Forte interests.

though Tuzo wanted to increase it as more soldiers had been killed and wounded in recent days than ever before. This, Whitelaw pointed out, was due to the killing of McCann, who had indeed been killed off by the troops when lying wounded on the ground.

I said how well he had done his public relations, and that in talk with all and sundry in Belfast there was no regret at the passing of Stormont. Whitelaw had attended a meeting of Tory back-benchers the previous evening. He said about half of them said that drastic measures must be taken to root out the terrorists and close the border. Whitelaw pointed out that the border is three hundred miles long, and in places has never been defined, and that no large body of opinion can be suppressed by force—look at Cyprus, India, Kenya, Ireland itself, or Vietnam. Hilary, the Foreign Minister in Dublin, had been to see him and said that a constitutional commission was to be set up and this would be announced shortly.

I said that in addition to prejudice and propaganda there seemed to be complete misapprehension of the facts. Paisley told me there was no discrimination in government or local government in the award of jobs, and Catholics I met told me that since Whitelaw took over he had detained more than he had released. Whitelaw said the discrimination for jobs was gross. On detainees, he had released 170 or so and not detained any, though some men had been arrested and would be charged.

Tuesday, May 2nd, 1972

Lunch yesterday with Norman Collins. I would not suppose he is a particularly good judge of the political prospects. I know he moves about a lot in Conservative circles, and would expect him to reflect the opinions of those around him. He seemed to me quite wildly optimistic. The unions were coming to heel; the level of unemployment is acceptable; the economy is on course; Ireland is regarded by the British voter as impossible and so does not matter. This sort of thing reminds me of British politics in 1938 when one was denounced as a 'jitter-bug' for pointing out that we were heading for war. Wild optimism in the teeth of the facts was the order of the day. In fact the whole situation becomes increasingly gloomy. The Americans and their allies are being pushed out of Vietnam. The unions are on a collision course with the High Court and the Government. In Northern Ireland, the big Courtauld plant at Carrickfergus has been disabled by eight carefully placed bombs. Who placed them so expertly? Was it a Protestant in this very Protestant area—or a Catholic? Inflation is very visible in rising house prices; industrial investment is not picking up.

Lunch at Warburg's with Eric Roll, who was in crashing form. He had no particular news, but one interesting story. In September 1970 he had one and a half hours with Ted, whom he knew quite well as they both have flats in Albany. He was advised that an incomes policy was not a popular subject. However, in the course of the talk he said that by the spring of 1971 it would be obvious whether Ted's policy of de-escalation of wage demands was working. If it was, that was the time to come to an agreement with the unions on the subject. If it was not, he would be in trouble and an incomes policy would be inescapable. Now over a year later, Ted, having done nothing, is having his face rubbed in the problem. But Eric thought it was now too late.

Friday, May 5th, 1972

Lunch on Wednesday with Noel Annan. He had no news but was fascinated by the problems of the Labour Party. They obviously would get nowhere with Wilson, who is so universally distrusted, but he sees no way by which he could be removed. What will be the outcome? He cannot wait to see.

Lunch yesterday with Gerald Thompson, chairman of Kleinwort Benson. I knew his family in Dublin before the First World War. He is alarmed by the progress of inflation. This is all very well for merchant banks—they are coasting downhill with the wind behind them, but what about the economy and the country? The inflationary situation favours the City at the expense of industry—particularly heavy industry. As a result an undue proportion of our bright young men are being sucked into the Stock Exchange and similar financial institutions.

The local elections announced this morning have gone even better for Labour than was expected. It is difficult to see how the new rent Act can be made to work with all the big local authorities against it. And on the industrial front serious trouble is brewing with the railways, the docks and the engineers.

Monday, May 8th, 1972

Lunch with Tony Keswick and Hugh Fraser. Tony Keswick spoke of B.P.'s oil find in the North Sea (he is a director of B.P.). He said for a time we may even have a surplus of oil. The pipeline on the seabed will be 400 miles long—I suppose a double one, as the wells are not that far out. These pipes cannot be made in this country, and will have to be imported from Japan! Keswick is still a director of the Bank, and a colleague is Sidney Greene, general secretary of the N.U.R.,* who is deeply involved in the current wage claim. He told Tony he is counting the days to retirement—being pushed around by his militants is intolerable and incessant. The railway unions' demands have not been settled, the dockers' demands look more threatening than ever, and the engineers' sit-ins in the Manchester area are a menace seldom referred to in the papers.

Tuesday, May 9th, 1972

The big news today is of the blockade of North Vietnamese ports by American mines, together with continued bombing by American aircraft of targets in North and South Vietnam. This is obviously a highly dangerous escalation of the war, and is only understandable if regarded from Nixon's personal point of view. American vital interests have little part in the decision. It seems to be assumed that the Russians will not retaliate. Is this a reasonable assumption?

Lunch today for Baylis of the Stationery Office—an intelligent civil servant of the same type as Alex Jarratt, now of I.P.C. Baylis said Jarratt was putting everything he had into I.P.C. but did not see that the editorial was any part of his business. It is said in the office that Jarratt regards his job at I.P.C. as that of Permanent Under-Secretary of a Government department.

The most interesting part of our conversation was on labour matters. Baylis has apparently bought Government policy in this area. We must be patient and in due time ordinary trades-union members will reject their Communist leadership and see that it is in their own interest to co-operate with Government policy. All we have to do is to show patience and forbearance, and the lion will lie down with the lamb, the desert will blossom like a rose, and the millennium will be here. It is hard for me to see how it can be supposed that in this age of violence, it is possible to achieve lasting results by giving in to militant minorities—by constantly turning the other cheek.

When I saw Tony Keswick on Monday he said his brother John had returned from Peking on Sunday. When there, he was told the

* National Union of Railwaymen.

201

Nixon visit was given the very minimum. Crowds of various sizes are ordered out by the authorities according to the warmth of the reception intended. But for Nixon no crowd at all!

Thursday, May 11th, 1972

An hour and a half with the Irish Ambassador, Dr O'Sullivan, at my request. I wanted to tell him of our trip to Ireland and our reflections thereon. I was trying to impress on him the necessity of implementing changes in the Irish constitution—and please don't say, as Lynch recently did, that it is being done to facilitate the reunification of Ireland. Say the constitution is being brought up to date in view of Ireland's entry into the Common Market—any argument will do but not the goal of reunification. To speak of this merely provides material for Craig and company. A two-party commission is being set up, but there is no certainty that it will produce useful results—or when. I said it really must come up with something concrete by next March when the present suspension of Stormont comes up for renewal.

I had lunch with Edwin Plowden at Bridgewater House. He was very depressed and seemed to be looking forward to retirement. The heavy engineering end of Tube Investments is about 60 per cent of their business and this shows no sign of picking up. The nearer their products are to the retail consumer the better they are doing.

After Plowden's party on Tuesday Harold Macmillan came in expressing surprise over the bungling of the miners' strike. Mac said he had fought with miners in the trenches—and they never give in.

Plowden is even more insistent than he used to be that we are heading for an authoritative Government. He hoped for one of the Right, but saw no signs of any move from that quarter, while the Communists were very active.

Plowden did not think our Parliamentary democracy was failing: he thought it had failed. Like others he thought Whitelaw and Carrington the two outstanding Ministers; he thought Peter Walker had done his political propaganda well—turning the subject of pollution to his political advantage; Davies he regarded with contempt; Sir John Eden with derision. He thought our kind of economy could not stand up to the current degree of inflation for more than five or six years. It was no use citing Brazil, which is a totally different economy and society.

Lunch yesterday with Dick Briginshaw of the newly divorced NATSOPA. I have known him for many many years. He is now looking forward to his pension in a few months' time, when he begins a two-year course at London University on anthropology! His importance is that he is a member of the General Council of the T.U.C. He had little news—had seen Barbara Castle recently, thought she had aged a lot and was no longer a positive factor in Labour Party politics. He agreed that the £50 million given by the Government to the Upper Clyde Shipbuilders was a bad investment, but said they had no alternative. The situation became very ugly and they were afraid of an uprising. Like Feather he made no mention of inflation or of the Communists in his movement.

At the Czech Embassy on Tuesday I was interested to meet the Imperial Father of the *Mirror* Chapel, Reg Birch of the A.E.U., and Hugh Scanlon of the same union—all very friendly. Scanlon is having lunch with Plowden soon and Plowden wondered why. I said, why not? He gets a good lunch, and can be sweet and reasonable, which impression may serve his purpose later on.

Friday, May 12th, 1972

Lunch for Derek Ezra. I always thought him highly intelligent, but lacking in personality. The latter is no longer true and he was most interesting about the coal-mining industry, about the energy requirements of the future, and about his relations with the Government. On the latter he said he liked Sir John Eden, his Minister. He was always very polite, though Ezra felt it was not much use arguing with him as he clearly had had his instructions. On any view he was better than Roy Mason, the last Labour Minister, who made snap judgments without consultation and was not even polite. The amount of interference by the Government in the running of the Coal Board is greater than it used to be, and is the opposite of the published policy of making enterprises stand on their own feet. Ezra had wanted to settle the miners' claim at an increase of about 10 per cent—or perhaps a little more—but was told he was not to offer more than the norm, 8 per cent or so. Ezra warned them that this would not be accepted, and that he could not afford a strike. However, when the strike began the Government was confident it would collapse. If they had not been so confident they would have introduced rationing at the start and so brought public pressure to bear on the miners. Throughout the proceedings he dealt with

Eden, and later Carr. The senior Minister in charge of nationalized industries is Davies, with whom Ezra has had no contact.

Ezra said that it is very noticeable that the Government operates on a hand to mouth basis—it has no long-term policy. Unlike Tony Keswick, Ezra says that by 1980 we shall need 450 million tons of coal equivalent, of which not more than 80 million can come from North Sea oil, and not more than 60 million from North Sea gas. Twenty million might come from nuclear power, and 100 million from coal. This leaves a gap of almost 200 million tons to be filled by imports of oil or coal, which puts us at the mercy of the Arabs, and shows how vital it is to keep up our output of coal. According to Ezra the nuclear power programme is a catastrophe. We have expended huge sums of money on optimistic forecasts that have proved wildly unrealistic. This was Alf Robens' recurrent theme, but the actual outcome is worse than he feared. Owing to corrosion, the Magnox stations have had to be held back from their full rated output, with the result that the power from them is expensive. So many snags have developed in the A.G.R.* stations that they may never be operative. In any case, instead of ordering only one—or at most two—until it could be seen how they worked, these experimental stations have been ordered six and eight at a time (one by Roy Mason plumb on the Durham coal-field). The future lies with feeder reactors, but for this you need an initial capital of plutonium, which we haven't got. To get one of sufficient size it is necessary to develop an intermediate type of reactor. Can the A.G.R. be made to work? If it can, that's fine. If it cannot, we should be stuck with a huge loss, and no plutonium. At the moment the Government is hesitating on this point.

North Sea gas has been sold too cheap and now the Gas Board has run out of gas to sell. A bit more will be discovered in the North Sea, but nothing very significant.

Ezra said the strike had added enormously to the prestige of the militants. The N.U.M. have a conference in July and the present agreement runs out in March. He assumes they will aim to achieve another victory over the Government next year.

The future of the nationalized industries is now quite obscure. They were to have been run like commercial enterprises to make money for the Exchequer. That idea has now vanished but nothing clear has so far taken its place.

* Advanced Gas Cooled Reactor.

Incidentally, another point is a world shortage of coking coal. Such remaining pits as produce it in this country are mostly uneconomic. If we have to buy it from abroad we shall be held to ransom, as over our oil needs.

Friday, May 19th, 1972

Paisley rang up earlier in the week and wanted to see me, so I fetched him from the airport yesterday, had an hour with him at home, and delivered him to the House of Commons. He did not want to discuss anything in particular but seems to value someone safe to talk to. Whitelaw, having made a brilliant start (having cleared the decks, so to speak), is now faced with the difficulty of keeping the initiative. Simply shaking more hands will serve no purpose. Paisley says he is already known as Willie Whitewash. The Protestants are getting increasingly restive, and the amount of bombing and shooting is keeping well up to previous levels. Paisley is still talking about integration with Britain. If H.M.G. says publicly this is not on, then an opportunity arises of another solution. Craig is arguing for independence which, Faulkner points out, is not viable. Paisley is under pressure to go in with Craig and Faulkner as the Big Three of Protestantism. Paisley hopes he can resist this pressure. He seems to think that, failing integration, it should be possible to organize a degree of independence for Ulster. He thinks it would be viable, with the same trade advantages enjoyed by the Irish Republic. In any case he is in favour of Ted inviting representatives of all parties in Northern Ireland to 10 Downing St, to tell them what is in the mind of the British Government. If no more, it would involve talks between the parties, which have at present ceased.

Some of the papers say the Government expected the abolition of Stormont to lead to peace. This was never likely.

To me the industrial situation looks even more threatening than Ireland. At the moment both the Government and the High Court are set on a collision course with the trades union movement—this at a time when the Government is weak and the trades unions are riding high.

Monday, May 22nd, 1972

Lunch with John Stevens. He is far more pessimistic than he was. Democratic government has clearly broken down and a dictatorial regime is all we can look forward to. He thinks a slow slide for five years and then the crash. He feels in his bones that the dictatorship will be of the Right—but under whom, or what organization? Inflation is roaring ahead; the Industrial Relations Act looks more like a disaster than a failure; there seems to be no solution to the Irish problem.

At the Bank he says they are fairly happy. The surplus for this year will be about £500 million, mainly owing to the huge American deficit and our invisible earnings. The lot of the merchant banks is not all that enviable—worth-while borrowers are already stuffed with cash. The Governor can get no answers from the Chancellor and finds it hard to meet Ted. Barber is doing some good work on tax reform but otherwise is his master's voice—and no more. The Bank cannot reduce the supply of money without causing a set-back to the business recovery. They should probably be calling in deposits from the clearing banks. The bank rate cannot well go up without drawing in even more currency from abroad. McMahon told the Court he detected signs of recovery in industrial investment, but both Robens (for Vickers) and Maurice Laing (for industrial buildings) said they had so far detected none.

Stevens had recently been in Washington, where he was told that Nixon had promised American aid for China in case of war with Russia, and was ready in Moscow to offer the Russians the same! Such crude diplomacy will get nowhere. Stevens was told that Nixon's visit will be interpreted by the Russians as an under-taking to let them take over South Vietnam after the election. American business recovery is going better than had been expected —law and order continues to deteriorate.

Later I spent an hour with Tony Bloomfield, chairman of Oddenino's. He is a very able property man and appalled by the political prospects. He sees no end to inflation, to industrial trouble, and to Ireland. Unlike most people he anticipates serious trouble in a matter of weeks, rather than months. It is interesting to see how gloomy these important businessmen are while Ministers are as gay as larks.

Wednesday, May 24th, 1972
Dinner last night with the Weinstocks. One of the guests was Chataway whom I had only met once before—at an Academy dinner. To me he seems a nice little man with no particular ability or personality. Arnold Weinstock is even more convinced than

previously of the total failure of this Government—and depressed by the knowledge that Wilson and his team would be worse.

At the French embassy earlier I had some talk with Smirnovsky, the Russian Ambassador, who said Anglo-Russian relations were still under a cloud following on the expulsion of more than a hundred Russian diplomats. I said I thought the Russians should welcome a united Europe as in time they could look to one Europe from the Atlantic to the Urals. However, Smirnovsky said the Russians don't see things in that light.

Friday, May 26th, 1972
Lunch yesterday with Willy Whitelaw at Buck's Club. I thought he was in good heart and seemed to have grown in stature since he took up his Irish job. He is appalled by the bigotry and fear so much in evidence among the Protestants. Lady Brookeborough, wife of the former Prime Minister of Northern Ireland, asked to see Whitelaw and then refused to shake hands with him when she arrived! Willy says his civil servants are excellent, but are quite irrational at the prospect of being absorbed into the Republic. I said that, with the abolition of Stormont, and his own good public relations, the time was approaching for a fresh political move. What about an offer of Ulster independence? This is what Craig and his Vanguard Party are asking for, and would be accepted by the Provisional I.R.A. as a half-way house. In any case to summon the leaders of opinion and tell them integration with U.K. is not on would set people negotiating. Even abortive negotiation would check the slide to anarchy. Willy said he was certain the only answer to Ireland's problems was the re-unification of Ireland, but he went on to say that his idea for the future of Northern Ireland is to give them a regional government like the Greater London Council. It would be a council with a chairman (no Prime Minister or Cabinet), and would be elected on a basis of proportional representation. The responsibility for security would rest with Whitehall. The Province would have twenty instead of the present twelve M.P.s. This to me amounts to integration and would be far harder to undo than Willy imagines. Willy seemed to think the influence of the Common Market would help to abolish the border. I think the Common Market will be only a minor element in Northern Irish affairs for some time to come and not necessarily beneficial at that. Meanwhile, Willy wants to talk to someone who represents the

I.R.A.—but someone he can be seen to be talking to. It was curious that in the course of our talk Whitelaw did not once mention Paisley.

The papers make much of demonstrations of Catholic women against violence and the I.R.A. This arises from the murder by the Officials of a Catholic soldier home on leave from Germany. It will have no long-term effect. Paisley is getting together a group of politicians of all stripes to talk about the future.

Sunday, June 4th, 1972

Just as Irish affairs looked a little better, Lynch has imprisoned three of the Provisional I.R.A. leaders including Cahill, but not including MacStiopháin who, with O'Connell, is on the run. Willy tells me he not only did not instigate the move, he had no prior warning. It looks as if Lynch, emboldened by the result of the referendum on the Common Market, has decided to clamp down on the I.R.A. This might have been helpful some months ago, but is merely embarrassing now. The I.R.A. are said to want a 'declaration of intent' from Whitelaw that will enable them to declare a truce. I gather the declaration might only have to say that the future of Northern Ireland will have to be decided by Irishmen; a further point which would be welcome, and might be added, would be that Stormont will not be reconstituted in its previous form.

The phenomenon in American affairs is the emergence of George McGovern. At the start he was given no chance at all. Now he seems to have the nomination sewn up, and might well beat Nixon if the tidal wave in his favour continues.

Thursday, June 8th, 1972

Mike to dine last night. He was talking of Davies, his boss at the C.B.I. for some years. He said he formed a low opinion of his ability and of his knowledge of industry. His experience was that, as a salesman and a Welshman, Davies was better at talking than doing; his knowledge of industry was picked up whilst at the C.B.I. Mike was in general very gloomy—more so than I have known him. In particular he is deeply disappointed by Ted, with whom he has been on good terms for a long time.

We saw Paisley today. He is in great form, his stock rising every day. He regards the current situation as more dangerous than ever. The Protestants are well armed and well drilled—they even have a tank. Whitelaw continues with his public-relations effort and is universally liked, but does not seem to realize that none of this amounts to political advance. Ministers are unduly influenced by peace petitions signed by Catholic women. Of course the women are in favour of peace, but they don't have the guns. According to Paisley, the Protestants have all sorts of moves up their sleeves— kidnapping Lord Windlesham (known as Little Windle!) being one. Paisley said he did not see why he should change the baby's nappies for Whitelaw. He will have to learn the facts of Irish political life the hard way. He obviously regards Whitelaw as naïve and amateurish to a degree.

Tuesday, June 13th, 1972

Lunch for George Bolton—in crashing form. He has been lecturing to the Naval Staff College at Greenwich. They tell him there that the Russian navy is now the best disciplined and equipped in the world. Their ships are on average ten years younger than the Americans'. Our own ships are too small, and even at that are under-gunned compared with the Russians. Bolton says the Russians, not the Americans, are now the strongest military power. The best equipped European navy is the Italian. Its military value may not be much but meanwhile, our admiral told George, it is the best yacht club in the Mediterranean.

Last time we met George said that Japan was working up to an output of 180 million tons of steel per annum and that this could only be absorbed by China. He says now that this tonnage was meant for the American and European markets. These are being partially closed to the Japs, so they will necessarily become the junior partners of China—perhaps the arsenal of China.

George is a member of an investment committee that looks after £450 million of Kuwait money. He says over the last four years they have sold all gilt-edged and all heavy industrials. They are now investing in banks, insurance companies, insurance brokers, property, and consumer goods.

With continuing inflation George thinks the Midland industrial complex will be lucky to stay in business.

He was always anti-Common Market—as an illustration of the lack of *entente cordiale*, he says, the Navy recently sent ships on a goodwill visit to three Breton ports. On the arrival of our ships each mayor shut down all bars for the duration of the visit.

There was a debate on Ireland last night at which Whitelaw seemed to be under pressure from his back-benchers. He promised stern measures and announced the arrival in Northern Ireland of another battalion. Meanwhile, the Protestants are getting increasingly aggressive. What is needed is not stern measures but a political initiative, now well overdue. When I saw Whitelaw on his appointment I stressed the importance of holding the initiative and keeping up the momentum. Of this there is no sign.

Thursday, June 15th, 1972

Lunch yesterday for Douglas Houghton. He reminded me that long ago he had wondered whether Ted Heath realized he is in a way the last trustee of our Parliamentary democracy. If he fails, the regime is finished. He said that anyway it is impossible to govern the country if the Party in power changes every four years. On the other hand, of course, it changes every four years because the voter takes such a poor view of both Parties. Douglas had one or two good remarks: Heath is a stronger man than Wilson—he has more *fibre*; Whitelaw said to him he had been called in to Irish affairs two years too late; Crossman said to him that the Labour Party would have to settle for Short as its leader—the nearest they could get to Clem Attlee! In general Douglas, who is the nicest little man, has given up hope of achieving anything worthwhile. Like others, he limits his thoughts to getting through the day's work.

The labour situation is getting steadily more confused. The Appeal Court having upset the Industrial Court's ruling on shop stewards, the Industrial Relations Court is now threatening to imprison some dockers. We are forcing a confrontation between the dockers and the High Court, and the unions and the Government; but the Government does not seem to realize that, as has been shown in the case of the miners and the railwaymen, this is all a trial of strength and the unions are stronger than the Government.

Sunday, June 18th, 1972

The Industrial Relations Court has had a second decision overturned by the Court of Appeal—this time at the unexpected intervention of the Official Solicitor. Everyone is now feeling bewildered, though the Government maintains (without any credibility) that all is going according to plan.

Things look a little more promising in Ireland at the moment. The Unionists are having to learn that their day of complete power is over; Whitelaw is having his introduction to real politics; and the I.R.A. are having to learn that, though they have won an important victory in the destruction of Stormont, re-unification is not just round the corner.

Wednesday, June 21st, 1972

Lunch for Hugh Fraser. His main theme was the strong feeling growing up on the back benches against Ted Heath. They feel he is doing nothing about inflation and unemployment. Moreover, the Common Market issue is not going well. Last night the Government majority fell to five, and Peter Shore gave notice that the Labour Party in office would repudiate the Treaty of Luxembourg, which is an essential part of joining the E.E.C. Mellish, the Labour Chief Whip, is feeling very confident, and is planning to press his advantage by keeping the House sitting through August and September.

In the last few days sterling has been weak on the exchanges and there is talk of devaluation. Our price level is not out of line, but no foreigner has any confidence in our ability successfully to conduct our affairs.

Fraser dined last night with Selwyn Lloyd, who said Ted's difficulties sprung from his working out his policy in detail before taking office. By the time he was in Downing St, things had changed and they were stuck with a fixed programme when what was needed was a different performance.

Fraser thinks Ted has landed himself with an Industrial Relations Act that will not work and cannot be dropped; ditto with the rent Bill; and with inflation the outlook is for rising prices but not for increased industrial investment.

Friday, June 23rd, 1972

A real surprise on the eight o'clock news this morning. The pound is to float and the currency market is to be closed today and Monday. There had been a run on sterling since last Friday, but this was wholly unexpected. Some devaluation was looked for, but not before next year at the earliest. The dollar devaluation earlier in the year amounted to a revaluation of the pound by 8 per cent; this will now presumably bring us back to where we were vis-à-vis the dollar, but not the other currencies. This is a nasty blow to the prestige of the Government and to the country as a financial centre.

Brian Walden to lunch. His health is evidently much better and he was in cracking form. He speaks for the Labour Party on economic matters and is confident of office when Labour gets back. He thought the present performance by the Parties could not go on. The public is fed up with feeble ineffective government and is becoming increasingly anti-House of Commons and anti-M.P. He thought the demand for a tough, effective government could not be staved off. He had no suggestions to offer on the source of this tough government.

He thought Powell had written himself off and would eventually be expelled from his Party. In politics you must keep one foot well within the Party boundary however much the other foot is extended beyond. He thought Maudling had the best brain in the House. He has given up reading Cabinet papers and often returns his boxes unopened. Brian thought this a real tragedy as he has so much to offer the country and his Party. He said how sad it is that recent Prime Ministers—notably Wilson and Heath—have no inner self-confidence, and so have to surround themselves with people they like who bolster up their self-confidence. He said there is good material on the Tory back benches—in particular John Biffen and Christopher Tugendhat—but Ted does not feel at ease with them so they are kept out. Brian assumed that Maurice Macmillan and John Eden owed their offices to their relationship to the previous Prime Ministers. Macmillan he likes, but says that he has lost all will-power. He regards Alec Home as useless and Quintin Hogg as a menace.

Brian knows Geoffrey Howe rather well and said that he always supposed that the Industrial Relations Act would at least be good law. But apparently not so, as Denning has pointed out in the Court of Appeal. The position of shop stewards is not now *more* clearly defined; it is *less* clearly defined than it was. He thought Communist standing in the trades union movement could have been destroyed by insisting that all elections to trades-union office would only be valid if there was a 40 per cent vote. His ideas for curbing inflation seemed to me inadequate, but clearly any action that promised to be effective would push up unemployment to levels that would not now be acceptable.

Brian thought that if there was an election today Labour would be in by fifty—not more, owing to the lack of confidence of the voter in the quality of their leaders, the coherence of the Party and the practicability of their programme. Incidentally, he said that in the last Parliament the Tribune Group was about fifty; now, in a smaller P.L.P., he is told it is ninety-three. This is climbing on a band-wagon which, at the moment, is clearly lurching to the Left.

Sunday, June 25th, 1972

The big news on Friday morning was the floating of the pound. It is amusing the way the newspapers vary, describing the move as a bold stroke, or alternatively, as a panic measure. I should have thought it was neither, but a very unwelcome step forced on the Government by foreign holders of sterling who thought devaluation would come sooner or later, and who had no confidence in our capacity to manage our affairs. It seems likely to lead to the break-up of the sterling area, which is probably overdue. It will annoy the Europeans, particularly the French, as it is only six weeks since we agreed a common exchange policy; the further effects on the dollar, the yen and world trade are unforeseeable.

Tuesday, June 27th, 1972

The Irish Ambassador and A.B. [a senior civil servant] to dinner last night with their wives: A.B. rather subdued, but O'Sullivan in crashing form. A.B. thought it was interesting that at the end of the miners' strike, when the Government was on its knees, the miners' leaders did not press home their advantage. So evidently the Communists do not wish to take over in this country—anyway not at the moment.

Wednesday, June 28th, 1972

Jules Thorn, chairman of Thorn Electrical Industries, to lunch—the nicest little man. He has lost all confidence in Ted Heath; thinks him cold and distant, and quite incapable of a useful relationship with the unions or anyone else. He has asked for an interview with Barber for himself, Bernstein, Thorneycroft and Spencer-Wills, but they are being fobbed off with the Financial Secretary. They want to talk about the incidence of V.A.T.* on the business of hiring television sets. The idea of Barber being too busy to see four men, all more important than he is, is quite silly. Thorn does

* Value Added Tax.

not think Ted will do anything about the future. He said that as he looks into the future he can only see a 'large dark cloud'. He has been offered directorships of Warburg's and Associated Newspapers, but sees no point in additional directorships. He likes John Davies, but does not think much of his capacity; likes Plowden, but cannot take him seriously as a commercial man; thinks nothing of Maudling; thinks well of Marcus Sieff, Israel Sieff's son.

He has made a formidable amount of money but is not money motivated. He wants to see his work people—85,000 of them—happy. He is modest and unassuming, and a man of irreproachable integrity. He wants to take me round one of his show factories near Liverpool.

Thursday, June 29th, 1972

Bill Barnetson to dine last night. The item of Fleet Street gossip he produced was interesting. The *Observer* announced that they were leaving Printing House Square and planned to print on the *Financial Times* plant and in Leeds. This move would be highly damaging to *The Times* who were furious. However, the whole matter is being smoothed over and any drastic action postponed.

Friday, June 30th, 1972

A busy day yesterday—talks with Paisley at the House of Commons, where I met Monnet, Caradon and George Thomson; lunch for Carrington; and forty-five minutes with Whitelaw in the evening.

Paisley had talked all one night to the leaders of the Ulster Defence Association. He had not met them before and found a couple of personal friends among them. They are not particularly close to Craig or Faulkner. The latter is trying to create a united front with Craig and Paisley, but Paisley will have none of this. The truce that began at midnight on Monday is working, but the days before were distinguished by a higher-than-ever degree of violence. The U.D.A.* are putting up barricades this weekend, but they will only be a gesture and on side streets. Whitelaw thinks he has an understanding from the I.R.A. to take down some barricades in Derry. As time goes on Ministers (notably Carrington) are more and more convinced that a united Ireland is the only long-term answer.

Faulkner has infuriated the Government by his duplicity, and the Stormont regime has surprised everyone now concerned with it.

* Ulster Defence Association.

They learn of the bias, bigotry, corruption and intimidation widely practised. This was all known to anyone interested, but Conservatives in the past did not want to know. Now they control the administration at Stormont, they have access to the whole sorry story. The real trouble at the moment is to get the British and Irish Governments, the I.R.A. and Paisley—all of whom have the same long-term objective—to act in concert. At a critical moment recently Cardinal Conway did a power of no good by an inopportune speech. Time is wanted to enable the Protestants to digest the fact that their tyranny is over; that the Catholic hierarchy have their own problems and are in no fit state to be a bogey for the Protestants—in fact that their state of terror has no real basis. Everything would be easier if there was any prospect of jobs in Ulster—or the South. But the economic prospects are not good in Ireland or Great Britain. Tony Bloomfield was saying yesterday that he thought there would be a financial crash by October—1929 all over again. No one has any confidence in the international financial set-up or in the Americans, who are the largest part thereof, but whether it will come to a crash or not—or so soon—remains to be seen. Carrington yesterday seemed overworked and far from happy over the situation on the industrial front.

Sunday, July 9th, 1972
In Dublin. Since the truce began there have been more deaths, though no operations against the troops. Of the thirteen deaths, two seem to have been of Protestants by Protestants for consorting with Catholics; two more were murders of U.D.A. men by the I.R.A.; the rest seem to have been murders of a completely random kind of Catholics by Protestants. The U.D.A. is becoming increasingly militant, it is not clear why. They are said to resent losing their power and to have a feeling of bloody-mindedness regardless of any objective.

Presumably the Government and the Army are afraid of heavy casualties and a civil war that would spread to Glasgow, Liverpool and perhaps elsewhere. But a delaying action to give tempers time to cool seems to have resulted in giving the U.D.A. the impression that H.M.G. is chicken.

Monday, July 10th, 1972
So the truce was called off at 9.00 p.m. last night. The I.R.A. put

out a statement alluding to the meeting with Whitelaw on Friday in London. Whitelaw has said the row over the Linadoon houses was a put-up job by the I.R.A. in order to end the truce. This opinion is unfounded, but its statement will give rise to distrust of Whitelaw. The I.R.A.'s statement is unwise and can only seriously embarrass Whitelaw and H.M.G. The outlook is even more bleak than it was before.

Tuesday, July 11th, 1972

It now appears that six I.R.A. representatives saw Whitelaw on Friday. Of these the three mentioned were David O'Connell, MacStiophàin and Seamus Twomey.

Whitelaw's statement in the House was taken well.

Wednesday, July 12th, 1972

Lunch yesterday with Hilary and his wife. He is a doctor, M.P. for County Clare, and Foreign Minister. It went very well—he is a familiar kind of shrewd Irishman. We impressed on him the *necessity* of altering the constitution if a united Ireland is to be achieved. He seemed genuinely unaware of the importance of eliminating the clauses about the special position of the Catholic Church and about divorce. I gather that the 'regulations' on the use of contraceptives and compulsory Irish are not in the constitution.

Saturday, July 15th, 1972

Since I last wrote, the I.R.A. has been stepping up its activities and the U.D.A. has naturally lain low. I think Whitelaw has made various mistakes. When I saw him first after his appointment I said I thought General Ford should be removed, but he is still there. In general terms, the most important point of policy was to keep the initiative. But this Whitelaw let go some weeks ago. I was against him seeing the I.R.A. as it would inevitably leak out, and the news has made it impossible for him now to talk to any Protestants—or indeed Catholics. His other mistake was to say the Army would not allow the U.D.A. to set up Protestant no-go areas—and then let them do it. A few Protestants will have to be shot before either side will believe that when the chips are down the Army will not always support the Protestants.

Meanwhile the confrontation between the dockers and the High

216

Court remains static, with the dockers holding their own. The international financial crisis gets minimum play in the newspapers but is steadily getting worse. McGovern's nomination is surprising, but all the prophecies in America that he is doomed to a shattering defeat seem to me to be premature. He is a nice man and an honest one, and has come so far that he may be a new phenomenon on the American scene. Nixon is so unattractive and so much a figure of the political past that I cannot believe his re-election is just a shoo-in.

Wednesday, July 19th, 1972

At Stoke-by-Nayland. Looking at the television news last night I was startled to learn two pieces of real news. Reggie Maudling has resigned owing to the revelations in the Poulson bankruptcy case.* This has been expected for some days, as Hugh Fraser told me on Monday and Gordon Richardson last week, but it has really happened—accompanied with a deluge of hypocrisy in Parliament and elsewhere. He should not have been let down so lightly as, in addition, he was a major disaster when responsible for Northern Ireland, and was a lazy and ineffective Home Secretary. However, I thought, here is the hole at the top which will enable Ted to reconstruct and strengthen his Government. But that is not what it looks like now as Carr, of all people, has been given the Home Office, as well as the Leadership of the House. He cannot keep both jobs for long but promotion for Robert Carr is no answer to the nation's problems.

The other item was a statement by President Sadat of Egypt that all Russian technicians are to be asked to leave the country, but that all military material will be appropriated. This appears to spring from the Egyptian demand for offensive weapons for use against Israel—a request which was very wisely refused. The Russians have done so well out of their pro-Egyptian, pro-Arab policy that I wonder whether they will accept this dismissal. There was no hint in the news bulletin, but would the Egyptians have done this unless they had been assured of help from elsewhere—and where else is there except China?

* When the Director of Public Prosecutions undertook an investigation into the affairs of the bankrupt, Mr John Poulson, Mr Maudling resigned because his name had been mentioned at the hearing. He explained in a letter to the Prime Minister that he considered it would be inappropriate for him, as Police Authority for the Metropolis, to continue to hold this office.

Sunday, July 23rd, 1972

The Economist this week publishes an almost hysterical paean of praise for Maudling. I am glad to see the *Sunday Times* this morning reveals fully and in detail his involvement with Hoffman. The story is even more discreditable than had previously appeared.

Five dockers are in jail, and we shall have something approaching a national dock strike from tomorrow. Workers at most of the national Sunday newspapers were on strike last night in sympathy. It is difficult to see how the Government and the High Court can get out of this without a climb-down.

Whitelaw has delivered a very militant speech in Northern Ireland saying he is going to 'crush' the terrorists. How?

Meanwhile a statement has been circulated that Ted is not going to have a Deputy P.M. He will appoint a different stand-in according to the business to be done, when he is away. This will isolate him still further.

Monday, July 24th, 1972

Lunch alone with Paisley. He is very depressed about affairs, both here and in Ireland. He has been in touch with the leaders of the Ulster Defence Association who, he says, are led by a man called Herron, of whom I had previously not heard. Paisley had a long talk with Whitelaw on Saturday but he told me little of what was said. Paisley thought Whitelaw had made a monumental blunder in meeting the I.R.A. Paisley thought Whitelaw believed he could talk them into some kind of agreement. This was never on. The best hope was to keep the truce in being to give the Protestants time to consider their new diminished position. Apparently the Government considered that the abolition of Stormont would itself produce peace in Northern Ireland. Paisley is using his influence to prevent a Protestant backlash—even in the form of a rent-and-rate strike. He thinks the only policy possible now is to crack down on all lawlessness from whatever quarter. This will require special courts, of which there is no suggestion yet. Under the common law, numbers of self-confessed terrorists and murderers have been released in the absence of admissible evidence.

Since the end of the truce the centres of both Belfast and Derry have been devastated with bombs, and feeling among the Protestants has never been so bitter. Paisley does not believe that a united Ireland is possible for fifty years or more. The Dublin Government knows this, and so is lukewarm and inactive. Paisley arrived in the House of Commons very ready to be impressed. He now regards the whole thing as a meaningless charade. The Government is desperately short of good men, but they are not to be found on the Conservative benches. Paisley mentioned Tugendhat as a good man unused. I mentioned Biffen (praised by Brian Walden). Paisley said he had had some conversation with him during which he told Paisley the country's affairs would get nowhere until Heath was replaced. In the House they take the labour problem seriously, but do not seem yet to have got around to the currency crisis which rumbles on.

Meanwhile Paisley's church activities continue with unabated success. The church he bought from the Presbyterians is doing well, though in a bad area where you preach to the sound of gunfire.

Tuesday, July 25th, 1972

The industrial unrest is mounting, and taking on the form of something like a general strike. Ted has said nothing, but Carr and Macmillan on television have been nailing the Government flag to its mast.

Ruth had a word with Mrs Peyton last night. As Minister of Transport John Peyton is up to his neck in the trouble in the docks. Mrs Peyton said Ministers do not know what is in Ted's mind but they think he intends to fight it out. How? Maudling has had to retire at the worst possible moment; Ireland is in a worse mess than ever; and the currency crisis has been temporarily swept under the carpet. It looks as if Ted's days are numbered, but Whitelaw is discredited, at least for the moment, and there is no other plausible successor on the horizon.

Wednesday, July 26th, 1972

Lunch with Mike. He had been to No. 10 with a C.B.I. delegation recently and knows the C.B.I. view of events. He thinks that essential Government policy is to provide copious evidence of their willingness to be reasonable, so as to have public opinion on their side when the crunch comes. It is with this sort of objective in mind that they are pressing the C.B.I. to continue negotiating into August with the T.U.C. on a voluntary prices and incomes policy. The chances of an effective policy emerging are about nil, but the negotiations would provide evidence of reasonability if a statutory policy is imposed later. In the meantime no steps are being taken for providing for a show-down and the appointment of Carr as Home Secretary is not impressive.

The Official Solicitor said on Friday that there was no more he could do on behalf of the imprisoned dockers. However, now, under pressure from the Government presumably, he is seeking their release and the House of Lords is reimposing the original fine of £55,000 on the Transport Union. Where this will leave the dockers is not clear, though they may accept the proposals of the Jones–Aldington Committee which, in effect, means buying off the dockers for the moment with Government money. Anyway we have one more demonstration of the Government's willingness to run away from determined opposition, and the Government will doubtless be taught another similar lesson by the new rent Act.

According to Mike, the Government received a much worse shock over the crisis that led to the floating of the pound than most of us realize. More money went out more quickly than they thought possible.

I asked why there were so many crocodile tears over Maudling's departure. Mike said he knew of Reggie's investments long before *Private Eye* took the matter up. Mike thought the sympathetic press was because he had always taken trouble with friendly journalists, and was popular with a number of them.

At present, strikers are subsidized by welfare payments and the Government has refused to do anything about it. The reason is that they are toying with the negative income tax idea and think that if they adopted it, then subsidies to strikers could be dealt with inconspicuously as part of the new departure. To deal with the matter by itself would be too 'provocative'.

A good many months ago a civil servant in the Cabinet Office came to have a drink with Mike at Lockeridge. He regarded an eventual general strike as 'axiomatic'.

Saturday, July 29th, 1972

So we now have a national dock strike. It will certainly hurt the economy, and the dockers' demands are so far reaching that it is hard to see how they can be bought off.

Four thousand more troops are going to Ireland, some of them from Germany. Whitelaw has said the bomb explosions in Belfast last week show that the terrorists are sub-human and he will have no contact with them direct or indirect. So he is to have talks with the Unionists and with the S.D.L.P.* Whitelaw must indeed be naïve to suppose that you can obliterate the I.R.A. with four thousand more troops, or that any political settlement is to be had from talks with former Stormont politicians of whatever complexion. I don't now see how any useful initiative can be made by either Heath or Whitelaw—and Whitelaw did look like the only alternative P.M. Ruth thinks Whitelaw's reaction is due to the fact that he has been desperately hurt by the I.R.A. leaking the story of his meetings with them.

Wednesday, August 2nd, 1972

Forty-five minutes with C.D. [a senior civil servant]. He said Whitelaw was very hurt by the suspicion and hostility he encountered in Northern Ireland. He is now recovering. The occupation of the no-go areas by a massive military operation was felt to be necessary after Bloody Friday, when much damage was done to central Belfast and a number of people were killed. I said of course the no-go areas had to be swept away and this could have been achieved voluntarily during an extension of the truce. The time to do it militarily was soon after Whitelaw took over—it would then have served as a set-off to the abolition of Stormont. I said the abolition of Stormont cleared the stage for a political initiative: it wasn't a political solution in itself. I said that Whitelaw and Carrington both agreed that ultimately a united Ireland was the only answer; that Stormont would never be restored with its old powers; and that integration of the Six Counties with the U.K. was unacceptable here. C.D. said that was indeed the view of the two Ministers mentioned, but they were the ones nearest to Irish affairs, and these views were not shared by all Cabinet members, still less by all members of the Conservative Party in the House. So far no definite decision had been taken on any of these points.

C.D. asked, 'What now?' I said that after the break-down of the truce, and the bias showed by the Army towards the Protestants, it would be difficult for a fresh start to be made effectively by this Government. C.D. thought this too pessimistic—what could be done? I said the only possible course was to send for representatives of Northern Irish opinion and tell them that the British Army could not possibly remain in force in the Six Counties for ever, and that

* Social Democratic Labour Party.

£300 million a year would not be available indefinitely for the Province; the return of Stormont with its old powers was out of the question, as also would be integration with the U.K. Would the representatives go away and return within a month and tell H.M.G. what was wanted. They would return with no clear answer and it would then be for the British Government to impose an answer, looking towards an eventually united Ireland. Since the break-down of the truce this is all more difficult, but something of the kind must happen some time.

I then went on to say how depressed I was by Ted's performance on 'Panorama' on Monday. Here he is in a sea of trouble but on television he contended that all was well—there was not a cloud in the sky. If he believes this, he should see a doctor. If he knows it is nonsense, he should realize that this is not the way to get the best out of the British public. C.D. said that not to show what was in his mind was an essential aspect of Ted. I said three key Ministers, Barber, Carr and Macmillan, were quite frighteningly unimpressive. C.D. said bricks had to be made with the best straw available. I said there was admittedly a shortage of good straw, but better material than these three men was available in the House of Commons. What about Rippon, kicking his heels doing nothing much, and what about the Lords—they were not all as bad as Windlesham? From C.D.'s laughter I gathered that Windlesham had not gained any golden opinions. C.D. seemed to agree that the unions would have to be fought through a general strike some time, but it would not be possible in the lifetime of this Parliament. The Cabinet is even dithering over declaring a state of emergency, and doing nothing to help the Guernsey tomato-growers and the Jamaica banana farmers whose fruit is likely to be dumped. No intervention seems to be contemplated in spite of the damage to the economy of these small islands.

Friday, August 4th, 1972

Hugh Fraser and Jonathan Aitken to dinner. Hugh thinks Ted really believes things are going well. He, like other P.M.s, has his sycophants. In general, Hugh thought he was now a liability and would have to go—to be succeeded, he hoped, by Whitelaw, though Aitken contended Powell had a 50 per cent chance.

It is generally assumed that the dockers will be bought off next week, but Hugh thought this was quite uncertain as part of their demands was not for money but for other men's jobs. He also thought that Ted might get angry and challenge the trades unions, pointing out how far he has gone in conciliation. I should have thought that with no background of propaganda, such a challenge would be defeated. Hugh said the whole trouble was caused by not more than 1,200 militants in the trades union movement.

Aitken had been talking to Higgins, who is the second or third man at the Exchequer. He is M.P. for Worthing, a safe Conservative seat, but an area with a number of troublesome right-wing extremists. Higgins told him he spends three evenings a week in Worthing speaking to various small groups. This on top of his ministerial and Parliamentary work may be necessary to keep his people in line, but sounds a quite impossible strain.

Thursday, August 10th, 1972

The dockers' strike is still on and Ireland remains as disturbed as ever. Whitelaw is dickering with the S.D.L.P. with a view ultimately to a round-table conference, but as the I.R.A. and the U.D.A. would not be represented—nor the Dublin Government—it is hard to see what could be achieved thereby.

Had lunch with Don Ryder at Reed International. He has been seeing something of Wilson, perhaps because he sees in him the next P.M. He went to Downing St with a deputation of industrialists last night and ended by having a whisky with Ted. Attempting to commiserate with a man in a sea of trouble, he said Ted was no doubt glad the Parliamentary session was over—implying that Ted had had a very rough ride. Ted said that on the whole it had been a good session, as he expected the autumn one would be too. He seemed extremely confident with no worries of any kind!

Saturday, August 12th, 1972

George Bolton—a more realistic observer than most—sends me a piece today in which he says the troubles in Italy look more and more like a Communist takeover. The Vatican is deeply divided and unable to help in the political sphere. Right-wing elements do not look like gaining ground. The armed forces are not politically active. Many of the business community have taken their money out of Italy and may emigrate. He also records a belief in some quarters that the Russians were readier than one would have expected to pull out of Egypt, because they see much better prospects in Italy.

Saturday, August 19th, 1972

I have had no interesting contacts this last week. The dock strike is over, very nearly on the dockers' terms.

We are apparently to accept 50,000 Asians from Uganda, which doubtless will mean fresh demands to find accommodation for further hordes of Asians from other East African countries and elsewhere. It is unpopular, but this Government never makes any attempt to make its policies acceptable.

In Ireland things are now as bad as ever—the immediate effect of taking over the no-go areas has worn off. Whitelaw is on holiday. A round-table conference is proposed for the end of September. Will any Catholics attend? Even if they do, no fruitful outcome is possible.

Tuesday, August 22nd, 1972

Whitelaw is having a fortnight's holiday while the situation in Ireland is as bad as ever. Perhaps he had to have a break, but he needn't gave been photographed shooting grouse—picture in the *Sunday Express*. This Government seems tone deaf to public relations, however elementary.

Thursday, August 24th, 1972

Tea with Alf and Eve Robens at Walton-on-the-Hill. He has had two quite severe bouts of illness in past months, but was in great form today. He has seen something of Ted and has had conversations with the important Ministers. Many of these latter agree that things are going badly, but evidently intend to do nothing about it. Robens thinks Ted really believes that Europe is what matters, and inflation and industrial trouble will in due course subside. Each month in which nothing is done makes it that much harder to make a stand. Alf feels he has done everything he can—he has no power. He can only peg away in conversation and be ready when confrontation does eventually take place. In the meantime Ted and Carr really seem to think that if one is patient, militants of all kinds will come to see the error of their ways.

Sunday, September 3rd, 1972

The holiday lull has reigned supreme for weeks. There is a continuation of the building strike; trouble in the prisons; and growing indignation over the admission of supposedly 50,000 Ugandan

Asians. Carr was holidaying on Corfu and was extremely reluctant to come home and deal with prisons and immigration, both matters for him as Home Secretary. Both he and Ted seem to suppose that admitting the Asians is generally acceptable, if not actually popular. Ted is so carefree he is off to the Olympic games today and to Japan later in the month.

Saturday, September 9th, 1972

The papers are taken up with the massacre of eleven Israelis at the Munich games. No one points out that this terrorism was initiated by Zionists at the time of the Palestine mandate, nor do they refer to the major error of the German security forces in only killing five of the eight Arabs.

The cod war with Iceland continues. Having got away with extending her territorial limits from three to twelve miles, she has now announced an extension to fifty miles. If everyone does this, the fishing opportunities for British trawlers will be drastically curtailed. The Icelanders are using gunboats to enforce their claim but we are doing nothing.

In Ireland there have, for the first time, been serious clashes between the Protestants and the Army, with two Protestants dead. The Unionists are preparing demands for the round-table discussions on the future of the Province, to be convened by Whitelaw at the end of the month. In particular they are demanding a council with greater powers than Stormont had. This seems to be wildly unrealistic.

The T.U.C. has had its Conference, at which Jack Peel was pushed off the General Council. The papers this morning are saying the Conference went quite well, when in fact it represented a pretty general victory for the Left—and the far Left at that.

There are no signs that Ted is beginning to see the red light—poor little Carr is responsible for Asian immigrants, as well as all the other chores of a Home Secretary, and is Leader of the House. On television he looks more and more like a valet—the perfect gentleman's gentleman. Barber has been appointed chairman of the Conservative Party Policy Committee, in succession to Maudling. These are not the appointments of a frightened man.

Monday, September 11th, 1972

In Teheran. We had arrived last night by Pan American Airlines.

225

We had not realized we were picking up their round-the-world flight, and that therefore we should be in a jumbo jet. I had seen an advance mock-up of the passenger accommodation at the Boeing works in Seattle, but had never travelled in one before. The plane was reasonably full until we got to Beirut, where for some reason there is always a big demand for tickets to Teheran. We filled up to the full capacity of 362. Most of the new arrivals looked as if they could never in a lifetime have raised the necessary air fare. Some were Americans, but most were assorted Levantines. We were very well looked after, but for those in the back of the plane the effect was that of an excursion to Blackpool on August bank holiday. As we left we read that Syrian air space had been closed to all air traffic, but we had no trouble or delay, flying over Lebanon, Syria and Iraq at a time of acute political tension.

Tuesday, September 12th, 1972

With a bit of a stretch of the imagination I should have put the population of Teheran at a million, but it is three million!

Ali, the Reuters man here, was telling us at lunch today how the present Queen came to be the Shah's third wife. When it became clear that Soraya would have no children, those near the Shah, started looking for a successor. Our friend, Ardeshir Zahedi (later Ambassador in London), was then married to the Shah's daughter by his first wife, and in charge of Persian students abroad. The present Queen was then an arts student in Paris; she came of a good but not outstanding Persian family. Zahedi met her in the course of his work and thought she might fill the bill. When she was home for her holidays he arranged for her to come to tea with his wife. She also approved and passed the recommendation on to her father, who also approved. Thus are marriages approved in high places. The custom here—pursued in this case—is for the couple to have the civil and religious ceremony and then part. For some months the girl returns to her father and lives as if engaged. Then two to six months later there is a big social occasion and the happy couple depart on their honeymoon.

Thursday, September 21st, 1972

In Shiraz after Isfahan. Travelling about this country I am very struck by the progress that is being made, and by the very sensible use of the oil money coming to them. The Shah has been on the throne for twenty years and has obviously been a courageous and able ruler. He insisted on distributing land to the peasants, and this in the teeth of much warning, but he has got away with it and the country is evidently prospering. The tourists, such as there are, are mostly French, but there are Germans and Americans and the occasional Briton.

One sees in Shiraz, and in the country round about it, women in the traditional peasant dress. The skirts are very full, and down to the ground, and the colours are bright and very attractive. The effect is rather like a Victorian ball dress. They come in, apparently, from the mountain villages. They have wider cheek-bones than most Persians, and we were told, (a) that they were nomads—does this mean that they move their flocks in autumn and spring?—and (b) that they are of Turkish origin, relics of one of the many invasions that have swept over this country.

Friday, September 22nd, 1972

Back in Teheran. Am struck with the way the quite deplorable fashions of Europe and America have penetrated here. The same fat elderly women in trousers waddling about; the same young men in side-whiskers and scruffy clothes, wearing hideous steel-rimmed dark glasses indoors and out. There can never have been a time when fashions have been so universally unbecoming, but that no longer matters. All over the Western world you follow the fashion, however ugly. Another feature of this country is piped music everywhere. It really gets me down.

Tuesday, September 26th, 1972

Home again. Lunch with Barbara Ward. In spite of being at death's door with cancer a few months ago she is now in excellent form. Back from Rome; previously at the Environment Conference in Stockholm; and shortly to Rome again. Like so many people these days, she was optimistic about the future. There are formidable problems to solve—for instance changing over from planned obsolescence and economic growth to stability on a simpler standard of living—but she attached little importance to the moral deterioration to be seen on all hands. These things move up and down. She saw no likelihood of more authoritarian regimes in the West—once people had tasted the sweets of democracy they would never go back.

I asked if the Pope is going to retire; he is seventy-five this week, I believe. Apparently, it is likely later in the year. But the conservatives want him to stay, and the Vatican liberals want him out as soon as possible, and it is not clear how this conflict will be resolved. She says the Church is showing great vitality in some areas —in Poland the convents are swamped with girls with vocations, and Sister Teresa in Calcutta gets far too many postulants from all over the world.

Thursday, September 28th, 1972

There are two areas in which there has been some movement. Whitelaw's conference in Darlington has ended with, predictably, no result. He says there will be a Green Paper soon, but no Governmental decisions till Christmas. The Government has now been dithering since March and the further delay is inexcusable. There is talk of an agreement to form an Irish council representing Northern Ireland, Great Britain and the Republic. This is not much, but a move in the right direction.

The other area where there has been some movement has been in inflation. At meetings with the T.U.C. and C.B.I. at Chequers the Prime Minister has suggested rises of £2 a week for everyone— which would benefit the low-paid worker most. This is combined with some undertaking about price rises. It has, of course, been rejected by the important unions, and in any case is not an element in the fight against inflation—more like the opposite. The proposals are to be discussed further in the coming weeks, but the unions have seen their power over the present Government, so why should they relinquish it? and anyway the proposals are half-baked.

Friday, October 6th, 1972

There is nothing much moving; the Labour Conference has come and gone, its debates having had less impact, if possible, than before. Wilson kept his leadership; Benn is said to have suffered a loss of face; the Party is only committed to remain in the Common Market on terms that are obviously unobtainable.

Lunch today with Mike, who takes part in the T.U.C./C.B.I. discussions on inflation at Chequers. He thinks Ted Heath wants an agreement with the T.U.C.—almost any agreement. The C.B.I. anticipate a very sticky winter, and whether the T.U.C. agreement is honoured by individual unions or not, an agreement would be good public relations for the future. Mike had some talk with Prior, deputy chairman of the Conservatives, just back from a tour of the North. Mike liked him, but thought that he showed no signs of ability. He reported Tory morale in the country as at rock bottom. Personally I think Ted's initiative unlikely to have any effect on inflation, and for any agreement it will have to be watered down. I don't think an agreement for agreement's sake will serve any purpose.

Mike says the Government for months has been looking for a new chairman of the B.B.C. They want a man of personality, versed in the media, and someone who will really boss the Corporation. They don't want a politician. The supply of such persons is indeed meagre. John Davies told Mike that when his retirement from the C.B.I. was announced he was horrified by the number of chairmanships he was offered.

Tuesday, October 10th, 1972
It is announced today that bank rate is to be abolished and its place is to be taken by a formula based on the price of Treasury bills. It doesn't matter much, as for so many years now timid Ministers have refused to move the bank rate when a change was indicated. It had become a football of party politics. At the same time what is needed is more control, not less, and the abolition of a system that has lasted nearly three centuries requires more justification than it receives this morning.

Thursday, October 12th, 1972
Lunch for Stonehouse. He was very expansive—said his life began at forty-five—he is now forty-seven. He feels he was in blinkers but now is free. What with his activities on behalf of Bangladesh, and making some money, he is far more confident—and effective. On the political front he is doing his best to see Tony Benn does not get elected to the Shadow Cabinet. He knows Dick Taverne well and says his trouble with his Lincoln constituency is largely due to his arrogance. He has resigned his seat, but it is unlikely the by-election will be called till March. He is then likely to be returned, and likely to be re-admitted to the Labour Party.

Stonehouse said clearly the trades unions will have to be moved back into their proper role: their present activities are purely political. This change will have to be forced on the unions and can only be done by a coalition. An imposed solution of the Irish question would also require a coalition. I said a coalition could not be led by Wilson or Ted, but who had he in mind? He said 'Jenkins', rather half-heartedly. Perhaps he sees himself in the role. At present he regards himself as 'taking a sabbatical year'. Anyway, he feels he should lie low for the present, in which attitude I am sure he is right.

Wednesday, October 18th, 1972

Lunch for Rupert Murdoch. He is fairly sure Hugh Cudlipp's job will be, or has been, offered to Harold Evans, editor of the *Sunday Times*. This did not seem to either of us a promising appointment as he is used to a paper at the other end of the social spectrum. Rupert admires and trusts Jarratt but does not regard him as a publisher and sees him as an aspirant for Don Ryder's job.

He thought Ted Heath may be aiming at an election in the spring, or he may be forced into one. Whatever is arrived at in the Chequers talks will be rejected by one or more unions, and there is a limit to how much a government can be humiliated without going to the country. He thinks Ted might win an election, as neither Rupert nor the *Mirror* could support Wilson, Benn and the Labour Party in an election. A friend of Rupert's dined with Ted at Chequers within the last fortnight and said he was quite relaxed and did not seem to have a worry in the world.

Rupert thinks Ted wants an agreement with the C.B.I. and the T.U.C. on prices and incomes—even though an agreement will not be honoured. Perhaps the idea is to use such an agreement—when broken—as an argument for a statutory wage and price freeze. If this is so, his preliminary propaganda is non-existent.

Rupert had not given serious thought to the fair rent Bill which I expect to lead to rent strikes.

Meanwhile, the situation in Ireland is going from very bad to much worse. The U.D.A. accused the Army of murdering two men and had a gun-battle with the Army on both the last two nights. Whitelaw is becoming discredited; his elections have been repudiated by all parties except the Alliance Party; and we still have no hint of the Government's policy for the future.

Thursday, October 19th, 1972

Ruth had some talk with Douglas Houghton on the telephone last night. He said we have two political leaders—one of rubber, the

other of wood! He said Ted is working on a new constitution for
Northern Ireland, to be announced in January. He also said Willy
Whitelaw is a changed man—tired, worried and limp. The Government is losing authority so fast that I cannot believe that any plans
put forward by Ted in January will receive serious attention. This
morning the news from Belfast is less bad, but no one supposes that
even this partial lull will last.

Friday, October 20th, 1972
Lunch with Derek Ezra alone at the Coal Board. He was very
friendly and has gained a lot of confidence since he took the chair.
Like other official figures he seemed optimistic about the industrial
outlook, and attaches great importance to the Chequers talks.* I am
still not clear why this is so. He agreed the proposals are inflationary
and any actual agreement will be still more inflationary, but thought
that an agreement—any agreement—would have a restraining effect.
He says the leaders of the N.U.M. do not want to be unpopular
and are unlikely to press their demands as strongly as last time.

Ezra reports to Boardman, Minister for Industry, and does not
know what part (if any) Davies plays, though he is the Cabinet
Minister in charge. The Coal Board wanted to close several
pits after the strike but were not allowed to by the Government.
It would be more difficult to do so now and these pits continue
to lose money. The Government continues to urge the Coal
Board to sell its ancillary undertakings, notably its brick works.
This is a piffling point financially, but a sale might easily lead
to a strike as it is a subject on which the N.U.M. has strong
views.

We talked about the coming world fuel crisis and the importance
of our coal-mining industry. If we make the right decisions we shall
be the only Western country to be self-supporting in fuel in the
coming decades, with half our requirements coming from the North
Sea, and the rest of our energy coming from coal, nuclear energy,
etc. The environmentalists in the United States—and to a lesser
extent here—are making serious difficulties over any new nuclear
plants, refineries or coal-fired stations. Looking into the future it
seems the United States and Japan will be dangerously dependent
on Arab oil.

* Chequers is the British Prime Minister's official country residence, often used for
official or semi-official meetings.

Dr Paisley had tea with us at Ruth's club. He is personally in fine fettle but in despair over Northern Ireland. He says Whitelaw's usefulness is over, and he should be transferred to other work as soon as possible. Channon is good in the House; Windlesham is useless and behaves like a frightened rabbit. Though Ireland is played down in the media, there is in fact a civil war, with much going on that is not reported here. The Protestants feel they have been let down and no longer trust Whitelaw; the Catholics are steadily being burnt out of their homes, when adjacent to Protestant areas; in return Protestant farmers are having their cattle poisoned and their barns burnt. Meanwhile, we have no word of Government policy. A plebiscite on the border was announced and cancelled; local elections have been announced, and are to be cancelled. The fighting is more and more moving from the Vanguard to the Ulster Defence Association, and now to the Ulster Volunteer Force, who control the Tartan gangs. The morale of the Army is going and Paisley described an angry scene with Tuzo, the G.O.C., who seems to have lost his temper. It is looking more and more as if we shall have to pull out of Northern Ireland because of events there and war-weariness here. Paisley would like to have a referendum of the whole U.K. population on the future of Northern Ireland. So far he is the only man to come out of the troubles with an enhanced reputation. The U.D.A. leaders Anderson and Herron are tough, working-class types, but do not seem to be of a stature to take a grip on the situation.

Monday, October 23rd, 1972

Lunch for Arnold Weinstock. He was in excellent form and in no way daunted by the difficult conditions of today. He had no special news to impart, but some of his opinions were interesting. He regards John Davies as very arrogant and totally ineffective. He is rather favourably impressed by Boardman. Geoffrey Rippon he thinks is by far the best Minister in this Government, which he is inclined to rate even lower than the last. He has no crystal ball, no picture of the future, but says the existing system is clearly not working, either on the ministerial or the civil servant level.

I asked him how Victor Rothschild was faring. He said Victor is very low—he can make no headway against the establishment. Harold Lever, on the other hand, is optimistic, saying that the system will adapt itself.

He says he has had to grant wage increases of 14 per cent per annum for five years without increasing labour costs. But economies in the use of labour cannot be continued indefinitely, and even his consumer goods prices cannot be raised, because of competition from Italy and Japan. Already all radios now come from abroad— Japanese imports being ousted by those from Hong Kong and now Taiwan. In his wage negotiations he finds the Communists quite helpful; the trouble-makers being the International Socialists and even more extreme groups.

I asked him why the Government is so keen on the success of the present Chequers talks. The proposals are inflationary even in their original form. He has evidently not been in close touch with these talks and did not know.

They have developed some advance control equipment for fast trains, but British Rail won't buy it because it is untried. Other countries will always try out their own new equipment. When successful it can then be sold round the world as having been tried out.

Weinstock says the Ministry require detailed information on every aspect of the nationalized industries, and then demand delays whilst quite trivial matters are referred to the Treasury. This is inevitable as the Ministry of Trade and Industry has established departments to deal with all aspects of the nationalized industries, and these departments must be given work to do.

Wednesday, October 25th, 1972

In Amsterdam giving a talk to the leaders of the Dutch newspaper, magazine and broadcasting world. Clearly Holland is an orderly and prosperous country, but in the conversations at lunch there is no confidence in the political stability of the country. Owing to the number of parties, every Government is a coalition, and these coalitions are becoming less and less effective. It is interesting that the main leader-page article in the *Daily Telegraph* yesterday was devoted to the fact that the only people not alarmed by the outlook are Ministers, and that clearly our whole political set-up has only a very limited future. When such dangerous thoughts get prominence in the *Telegraph* of all papers we are in trouble.

My neighbour at lunch was explaining that from research done in Holland it is evident that the limit of the social services is set by the available amount of competent staff. Philips of Eindhoven have

233

also found that their expansion, anyway in Holland, is limited by the available skilled manpower.

Saturday, October 28th, 1972

Lunch with Tony Bloomfield—very pessimistic, sees a Communist takeover within ten years. You can buy shares or farm land as a hedge against inflation but it won't do much good in the long run.

Hugh Fraser to supper at home. He says Ted Heath seems optimistic, but the people round him are becoming scared. He anticipates an election in the spring, probably in April, because of the Government's loss of any ability to govern. In such an event he assumes the Tories would lose. He was at the Tory Party Conference and thought about 40 per cent were behind Powell. Powell told him he did not want to speak, but he felt compelled to do so by the pressure of his supporters, and for the same reason the subject had to be immigration. Hugh saw no fresh leadership emerging in the Tory Party, except for Powell, who is a loner, and he doesn't like the idea of Powell in 10 Downing St any more than I do.

The tri-partite talks between Heath, the C.B.I. and the T.U.C. on Thursday lasted from 9.00 a.m. to 2.00 a.m. on Friday morning. This seems to me to be daft. After three hours—at most—people get tired, inattentive and repetitive, and if they do get bored into an agreement they may well go back on it later. The outcome seems to be nil. There is really only one objective, to check inflation; but the Government has added in the plight of the low-paid worker, and 'growth', the last two items being inflationary. There is to be a further meeting on Monday, but (a) the T.U.C. chiefs taking part are as intransigent as ever, and (b) if they did soften up, no undertaking to lessen wage demands would be honoured. Ted seems to be desperately keen on an agreement. I suppose this is to show how hard he tried, and to put the blame on the unions for any breakdown. Is this to provide a background for an election?

Meanwhile, the foreign exchange market has gone berserk. The Government agreed at the Smithsonian Conference to $2·60. This could not be held, and in June the pound was floated initially at about $2.45–2.48. Yesterday it plunged to $2.31 and was only brought back to $2.34 by the intervention of the Bank. This seems to reflect a total lack of confidence in our ability to run our affairs by the Continentals, particularly the Germans. It would seem that our half-promise to have a fixed rate from January 1st will have to be postponed.

Tuesday, October 31st, 1972

The Government/C.B.I./T.U.C. talks continued for another seven hours last night. Qualified optimism is expressed, but my impression is that the Government and the T.U.C. are each trying to lay the blame for failure on the shoulders of the other. I cannot see any significant outcome.

The pound fell another $1\frac{1}{2}$ cents yesterday, in spite of support by the Bank.

The Irish Green Paper is out. The newspapers are pleased with the reception it has received. But the favourable remarks are from politicians: the U.D.A. and the I.R.A. (the only people who matter) have damned it out of hand. It does go so far as saying that the responsibility for security will remain with Westminster and, by implication, that the old Stormont will not be revived.

The most dramatic news has been that two Arabs hijacked a Lufthansa plane with a crew and passengers of twenty and threatened to blow it up if the three surviving Arabs from the Munich massacre were not released. The craven German Government gave in and flew all five Arabs to Tripoli! The Germans paid the ransom for a German Ambassador in Central America—$800,000 I think; they paid £2 million for a hijacked jumbo jet in Aden; and now this —an encouragement for blackmail not only by Arab terrorists but any dissatisfied political groups or ruthless criminals.

Thursday, November 2nd, 1972

Lunch for O'Sullivan, the Irish Ambassador. He said the Dublin Government was pleased with the Government Green Paper. It abolished Stormont permanently; allowed for a Council of Ireland; and provided for elections on a proportional representation basis. I said the plebiscite would be no help: the Protestants would never consult the Council of Ireland, and the elections might be disrupted and frustrated.

He had seen Heath lately and said he was in excellent form—confident, relaxed, euphoric. He would regard it as a disaster if Whitelaw was withdrawn from Ireland. He said Whitelaw's department had done much to make the Green Paper realistic. If it had been left to the Foreign and Commonwealth Office it would have been far more negative.

With regard to the current negotiations between the Government, the T.U.C. and the C.B.I., he said that holding prices was quite out of the question for this year anyway. What with V.A.T. and joining the Common Market prices would certainly rise.

Until recently his Labour friends assumed an election would be won by the Conservatives. In the last few weeks they have changed their tune and are far more optimistic about Labour's chances. O'Sullivan seemed to think an early election would bring a Conservative victory. I think this is possible, though unlikely. Heath's only assets are Wilson and Benn, but the popular contempt for both Parties is so complete that any result is possible.

Saturday, November 4th, 1972

A word with Mike on the phone last night. He was present at the Downing St talks with the C.B.I. delegation. I asked why Ted was so desperately keen on an agreement, though any agreement would not be honoured by the unions. He said Ted had realized from the miners' strike that he couldn't win a confrontation, so an agreement was the only alternative. Now that has failed he is thrown back on statutory controls, which will probably not work and will get the Government into yet more industrial trouble. Mike said Clapham, the president of the C.B.I., is a very nice man but incapable of putting his case across.

Monday, November 6th, 1972

The long-expected Cabinet and other Government changes are out. Asquith (I think) said that a Prime Minister must be a good butcher. The evidence is at last available—Ted is not a butcher at all. No one has been sacked, though Noble leaves the Government. What it amounts to is that Rippon moves up; Davies moves down; Geoffrey Howe comes into the Cabinet; and there are yet more Junior Ministers in the Foreign Office and Northern Ireland. The architects of the disastrous Industrial Relations Act have been promoted, and the unwieldy Trade and Industry Department now has two Cabinet Ministers, instead of one, and Howe has 'special responsibility for consumer affairs'—a gimmick well worthy of Wilson.

Lunch for Douglas Houghton. He had no particular news, but

was obviously trying to keep his spirits up in spite of adverse circumstances. He said how excellently Ted does a job of exposition, as over his proposals to the T.U.C. and over the Common Market in earlier days. He is an excellent bureaucrat but is no politician. I might add, a very poor picker of talent. Douglas seemed to think a gentleman's agreement with the unions was still possible for a Labour Government and he is working for that possibility.

In Ireland it appears that the Army has a much better grip on the situation and has been pulling in a number of I.R.A. members, as well as Gusty Spence, the convicted murderer who is a leader of the U.V.F.* I cannot feel that a referendum has any meaning, even if it is not boycotted by the Catholics.

Wednesday, November 8th, 1972

Lunch yesterday for C.D. [a senior civil servant]—most friendly and communicative. He agreed that the present Government proposals are inflationary—not anti-inflationary as Ministers have been arguing: he also agreed that the talks at 10 Downing St were so long-drawn-out because both sides were seeking to plant the blame for failure on the others. He said that an attempt to run the economy by agreement between Government, C.B.I. and T.U.C. was a syndicalist policy. Would it work? Douglas Houghton, the previous day, thought it was the first signs of the corporate state (à la Mussolini). I don't think this is any part of the intention and is merely due to the weak position of the employers and the spinelessness of the Government. Government cannot be conducted by agreement between three normally antagonistic bodies. In the end the Government must be supreme. C.D. put in a brief plug for Alec Home—said that whatever you may think of his ability, he was the only man in public life who would voluntarily resign the leadership of his Party as he did. I seem to remember that when he became P.M. it was said that he would have been wiser to become king-maker rather than king.

Lunch today for Brian Walden, in excellent form. He sees as the principal weakness of both Wilson and Heath that they are unable to work with people who disagree with them. He likes Barber, but says he is merely his master's voice. Macmillan is quite incompetent, and his appointment can only be explained by a desire to please old Harold Macmillan. He does not like the look of things in Ireland —the situation is deteriorating week by week and may end in general

* Ulster Volunteer Force.

chaos. He thinks the Industrial Relations Act will be amended drastically. He agrees with the principle of the new rent Act, but says it is inflationary and badly timed. The same is true of V.A.T. He says recent Prime Ministers have no coherent idea of what they are trying to do, so that often one department is nullifying the efforts of another.

The most interesting part of our discussion was when he said his constituents are essentially conservative people who deeply believe in the old principles of conduct which are being so widely flouted. If a dictatorial regime emerged, he thought it would be of the Right and involving the Army. Stanley Orme, a left-winger, was recently in Northern Ireland and returned lyrical about the Army and its officers! Walden himself had had lunch with one of the brightest of our young generals, who showed no interest in a Defence White Paper, but talked politics of a kind which Walden said used to be called treason. And if officers are thinking in political terms, Northern Ireland gives them experience of politics and of civil riot and commotion.

Saturday, November 11th, 1972

Lunch yesterday for John Fforde of the Bank. Not in good form— perhaps reticent because of my forthcoming book!* He said it was indeed fortunate that the Government was facing the inflationary crisis with a floating pound. It would have been intolerable if, in addition to everything else, they had had the I.M.F.† breathing down their necks. The special deposits are now to be spread over various financial houses as well as the clearing banks. Fforde did not think the impact would be great. It will not reduce the present money supply but will help to keep it growing even larger over Christmas. He evidently did not think Barber, Carr and Macmillan carried enough weight to help Heath in his present difficulties. In general, I think Fforde was not optimistic over the present freeze but did not know what else could be attempted. In spite of the polls he, like others, seems to think Heath might win an election.

Wednesday, 15th November 1972

My book came out on Monday—a great hoo-ha. An abusive review in the *Sunday Times* by Woodrow Wyatt; a flattering one in the

* *The Cecil King Diary 1965–1970* (London: Cape).
† International Monetary Fund.

Observer by Bernard Levin. But for the most part reviews are likely to be hostile. The book, however, is going well—a printing of 10,000 and 6,000 subscribed before publication. In the *The Times* the first letter today, and yesterday, was hostile: today from Peart; yesterday from Dick Marsh, for whom I have done a lot, who complains that I said he said his Labour fellow Ministers were a grubby lot—one of the milder epithets he has applied for a long time past, and given to me as the reason why he will never return to politics.

Dinner last night with the Mosleys. He is very cagey, but evidently very active—comes over from France every fortnight.

Diana Mosley said she was talking to the Duke of Windsor shortly before he died. He was recalling with what relief, when he was a small boy at Court, after the English courtiers and officials had cleared off, the Royals relapsed into German. Edward VII was known to the family as Bertie pronounced *Berrrtie*.

Today lunch with Dick Crossman at the Garrick, to talk about a television programme in February. We met Perry Worsthorne in the bar. Much talk about the ethics of my book—the upshot being that it is published too near the events—an interval of ten years should elapse.

Crossman, who had read the book as he is reviewing it for the *Listener*, said he could not see my point about the importance of administrative experience and the value of introducing some businessmen into the Cabinet. If they tried to do anything different from what was done by other Ministers they would be taking on the Civil Service—with no possible success. His assumption was that nothing in the present system can or will be changed—including the present custom of changing Ministers around every two years. He said the part that hurt Wilson was where I disclosed that I had passed on the date of the 1966 election to Ted Heath.

Friday, November 17th, 1972

The torrent of abuse in the papers over my book continues—further forcing up the sales. I have had two letters only so far: one very friendly; one mildly hostile. Worsthorne told me the *Telegraph* had had none. My reflection is that those in high places must indeed be vulnerable if they make all this fuss about the book.

Yesterday at lunch sat next the Mayor of Cheltenham—a very able young businessman, a Conservative but a rather independent one. He said he notices in Cheltenham and the constituencies around a very definite move to the Right, at any rate in the Conservative Party.

Lunch today for John Stevens, in no way put off by all the hoo-ha. He says he is just back from Hungary where he was told by his banker friends that there is an important debate taking place in the Kremlin—the hard-line conservatives versus the very moderate liberals. Stevens's friends thought that the result would be the retirement of Kosygin, and perhaps Brezhnev, though more probably Brezhnev would keep his job by a shift to the Right.

He said that the performance of the Shah's regime in Iran is not as good as superficially appears, as much is done for effect where it will be seen. Even so his performance is far better than that of his neighbours.

Stevens said the Japanese are seeking to set up steel mills in Iran, East Africa and South-East Asia. Apparently they realize that the forces of nationalism will prevent them exporting as much steel from Japan as they had hoped. Stevens said the exchange and currency problems will really be worked out between Japan and the U.S. The former is running a surplus of $9,000 million, whilst the latter is running a deficit of $8,000 million. These figures are so much bigger than the European ones that Europe hardly counts in the matter. He seemed rather doubtful whether the Japanese would in due course enter into partnership with the Chinese: they might try to go it alone. On another subject, he said that both Britain and West Germany will be in deficit on their balance of payments next year.

Looked into S. J. Phillips in New Bond St* and had some talk with the younger Norton. He is flabbergasted by the rise in the prices of the sort of antiques in his field—silver, jewellery and small *objets d'art*. I said it was merely inflation, but he said 90 per cent of his trade is for export to countries where inflation is not what it is here. I said then it must be fear that inflation similar to ours will shortly spread to those countries.

Monday, November 20th, 1972

Lunch with Dick Briginshaw. I arrived late because of the Silver Wedding traffic,† and he had to leave for a meeting of the General

---

* A well-known London firm of antique silver and jewellery dealers.

† Celebrations concerned with the Silver Wedding anniversary of Queen Elizabeth II and the Duke of Edinburgh impeded movement in Central London at this time.

Purposes Committee of the T.U.C., so our lunch was more hurried than I would have wished. He is not very clear in his views, but his present thought seemed to be as follows. Trying to hold the centre in politics today is a mistake. The day of centrist politics is over. Wilson's failure in the last election was not that he frightened the uncommitted voter, but that he kept the committed Labour man from voting at all. Benn is therefore no asset to the Tories, but is an asset to the Labour Party at the grass-roots level. Last week Briginshaw was in Glasgow at a celebration of the success of Reid and his allies with their work-in at Upper Clyde Shipbuilders. Reid incidentally proved to be thirty-nine, and not in his middle twenties as we have been told in some newspapers. At this gathering Benn's name was mentioned with warm approval and several times.

Briginshaw thinks a spring election out of the question—it could not now be launched on an anti-union basis. He thought Ted could have had an agreement with the T.U.C. but didn't want one. This can only be true if the T.U.C.'s terms were so humiliating that Ted could not have got his Party to accept them. He thought that no future regime could be viable without mass support, and he does not see how the Tories, whoever their leader, could win such support. He assumes a dictatorship of the Left on the model of the rule of Señor Allende in Chile—a mixed economy, but under authoritarian left-wing control.

Thursday, November 23rd, 1972

Two new developments that may show that opinion in the Conservative Party is turning against Ted Heath. (1) Du Cann has been elected Chairman of the 1922 Committee—a post usually reserved for a real back-bencher, someone who has never held office. (2) Last night the Government was defeated on an order arising from the new regulations for immigrants under the Common Market agreement. It was said these regulations put immigrants from the Old Dominions at a disadvantage. The point has not much substance, but arises from the opposition to the Common Market plus the resentment over the Government's policy on coloured immigration. On the Labour side there is the rather unreal fear of the immigration of cheap Italian labour.

There is a one-day national rail stoppage today because ASLEF objected to the staff moving a new experimental train 400 yards into a shed. It has been out in the rain for four months. This seems to me to be ASLEF* just flexing their muscles, as there is no excuse for such a stoppage on such an issue. Dick Marsh on television just looked peevish.

Friday, November 24th, 1972
The Times and the *Financial Times* today both make the point that the election of du Cann and the defeat of the Government over the immigration rules are to be linked, and seen as a set-back to Ted's authority.

Saturday, November 25th, 1972
Lunch with Alf Robens yesterday. He was in good heart—bigger and more confident, perhaps from his success at Vickers and Johnson Matthey. He says world trade is picking up and the Government's inflationary policy is at last taking effect. The result will make 1973 a boom year. It may provide Heath with a favourable opportunity to go to the country next autumn, or in spring 1974. The boom here will be in consumer goods and in services—heavy industry remains in the doldrums. Vickers make heavy presses for motor-car bodies. They cost up to £750,000 and Ford Motors were to have bought one. They have decided to pay more for one made in Germany and to install it in Germany, rather than battle with the labour troubles here. If necessary, bodies from the new press will be shipped here by road. The story of escalating costs and broken delivery dates due to labour indiscipline means that we are just losing out in heavy industry. Vickers heavy-engineering departments are doing badly and show no sign of recovery. Alfred Herbert's great Manchester factory for machine tools has closed down. Alf thinks we shall rely on imports for our heavy equipment. He thinks it may be a long time before the present policy of both Parties to buy off trouble need lead to an inescapable crisis. Both Parties are essentially bent on staying in office once in. All other considerations are subordinated to this one.

Afterwards I had some talk with one Boyle, who runs the B.B.C. 'World at One' radio programme and is contemplating a book on Brendan Bracken. He says the story—quite untrue—that Bracken was the illegitimate son of Churchill was put about by Bracken but, and this is the strange part of the story, actively propagated by

* Associated Society of Locomotive Engineers and Footplate men.

242

Randolph, who may have been jealous that Bracken was treated more like a son than he was.

Monday, November 27th, 1972
Lunch with Vic Feather—in excellent form. The New Zealanders have just had a general election with a large and unexpected swing to Labour. Vic said he was certain that this last-minute change was due to the debates here over the conditions for immigration from the old white Dominions. As our Government seemed to be restricting their right to entry, so they voted Labour. Vic was sure that the Australians would do the same when they have their election in a few days' time.

I asked about Jack Peel, who lost his place on the T.U.C. General Council. Vic is sorry because Peel is able, but Vic said he had been spoilt with a seat on the Coal Board and so on, and that he had moved too far to the Right, regardless of the members of his union. His biggest blunder, when he was appointed a Deputy Lieutenant for the West Riding, was to consent to be photographed in a Deputy Lieutenant's uniform—complete with cocked hat and sword—for the *Daily Express*.

On the larger question of prices and incomes, the freeze and all that, I don't think Vic really has any very clear ideas. He thought the rise in prices would be 'blunted' (his expression). In the long long run he thought a national schedule of wages inevitable. He thought the election would take place in boom conditions in the spring of 1974. He was very severe on the wage supplement policy which, as he said, goes right back to the Speenhamland one—which has been damned by every economist for nearly two centuries.*

He said he was not critical of the Communists in the trades union movement. They took advantage, as they were entitled to, of the apathy of the ordinary union member.

Tuesday, November 28th, 1972
Dinner with the Foundation for Business Responsibilities to hear the Earl Memorial Lecture. The lecture, by a Frenchman, one Berthoin, was long and dull. I sat between Nicholas Ridley, a former Minister in this Government and M.P. for Cirencester, and

* The Speenhamland system of 1795 was that, in order to alleviate the poverty of agricultural labourers when wages fell below a certain fixed level of subsistence, which was related to the price of wheat, the difference should be made up out of the poor rates.

a Professor Roberts, of the L.S.E.* Opposite was Martin Jukes, director-general of the Engineering Employers Federation. I had a little talk with these last two, who surprised me by speaking in favour of the Industrial Relations Act. Jukes said he found the N.I.R.C.† useful and Roberts argued that some such Act was necessary anyway.

Nicholas Ridley was a Junior Minister in the Department of Trade and Industry. He did not impress anybody and was sacked. He is a terribly nice man—like nearly all the Tory Ministers. I know nothing of his work in the Government but he talked very sensibly. He said he had been one of a group before the election working out the proposed Industrial Relations Bill. He disagreed with the form it took so strongly that he resigned. He implied that it was largely designed by Carr, whose experience of labour relations was in a very small firm with no militancy to contend with. He was discreet, but seemed to be out of step with Heath. He thought the popularity of the Conservatives had slumped since they had abandoned their tough, self-reliant policy and taken to appeasement. Coming from the North-East he knew a lot about shipbuilding and was appalled by Upper Clyde Shipbuilders and all that. We are pumping in £35 million, on top of Labour's £20 million, and also £12 million for the American who is taking over Clydebank. But the troubles of Clydebank were due to weak management and outrageous behaviour by the men. They had built a tunnel under the yard wall, so that they could clock in and out at the right times but spent the rest of the day elsewhere.

After dinner I had some talk with Dr O'Sullivan, the Irish Ambassador. Stevenson is on hunger strike and is expected to die. O'Sullivan was hoping and praying he would change his mind The Irish Government has charged MacStiophâin, has dismissed the Radio and Television Board, and is altering the rules of evidence to make convictions of the I.R.A. more possible. Meanwhile the British Army is having more success in picking up I.R.A. officers in Belfast. O'Sullivan is evidently hoping that all this betokens a turning of the tide in Ireland—a repression of terrorism on both sides of the border plus a clearer realization both here and in Dublin that Northern Irish affairs concern both Governments, and not only an assembly at Stormont.

* London School of Economics.
† National Industrial Relations Court.

Ridley said Enoch's latest idea on extravagant wage claims was that essential workers should be given more or less what they asked for, but the money supply should be curbed. Then the engineers (say) would find the electricity workers getting four times what they were, and as there was no more money for them, they would seek to liquidate the power workers' monopoly. The Government, in fact, would set militant against militant and sit back to watch the result. If this is Enoch's idea, it seems to me wholly impracticable.

Saturday, December 2nd, 1972
In Nottingham for a talk to undergraduates on politics. We stayed with one Owen, the excellent university chaplain. I said it seemed to me that undergraduates, though now legally adults at eighteen, are even less mature than they used to be. Owen said this was indeed so. Ruth thought the university more of a youth club than a seat of learning. Though half the students live in, they mostly go home at weekends to be with their girl-friends!

Tuesday, December 5th, 1972
Lunch yesterday for A.B. [a senior civil servant]. In spite of all the hoo-ha over the diary he was as communicative as ever. I asked him why Ted had been so very keen on an agreement with the T.U.C. and the C.B.I. If there had been an agreement it would not have been honoured. A.B. took part in these talks and said Ted showed all the enthusiasm of the convert. He had tried a rather muted form of confrontation, which had been defeated by the miners, and he then decided conciliation was the only course. But, according to A.B., his timing is too short and he thought he could go into reverse at short notice and take the T.U.C. with him. I said, but surely any worth-while agreement must be negotiated by the Government from a position of strength. If you allow our education policy to be decided by the N.U.T., and any economic policy to be ruined by the big unions, in the end there will be chaos. The only alternative is a confrontation pressed to the point of a general strike with all the power stations down. It was clear from what A.B. said that the latter has never been considered. But surely some government at some point in the future will have to assert itself at whatever cost.

He had not been in on any Irish discussions, but had seen White-law last week. He said he had obviously had a terrible bashing. A.B.

said Whitelaw is a quick-tempered man, and the necessity of keeping his temper under control under very difficult conditions had obviously entailed a very heavy price.

I asked him about Alex Jarratt, now managing director of I.P.C. He is showing no sign of wanting to learn the publishing business. Does he plan to return to the Civil Service? A.B. thought definitely not. Jarratt resented being responsible to Ministers ('a cross they all have to accept and to bear,' as A.B. said). He was told more or less clearly he would be Permanent Under-Secretary at the Ministry of Agriculture from January 1st, 1973, but was not tempted.

I said surely it would be a good idea to have a Deputy Prime Minister to perform the Prime Ministerial chores the actual P.M. had no mind to do. I had suggested this to Wilson but nothing had come of it. A.B. said that jealousy and fear of a rival would prevent any P.M. adopting such a suggestion. The Prime Minister's patronage is inadequately covered as there is too much of it. A.B. implied that ecclesiastical appointments have regrettably fallen into the hands of the archbishops. But Civil Service appointments at the top do get serious attention from Heath. When a top appointment falls vacant Heath is offered alternatives, and told the virtues and deficiencies of each man. If the P.M. does not know the man recommended he is told which Minister would be familiar with his work.

On the economy, A.B. said no one has discovered the secret of steady economic growth. The Japanese had achieved this, but no one knew quite why. He thought we should have a boom extending into the second half of next year, but towards the end of next year, or the beginning of 1974, the economy would 'run into the buffers' and we should be up against the stop phase of the stop-go cycle. He said the public are demanding more and more benefits, with an increasing reluctance to pay taxes. Indirect taxes put up prices, and direct taxes are high and invoke endless efforts to dodge them. The result at the moment is a huge budget deficit. But in time nationalized industries will have to pay their way, and Government expenditure will have to be met by methods other than the printing press.

I went on to talk to Tony Bloomfield at Oddenino's. He is very gloomy indeed, though not in himself a gloomy type. He thinks the economic situation different, but worse, than it was in 1929. People's faith in money is disappearing in all advanced countries, hence the fantastic advance in property prices—property being his own line of country. In St John's Wood where he lives, a semi-detached house which he valued, even at present prices, at no more than £25,000, has gone for £100,000. Also in the same neighbourhood is a block of flats built to sell at £25,000 a flat. The block was completed last week and the average price received will be £40,000. Everybody is looking for an investment which will hold its value through some major catastrophe. Tony thinks the basic trouble is our abandonment of spiritual values and that man will only be led back to these by some appalling calamity of world-wide dimensions.

Saturday, December 9th, 1972

The big news these last few days has been the result of the by-elections at Uxbridge, and at Sutton and Cheam. In a low poll—56 per cent—the Conservatives scraped home at Uxbridge, and lost to the Liberals at Sutton, where a 12,000 Tory majority was turned into a 7,000 Liberal one. The Labour man lost his deposit. Both results are bad for Labour, and the second is a disaster for Ted. Needless to say, the papers report a 'triumph' at Uxbridge and say the other result was a freak one. Actually they both follow the result at Rochdale and are a vote of no confidence in both major Parties.

Monday, December 11th, 1972

Lunch for Nicholas Ridley. He is now chairman of the back-benchers Finance Committee; du Cann is chairman of the 1922 Committee; and Biffen chairman of the third important back-bench committee. These appointments of men rejected by Ted were done on purpose, as it was thought these are men who would stand up to the Prime Minister. Though this is some check on the Prime Minister it isn't much, as he has the party organization in his hands as well as political patronage. Ridley said Ted is good at hiding his feelings—he was in despair three days before the last election but did not show it. So all his present show of confidence may not be real. Ridley also said that Ted's present assertion of an anti-inflation policy, when it is in fact violently inflationary, may be due to ignorance more than deceit. Ridley thinks he just doesn't understand what he is doing. Barber is clever in side-stepping difficult questions and his tax reforms are good, but his constant talk of the coming boom is dangerous. He is entering on a boom while holding back the increase in the money supply.

Ridley remarked on the very strong position in the country of Enoch Powell. If he put up three hundred candidates in the strongest Conservative areas he would win every seat. Strangely, he shows no sign of doing this, and it is hard to see how he could be voted into the leadership of the Tory Party in the House, where at present he has only two followers. Nevertheless, the situation, even in the House, is unstable with increasing dissatisfaction with Ted. Ridley thought the best available P.M. is now Roy Jenkins. How could he come to the fore? I said only in the event of a national government, however named. He did not see how such a govenment could come about. He could see the necessary 100 Labour members, but not the 250 Tories.

Ridley said Whitelaw had lost a lot of ground before he went to Ireland, and that Ted had sent him there to get him out of the way. His weakness is that he is the arch-compromiser. It is not thought that he now has any great future. If we can get away from the Wilson–Heath confrontation, we shall have the Benn–Powell one.

Over labour relations, he did not think the Industrial Relations Act could be made to work, nor that the unions could effectively be called to order. I said to keep on buying them off will lead ultimately to chaos; to confront them firmly after an election would lead to a national stoppage with most damaging consequences, but the result would be better than just letting things rip. Whatever the theoretical merits of such a course, he did not think it a matter of practical politics.

He thought Enoch an opportunist. He compiled with Ridley a pamphlet in favour of the Common Market and only turned against it when he saw it was unpopular. His present attitude is that it is his business to interpret the popular will—whatever that may be.

Thursday, December 14th, 1972

A man called Swann is to be the new chairman of the B.B.C. He is a distinguished zoologist and vice-chancellor of Edinburgh University. From the official statement and newspaper comment, it is obvious he has no qualification for the job, which means the B.B.C. will be nominally under the control of the director-general, Charles Curran, who has so far made no impact on anyone. The B.B.C. is such a powerful medium that it is irresponsible to have it under the control of no one in particular—especially as there are generally believed to be a number of extreme left-wing militants in positions of influence.

Whitlam is the new Australian Prime Minister. Mike says he is only a front man, and that the real power is in the hands of one Hawk, who represents the trades unions. Hawk is said to be in his early forties and a man of great ability. So far I have seen no mention of him in the papers.

Whitelaw announced today that the Northern Ireland referendum is to be on March 8th. Pressed to give a date for the White Paper, he declined, saying he is still involved in consultations. The consultations are a waste of time and the continued delay is dangerous. According to Peter McLachlan, the Protestants are numerous and armed to the teeth. It is increasingly supposed that unless the Protestants get what they want, there will be a blood battle—and it is difficult to see how the Government can restore Stormont, let alone anything else.

1973

In the United States, this was the year in which 'Watergate' became a household word. A continuing saga of apparent deceit and corruption was to preoccupy the attention of the nation and, vicariously, the rest of the Western world until the end of the following year. The Vice-President resigned, a former Attorney-General was indicted and several White House officials were tried on criminal charges and convicted. The President himself came under deepening suspicion. And, in the meantime, the Vietnam war continued. The Middle East exploded once more in October, when Israel again survived a combined Egyptian–Syrian attack.

The world as a whole was facing major economic disorder, as inflation continued and the prices of raw materials—especially oil—rose to unprecedented heights. The age of cheap energy seemed to be over, and the adjustment proved difficult.

In Britain, especially, the economic situation was a cause of major concern and the statutory control of incomes and prices remained the most controversial feature of the Government's programme. Phase One of the wage-freeze, which had been introduced in November 1972, was followed by the slightly less rigid Phases Two and Three in April and November 1973. These controls and their implications were the root of interminable industrial strife and bitterness, culminating at the end of the year in the worst labour and economic crisis for many decades.

Civil strife in Northern Ireland continued without pause, while the British Government, now directly responsible for the affairs of the Province and with many thousands of troops committed to the maintenance of law and order there, sought the co-operation of moderates in forming a new all-party Executive.

This was also Britain's first year in the Common Market, though the nation remained divided on both the significance and the usefulness of entry. Argument within the Market dwelt mainly on the Community's regional policies, a part of the programme from which Britain hoped to derive some financial benefit.

Wednesday, January 3rd, 1973

It has been nearly three weeks since I last wrote in this diary. At Christmastime the world goes dead and this now extends into the New Year. Ireland remains as violent as ever; we continue to offer the other cheek to Uganda and Iceland; labour relations have been relatively quiet over the holiday; the Vietnam war is on again, off again; Nixon begins his new term of office with an appalling world press; the newspapers, of course, are filled with our joining the European community. I supported this cause in the *Daily Mirror*, urged thereto by Barbara Ward, long before other newspapers or Macmillan took it up. I still think it is not the best policy; but it is the only one, and the antics of Wilson and the Labour Party are contemptible. But is it not mistimed? All European countries are faced with uncontrolled inflation and, as well, we have many problems unsolved from Ireland to labour relations. Italy is hanging on the edge of civil war and France is not all that much better. May we not have signed the Treaty of Rome just before the collapse? Official comment is so wildly optimistic on every subject that it is hard to judge what is really happening. We even have a new doctrine that optimism is a patriotic duty—criticism or even cautious comment are little better than sabotage. And in the meanwhile every problem is to be settled by negotiation and goodwill. No one must actually stand firm on anything—except in a demand for more money.

Thursday, January 11th, 1973

The Rohans to dine last night—no particular news about Czechoslovakia. He now runs the London end of an independent German news agency. He has a great admiration for *Le Monde* under its new editor—also for the international part of *The Economist*, which I have not heard praised for a long time. Rohan said that Enoch Powell charges for his public appearances and even for interviews. Rohan thought that Heath was now coming up to a whole semicircle of road blocks. Can he survive? The papers are full of confident accounts of his plans for a wage freeze, though they are not co-operating. Meanwhile, the balance of payments is going against us more quickly and more heavily than anyone expected.

Tuesday, January 16th, 1973

At lunch with the Griersons I met one Monty Finniston, deputy chairman of the Steel Board. He is one of three Jews at the head of the Steel Board and remarkably unimpressive. Melchett, the chairman, is always getting ill—perhaps owing to his inadequacy for the job. Anyway, Finniston was saying that there is bound to be a clash between the Government and the unions on Phase 2 of the prices and incomes legislation—and what happens then? I said the Government had been thrashed by the miners and could hardly win a second round at this late stage in the Government's history. If defeated, would Heath go to the country? Finniston thought this most unlikely as the result would be so uncertain. He thought a defeat by the unions might be the moment for Powell to emerge, and Finniston found more and more people—even those left of centre—looking to Powell.

Wednesday, January 17th, 1973

Lunch with Jules Thorn, such a dear little man, so straight, so nice, so able. He is not happy about Ted and his Government. Ted, he thinks, has no idea how to handle people. Thorn has been having business dealings with Sir John Eden, Minister for Telecommunications. He regards him as totally useless. He doesn't think much of industrial management in this country anyway, and was very critical of the performance of the Clarks at Plessey.*

Friday, January 19th, 1973

Ted came out on Wednesday afternoon with his new prices and incomes policy—the very measure he had damned out of hand when he came into office. He did his best to make it a big occasion; so it was at Lancaster House with four hundred assorted journalists present. He was supported by Maurice Macmillan and Tony Barber, who hardly added any weight to the occasion. The plan is that wage increases were to be limited to £1 a week plus 4 per cent, with a limit of £250 per annum. This apparently works out at about 8 per cent. Prices are, on the other hand, to be frozen except by

* The Plessey Company is an international enterprise, mainly concerned with radio, electronic and telephone manufacturing and with aircraft and mechanical engineering.

special permission, though imports and fresh food-stuffs are exempt. The comment has been that Ted is trying now to control inflation through prices, while in the autumn he was seeking to do so through wages. The plan has been damned out of hand by the T.U.C., the Monday Club and Enoch Powell. I cannot myself see it working as it is too late in the life of this Parliament to get away with a complete reversal of his whole anti-inflationary policy. Ted claims to have the overwhelming support of the public. Of this I see no sign, but its existence is what the whole policy rests on.

Last night we dined with the Murtons. He is a Whip and M.P. for Poole. Also there was one Weatherill, also a Whip, and M.P. for Croydon. It was difficult to get any clear idea of their thinking. This is largely due to the fact that all M.P.s are too close to political events. They can't see the wood for the trees. I had very little talk with Murton; Weatherill appeared to believe that we are on the threshold in this country of an unparalleled period of prosperity. This is an opinion sometimes put forward by Ted. Meanwhile, a survey commissioned by the French Government came up with a report that by 1980, of the advanced Western countries, we shall be with Spain at the bottom of the league. Weatherill seemed disturbed by the amount of subversion in this country, notably in the trades unions and in the universities. This seems to me a danger to which far too little attention is paid, either by this Government or the last. Weatherill wondered whether the subversion is centrally directed. It seems to me that it is not. The Russian and Chinese Communists are profoundly hostile to each other; and all Stalinists are hostile to Trotsky-ites; and then there seems to be an evil element, whose objective is demoralization and not political change. But these groups might well see their end being served by inflation and the permissive society.

Sunday, January 21st, 1973

Toby Jessel to tea yesterday. He is no independent-minded politician, but reflects what goes on around him. He has evidently been informed that the balls-up over the miners' strike was due to Derek Ezra, while in fact it was the fault of the P.M. and the P.M. alone. In spite of adverse opinion polls it is assumed that the Tories will win next time; it is also assumed—partly because of a lack of hostile letters in M.P.s' post-bags—that the voter is solidly behind Heath in his prices and incomes policy. While assuming that the policy will come off, Toby anticipated many strikes and much trouble in the period ahead. He thinks the Government is determined to press on, come-what. But Ted found that he had neither the authority nor the power at the time of the miners' strike. Will he have to be taught the same lesson again?

Thursday, January 25th, 1973

In Freetown. I calculate I was last here in 1963 and since then we have had independence and much else. A recent mark of independence is that all cars now drive on the right. However, the old Africa still raises its head from time to time.

Friday, January 26th, 1973

We paid a visit to the Diamond Office, whose boss told us that about half the Sierra Leone diamonds are being smuggled out—about £12 million per annum. The smuggling is all organized by the Lebanese. Any attempt to curb the more flagrant operators comes to nothing because £150,000 per annum is paid by their syndicate into party funds, besides lesser sums to individual Ministers. Recently a large stone was found and sold to the Diamond Office for £250,000. The seller had no bank account and asked for the payment to be made in cash. It took three taxis to take all the notes. When the money was aboard, the taxis set off up country, though it is hard to imagine what one would do with such a huge sum in the bush.

Later we called on the President, Sir Siaka Stevens, who was the general secretary of the Mineworkers Union when I met him last nearly twenty years ago. Since then he spent time in prison before emerging as President. He has a strong face, pitted with smallpox. I should judge he is stronger than Dr Milton Margai, and much more direct than Albert Margai. The Sierra Leoneans are lucky to have him.

We had lunch with the Tolon Na, the Ghanaian High Commissioner today and with the Nigerian High Commissioner yesterday. The Tolon Na is a very impressive character—far more so than most of our overseas representatives. He seemed to me very masculine, highly intelligent and very competent.

Lady Tweedsmuir has been here these last two days, but I haven't seen her. She seems to have made a favourable impression, but it is hard to discern her function, as a week or two ago she was in

Iceland coping quite unsuccessfully with the Icelanders. Alec Home is due in these parts soon, though not here. He seems to be enjoying himself, travelling hither and thither at public expense. Peter Walker, who has an impossibly large department to manage, has announced a year's programme of foreign travel—so much for Trade and Industry.

Saturday, January 27th, 1973
Spent the day flying to Yengema and back, to see the diamond mine. Owing to widespread illegal digging, the lot of the Diamond Office is a hard one. However, they expect to battle on for another ten years, when all the diamonds will have been worked out. The great thrill in this industry was the discovery of the 'Star of Sierra Leone' about two years ago. This is a half-pound diamond sold to Winston, the American diamond dealer, for £950,000. It was apparently pure chance the diamond was recovered, as in the course of processing the diamondiferous gravel they sift out the large pebbles to begin with, before they make any inspection for diamonds. But by a million to one chance this one caught up on some projection and was spotted by one of the staff.

The Lebanese have the political end so well sewn up that culprits caught stealing stones or digging illegally are always let off by the magistrates. Regulations have been brought in that staff may not be searched or even X-rayed for concealed stones. The illegal digging used to be for the larger stones, but they are now recovering stones down to a value of £1.

Tuesday, January 30th, 1973
In Nigeria. We are now in Enugu, having driven over from Benin. There is no sign of the war until you reach the Niger bridge. Some of the Bailey bridges we passed over replaced permanent bridges blown in the Biafran war. But most bridges were temporary, being replaced by the German firm which is building a wonderful new road from Benin to Onitsha. I gather the road—and other work, and some in Sierra Leone—is a gift or loan from West Germany.

From Onitsha on, the war damage is very evident, though Enugu was not much damaged. The great new market at Onitsha was completely destroyed and is being replaced by something cheaper and one hopes adequate. We called on Sir Louis Mbanefo, at one time Chief Justice of the Eastern Region, and the father of an excellent son who we met at St Thomas's Hospital. He said the victors had been in general generous. The North is at the moment actively recruiting Ibos; most Army officers were received back, though this was less true of the police. The Biafra currency was exchanged on very harsh terms. Most Ibos found no difficulty in returning to work in Lagos. The Ijaws have made great difficulties in allowing Ibos back to Port Harcourt, but they have not the enterprise to make a success of the city on their own and are beginning to realize the fact. Before the war, though it was in Ijaw country, it was an Ibo town. He thought that Port Harcourt, not Onitsha, would end as the second city of Nigeria.

Apart from all the war damage between the Niger bridge and Enugu, the main differences between now and our last visit three years ago are, (1) the enormous increase in motor traffic everywhere, and (2) the very much more numerous military camps to be seen on the main roads. The regular Army must be enormously larger than it was before the war.

Friday, February 2nd, 1973

Back in Lagos. We have spent the last two nights in Port Harcourt, the capital of Rivers State, and in the last few days we have travelled through most of what was the war area. Last evening we were given a drinks party by one Savo Wiwa, the Commissioner (i.e. State Minister) for Information and Home Affairs. He is a charming little man, and very clear and sensible in what he had to say. At the party were the Commissioners for Health, Education and Economic Development, two senior civil servants and the colonel in command of the troops in Port Harcourt. He was, so I was told, the officer who led the attack on and capture of Enugu. He is a Hausa and seemed to me an excellent officer—in his early thirties I should say. He refuted what the Commissioners said about the anti-Ibo policy in Rivers State. He said it had been so pronounced that the people of Benue Plateau, of Eastern, Central and Mid-West States were planning to by-pass Port Harcourt and use Warri instead—or even Lagos—as their main port. This officer said Mbanefo would speak up for Port Harcourt, as his house property was in Port Harcourt not Onitsha. He also said that the Army before the war was under 10,000 and is now over 200,000. It is mostly stationed where it was at the end of the war, and will have to be spread out more evenly over the country. The difficulty over this is the large amount of money brought to an area by the troops—about £150,000 per battalion per month. It is the Army's expenditure in the war area that has enabled the local inhabitants to make a fresh start so quickly, but their economy would take a serious knock if the troops moved elsewhere.

The oil is not a bonanza for Rivers as it is spread along the coast from Mid-West to South-East, and the Federal Government is at pains to see that all twelve States participate. The Rivers government thinks it can grow enough rice for the whole country, and increased rice growing is their major preoccupation: other priorities being education and roads. Though the Ijaws are the most numerous tribe, there are many Kalabaris (who do not live near Calabar) and smaller tribes who are at last being given a say in their country's affairs, which hitherto have been almost monopolized by Yorubas, Ibos and Hausas.

Wednesday, February 7th, 1973
In the plane from Lagos to Geneva. Our visit to Nigeria lasted nine days and we saw prominent citizens in Lagos, Onitsha, Port Harcourt, Ibadan, Ijebu Ode and Abeokuta. I should say the country is recovering very fast from the civil war and that the future is set reasonably fair. The Ibos are as pushing and hard-working as ever, but the new constitution, with twelve states, gives the smaller tribes a chance to assert themselves. I have heard twice from Europeans that the day is fast approaching when the Hausas and the Yorubas will be at each other's throats. From the African side I have heard no hint of any such thing. Obviously tribal friction is with Nigeria for a long time yet, but no Nigerian I met thought an open conflict at all probable.

After all the talk of massacre in the civil war, a frequent question now is who did actually die? When we were in Lagos last General Gowon said all the well-known Ibos had emerged unharmed except one, and he was thought to be safe. This morning we were talking to the man in charge of Lennard's shoe shops in Nigeria. They have ten shops in the East. No single one of their employees was killed or injured in the fighting. It seems that those who died were mostly obscure peasants who were unable to get out of the way of the shooting.

Friday, February 9th, 1973
Dr Paisley to supper last night. We wanted to see him to ascertain

261

what is happening over Ireland, and to urge on him the conviction that at some time after the production of the White Paper, he will have to take the initiative and become the Northern Ireland spokesman. The British Government has made too many mistakes and there is no one else in the North.

He said the long delay by the Government in formulating any policy is due to, firstly, that when they abolished Stormont they had no consequential moves in prospect; and, secondly, that, for Parliamentary reasons the plebiscite had to be postponed and postponed and no White Paper could be produced until after it was held. Paisley was very critical of Whitelaw: often in a state of high tension, but even so the best man they have for the job. There is to be an election in the South at the end of this month and this may be Lynch's idea of a set-off to the referendum a few days later. If Lynch wins, which is by no means certain, he will be in a good position for negotiating with H.M.G. after the White Paper. Paisley is sympathetic to the U.D.A. If the Six Counties have their own government recognized by Dublin, then all sorts of deals are possible. It seemed clear that Paisley is coming round to the view that the whole problem of Belfast and the North could be best dealt with by Irishmen in the absence of H.M.G., though with financial (but not military) backing from this side.

A few weeks ago the Government seemed to be under the impression that they were succeeding in restoring law and order, but while we were away the whole situation has seriously deteriorated.

Paisley thought the Government was doing badly, and that there is a likelihood that Ireland will split the Government and destroy the Party. Whether this is so or not, in the debate on the prospective airport at Foulness last night the Government did badly in debate, and hostile speeches from the Tory back benches were cheered by Tories. The Government is on a collision course with the unions, and with the Protestants of Northern Ireland; the Tories in the House are disenchanted with Ted, while Prior, the new Leader of the House, is totally inept. Nevertheless, Ted gives the appearance of being as happy as a sandboy.

Meanwhile, the world currency markets are in serious disarray owing to an onslaught against the dollar. The Germans are the main target, and are trying hard to stem the flood of dollars but do not seem likely to succeed. Our position has so diminished that we play a negligible part in the whole business. The American attitude seems frivolous and irresponsible.

It was announced this morning that Gordon Richardson is to succeed Leslie O'Brien as Governor of the Bank in July. It was understood, when Leslie was appointed for a second term that he would not serve the whole five years, and it has been known for a long time that Gordon Richardson wants the job. I should think this is a good appointment. It is thought in the City that Gordon is not a good administrator, and not really a banker, but a very intelligent lawyer and a brilliant draughtsman.

Paisley has been deeply disillusioned by the House of Commons —thinks the M.P.s a lot of puppets, and Enoch Powell the only man of stature among them all.

Paisley thinks Peter Mills, a new Junior Minister in the Northern Ireland Office, to be the best of the Junior Ministers there. He went to Brussels and did a good job for the Ulster farmers, though Ted Heath was very reluctant to let him go there.

Tuesday, February 13th, 1973

The big news today is that the dollar is to be devalued by 10 per cent and the yen is to float. This is the second dollar devaluation in eighteen months and humiliating evidence of the mismanagement of American affairs. Having the strongest economy in the world in such weak and irresponsible hands makes life difficult for everyone else.

Had lunch with David Williams, whom I had not seen for a long time, to talk about West Africa. He says the present Ghana regime is the one shining example of an African government that is not corrupt. Apparently the Nigerians are so incensed over the reporting of the Biafra war that they will not grant visas to journalists—any journalists. David Williams is exempt. According to David, I rate high in Sierra Leone because at a lunch or dinner given by the then Governor, de Zouche Hall, I said that Albert Margai and Siaka Stevens would both go far. This has been frequently recalled, though Hall thought at the time that I was talking nonsense.

One of the Sierra Leone diamond smugglers and organizers of illicit digging really went too far, even for the Freetown administration, and so was to be sent as Ambassador to Cuba, but the Cubans are showing great reluctance to have him.

In Ghana the currency is nearly useless and any attempt to keep

263

out luxury imports is frustrated by smuggling. Recently a trawler was stopped off the Ghanaian coast and found to be carrying a cargo of wigs!

Saturday, February 17th, 1973

Lunch yesterday with Hartley Shawcross. He was despondent, and could see no light at the end of the tunnel. Communist influence is very visible in the *Sunday Times*, I.T.N. and other media. It is not thought proper to mention this sinister influence, either in the media or in the trades unions. When in the Labour Government years ago he was on an emergency committee, who could not see how a government nowadays could fight a general strike. The power workers alone could bring the whole country to a standstill.

I said that sooner or later some government would insist on governing, and the longer a confrontation was postponed the bloodier it would be. He said the police establishment was too low, and in any case they were thousands below their quota. He discounted the Army altogether, which surely, in the end, will be the decisive force.

I spoke disparagingly of Barber and Maurice Macmillan. He thought nothing of the latter but said the former was as good as any other available Tory. I asked what about du Cann? He said du Cann had made too much money too quickly, and his appointment to the Exchequer would be badly received in the City.

On the same theme he said that there is nothing in the City for Reggie Maudling. He said Reggie was picking up pennies writing articles. Hartley sat with him for two to three years on some board, and in that period he never once opened his mouth. He seemed to think his duties as a director ended with the acceptance of his fee and the absorption of a champagne lunch after board meetings.

Wednesday, February 21st, 1973

We gave a party yesterday at the Hyde Park Hotel, to which a number of important people came. I had some conversation with Geoffrey Rippon, now Minister for the Environment. His optimism was total. The Government had been dishing out nasty medicine so far, but from now on it would be goodies all the way. The unions did not want confrontation, nor did anyone else. Everything was going well, and would lead inevitably to an electoral victory in 1974. He left himself no doubts, no hesitations, no escape clauses of any kind. I have known Rippon since he was P.P.S. to Duncan Sandys long ago, and I cannot believe he would say all this if he did not substantially believe it. But how is it possible?

John Stevens was interested in Peter Walker's move to set up a 'task force', to be the link between Westminster and the City. This is to usurp the traditional function of the Bank of England, immediately after the appointment of a new Governor—a Prime Ministerial appointment.

It is difficult at a confused party of a hundred persons to recall who said what, but Paul Bareau, George Bolton and Plowden felt the financial and currency situations were very dicey indeed.

Later. Lunch for C.D. [a senior civil servant]. He was in good form but had no specific information to impart. I said Rippon last night had been absurdly optimistic. C.D. said, he probably meant most of it. He was, anyway, more hopeful than some of his colleagues. I told C.D. that Peyton had said we should get nowhere until we had been subjected to some deep humiliation. C.D. was much interested and wondered what kind of humiliation he had in mind. We had been humiliated on several occasions since the war—Suez and three devaluations. I said these had passed unnoticed by the man in the street. Every now and then the Government of the day announced a crisis, but to the ordinary citizen nothing unusual was visible.

C.D. said he supposed that if there were an election today, the Tories would win. I said I thought the result was quite unforeseeable—the Tories would run an anti-union campaign; the Labour Party a campaign against high prices. No one wants either Heath or Wilson, and there would be a number of freak candidates who would further confuse the result.

C.D. could not see what the militant unionists want. Having destroyed our society, what then? I don't think they think that far, and anyway on the Left there is a strong factor of envy.

We talked about Ireland, and I said we have been trying to persuade Paisley to come out in favour of an independent Ulster at some date after the publication of the White Paper. It did seem as if important Protestant and Catholic elements would be attracted by the idea of settling their own affairs without stupid meddling by English politicians. I said the Government White Paper should have come out last June. But apparently the Government was looking,

and still is, for some agreed solution. This is its besetting sin—
looking for painless solutions for difficult problems. C.D. asked
how high I put Faulkner's influence now. I said surely he was water
over the dam. Power in Protestant Ulster had passed from the
Unionist Party and the middle class and gentry to the militant
working class, to whom Faulkner made no appeal.

I made some reference to the merits of Biffen and Tugendhat as
possible Ministers, but Biffen is ruled out as a 'rebel'. I suggested
that poachers often make the best gamekeepers, but this theory
apparently does not appeal to Ted.

'But anyway,' C.D. said, 'we have got into Europe.' I wondered
whether we had not done so just as it was breaking up.

He said, as we parted, 'How depressing it is to live in a period of
decline'.

Monday, February 26th, 1973

Lunch for John Peyton. The more I see him the more I like him,
and the more impressive I find him. He has an odd face and often
does not speak very clearly, but he seems to me both tough and
capable. His opening remark was to the effect that all important
people in our society, from Government to newspaper proprietors
and beyond, should be more humble and cease claiming both
power and influence they do not possess. He thought the most
important requisites of government were humility and guts. I
asked him if he thought the Government would press on with their
Phase 2 to the point of a general strike. He said he thought they
would. I said surely with an inadequate police force and no propaganda build-up, the Government would lose. He thought the outcome would be unforeseeable.

I said I understood the ASLEF executive had a majority of Communists, 4–3. He said, 'There are only two certain Communists on
the executive and they often disagree.' He said he knew Jack Jones
well, and as with all these union leaders, he has no clear objectives.
They all exist from hand to mouth and are pushed around by their
militant shop stewards. The only union leader whom he thinks
knows where he is going is Clive Jenkins, whose objective is the
maximum benefit—for Clive Jenkins. If there is a confrontation
between the Government and the unions it will be because they
drifted into it, not because it was planned by anyone.

I said I thought if you wanted to convince everyone that the

Government is not serious about its labour relations, make them over to Maurice Macmillan who is a burnt-out case, and looks like a clown on television. Peyton spoke up for Macmillan. I should gather he likes him personally but does not regard him as a ball of fire in his office.

Anyway, we are in the Common Market, which should give a lot of hidebound industrialists, and others, something to think about. Peyton is not impressed by the C.B.I. people, particularly Partridge and Campbell Adamson. In his dealings with the French he finds them even more selfish than he had expected.

Peyton is now in charge of roads, and is disturbed that engineers —but particularly civil engineers—have no standing in our society, in spite of their importance. In the last century the Brunels, Telford and Watt were household names (and still are) while their present successors are unknown. Why is this? Why do we not give our leading policemen more prestige? Why not have a policeman peer? The whole of our society needs a good shake-up, hence the importance of entering the Common Market.

To my surprise he did not agree with my high opinion of Dick Beeching, but did not give his reasons. Over the railways, for which he is responsible, he says you can cut out lines that lose money and thus uncover more lines that lose money. It is like peeling an onion. You would end with no losses—and no railway.

Wednesday, February 28th, 1973
Lunch with Edwin Plowden. He said Tube Investments consists of about 40 per cent consumer durables and 60 per cent heavy industry. For two years now the first has been booming while the second has been in the doldrums. Suddenly, at the beginning of November, the heavy end of the business picked up—but for how long? No serious amount of investment is to be looked for until industrialists have confidence that the new investment will earn an adequate profit over a period. They have no such confidence at the present time.

He said—which is a new thought to me—that much of the complaint against rising prices comes from the housewife. This is because the husband, who is earning more money, is not passing on a comparable increase to the wife.

He had some talk with Carrington at a party lately. Carrington seemed confident that if there were an election now, the Tories would win. Plowden does not share this belief. Carrington also said that the Government has no alternative but to soldier on, whatever the unions may do.

Plowden says he has been convinced for five years that we are heading for a revolution and for a dictatorship, whether of the Right or the Left. How we get to such a point—and when—is as obscure to him as it is to me. Like others he does not count on the Army in his calculations. But in a revolutionary situation the Army is the decisive element, though in what direction it would throw its influence is quite incalculable at present.

Thursday, March 1st, 1973

Dinner last night with Hermione and Paul Crosfield—du Cann was one of the guests. I had little talk with him but Ruth had much more; she thought him a sensitive man with great charm, great clarity, great intelligence, but not a strong man and not really a leader.

Du Cann thought, he told me, that the Government and the country are in trouble. In particular, the policy document put out some months ago about competition between the banks had clearly not been thought through. Urging the banks to be more competitive meant that they would bid against each other for deposits, thus raising interest rates. With rising interest rates, banks become more profitable and are then attacked for profiteering!

Lunch today for Rupert Murdoch. In the last few days he had had Geoffrey Rippon to lunch, and had been a guest at Chequers. On both occasions he was treated to a long sales talk. Everything is going well—there is no trouble anywhere.

In Fleet Street the *Mirror* has fallen back to 4,200,000 copies, while the *Sun* is up to 3,000,000 and is doing surprisingly well in the North; not so well in London. The provincial papers are making a lot of money—Thomson's *Newcastle Chronicle*, £2 million, his Cardiff paper, £1 million. It is assumed that on Roy's death his English papers will be for sale.

Don Ryder is still trying to get Harold Evans to succeed Hugh Cudlipp at I.P.C. It seems he may yet be successful. It is customary in Fleet Street that when a man is to leave he leaves that same day, but Hugh, after his announced retirement, is still in charge at the *Mirror* and will be so for some months. It is not clear why Ryder is so keen on Evans.

The newsprint mills asked for an increase of £7 per ton, but the

Government, to please the newspapers, only allowed £2. As a result imported newsprint is up £7, home-produced up £2. In consequence Bowaters are planning to close their Kemsley mill and Dixon's are likely to drop newsprint manufacture altogether.

Sunday, March 4th, 1973

Two political events of the last few days are interesting. The more important is Lynch's defeat in the Irish elections. He must have been fairly confident of victory, and planned that the election theme would be his policy towards Northern Ireland. The result, it was hoped, would strengthen his hand in dealing with Ted and his Irish White Paper, due out this month. But the election turned on domestic issues and Lynch is out. Liam Cosgrave, the new Prime Minister, may be tougher on the I.R.A., on the other hand Fianna Fail, without the restraints of office, may pursue a more actively nationalistic policy.

The three by-elections were of seats held by Labour: Dick Taverne overwhelmed the official Labour man at Lincoln; the Tories came last in all three constituencies; the Scottish Nationalists did well in Dundee; and the Liberals in Chester-le-Street. The result can be seen as a condemnation of both major Parties. Will either of them react? I doubt it.

Meanwhile the international currency crisis is looking fairly menacing, and is coming at a bad moment for us, with the Budget due on Tuesday. The two main international currencies are the dollar and sterling. Nixon seems to be taking a frivolous and irresponsible attitude over the dollar, and we seem to be saying that the pound is floating so we are not under attack. Let the Germans and the Japanese cope with the situation. This is all very well, but a neo-1929 cannot be far away, and if it came upon us it would find a public far less ready to accept unemployment, or any of the inevitable consequences of a severe set-back to international trade.

Tuesday, March 6th, 1973

Yesterday the T.U.C. called a special conference to decide on the policy to be pursued with regard to the Government's Phase 2. The proceedings had been agreed in advance and were to have been innocuous, but Joe Gormley—normally a moderate—moved that the motion be referred back, and in the outcome there was a large measure of endorsement for a day's national strike. This is on top of real trouble from hospital workers, gas workers, civil servants and train drivers.

I met Jules Thorn at lunchtime. He was with William Ryland of the Post Office. Thorn had been at what he described as a trades-union dinner. He said the mood was one of black despair. 'Ted,' he said, 'is so inflexible.' Personally I think Ted has given too much to the unions already and has to stick somewhere. His trouble is that he is trying to assert the Government's authority too late in the life of this Parliament, and when his changes of course have discredited him.

Lunch for Hugh Fraser, who has just been to Ireland. He thinks the Government has not yet decided what to put in its White Paper for publication later this month. Whatever it says will be rejected out of hand. He says the Army is being compelled to do all the police work and is being destroyed. His idea is that we should install a new council with limited powers, set up the best executive organization we can devise with local police forces, and in two years walk out. The Irish are more likely to solve their problems if left alone. He rates the currency crisis and Ireland above the trouble with the unions. He thinks if things get worse we might have an election, which the Tories might well lose, and even if they won it would have no effect on the Irish, the unions, or our fellow Europeans. A national government might be an interim measure in case of real trouble but under whom? Enoch Powell?

The European exchange markets are closed this week. Barber has laid down quite unacceptable terms for joining a European floating exchange. This leaves us looking foolish; having made such a fuss about joining the Market, we are declining to honour our undertaking to fix the rate of exchange as from January 1st.

Wednesday, March 7th, 1973

The Budget yesterday got high praise from the B.B.C. and the *Telegraph*. The *Financial Times* was a thought more realistic. The twin aims were said to be, (1) growth, and (2) anti-inflation. The first aim is of course inflationary, so the two cancel each other out. In fact, the Budget made some concessions to the badly-off and did nothing about inflation. Like all Government, and many non-Government, commentators it is assumed without question that the unions will fail in their attacks on the Government; that its anti-inflation policy will succeed; that Ireland will settle down; and that the world currency crisis must fade away. At the moment none of these predictions looks likely to come off. The gas men, the hospital workers and the train drivers are being troublesome, with the teachers and civil servants not far behind.

Friday, March 9th, 1973
A brief lunch with John Stevens. He seemed principally concerned with Government changes, of which there has been no hint in the newspapers. Alec Home at last wants to retire, and is to be replaced by Carrington. Barber is to go to Defence. The Treasury is concerned that Whitelaw should succeed Barber, but Peter Walker is pushing hard. Leslie O'Brien was sacked under rather harsh circumstances, as he was not felt to fit in sufficiently quickly with Ted's financial and commercial ideas. Gordon Richardson was appointed to succeed him by the P.M. No other names were mentioned. I asked why Gordon was so keen to get the job, but John did not know.

According to John, the Prime Minister has been saying that a 5-per-cent growth rate is an absolute minimum. The Government should aim higher and count on exchange rates, interest rates, etc., to 'fall into line'—in other words let them rip.

John dined last night with Lord Limerick, a Junior Minister, who reflected the euphoria current among Ministers at the present time. He said Gormley's intervention at the T.U.C. special conference on Monday was very helpful—it ensured the general strike only being on for one day. Actually, his intervention meant the rejection of the council's very moderate resolution and its replacement by a much more militant one.

John said our monetary affairs are so badly conducted that short-term interest rates are now higher than long-term ones. So you can borrow an overdraft at $9\frac{1}{2}$ per cent and lend at seven days' notice for 13 per cent; the Chase Manhattan Bank had made £5 million doing just that. The City's reactions to Barber's announcement of two new gilt-edged issues had not been expected—one stock fell $2\frac{1}{2}$ points. The money supply is to go roaring ahead and there is no reason to suppose there will be any end to inflation this year.

Tuesday, March 20th, 1973
Lunch with Norman Collins. He had no particular news. He said recently he and three or four friends had entertained a Minister

and asked if they could help in any way. But the Minister said that things were going so well they had no need of help. Ted is still incapable of making a speech with even one memorable phrase. Co-ordination of ministerial speeches is usually the job of the Lord President. Perhaps because of Prior's incompetence, Carr offered to take it on. But Carr is much too busy and the job is not done.

The allocation of the principal commercial radio station left much to be desired.* At a cost of £30,000 A.T.V. put together much the most impressive group, with no one interest having more than 20 per cent. However, the I.B.A.† allotted it to Richard Attenborough and his friends, who are without any experience or expertise. It would have been better, if this was in their minds, to say from the start that the big groups need not apply. Apparently, they are likely to make 100-per-cent profit per annum on an outlay of £750,000.

The White Paper on Northern Ireland came out at two o'clock this afternoon. Paisley rang up early this morning quite cock-a-hoop. But on the radio at six o'clock he expressed disappointment. Perhaps the Paper was not quite what he had been led to expect. From what I picked up while listening in my bath, I would suspect that it will not work. The All-Ireland Council has no powers: the idea of uniting Catholics and Protestants in running the Six Counties is unworkable in the present state of inter-sectarian feeling. There is no use blathering about the evil of violence if nothing is done to satisfy the violent. Two definite pledges are made: (1) to keep the British Army in Northern Ireland indefinitely; and (2) that the status of Northern Ireland will not be changed, except with the consent of the majority of its inhabitants. Neither in the long term can be sustained. To wait until the last moment, and then for the mountain to produce such an undernourished mouse, is indeed a disappointment.

Later. On television Craig denounced the proposals out of hand—said they would use the elections to gain a position of power from which to enforce their own ideas. Craig, Paisley and other Unionist leaders are to meet tomorrow. We shall know more then. There is

* Commercial radio broadcasting was to commence in Britain in October. A number of groups had applied for licences, and the allocation by the Independent Broadcasting Authority was announced in March.
† Independent Broadcasting Authority.

nothing tangible for the I.R.A. or for the Dublin Government. Why no increase in the twelve Ulster M.P.s? Is this the price for Labour co-operation?

In his remarks on television Whitelaw clearly gave the impression that he will not remain as Northern Ireland Secretary for much longer.

Wednesday, March 21st, 1973

Lunch for Vic Feather. He was in good form but, as usual, discreet. He said there were now two power centres in politics—the Government and the T.U.C. The employers did not constitute a third. He had little use for the C.B.I. and thought they had made a mistake in having a fifteen-month price freeze. He said Ted treats his Ministers not as the headmaster treats his staff, but as the headmaster treats his sixth form. He had little use for Ministers: Geoffrey Rippon he once saw as a future P.M. but not now; Peter Walker he thinks able, but a 'fly-boy'. He did not expect a confrontation between the Government and the unions, as the latter would get what they want by a fiddle. The gas workers had got it as the result of some fiddle over pensions, and the railwaymen would settle for some similar wangle. He thought balance of payments difficulties and increased unemployment would show up soon, and he thought we should have a lot of trouble in August and September. Phase 2 is to be replaced by Phase 3 'in the autumn'. He thought the autumn would be December, if we ever get to Phase 3. He expected no let-up in the rate of inflation.

Later to Tony Bloomfield. Last time I saw him he said the dollar devaluation would not last three months. It lasted two weeks. He thought measures to correct the currency problems would not work, and could not be made to work, except under controls that could only be effective in an autocratic regime. He thought the Government's measures against inflation were mere patching. If we are not careful we shall see the collapse of world trade.

On the radio this evening it is announced that all Protestant organizations in Northern Ireland, except Faulkner, have rejected the White Paper but plan to get what they want by democratic means.

Thursday, March 22nd, 1973

Lunch with Alf Robens at Vickers. He had just come from the weekly Court at the Bank. They had had their monthly economic talk from Christopher Dow, who has succeeded Christopher McMahon, who took Maurice Allen's place. Dow told them unemployment was falling faster than had ever happened before. He thinks there is a danger of the economy becoming overheated, but not before the first quarter of next year.

Alf said that the foundry and heavy-engineering side of Vickers started picking up in mid-February, and is now going great guns. He said the big orders for British shipbuilding yards, and the orders for machine tools, are no sign of greater international confidence in British industry. We get the orders because everyone else is already full up.

He said it is generally believed that Barber is tired of the Treasury and wants to move. Hugh Fraser this morning said that Barber had had a tiff with the P.M. Heath has wanted to take part in a joint float with the other E.E.C. countries,* but Barber had got his way with a separate float. Alf said the most powerful member of the Cabinet after Ted is Peter Walker. He is more arrogant than Ted dares to be, and so far has got away with it. He wants to be Chancellor, and Alf assumes he will get it. At a pinch, he will make himself awkward if he doesn't get it.

Alf was in much better form than he has been in for a long time, and his political attitude has changed a lot. He said the Government was getting away with its wage freeze—there were some strikes, but an awful lot of settlements on the basis of £1 plus 4 per cent. He doubted if the miners would vote for a strike, and thought Ted would get away with the toughest policy of any Government for some years. By the autumn there would be a shortage of labour, and it would be the employers who would break the wage freeze. I said surely there would then be a serious degree of inflation? At this point Alf became self-contradictory. On the one hand the Government is having success in damping down inflation, and on the other hand, under modern conditions, inflation did not matter. After a time, like the French, you lop a nought off the end and start again. People's savings don't really suffer, because nowadays there is no point in saving. It is all looked after by some form of pension. It is true that trades-union pressure and inflation have eroded the status of the professional classes, but as far as he could judge from the doctors at Guys Hospital (where he is chairman), they do not mind. It is true that in most ways we are falling behind

* European Economic Community.

other countries, but young people are content with a rising standard of living and have no interest in greatness of any kind. It may be we shall sink to importing much that we should make ourselves. But we can always make the money to buy what we need by tourism and the sale of souvenirs. In any case, there is bound to be a huge demand for industrial products of every kind from the undeveloped countries of Asia, Africa and South America, and this should help to keep us going to the end of the century. 'But', I said, 'how do you have a rising standard of living in a world that doubles its population every thirty years?' 'Well,' Alf said, 'we may have difficulties over food.'

In fact, Alf is now contemplating the painless decline of this country into a position of total insignificance—material, spiritual or aesthetic.

Friday, 23rd March, 1973

Lunch for Brian Walden—quite one of the most intelligent members of the Labour Party. He had one item of news which I found interesting. At the Commonwealth Prime Ministers' Conference in Singapore last year, President Obote of Uganda was rude to the British—a discourtesy which was much resented. Later our Intelligence learnt that there was a tribal plot to oust Obote and replace him with General Amin. The Intelligence people wanted Obote to be warned. However, Obote was not warned, and the Labour Party chiefs believe this helped the rebels and so landed us with General Amin.

Brian is now Shadow Financial Secretary to the Treasury. His views on finance did not seem to be consistent: money supply was being increased at a reckless pace; the balance of payments would be in serious trouble before the end of the year; but on the other hand he thought inflation would ease off slightly, and that industrial investment would continue to pick up. He thought our inflation was due to the money supply, and that wage demands would be kept at, or near, £1 per week plus 4 per cent.

The composition of the Government was partly based on the assumption that Alec would retire. But he has not done so, and shows no signs of going. He is the one unsackable member of the Cabinet. If he were to say Heath's policy was not that of the Conservative Party as he understood it, Heath would be in desperate trouble. As Foreign Secretary Alec is quite useless, but he is entirely honest. Still quoting Brian—Peter Walker is emerging as the strongest member of the Cabinet; capable in a rather fly way and very ambitious. Our great Prime Ministers of the past, from Gladstone to Baldwin, would not have had such a man anywhere in their administrations.

Brian confirmed that the proposal in the White Paper that the Northern Ireland representation at Westminster should remain at twelve M.P.s was the condition laid down by the Labour Party for a bi-partisan policy on Ireland. Nevertheless, Ted will be under very great pressure from his Party in Westminster, and from Northern Ireland, to raise the representation to twenty.

Brian thought Government expenditure wildly excessive, particularly on Defence. He thought Barber had been weak. If Barber goes Brian hoped, and believed, he would be succeeded by Keith Joseph.

Brian's present constituency is at least half coloured—mostly Sikhs. They are model citizens in every way, except perhaps for a tendency to fiddle on their tax returns. Any aggressive tendencies they may have are concentrated on the Pakistanis. This is historic, though none the less real. I believe the Sikh sect was established in the seventeenth century as a fighting sect of Hindus to fight Mohammedans.

Wednesday, March 28th, 1973

At a Foyle lunch for Enoch Powell, I sat next Mary Whitehouse. The latter says she travels all over the country speaking several times a week to four or five hundred people. A few days ago she was speaking at Rugby School. She notices a great change in the young people—twenty-one and under—serious, with a great interest in religion. She had a tremendous reception.

Enoch good as always—on the whole blaming the public for the mess we are in. The voter wants to be told he can have hospitals, schools, a high standard of living, and everything else without working for them—and he gets them at the price of inflation. He ridiculed Heath's promise of 6-per-cent growth in the economy. He said this would mean that if a man lived to be seventy he would be enjoying, at the end of his life, a standard of living twenty-seven times as high as at the beginning. Though Enoch is usually a very popular speaker the audience was smaller than it sometimes is.

Thursday, March 29th, 1973

Last night Ted introduced the Northern Ireland White Paper debate with a violent attack on Paisley. He was not named but the attack was not only on his policy but also on his integrity, saying he had rejected the proposals in the White Paper out of personal ambition. This reaction by Ted is one of personal pique, which will do nothing to help along a peaceful settlement in Northern Ireland.

Later. Lunch for Fforde of the Bank. He said, when the Government took over there was rising unemployment and growing inflation. They were advised—presumably by Treasury officials—that unemployment would level off, and were encouraged to go ahead with their policy of wringing the necks of lame ducks. But when unemployment went up and up, they panicked and adopted their present policy. I said surely their present policy was wildly inflationary. He said some indicators suggested this—notably on the money supply. On the other hand, house prices had levelled off. It seemed that the unions, or their members, were less militant and it is quite possible that Ministers' optimism might be justified in the short run. They have taken a strong stand against union demands and have no option but to stick to it.

Fforde thought it quite an idea for the D.T.I.* and the Bank to get closer together. It would be a set-off to the growing power of the Treasury in Bank affairs. He didn't seem to know anything about changes at the Exchequer though he thought it quite likely that Barber and Heath had differed over the independent floating of the pound (said to have been insisted on by Barber). On floating currencies, Brian said it was not a particularly good idea, but at a time when all Western currencies are inflating at different rates, it is the only possible course.

I asked about Jeremy Morse, who has had some months as chairman of the Committee of Twenty, of the I.M.F., and does not seem to be doing well. Fforde thought he was being blamed unfairly, but that he is a rather authoritarian official with no political gifts. These latter would have come in very handy.

It appears that Lynch had been 100-per-cent certain that he would win the Irish election.

* Department of Trade and Industry.

Tuesday, April 3rd, 1973

Lunch for George Bolton. He was in great personal form, though very unhappy about the outlook for the country. He says Enoch Powell expects the collapse of the prices and incomes policy by September, an opinion with which George agrees. He says there is a group of some forty Conservative M.P.s determined to ditch Ted, and thinks the opportunity will come in the autumn, perhaps over the soaring price of food. There is another, loose, group operating on behalf of Soames. The City is very critical, and distrustful, of Peter Walker. They regard him as Jim Slater's lap-dog, and do not trust him anyway.*

George says there is a complete lack of confidence in our engineering industries. No stockbroker would put his name to a prospectus offering shares in engineering today. Our investment in industry has for years been quite inadequate, which is one of the reasons why British firms cannot provide much of the equipment required for North Sea oil. Recently Ted addressed a party of bankers at No. 10. Tuke, chairman-designate of Barclays Bank, told him Ted had lambasted them for not investing more in British industry. This went down very badly.

According to George, all currencies are suspect these days—Keynsian policies of inflation to keep the economy moving forward have led to this result. In Switzerland prices are soaring, trade is indifferent and foreign workers have been sent home in large numbers. He implied that the Swiss economy is pretty rocky, and if Switzerland is in trouble how much more so are other countries. We have liquidated the last remains of the British Empire and sterling has become a provincial currency of no importance.

George thought it amazing that Nixon, after winning the election in a landslide, had already seriously undermined his own position over the Watergate affair. Though the dollar is weak, the American economy is doing well. He assumes Nixon will 'bring the boys' home from Europe, and also assumes there will be something of a trade war later in the year over GATT.†

George was rather sarcastic over Sam Brittan of the *Financial Times*. Brittan has come out these last few days as a severe critic of

---

* Slater Walker Securities was about to merge with Hill Samuel to form one of the world's largest merchant banks.

† General Agreements on Tariffs and Trade.

278

Government policy—very different from the sunny optimism a short while back.

George confirmed that Leslie O'Brien was sacked, and not allowed to suggest his successor.

He thought it odd that the Dutch, whom we regard as a stolid but reliable people, have become the exact opposite. They have had no Government for four months, and the Catholic Church in Holland has virtually seceded from Rome.

George said Ted's closest advisers are Peter Walker and Toby Aldington.

George said industrial England stretches from Oxford to Stirling. In that area there is little opportunity for a young man to make a name and a career. So they come to London, and the industrial North sinks still deeper. Is it possible that it is from this area that a movement might start for the rebirth of England?

Wednesday, April 4th 1973

Lunch for Bill Barnetson. He was interesting about the new-found prosperity of the newspaper industry. United Newspaper profits are up 150 per cent on last year—a good year for them. *The Times* loss is down to £700,000, more than made up by the profits of the *Sunday Times* and the *Times Educational Supplement*. The *Manchester Evening News* made £2 million last year, more than enough to pay for the *Guardian*. The consumer boom is benefiting newspapers in two ways—columns and columns of classifieds, good retail advertising, and cover prices high but acceptable.

The miners have voted against striking and the civil servants' strike has petered out. There are still the Ford workers, the railways, and the hospital workers. The unions have agreed to the Phase 2 rises, which are between 8 per cent and 9 per cent (and so inflationary), but some slight progress has been made. Ted is still anxious for a tripartite agreement on wages, but I do not see how the T.U.C. could sign any worth-while agreement—or at any rate, if they did sign one, how they could make sure it was honoured. The unions are as anti-Ted as ever and will make their displeasure felt in due course. Barnetson did not think there would be trouble till next year, and did not think any intrigue against Ted could be effective until there was serious trouble with the economy. So it was quite possible Ted would get away with a successful election before the storm.

Barnetson had some talk with Alec Home recently. He is enjoying himself enormously at the Foreign Office—so is his wife—and he shows no sign at all of retiring. He takes a very short view of politics in general, delegates awkward subjects like Iceland fish to others (in this case Lady Tweedsmuir), and goes on his way swanning around the world on goodwill missions.

Thursday, April 12th, 1973

Lunch with Hugh Fraser. He had had a long talk with Willie White-law, over (as he said) a fantastic number of double whiskies and soda. Willie was pleased his White Paper had been so well received, spoke of the great strain imposed by his work in Ireland, and clearly expected to return to office in London before long. Fraser hoped it would be the Treasury.

Fraser quoted the name of someone who he said was the great expert on opinion polls and voting trends. He said, in the new Northern Ireland Assembly he calculated that the number of members prepared to work the White Paper and those not so prepared were about fifty-fifty. Under these circumstances men like Faulkner—prepared to work the White Paper as it is—would be forced, Fraser thought, to fight for an extension of the Assembly's powers to something like what they were at Stormont. It is out of this situation that a demand for U.D.I.* might develop. A curious development of this idea is that the Duke of Devonshire, influential in Southern Ireland because of his property at Lismore, has come out for U.D.I.

Fraser thought Ted is now doing better—the wage freeze has gone off better than at one time seemed likely. Fraser said he is anxious to get rid of Alec Home. I said, surely Alec can get rid of Ted but not vice versa. Fraser said a lot will depend on the result of the local elections being held today—to strengthen Ted's hand or otherwise. The general impression is that the Tories will do badly, perhaps very badly.

Fraser is amused over our troubles with the Common Market, which he has always opposed. He says the next shock from that quarter will come when our partners demand a share of North Sea oil.

Fraser also said that Ted can hang on till October 1975. Parliament runs out in June, but an election need not be held till three months later.

* Unilateral declaration of independence.

Saturday, April 14th, 1973

At Northampton General Hospital for the annual meeting of the Psoriasis Association. At lunch the secretary of the hospital made two points I thought interesting. He had had some talk with Maurice Macmillan when he was Shadow Minister of Health. He said Macmillan knew less about the Health Service than the average patient in the hospital. He also said the strike of hospital workers seems to be fading out, but one result will remain, the knowledge that hospital workers may—because they now have—go on strike again. The relations between a hospital and its auxiliary workers will never again be the same.

In the local elections Labour has won London, the six Metropolitan Counties and much else. The Liberals have done better than before. It is interesting that all the comment is on familiar lines: 'Indeed Labour has done well but there is quiet satisfaction among Conservative leaders, as it might have been much worse.' Though the elections have taken place in the new counties they are not implemented till next *April*. This seems odd—and why should the Conservatives bring in a new organization of local government that will always give an advantage to Labour?

Monday, April 16th, 1973

Lunch with Tony Bloomfield and Humphrey Trevelyan, the latter just back from China and Russia. He found the Chinese suprisingly ready to talk on a wide range of subjects that would be barred in Russia—international politics, defence policy and so on. The principal impression was that the politburo is old—very old—and the regime cannot be regarded as safe until a new set of younger men is installed. Many important posts are still vacant from the Cultural Revolution. Mao's pictures are not as prominent as they were; his little Red Book is not much in evidence. It is also surprising that Stalin is still looked up to, though Krushchev is execrated. In Russia nothing has changed. It is a very static society.

On the Middle East (Humphrey was our ambassador in Egypt), he said the Six Day War was not started by the Egyptians. They had been told (falsely) by the Russians that the Israelis were about to attack Syria. The Israelis felt this was an opportunity for an attack and took it. The fault lay with Nasser, who knew he would lose a war but manoeuvred himself into a position where war was probable. Humphrey said he told Smirnovsky, the Russian Ambassador here, that he thought the Russians were lucky to have been expelled from Egypt. There were too many of them for safety, and this was a convenient way of pulling out. Smirnovsky agreed.

One last point Humphrey said the Chinese time-scale is quite different from ours, and that they will never accept a temporary advantage at the price of a serious disadvantage in the next generation or century.

Humphrey lived in India for seventeen years (I think he said). He thought the country too large, too inchoate, ever to mean anything on the international stage. He doubted whether the Chinese would, or could, take it over and organize it.

I said the Opposition thought Heath had the makings of a superb civil servant but not those of a politician. Humphrey agreed and said, when under Macmillan, Ted was negotiating our entry into the Common Market, he did Macmillan's permanent under-secretary's work for him.

Wednesday, April 18th, 1973

On our way back from Stoke-on-Trent Humphrey Trevelyan stepped into our carriage. In the course of a long conversation he spoke about Peter Walker, of whom he had seen quite a bit in China recently. I tried to argue that he is an unattractive man with no political gifts—but able. Humphrey would only concede that he is a good card-player. Walker made his big speech impromptu, which is dangerous as you may say something you shouldn't, and the interpreter may get wrong something you said. In the course of his speech he referred to the Chinese as Chinamen, which to them is a term of contempt. He also referred to Chairman Mao as a statesman of world stature but, (a) Mao is trying hard to subvert the democracies of the West, and (b) such praise would annoy the Russians, whom he was to visit on his way home.

Humphrey asked Walker if he did not find his huge department, D.T.I., a major burden. 'Not at all,' said Walker, 'at 9.15 I have in all my Junior Ministers'—I think he said there were nine. The day's business was discussed, duties assigned, and in no time at all they were all back in their offices getting on with the job. Humphrey could not have been more contemptuous. It all sounds quite nice in principle, but when you realize two of the principal Junior Ministers are now Chataway and Boardman you can see what a lot of nonsense it is.

Over the British Museum, Humphrey said the civil servants are impossible. Quibbling over small sums of money and then wasting far larger sums through delay. It is impossible to get decisions and there seems to be no clear line of command.

Easter Sunday, April 22nd, 1973

It is announced in the *Sunday Telegraph* today that William Whitelaw will not be leaving the Northern Ireland Office in the foreseeable future. The P.M. is said to be well aware of Whitelaw's highly nervous state; but Whitelaw would not agree to his removal until he had defeated the I.R.A. He wants his revenge for being shown up by the I.R.A. as having direct contacts with them. This is not sensible. The reason for the I.R.A. giving the show away was because Whitelaw's civil servants had put out an entirely false story that the Linadoon affair was staged by the I.R.A. to bring about the end of the truce.

The *Sunday Times* today says Whitelaw is going, but only after the new Assembly is well under way. Meanwhile, Paisley in conversation on the telephone some days ago spoke as if he thought the White Paper could be frustrated.

Monday, April 30th, 1973

The only matter of political interest in the last week has been the Watergate affair in Washington. The scandals continue to proliferate and Nixon does nothing. His only honourable course is to resign, but I imagine that is the least likely outcome of the affair. If he sacks his closest associates—Haldemann and so on—they may well take their revenge on him. If he doesn't the whole credibility of the Presidency goes.

Yesterday Ruth met a Romanian, Ionescu(?), with a message from Istinki who was Pan's violin instructor in Bucharest. This Romanian is an anaesthetist of international repute. Ruth asked him what struck him on this his first visit to England. He mentioned three things: (1) The Radcliffe Infirmary, at Oxford, is old-fashioned by Romanian standards; (2) the way in which appointments with doctors could be arranged immediately with reference to their engagement book. No higher authority evidently was required; (3) he found the younger men he met very hard to understand. They spoke the words indistinctly and kept on saying 'ye know' when he didn't know. With older men he had no difficulty.

Paisley spent a couple of hours with us on his way from Heathrow to the House. He was tired and not very communicative. He seemed fairly sure that in the election for the Assembly at the end of June, his group would have, or could gain, a majority. What I had not realized is that the elections are still two months off and the Assembly is not to meet until October! To allow a very dangerous situation to drift for months and months seems to me insane. Paisley said the Government seems to think that one day they will wake up and find the Irish problem has just gone away. Paisley said Straubenzee, the Minister of State in the Irish Office, is a figure of pure fun. The only Irish Minister of any quality is Mills, the Under-Secretary, who does not pretend to knowledge he does not possess. Also, according to Paisley, Prior, the Leader of the House, is quite hopeless—and arrogant as well. Heath is to be seen in the lobby far more often recently.

Tuesday, May 1st, 1973

Supper and the *St Matthew Passion* with the Weinstocks last night. It was a friendly social occasion and there was no political talk. Arnold said he had been asked to take on the sorting out of our atomic energy affairs because there was no one else. He was reluctant and offered to help—free—anyone who took it on, but there was no one else. Further acquaintance has raised his opinion of Boardman—Minister for Industry. He is a solicitor by trade, and was publicity man for the beer trade. Arnold says he knows nothing about industry but has sound judgment. Arnold's opinion of Heseltine, the Aerospace Minister, has, on the other hand, fallen to a low level. Arnold, like others, neither likes nor respects Peter Walker. He says it is nonsense to talk about delegation—as Walker does—unless you choose the men to whom you delegate. Walker has seven or nine Junior Ministers, chosen for various reasons by the P.M. They are no band of brothers chosen by Walker to make a success of his Ministry.

Monday, May 7th, 1973

There is a violent attack on Government economic policy by Peter Jay in *The Times* today—a great contrast to Tony Barber's complacent utterances on the radio yesterday. Jay's general theme, which seems to me unanswerable, is that to generate a consumer boom by running a huge Budget deficit is bound to run the country into serious trouble, and that before very long. To me it looks like an exaggerated version of Maudling's 'dash for freedom' in 1963. And to argue that by floating the pound you can ignore balance-of-payments problems seems to me obviously unsound.

Meanwhile Ted is to meet the T.U.C. to hammer out an agreed Prices and Incomes Policy for Phase 3. I cannot imagine the T.U.C. agreeing to anything really practical, and even if they did, they cannot impose any policy on all their members. And Ted's declared policy—renewed from time to time—that more must be done for the low-paid worker, for the pensioner, and for women, accentuates the impact of the consumer boom while doing nothing for the welfare of the economy as a whole.

The main political interest these days is in the Watergate affair in the United States. This has now been dragging on for ten months. It is only in the last three that it has really caught the public attention. According to English ideas the President has no alternative but to resign; according to the ideas of other countries and other times he has no alternative but to commit suicide. In the United States, neither course is likely and impeachment is such a clumsy weapon that its employment might well destroy the whole political fabric of the country. Meanwhile, Nixon has nearly four years to go. He has had to dismiss all his senior staff except Kissinger; fresh revelations are published daily in one or other of the papers. Last Monday, Nixon said the whole matter was to be probed to the bottom, and yet on Friday he forbade any past or present member of his staff to reveal particulars of anything that occurred between him and them. If this means anything, it means that Nixon now knows he is a desperate man in a very tight corner. It has always been said that Mrs Nixon is the best part of the Nixon household, and it is interesting that she has kept right out of sight in all this.

Tuesday, May 8th, 1973

We met the Eccleses at A.G. Benney's party at the Goldsmiths Hall. Ruth asked David how Ted is these days. Eccles said he was fine, very confident that he has everything under control! I suppose this has to be read in conjunction with Nixon's flounderings. Nixon has evidently, until very recently, had no idea of what a mess he is in. These top chaps do manage to isolate themselves from what is going on.

Canon Bolton told Ruth on the telephone that his son-in-law's father, the head of the Firestone company, was to have been the new American Ambassador in London. Following the Watergate affair he has asked not to be considered any longer for the post.

Wednesday, May 9th, 1973

At a *Financial Times* conference yesterday Barber delivered a lyrical survey of the economy—the usual stuff, only more so: the British economy had never been in such fine shape, etc., etc. At the annual Plowden party yesterday Beeching, Weinstock, Plowden and Ezra offered no confirmation of this glowing picture. What may be more significant is that the Stock Exchange is, and remains, weak. Good company reports evoke no response at all. Beeching's and Weinstock's point is that the economy is slow to respond, and corrective steps should have taken place months ago. Following Peter Jay in *The Times* on Monday, we had the *Financial Times* leader yesterday warning the Government that the economy was becoming overheated, and that 'red lights were flashing'.

Later. Lunch for A.B. [a senior civil servant]. I asked what was the point of the tripartite talks on which the Government seems so keen? The C.B.I. did not really matter in this context, and the T.U.C. in the end would not agree to anything, and anyway would be unable to honour any undertaking entered into. He said this was a correct assessment, but that it was hoped that while talks continued it would be easier to keep rank and file trades-union members in their present co-operative mood.

I asked why Barber is so optimistic in his public pronouncements? A.B. said this is because he is a very optimistic little man. I said it is generally supposed that he wants to be moved from the Treasury; is this because at heart he is not as optimistic as he sounds? A.B. thought this is not the explanation, and said that he had been talking of a move since last summer. The Treasury is a gruelling job anyway, and of recent years they have felt compelled to add a lot of foreign travel to the inevitable burden. I said it has been supposed that any big Government shuffle depended on Alec Home's retirement, but he shows no signs of going. A.B. says that friends of Alec's say he has no intention of retiring, but one close friend told A.B. recently that he will go this summer (he is seventy in July).

A.B. seemed to assume a balance-of-payments crisis in the not distant future. He said it could be taken on a sinking exchange rate, but this would lead to a rise in the price of imported food. I asked if the dicky exchange rate would not earn us sour looks from our Continental friends. He said so what! Ted was so keen to get into Europe, but now seems quite indifferent to the views and wishes of our new-found partners.

A.B. thought our efforts at a managed economy had produced trade cycles of about four years, instead of the seven-year cycles of Victorian times. He thought price control a bad idea—rising prices have a deflationary effect. In any case, control of prices would not reduce the cost of living by more than a quarter of 1 per cent.

I said I was interested in Ireland, and sorry that Whitelaw had shown evidence of a velvet glove but none of a steel fist inside. A.B. said, in so far as there was a steel fist in that office it was that of Sir William Nield. When he moved to become deputy chairman of Rolls Royce (1971), there was no more steel fist.

Kissinger is here just now, and the great problem in dealing with him is his insistence that anything he says to H.M. Government must not be passed on to the American Embassy here, or to the State Department in Washington. I asked if this is on instructions from Nixon, or if it is Kissinger protecting his own position? A.B. did not know—but what a way to run a railway!

The recent strikes or semi-strikes by gas workers and hospital auxiliaries got nowhere because they were not prepared to be ruthless and cause hundreds or thousands of deaths. The miners' threatened strike came to nothing mainly because of the absence of Lawrence Daly, the miners' secretary. A.B. did not know what the trouble was (and is?), but at the time Daly was in hospital and not allowed to use the telephone.

Thursday, May 10th, 1973

Reflecting on my talk with A.B. yesterday, two further points come to mind. They arose from my saying that it is surprising that socialists, who believe by definition in nationalization, are so little interested in making a success of the nationalized industries. A.B. said he thought the drive towards nationalization was not due to any underlying philosophy, but to a vague hostility to capitalism as such. In a mixed economy, such as we admittedly have, the only dynamic sector is the private one. If the private sector is sufficiently trammelled and confined the whole economy will slow down. I said the Government departments responsible for the nationalized industries will not leave well alone. A.B. agreed, and said that a satisfactory relationship had never been established. Under the Labour Government they had thought they had arrived at the right formula but eventually this had been killed by Lord Diamond. Now under this Government any pretence that nationalized industries are to be treated like commercial concerns has been totally abandoned.

Lunch today for Dick Briginshaw of SOGAT. He is getting old and losing interest. However, in the course of the meal he volunteered the opinion that it would be impossible for any future government to back out of the Common Market—and he was a strong anti-Marketeer. He also agreed that talks between the Government and the T.U.C. could get nowhere. There is no policy on which the two sides could agree, and anyway (as Briginshaw said) there is no means by which the T.U.C. negotiators could ensure the carrying out of an agreement, if they made one, by the individual unions and their members.

Sunday, May 20th, 1973

On the Irish front little has been happening of recent weeks—the violence continues; preparations go forward for local elections next week, and for the Assembly elections at the end of next month. Paisley is quite confident that whatever the results of the latter he can make the Government White Paper policy unworkable. He wants integration with Great Britain; but if this is not to be had, sees a way out in self-government within the Commonwealth. There are reports from Dublin that the new Government there is considering the recognition of the independence of the Province.

The economic situation is more prominent in the news than Ireland. The consumer boom has spread to some extent to heavy industry, and all the unions with wage claims outstanding have settled for raises within the £1 plus 6-per-cent guide-lines. Prices are rising faster than had been expected and no one has any clear idea what the Government has in mind for Phase 3 from October. The T.U.C. are having talks with the P.M., but it is difficult to see how there can be any constructive outcome. Does Ted even expect one? The unions evidently do not. The boom may end in a successful election, but the price is bound to be high and prolonged. An aspect of the economic affairs that is increasingly worrying is the lack of confidence in the dollar and the soaring price of gold, which has been as high as $110. The Stock Exchanges here and in New York are sluggish, if not weak, which can only mean that the international financial community has no confidence in the present set-up.

Nor is this helped by the Watergate affair, which makes fascinating reading. There is now no effective American Government, nor any means of knowing when one will be firmly in the saddle. It would clearly be best for everyone if Nixon were to resign. If he won't, the effect of prosecutions, senatorial inquiries and newspaper revelations can only be to discredit the American constitution as it has recently operated. The Americans may get themselves into a situation where the President can't govern, won't be impeached, and won't resign, while all his intimates are totally discredited. It has always been said by constitutional pundits here, that in a grave emergency the American constitution won't work. In the coming months we shall see if this is true.

Thursday, May 24th, 1973

The Watergate affair rumbles on. The President's position gets more and more difficult, but it is not clear that he realizes this.

Here at home we have a rerun of the Profumo business—Lords Lambton and Jellicoe have confessed to having employed call-girls in Maida Vale and have resigned. They are quite useless as Ministers, and there will be no difficulty in finding someone else to lead the House of Lords in place of Jellicoe. Ted, in making a statement this afternoon, went out of his way to say he knew all about it before it was headlined—without names—in the *News of the World*. It would have been better for his press relations if he had praised newspaper vigilance, as they knew of the story months before he did.

Lunch yesterday for Gerald Thompson, chairman of Kleinwort Benson. I asked why the Stock Exchange was so sluggish when the Government was so euphoric. In any case, reports are good, but shares don't respond. In a time of inflation surely ordinary shares should boom—as land and antiques are booming? He said land and antiques are in limited supply—a supply that cannot be increased. The value of shares ultimately depends on the well-being of the economy. Our economy is being destroyed by inflation, and the effect on ordinary shares is not readily foreseeable. Once a week he and his chaps meet to talk investments, but they are inclined to keep liquid and earn interest in the short-money market until they can see their way ahead more clearly.

I said that in a time of inflation banks should do well—merchant and other—as they deal in money and there is plenty of that. He said that was so, and though the City performed an essential function and was one of the only successful areas of our economy, there was too much money to be made there too easily. George Bolton's son was making £30,000 a year before he was thirty, and he was not the only young man making £1,000 per annum for every year of his age.

He spoke about the two-tier boards of German companies. There is talk here of adopting the idea as a sop to the trades unions. Thompson said this idea emerged in Germany for quite a different reason. During the inflation German banks acquired big blocks of shares in most German enterprises. The two-tier board was a device to eliminate—or anyway reduce—the overwhelming influence of the banks in running industrial enterprises.

Thompson was asking why the standard of integrity in our affairs had gone down over the last century. I said surely the reason was the decline of religion. He said, 'Too true, and how can a real sense of responsibility be recovered until we return to a belief in a Higher Power to whom we are all responsible?'

Friday, May 25th, 1973

The results of two by-elections were announced today. They were safe Labour seats, but the Conservatives did very badly. The interesting aspect was that at West Bromwich the National Front candidate got 16 per cent of the vote—presumably by playing up the immigrant aspect.

Lunch for Stonehouse, who said he was enjoying life as never before with his Bangladesh Bank and other business enterprises. He said he believes in public ownership, but the use of the profit motive to keep nationalized businesses on course.

He said most of his fellow Labour M.P.s were dreamers, with no sense of the practical or the possible. He thought Wilson was growing old, and his leadership would not survive another defeat at the polls. He thought the boom would last into next year and might well give Ted another victory. He said Ministers are only concerned with one thing—to win the next election. He said Tory M.P.s show a marked deterioration from their standard of twenty years ago. They were now opportunists who sought office, not power, and their ambitions were not buttressed by principles of any kind.

Of Ministers, he thought Keith Joseph was an asset and that Tony Barber was coming on.

The *Daily Mail* says today the call-girl scandal has badly shaken Ted's Government. I am more inclined to agree with the *Financial Times* which says that this event is so foreign to Ted's administration that it will not affect it. Why the Watergate affair is so damaging to Nixon, is that it fully bears out everything Nixon's enemies have said about him since 1946.

Monday, May 28th, 1973

The papers are still full of Lambton and the call-girls—and another Minister may be involved. But the cod war with Iceland is warming up and may prove important. Not many years ago Iceland put its territorial limits out from three miles off-shore to twelve. Then a few months ago the Icelandic Government extended the limits to fifty. This was important, because fifty miles out from all the shores bordering the Arctic Ocean would deprive us of almost all our fishing grounds. We took them to the International Court, whose jurisdiction the Icelanders repudiated, and since then we have been bleating for 'talks' while the Icelanders have done their best to prevent our trawlers fishing within fifty miles of their coast. Now they have fired on one of our trawlers and very nearly sank it, while we have moved three frigates into Icelandic waters. Surely on the original unilateral announcement by the Iceland Government we should have reverted to the three-mile limit and moved all available trawlers and naval vessels into Icelandic waters. If it had been done at once, the Icelanders would have come to heel. Now they see no reason why they should make any concessions, particularly when our negotiator is Lady Tweedsmuir.

Saturday, June 2nd, 1973

The news today and yesterday has been the local elections in Ulster. The papers represent the result as a triumph for Faulkner and do not mention Paisley. Paisley has been on the phone and says this is nonsense. The new local authorities have hardly any power and Paisley has not bothered with them, but some of his followers have put themselves forward and are in. The Unionists are nominally Faulkner's followers, but no one knows what proportion accept his views on the White Paper. I expected the Alliance Party to do badly—which it did. Northern Ireland Labour has been all but wiped out. The Protestants, in spite of proportional representation, have done well except in Londonderry, which is a mainly Catholic town. I think the outcome of the elections at the end of the month will be that the White Paper is dead. However, so far the newspapers and television have followed Faulkner and Ministers in their optimistic propaganda.

Yesterday lunch with Weinstock and the directors of G.E.C. There was considerable agreement that our present Parliamentary set-up is not working and will be replaced. Weinstock was contemptuous of insurance salesmen in politics—Edwin Leather, ex-M.P., and the new Governor of the Bahamas and Peter Walker. The result of the next general election was thought to be quite open. Humphrey Trevelyan spoke highly of Windlesham and Lady Tweedsmuir—God knows why. The main discussion was over a consortium they were forming for bidding for the underground railway contract in Hong Kong. The first phase might cost £300 million and involves a lot of unknowns. The equipment would be sold at the normal profit, which would not exceed 4 per cent and which involved great risks. They would be competing against a Japanese consortium organized by Jardine Matheson & Co., a French group and an Italo-German group. With the recent exchange changes German and Japanese prices tend to be higher than ours. The sharpest competition comes from the Americans.

Tuesday, June 5th, 1973

Had a few words yesterday with O'Sullivan, the Irish Ambassador, at Lady Kelly's party. Two surprising facts emerged: (1) the Irish Government is strongly opposed to the Ulstermen getting twenty Westminster M.P.s instead of the existing twelve. I wonder why this is so; (2) he asked if there was any chance of Paisley becoming non-violent. He is apparently unaware that it is Paisley who has done more than anyone else to damp down violence on the Protestant side. Why are Governments not better informed?

Friday, June 8th, 1973

Mrs Paisley rang up to say the English newspapers seem reluctant to mention Paisley's name, and play down his activities as much as possible. However, he has seventeen Paisleyite candidates, and twenty-eight others running under different names but pledged to work with him if they get in. I don't think Paisley expects a majority of the 78 or 80 seats, but he is fairly confident that he will have a large enough bloc to make the White Paper unworkable.

Tuesday, June 12th, 1973

Two nights near Gloucester. At dinner we met one Burnet, now second or third man at the National Westminster Bank. The banks are being blamed for making too much money, but this is an inevitable consequence of soaring money supply and inflation. Burnet thought the banks do too little to state their case. He seemed to have no illusions about the Government's allegedly anti-inflation policy. In the case of the National Westminster, while deposits and advances balance the banks' capital is largely in cash, depreciating in value at 10 per cent per annum.

Peter Walker at lunch today delivered a speech saying our economy is now on the threshold of a golden age. Can he really believe this? The Bank of England has put out a statement in its Bulletin that any signs of over-heating must be treated immediately. As O'Brien lost his job for not being subservient enough, I take it that the interpretation of this warning is that the economy is already over-heated and remedial steps should be taken now.

Saturday, June 16th, 1973

In Warsaw. I have not been here for eight years, and the improvement in the general well-being of the public is very obvious. Clothes are of poor quality, and mostly made at home, but there are no poor, as that condition used to be understood. The new housing is unattractive but there is an enormous building programme in hand. If it is a police state there is nothing of the kind obviously apparent. The rate of exchange is officially 85 zlotys to the pound, but the head-waiter in the hotel restaurant offered me twice that for £1, and three times for £10—offers I did not accept. 85 may be unrealistically low, but 240 seems to me to have no bearing on our respective price levels. Pay seems very low. At the *Prasa* magazine printing works we were shown the pay sheets for a number of ordinary workers. Assuming a forty-hour week, and the official rate of exchange, wages worked out at around £12 per week. At the black market rate the wage would be half or less. Women are paid the same as men for the same work, and the proportion of women in the factory was far higher than it would be in the U.K.

The Polish word for German is 'Niemiecki'. I asked the derivation of the word, so different from ours and the French. I was told it meant, 'the people who cannot speak'—presumably speak Polish.

I had an hour with one Krasko, pronounced Crashko. He is an eminent Parliamentary figure. The presidency is a Commission and he is one of the Commission. He is also chairman of the Foreign Affairs Committee of the Sejm (Parliament). He is a very nice man and an intelligent one. I suggested that the long-term policy of the United States must be to withdraw from Europe, so why do not the East European countries welcome the Common Market, as a first step towards the unification of all Europe 'from the Atlantic to the Urals'? No response. I said we find Russians very hard to understand and isn't there a role here for the Poles—Western and Catholic on the one hand but East European and Slav on the other? I got the impression that they find the Russians as difficult as we do and do not see themselves as effective intermediaries.

I asked Krasko and others about the Watergate affair. The official line is that this is a minor affair, blown up by sinister forces in the United States to unseat Nixon and stop the American–Russian rapprochement. This seems to me total nonsense. The witch hunt, as it would be called here, was for months the work of Kay Graham of the *Washington Post*, almost unaided—and she certainly had no axe to grind. Moreover, there is no reason to suppose that if Nixon were unseated he would be succeeded by a President pledged to any different policy vis-à-vis the Russians. What I find so frightening about international affairs is the way the super-powers are often ill-informed and display appallingly bad judgment, e.g. over Vietnam, the Bay of Pigs, the missile crisis in Cuba, etc., etc.

Wednesday, June 20th, 1973

Last night at a music party at Windsor we met an immense variety of well-known people—Harold Lever and Denis Healey particularly friendly. Douglas Houghton said he was afraid the Government White Paper plan for Northern Ireland would not work, but that no one seemed to be looking beyond the end of this month. Ted Heath seemed to be the only Tory Minister present, but I had no chance to talk to him. Angus Ogilvy has had a lashing over the Lonrho affair. He was strongly advised not to offer any explanation of his part in the company's affairs. What did I think? I said I always believed in telling the truth, whatever misuse might be made of it. In fact his case has gone by default, which is a pity. Mrs Lever told Ruth she could never be sufficiently grateful for my book. It was the first Lever had to read after his stroke—and he was enthralled! Roy Jenkins looks diminished, as well he may be—perhaps he never really recovered from the Party's defeat in 1970. Healey, on the other hand, seems much more resilient.

Friday, June 22nd, 1973
Reflecting on the Windsor party on Tuesday, a surprising aspect was the behaviour of Ted Heath. He was seated next Princess Anne at the Duke of Edinburgh's table, but both before dinner and after he was seen talking to no one else except Anne! It was a distinguished gathering and he could have taken the opportunity to talk to people he might not often meet.

Sunday, June 24th, 1973
Paisley on the telephone—very tired after weeks of campaigning. The newspapers forecast great victory for Faulkner, but Paisley says this is rubbish. His tour through two counties yesterday was like a royal progress, while Faulkner has had an unfriendly reception. Paisley wonders why the English newspapers are so ill-informed or biased. Perhaps they are too readily talked into agreement with the views of Whitelaw and Faulkner.

Gordon Tether in Friday's *Financial Times* was deeply pessimistic about the future of world trade under the impact of continuing inflation. Meanwhile, the unions are reasserting their militancy. Chrysler—formerly Rootes—has had to undergo a total humiliation at the hands of its strikers, while Scanlon has been instructed by his members to boycott the Downing St talks. The Government is now coming round to the idea of food subsidies to restrain wage demands. These would be inflationary and the impact on wage demands would be only temporary.

Saturday, June 30th, 1973
The two important items of news are the further revaluation of the mark—and the Irish elections. The first is due to the weakness of the dollar, due in its turn to a very unfavourable balance of trade, to growing inflation and to a lack of any leadership from the White

House. Financial opinion in the City still lacks confidence, either in the Heath Government or in the future.

The Government, and the media, seem to have assumed that Faulkner would emerge triumphant from the Northern Irish elections. Much as Heath dislikes and distrusts Faulkner, he was, for some not obvious reason, preferred to Paisley, who has been consistently played down. The results of the election are not all in, but it seems that the Paisley coalition has 26 seats to Faulkner's 19, the S.D.L.P. has 18, and Alliance 5, with 10 to go. Alliance has done very much worse than the Government thought and hoped; they are probably now supposing that Paisley's coalition will be a fragile affair. According to Paisley, however, Faulkner's following includes a number whose loyalty to Faulkner is very uncertain. When they see how badly he has done they may well rat on him.

Monday, July 2nd, 1973

The final Irish results were 22 Official Unionists plus one other Faulknerite, 27 Paisley–Craig coalition, 19 S.D.L.P., 8 Alliance and 1 Northern Irish Labour. The S.D.L.P. did better than anyone expected: Alliance and Faulkner did worse than the Government expected. Judging by the papers the Government is desperately hoping that a Faulkner–S.D.L.P. administration can be made to work. In all the material put out by the media Paisley is played down and Faulkner grossly played up. From our various contacts the Republicans sounded depressed; Paisley triumphant; and No. 10 badly shaken by the results.

Tuesday, July 3rd, 1973

Paisley looked in this morning on his way to the House. He is very pleased with the way things have gone. Of Faulkner's 22 members, 3 are opposed to the White Paper, and others will desert him if they see he is on his way down (as Paisley thinks he is). Paisley saw Whitelaw yesterday—thin, white and jittery, and deeply disappointed by the result. The Government apparently expected the Alliance to do well and, failing them, big support for Faulkner. There is now talk of a Faulkner/S.D.L.P. executive. Paisley says this could not work, as a partnership with Faulkner would split the S.D.L.P. Paisley's policy is to demand full integration with the U.K., with control of the police, as elsewhere in the U.K., and with the appropriate number of M.P.s.

The Northern Irish are, quite unjustifiably, terrified of a deal between London and Dublin over their heads, so Cosgrave's remarks about the cordial nature of the talks between himself and Ted will have a sinister sound in Belfast. I imagine they are courtesy phrases, with no more than superficial meaning.

We heard last night to our surprise that Peter McLachlan, who was Ruth's secretary at the National Youth Orchestra, has been elected as a Faulkner Unionist.

Lunch for Hugh Fraser, just back from Japan. He told Whitelaw some months ago that Paisley would come well out of the election but Whitelaw would not believe him.

Hugh has a friend, an officer in the Brigade of Guards, just back from a tour of duty in Northern Ireland. While they were there forty of his men bought themselves out of the Army, as their wives would not have them being shot at in Ireland. Meanwhile, partly because of the boom, but partly because of Ireland, the recruiting figure for April this year was half the number for April 1972. Elworthy, who was Chief of the Air Staff when Fraser was Minister for Air, subsequently became chairman of the Chiefs of Staff, and in that position warned the Government that after two years the morale of the Army in Northern Ireland could be expected to slip. The Government has ignored the warning. Denis Healey, when Minister of Defence, told me that troops could only be used for a limited time on police duties.

Fraser is, in fact, a merchant banker and says that in the City there is no confidence in the Government. There are very large sums being held liquid as no one has sufficient confidence to give them a permanent home. Fraser does not think there will be an election this autumn. He does think we shall have exchange controls within twelve months.

Wednesday, July 4th, 1973

Lunch for Nicholas Ridley. He figured prominently in today's papers because yesterday he presided over a meeting of the Finance Committee of Conservative back-benchers. He may not have been a very effecctive Minister, but he is an attractive and highly intelligent person. He thinks he was dismissed from office for having a mind of his own. He said he had recently sent in to three newspapers pieces critical of Government policy. They were all returned with an apologetic note from each editor explaining that he was not publishing attacks on the Government at the present time. Ridley thinks Ted has put pressure on the proprietors, as the editors on their own would have published his contributions.

Ridley's main theme was that until recently Ted honestly believed his policy was working. Any extravagance would be looked after by 'economic growth' without inflation. Now he knows that this is not so—that the money-supply explanation of inflation contains after all an important element of truth. So there will be yet another U-turn: family allowances to be increased; food subsidies; threshold wage agreements—the lot. The effect of course will be to treat some of the symptoms of inflation, while making the disease worse. Ted's sudden realization that his policy is not working makes an October election quite possible—contingency plans, anyway, are already being laid. Hitherto Ted has been confident that he has the next election in the bag. Now he feels that if something effective is not done about prices he will not win the election, whenever it is held.

Ridley thought Biffen the ablest member of the House of Commons. He thinks well of Tugendhat (M.P. for Westminster and the City) but says he is a socialist, all in favour of food subsidies and increased Government expenditure.

Ridley had a wonderful example of the sycophancy of M.P.s. He put forward an amendment to the anti-inflation Bill that was ultimately successful, limiting the life of the Act to three years. He approached twelve M.P.s, who he knew were favourable to the amendment, for their signatures—three signed; four said they were not standing again at the next election, and were afraid their signatures would damage their chances of a reward for twenty years of faithful service to the Party; the remaining five also refused to sign, giving as their reason that they were new to the House and did not want to prejudice their chances of future ministerial office!

Ireland is still hitting the headlines. Ruth saw A.B. at No. 10 this evening. The Government is bent on down-pointing Paisley, in spite of his success at the election. They are hoping that a coalition of Faulkner, the S.D.L.P. and Alliance can be cobbled together to make the new executive work. I do not think this plan will get off the ground, but even if it does the divergence of outlook and personality in such a heterogeneous collection of people makes it certain that a break-up would not be long delayed.

Thursday, July 5th, 1973

Tony Bloomfield rang up in something of a tizzy over the currency situation. The dollar and sterling are still going down; the mark has been revalued but is still strong; antiques and works of art are booming; property is still in strong demand; equities are not strong; gilt-edged are weak. Tony has some millions to invest and does not know what to do, so they remain in the short-loan market, earning 6½ per cent—less than the rate of inflation. Inflation should produce a strong equity market but it has not done so here or elsewhere.

Tether has a very gloomy piece in the *Financial Times* today. It is difficult to know what to do; even more difficult to get the advanced countries to agree on anything; and, in the case of the United States, the Watergate affair means that at the moment there is no real government in Washington at all.

The House of Commons is becoming seriously worried about rising prices. But these are symptoms and proposed measures are likely to make inflation worse.

The pessimists are afraid that we are in for another 1929; of course it will be different in form, though it might be equally disastrous in effect.

Tuesday, July 10th, 1973

We dined with the Murtons on Friday (he is Tory M.P. for Poole). He had no news. He spoke highly of Carr as Home Secretary, and of Prior as Leader of the House. Toby Jessel came to lunch on Sunday—a wee bit less optimistic than usual, and making contingency plans for an autumn election. Neither of these M.P.s gave any impression of uneasiness—let alone alarm.

Meanwhile the economic and financial situation is once more a shambles. Friday was very bad and yesterday not much better. The dollar and the pound have been under great pressure, while wholesale and commodity prices of all kinds have been rising. The central bankers had their monthly meeting at Basle and came up with one of the most meaningless comminiqués ever. The Americans seem disinclined to do anything, and without American co-operation it is hard to see what others can achieve. Barber said yesterday that whatever happened in the currency market the Government is going to press on with 'growth'. Their only cure for inflation is more of the same—apparently. Gordon Tether, on the back page of the *Financial Times*, has been very alarmist these last few days—and rightly so.

To add to the general confusion, the unions are becoming increasingly aggressive—engineers, miners, newspaper workers, and now railwaymen, with transport workers to follow later this week.

On 'Panorama' last night the manager of the Dresden Bank was asked what he thought should be done, and he recommended a mild degree of deflation. Brian Walden dismissed this idea out of hand, said it would lead to $1\frac{1}{2}$ million unemployed, and no Government concerned with re-election could look at such a policy. I admire Walden; he has a very clear head and says out loud what other people conceal. What he said was the normal political reaction, and proves that our Parliamentary democracy is no longer a viable form of government. The refusal to face issues and the constant postponement of unpopular decisions must mean the crash will be that much worse when it does come.

Wednesday, July 11th, 1973

Dinner last night with the John Stevenses. John had recently spent three days in Peter Walker's company on an official trip to Moscow. He said Walker is able, intelligent, ambitious and energetic, but he would hate to be deeply involved with him in any transaction. Walker intends to be Prime Minister, but has to shake off his association with Jim Slater, who has been under fire lately and does not seem to have cleared himself completely. Stevens confirmed that Barber is anxious not to bring in another Budget. His stock with the P.M. is not as high as it was, as he incurred Ted's wrath at the time Leslie O'Brien was sacked.

Some time ago a report was published suggesting that the Department of Trade and industry should have a bigger say in City affairs. This did not get much attention and disappeared from view. However, at Gordon Richardson's first Committee of the Treasury meeting this report was brought forward again. Walker evidently does not give up easily. It infuriates the Bank which, in any case, is becoming more and more a department of the Treasury.

Stevens has had private information that the possibility of an autumn election is being considered. It appears that Ted is not concerned over the fall in the exchange rate of the pound. This is hard to understand as he *is* concerned over rising prices.

Stevens was recently in Washington, where he saw something of Rowley Cromer, who is getting towards the end of his period at the Embassy. Apparently he was to have been succeeded by Jellicoe.

The appointment had almost got to the point of seeking the agreement of the American government. Now that is off and no new appointment has been decided on.

Stevens is chairman and managing director of Morgan Grenfell, who are the financial agents of the Vatican in this country. They have dealings with the Vatican over two funds: one presided over by a Monsignor of the greatest culture and discretion, a real eighteenth-century figure; the other run by an American bishop, of Lithuanian origin, from Chicago. Of the two Stevens thought the first the better financial man.

In the course of his activities Stevens has had to transact business in the financial departments of both the Vatican and the Kremlin. The setting in both cases is remarkably similar—austere, bare rooms and a green baize-top table with a carafe of water. The main difference was that the only picture was in one case of the Pope, and in the other of Lenin.

Stevens said the behaviour of the Prices Board is a bit hard to follow. A friend of his, one Borthwick, is a meat importer who recently bought up a firm making meat pies. These people put in a request to the Price Commission for a 14 per cent increase in price which was immediately granted. Borthwick had had nothing to do with this, but said there were quite inadequate grounds for the increase.

Thursday, July 12th, 1973

Lunch yesterday at the *News of the World* with Rupert Murdoch and senior members of his staff.

On Fleet Street, they said the *Mirror* and *Express* were losing money; the *Express* was also losing sales. The *Daily Mail* was doing better. Roy Thomson was losing a lot on his travel business. At I.P.C. the magazines and trade papers were doing brilliantly; the newspapers were not doing well, except for the *Sunday Mirror*. They thought it gained from being the only Sunday tabloid. They thought the *Sunday Times* had moved so far to the Left it made things very difficult for the *Observer*.

The *Express* group was losing money on the daily, making money on the *Evening Standard*, and making a packet on the *Sunday*. Jocelyn Stevens is very active in its affairs. Recently they had a plan to reduce the size of the editorial staff and offered special redundancy payments to those prepared to go. Naturally the best journalists all applied—as they could get jobs elsewhere. One man on £6,000 per annum took £10,000 and went to the *Mail* at £7,000. The *Express* had lost so many good men they felt they had to have this one back—which they did at £9,500 per annum!

Tuesday, July 17th, 1973
Lunch with C.D. [a senior civil servant] yesterday. From what he didn't say I got the impression that he has been sadly disappointed by the Heath administration, does not like the outlook, and is counting the days to his retirement. He urged me several times to see William Whitelaw, which I will endeavour to do. I have not seen him for many months as I thought he had lost his way, and any talk we had would necessarily be critical on my side. However, if C.D. thinks a talk would be helpful, I will have a go.

Thursday, July 19th, 1973
Lunch yesterday at Kleinwort Benson, my hosts being Gerald Thompson and Cyril Kelinwort. The latter is a very nice man but no ball of fire. They were wondering what the City could do about our inflationary troubles. I was wondering why, judging by prices on the Stock Exchange, investors did not see ordinary shares as the main available hedge against inflation. Clearly, only the Government can effectively tackle inflation, though so far its policy has been to apply palliatives. On the second point they all said inflation was destroying our society, and that in a destroyed economy shares would have no value. I should have thought the same would apply to land, antiques and works of art, but they did not see it that way. Kleinwort's great source of comfort was that public opinion was the decisive factor, and the public would never let the trades unions destroy the currency.

Friday, July 20th, 1973
I spent the best part of an hour with Willie Whitelaw in his office this afternoon. I had not seen him for about a year and the meeting was at the urgent suggestion of others. In spite of all that has been said about the deterioration in Willie from the strain of Ireland, I saw little difference. The purpose of my visit was to expound the views I had expressed to others: (1) power-sharing could not possibly work; (2) Paisley is the dominant personality in Northern Ireland; (3) he wants integration with England—a demand which includes

twenty M.P.s at Westminster instead of twelve and control of the police (to raise the number of M.P.s would end the bi-partisan approach to Irish affairs, so Paisley's request must be rejected); (4) the British public don't want integration, and the Government could not grant control of the police; (5) in that event, he might have to ask for independence within the Commonwealth—this would involve the withdrawal of British troops, but a continuing financial commitment; (6) the Government's attitude to this idea is said to be that it would lead to a blood-bath—the Catholics would be massacred—but I had been informed by Paisley, and by militant Catholics that they did not think this would happen; (7) the latter would see the departure of the British Army as a great step forward.

Whitelaw was very discreet, but gave me the clear impression that he had not considered the possibility of independence. He said Paisley has said such outrageous things that he is regarded with horror by the S.D.L.P. and by the middle-class Protestants who look to Faulkner. I said that Irishmen do say outrageous things about each other, and such pronouncements are not to be taken too seriously. Willie said Paisley had denounced Catholics in the most offensive terms, as well as the Government in Dublin.

Willie was well aware that though they got few votes, the men with the guns—on both sides—are to be taken very seriously.

Talking about integration, he agreed that the British public would not welcome the idea and he did not see how H.M.G. could relinquish control of the police, but he thought the number of M.P.s was negotiable. He thought that out of twenty, seven or so would be Republicans. Hitherto it has been assumed that they would be Unionists and so would generally vote with the Conservatives. He seemed doubtful about a continuing financial commitment, anyway for any prolonged period. But I pointed out that the Irish Republic received many economic and financial benefits from this country.

Willie agreed that Paisley is a dominating and eloquent personality, but complained that his words and his deeds often conflict, and that it is hard to be sure what he is really up to. The Assembly meets on July 31st, and has to be working at latest by next March. However, Willie will not drag out the probationary period for as long as that. He will want to have it working fairly soon—or else close it down as an executive body.

Saturday, July 28th, 1973

On Friday of last week the Government put up the minimum lending rate from $7\frac{1}{2}$ per cent to 9 per cent and yesterday it was further increased to $11\frac{1}{2}$ per cent. The first increase had no effect; the second seems to have halted the slide in the exchange rate of the pound. Interest rates on the Continent are far higher, so it remains to be seen how effective this move will be. The money supply is growing fast, and the unions are increasingly intransigent, but Ministers are apparently quite happy. Yesterday the by-elections at Ripon and Ely were won by the Liberals. These were regarded as absolutely safe Tory strongholds.

There is an article in *The Times* this morning by Julian Critchley M.P., saying that these days the smoking-room and the Chamber of the House of Commons, nominally the two most important areas of the House, are very poorly attended. Debates arouse little interest outside the House and, he suggests, back-bench M.P.s are losing interest in their own institution.

Last night Ruth met young Lord Baden-Powell, grandson of the founder of the Boy Scouts, at dinner. He is a very unpolitical man, but he does attend the House of Lords. He told Ruth he gave the present Parliamentary set-up two years before it dissolves in anarchy. If the regime cannot keep the Baden-Powells of this world on their side they are in deep trouble.

Monday, July 30th, 1973

Lunch for Edwin Plowden. He had no particular news. His company, Tube Investments, is going great guns, but the shares are low and falling. Plowden thinks the dismal prices on the Stock Exchange are a mixture of no confidence in the Government and the anticipation of really serious industrial unrest in the autumn. His company's order book is so full, that he thinks the boom may well last over most of next year. When this Government came into office he thought they were right to continue Roy Jenkins's deflationary policy. But they kept it on too long, hence the million unemployed, and hence the subsequent panic and our present inflationary troubles.

Recently six M.P.s on television were to meet a representative audience of the general public to discuss why the prestige of politicians was so low. The 'representatives' of the general public proved to be selected left-wingers who abused the M.P.s, and the programme was a shambles. Swann, chairman of the B.B.C., after consultation with two senior members of the B.B.C. staff, wrote and apologized to the M.P.s, whereupon a Mr Wilcox, who organized the programme, complained he had not been consulted about the apology, and he and his friends have been making a great noise. The whole episode goes to show how the media have been influenced, and how unwilling to do anything about it are the authorities —in Fleet Street or in the B.B.C.

Plowden thinks we are heading for a dictatorship, but sees no candidate for the post of dictator. He thinks Powell too old.

Wednesday, August 1st, 1973

Went to see Mike at Lockeridge yesterday. He takes up his new job at Imperial Tobacco on Monday. He says Heath's unqualified optimism is due to boom conditions in industry, as reported by the C.B.I. When I said this optimism was not reflected in the City, where the Stock Exchange sees declining share prices, Mike held forth on the poor judgment of the City. I take it that this is the Establishment view. Actually, prices are not determined by the City but by the majority of the investing public here and abroad. Soaring prices for commodities and declining prices for shares show the entire lack of confidence in the economy and the Government felt by the commercial, industrial and financial leaders.

Lunch for John Peyton, Minister of Transport. Of course he is very discreet and talks mainly in generalities—no names, no pack-drill. However, he was clearly in favour of the Channel tunnel and hoped and believed it would be proceeded with. He evidently thinks the proposed Foulness airport (now called Maplin) is a mistake, but mercifully it is not his responsibility. He thought again, as he told me last time we met, that the situation in this country would continue to deteriorate until people were frightened. What we needed was a sense of national unity, which was not to be had under present circumstances. Time-keeping in business (and elsewhere) is bad, malingering is common, dishonesty is rife, but none of this can be corrected without a crisis in which the ordinary man in the street is frightened. In this connection Peyton spoke up for the House of Commons as a marvellous reflection of the English people with all their faults. He believed that if there was a more constructive mood in the country it would be reflected in the House within hours.

Peyton had thought until recently that the Tories would win an election, but now he is not so sure. The disastrous defeats of the Tories at Ripon and Ely have clearly some serious significance. One result is assumed to be that there will be no election this year, though Peyton thought a lot could happen in the next two months.

I got the impression that Peyton sees no useful outcome of the T.U.C. talks at 10 Downing St, and does not believe that inflation is being brought under control.

Mrs Peyton told Ruth the other day that her husband has unbounded admiration for Peter Walker and had never liked working for anyone so much.

A man from *The Times* rang me up this evening. He said he had been in Australia when my 1965–70 Diary was published last year. He wanted to know if there had been any reaction to my revelation that Bank of England and Treasury figures were faked. I said there had been none. He asked if the evident disbelief abroad in optimistic Governments statements was due to a suspicion that official figures were still being faked. I said I didn't think so. I had not seen any facts that I found hard to believe; it was the opinions and the projections which were incredibly optimistic.

Thursday, August 2nd, 1973

John Peyton yesterday said people are reluctant to face the fact that causes have effects—they seem to regard the two phenomena as separate!

Monday, August 13th, 1973

Lunch with Alf Robens at Vickers. Alf is still in a state of great euphoria. We have discovered the secret of perpetually rising prosperity! Prices will go on rising, so will wages, at an ever increasing rate. I said the world cannot double its population every thirty years on a rapidly rising standard of living. Alf agreed that in the long run this is not possible, but this is a problem for the next century not this one. The feckless at the bottom of the social pyramid can always be looked after. If he was P.M., he would have equal pay for men and women next year, and a minimum wage now of £22·50 per week. The steep rise in food prices—wheat went to £88 a ton last week, a rise of £10 in a week—will be resented at first but will have been forgotten by the time we get around to the election in October 1974 or April 1975. Modern technology is proceeding at such a pace that the necessary raw materials can be produced—and with less labour. Vickers are developing a small submarine worked by cable from a mother ship that can explore the ocean floor at unimaginable depths. What has been done in the North Sea for oil and gas can be done for other products elsewhere. Outside the circle of Ministers, who have an axe to grind, I have heard no one else who took the view that we can live happily with inflation at an ever-increasing speed.

Vickers have been building a cement plant in Uganda; their Europeans have not been harassed, and the money due has been paid on the nail. Today Alf had a call from the commercial attaché at the Cuban Embassy asking Vickers to tender for a large cement plant in Cuba. The attaché said the Danes, Germans and Americans had all tendered, but not the British. The time for the tender to be in had run out but never mind! This was a curious episode and left Alf with the impression that perhaps the other countries' firms had in fact not tendered.

Alf said the Bank is becoming more and more a department of the Treasury. He thinks any financial or economic policy is determined in the Treasury, and the Bank merely implements the instructions received. The directors fulfil no function. He implied that the new minimum lending rate, to be announced on Friday instead of the bank rate announcement on Thursday, was a change made to put the Bank even more under political control, and deferring the announcement to Friday made Parliamentary questioning less immediate. He thought Gordon Richardson had taken on the Governorship for prestige. It was clear that he was getting more money from Schroder Wagg than he is now. Alf had had some talk with Jeremy Morse, who chairs the Committee of Twenty on the future of international currency regulations. Morse is apparently optimistic that something worth-while will emerge in the autumn. I should have thought the American administration is too paralysed by Watergate to implement anything so far-reaching as a currency agreement. Alf thought Nixon would find himself so isolated and powerless that he would resign on the grounds of ill-health—not now perhaps but in a few months' time.

Our government is in trouble over the claim of the Littlejohn brothers, convicted of bank robbery in Dublin, to have been working for British Intelligence. The impression left is of the incurable amateurishness of our security services and of the Ministers responsible for them.

Tuesday, August 14th, 1973

At the time, it was said in the papers that the Dublin explosion some months ago was an I.R.A. outrage.* This seemed incredible, and the alternatives seem to be, (1) the Irish Secret Service, (2) the English ditto, or (3) some Protestant extremist group in Belfast. What the Irish want to know is whether British Ministers knew, then or later, what their secret police were up to. I should think the answer was that Heath, Carrington and Whitelaw are not men to engage in cloak-and-dagger work. If they suspected *ex post facto* that it was their men who were responsible, they would be at pains to look the other way and make no embarrassing inquiries.

Thursday, September 6th, 1973

Have been away in the Eastern Mediterranean, and return to find things much as they were when I left. The unions are, if anything, more intransigent; the pound is even weaker; and the P.M. even more truculent. He has said twice this week that his policy is still full-steam ahead. Previous governments had held back when they reached this point in the inflationary cycle—but not our Ted.

Sunday, September 9th, 1973

When buying two pounds of tea at Fortnum's on Friday I had some chat with the hard-pressed manager of the tea and coffee counter. He said he had been advertising for staff for four weeks at £30 a week, plus commission. They will accept immigrants or anyone, but have so far had not one applicant!

Monday, September 17th, 1973

Ted is in Dublin today. Clearly this is a feather in Cosgrave's cap but how will it help in Northern Ireland? Herron, the vice-chairman of the U.D.A., was kidnapped on Friday and found murdered last night. Both Protestants and Catholics in the North think this was the work of the British security forces. Ted Heath, Willie Whitelaw and Peter Carrington are the Ministers who would be responsible, but I cannot see any of them resorting to political assassination.

* In December 1972 two car bombs exploded in Dublin, killing two and injuring over a hundred.

However, the Dublin bombing of some months ago, and the Littlejohn affair, make such suspicion understandable.

The trade figures are bad, the pound is weak, the industrial outlook is for several serious strikes, but Ted remains defiant and optimistic in spite of the opinion polls, which show the Conservatives only 1½ per cent ahead of the Liberals!

Tuesday, September 18th, 1973

Now that Irish bombs are going off in England, there has been a marked decrease in the sale of Irish butter and beef, as I am told by a village retailer in East Molesey.

Wednesday, September 19th, 1973

On Monday, before he left Dublin, Ted gave two television interviews, one to the B.B.C. and one to I.T.N. In the course of these two separate interviews he was asked what would happen if the new Assembly did not get off the ground. He said the legislation would lapse in March and a grave situation would arise. We could not go on having dribs and drabs of direct rule, and the sensible course would be full integration with Great Britain. Last night he was speaking at a dinner and had an opportunity to retract what he had said. But he said the same thing in a less direct form. He seems to have no idea that this is a complete reversal of the position in the Green Paper, which rejects integration out of hand. The statement has united an astonishing assortment of people—Harold Wilson, the I.R.A., the S.D.L.P., Brian Faulkner and Jack Lynch are all appalled by this sudden change of front. Evidently Ted had no inkling of the political implications of what he was saying. His attitude these days is very arrogant—he has decided what is best for Northern Ireland and is indignant and angry that the Ulstermen are not grateful and acquiescent. The result is that any good effect from his visit to Dublin is nullified, and it is less likely that the Assembly can be made a going concern. Neither result can possibly have been in Ted's mind when he spoke. If he realized he was announcing a change of Government policy he shouldn't, and presumably wouldn't, have announced it in a casual television interview in Dublin.

Thursday, September 20th, 1973

Both Paisley and the I.R.A. are said to suspect that Tommy Herron was murdered by the British security forces. I cannot believe this is true, but it can do no harm for Ted to know with what suspicions he is confronted.

Paisley has written to Ted to insist on a clear statement of Government policy. Since his statements on television in Dublin on Monday everyone is baffled. He has partly withdrawn what he said on Monday, but no one has any explanation of what Ted thought he was doing.

Paisley thinks Northern Ireland is moving towards independence within the Commonwealth. Perhaps Ted, by his indiscretions, will have contributed to this end.

When Ted was in Belfast he saw Paisley and his group last of all the Ulster politicians. Paisley was amazed that at this interview much time was occupied by a violent difference of opinion between Ted and Willie Whitelaw.

Wednesday, September 26th, 1973

We have heard more about Paisley's meeting with Ted last week. When he and his group were about to see Ted, Whitelaw urged them to tell Ted straight the situation as they saw it. This they did, but Ted would not accept their assessment and got into a violent argument with Whitelaw, who more or less did. Paisley said he was still puzzling over Ted's gaffe in Dublin, when he said that if the Assembly did not function by next March there would be full integration. It was understood by everyone that he meant integration with the U.K., but Paisley now wonders whether, under the influence of a good dinner, he had really meant integration with the Republic. Paisley was recently at an ecumenical function in the Republic and was well received.

Thursday, October 4th, 1973

The opinion poll out this morning shows the three Parties neck and neck, with about a third of the electorate each. Labour is slightly in front and the Tories in third place! Ted pleases only 36 per cent, while normally a P.M. rates 70 per cent *ex officio*. You would suppose such a disastrous figure would provoke some reaction, but there is none at all. I imagine the Tories suppose Ted's reckless inflation will somehow come right on the night. The newspapers say (inconspicuously of course) that the Government's advisers—presumably Treasury officials—are appalled.

Monday, October 8th, 1973

The big international event has been the Arab-Israeli war. Both sides are clearly lying, and the truth is hard to discern. That the Israelis will lose seems to me out of the question, but that the war will be a six-day fiasco does not seem to me likely either. Once wars start they can take on a life of their own and produce consequences unexpected by anyone. At least it can be said that the Arab world is united as never before.

At a press conference in Lancaster House, Ted launched Phase 3 of his economic policy. A serious effort is to be made to put it over to the country. The spearhead of the propaganda is to be a series of ministerial speeches. Why *do* Governments imagine that ministerial speeches carry any conviction?

The new phase is generous on wages—allowing 10 per cent to everyone, and more to women, pensioners and the underpaid. There are to be small cuts in Government expenditure. The package is inflationary—with still more money going into personal consumption and presumably still less into capital investment. Dividend increases are to be limited to 5 per cent, which is unfair. I do not expect the unions to accept the package. The militants will think they have the Government on the run, and prices will continue to rise.

Sunday, October 14th, 1973

The Tory Party Conference passed off with no outstanding feature. Barber launched an absurd attack on Enoch; Ted made wild claims for the success of his policies; Whitelaw poured fulsome praise on Faulkner.

The Arab-Israeli war continues. It is very hard to guess what happening as the Arabs say little and the Israelis are clearly lying. They have suffered heavy losses, but have had the best of the fighting against Syria. In Sinai the Egyptians seem to be awaiting an attack. They are over the Canal and about five miles into the desert.

The serious aspect of the war is the extent to which the Americans and Russians are pouring arms into the hands of their respective allies.

Agnew has resigned and it seems that an undistinguished Congressman, Ford, will succeed him. The damage done to the prestige of the U.S. abroad is the one aspect of the succession of scandals which is never mentioned, in all the millions of words of American comment. The damage done to the prestige of the American con-sitution within the U.S. is given much less than its appropriate weight.

Friday, October 19th, 1973

Paisley looked in for an hour or so this morning. He thinks an Executive will be formed and that he will quickly make it unwork-able. He says the British Government spent £500,000 to launch the Alliance Party. Without Government money and backing, it has no future.

Heath's attitude when in Northern Ireland was deplorable; school-mastery to an absurd degree. He sent for Paisley and his group, and apparently expected them to open the dialogue, which they failed to do. His main theme was that the new constitution was now the law of the land, and therefore Paisley and his friends should get cracking. This was also his attitude over the Industrial Relations Act. Evidently he has learnt nothing.

Ted was contemptuous of the size of Paisley's audience outside the Town Hall on a memorable occasion in Belfast, and had to be reminded by both Paisley and Whitelaw that Paisley's intervention at that moment had saved civil war.

The inflationary boom goes from strength to strength. The *Kingston News* (a throw-away advertising sheet) had advertisements from two branches of the Civil Service seeking men aged up to fifty-nine years of age! London Transport and the G.L.C. are both complaining that the boom and wages restraint are causing a steady drain on their manpower—and services must suffer. The Inland Revenue are losing staff more rapidly than they can be replaced. Everyone except Ministers is frightened, but today there is an official announcement that public bodies are to be encouraged to borrow in foreign currencies, and no longer only in dollars.

We met Peregrine Worsthorne at a party given by *Encounter* last night, who seemed to assume that Ted had now destroyed the Tory Party. John Foster was also at the party and said he is giving up politics and returning to the Bar.

The war continues, but the Russians and the Americans are said to be bent on a cease-fire. We are so deluged with optimistic news of all sorts, it is hard to say how much truth there is in these reports. I should have thought peace was not yet on the cards. The Israelis evidently defeated the Syrians on the Golan Heights. They then twice reported that the Syrian Army was in flight. Instead, it seems the Israeli advance was checked and thrown back. The Israelis are mostly within the 1967 ceasefire line on the Syrian side, but the initiative seems to be with the Syrians and Iraqis. On the Suez front there is some propaganda but no hard facts. The Egyptians seem to be holding their ground. The Israelis claim to have forces on the west bank of the Canal, but this sounds like a commando operation undertaken for morale-boosting purposes. Losses in material on both sides are very high: on casualties what little information has been given is certainly untrue.

Wednesday, October 24th, 1973

I met Maurice Laing in the street yesterday. I like him very much. He was saying that while business is good, the conditions under which it has to be conducted are bad and getting worse. I suppose he was referring to the fact that small builders can get round the wage controls while the big firms cannot. The result is that they are desperately short of tradesmen—notably bricklayers and plumbers. He said he thought the Government had had a chance, though only a chance, of getting away with Phase 3 but the Arab-Israeli war had put paid to that chance.

We had lunch with the Irish Ambassador and his wife—just the four of us. He was present at the Heath/Cosgrave talks and said they had much to talk about, apart from Northern Ireland. I said it was a highly inopportune visit, as it gave the impression in Belfast that London and Dublin were selling Ulster down the river. The Ambassador, rather naturally, did not agree with this, as the visit was a diplomatic gain for the Dublin Government. But he did say that Heath's threat of integration was deliberate and intended. Heath had no idea what a storm he would raise, and so had to eat his words in three instalments.

Much of the talk was about Paisley, with Ruth proclaiming his virtues, and our host saying he had been regarded as an ogre, a wrecker and an evil man. It was clear that the Irish Government had no link with Paisley or his people. They seem to pin their faith on power-sharing and Faulkner. I said power-sharing could not possibly work; the Ambassador thought it would get started but might well break down later. I propounded the idea of an independent Six Counties. The Ambassador seemed unfamiliar with the idea, but thought it might be a fall-back plan if everything else failed. The Ambassador said his information was that Faulkner would get his majority in the Unionist council which met yesterday. In today's papers it is reported that he did get his majority but its size and composition was such as to weaken rather than strengthen Faulkner's position.

Friday, October 26th, 1973

On Wednesday Hartley Shawcross had lunch with me. He was rather hard-pressed—back from Paris the previous night, and off to New York in the immediate future. He gives dinner to a small group of right-wing trades unionists and so is much interested in the Communist infiltration of the trades unions. He thought that probably this had gone too far to be eradicated. The Government apparently does not now even dare to mention the menace. On balance, he thought we would have a Communist dictatorship in this country.

He is chairman of Thames Television and has been disturbed at the volume of left-wing propaganda put out by commentators from his station. He had up the man responsible, and questioned him about the bias shown by his department. The man said he was a left-winger himself, as were most of his staff. He would not brook any interference with his work, though of course the directors could dismiss him. If they did so there would be a strike and the station would close down.

Meanwhile, we are once more not far from nuclear war. The Americans and the Russians called for a cease-fire in the Arab-Israeli war. Trying to sift out the truth from the barrage of propaganda it would appear that the Israelis, to improve their position on the west bank of the Suez Canal, violated the truce. Whereupon the Egyptians asked for Russian and American troops to come in and enforce the truce. The Russians were willing; the Americans were not. The Russians are said to have alerted seven airborne divisions to fly to the Middle East; the Americans countered this by alerting their nuclear forces throughout the world. The Russians are not now sending their troops, and the maintenance of the cease-fire is to be left to a quite futile U.N. force consisting of Finns, Austrians and Swedes.

Clearly, when the Russians and Americans demanded a cease-fire and immediate peace negotiations, they must have been prepared to put pressure on the belligerents to see the programme was carried out. But now it looks as if the Israelis are triumphant and defiant, and that the Americans are not exerting any worth-while pressure on them. It is hardly likely that the Russians will accept the bad faith of the Israelis lying down, and the Arabs certainly won't. They have put up the price of oil, to an extent that will cost us alone £400 million a year, and are reducing their output substantially. This may not hurt the United States very much directly but will cause huge trouble everywhere else. The world is paying an enormous price for American support of Israel—in which real American interests are not involved.

And of course this crisis occurs with Nixon in desperate trouble over a wide range of crimes and blunders of which we may not yet have seen half.

Sunday, October 28th, 1973

Last night at a music party and buffet supper at Chequers. I had some talk with Robert Carr—just social chit-chat. He is an exceedingly nice man but he carries no guns at all. Ted was very friendly. When we left he saw us down from the Long Gallery to the front door. He looks well and confident. He clearly enjoys being P.M. Any idea that he is a deeply worried man putting a brave face on things is quite untrue. Obviously on an occasion like this there is no opportunity for any serious talk. But he did say he was sure the Israelis would not pull back and that the Americans would do nothing to compel them to do so. He said he thought the Americans had handled the situation in the 'worst possible way'.

Ruth had some talk with a senior civil servant, who said our present regime has now gone, and he wondered if the new one would be ushered in by some material calamity. Max Rayne said to me—apropos of labour troubles in the printing industry—that the whole of our society seems to be crumbling. Gordon Richardson was there—I thought looking tired and worried, but evidently delighted to be governor of the Bank. God knows why, as he is really only head of a Treasury Department. He told me that John Stevens died in his sleep on Friday night. This was wholly unexpected. I am sorry, as he really did make a contribution to our trade with eastern Europe, and personally we got on well.

I had some talk with Denis Hamilton, in despair over labour problems in Fleet Street. He said the strain on management is more than can be borne. The trouble-makers at the moment are the

315

clerks, who have fallen behind in wage comparisons with the workers in the mechanical departments. They cannot be brought more into line because of the Government's wages policy. This policy is also causing trouble in London Transport, where they are unable to obtain enough busmen, underground-train drivers or maintenance engineers. The Government says—I dare say inevitably—that they cannot make exceptions. But if you get a wild boom going it is to be expected that it is the essential industries that will first feel the effects of labour shortage.

Incidentally, Ted said that when he visited Dublin the airport was surrounded by *tanks*, and 7,000 troops were deployed for his protection!

Tuesday, October 30th, 1973

Lunch for Brian Walden. He was in excellent form and very communicative. In the Queen's Speech today it is announced that the Government's tax reform is to be brought forward. In itself the tax reform is a sound idea, but it has been announced that it will cost £1,300 million when fully operative in some years' time. In other words, it is not really a scheme of tax reform but a colossal handout to the poorer and needier parts of the population. Walden says this is part of the run-up to the election. Wages will be allowed to rise without much hindrance, so that in a year's time everyone will be feeling prosperous and ready to keep Ted in office. I said elections tend to be treated by voters as an occasion to get the rascals out, rather than as a vote of confidence, and prices will be much higher.

I said the Germans had had runaway inflation and six million unemployed, and regarded the first evil as worse than the second. After all it was the destruction of the middle classes by inflation that led to Hitler. Brian said this operated in two ways—some of the middle classes, ruined by inflation, joined Hitler to get their own back; others, who should have been the moderating influence in German society, just let things take their course out of bitterness.

Walden had a meal with Barber a couple of weeks ago, and taxed him with misleading the public about 5-per-cent growth. Walden said there is little real growth; what you see is unused capacity being taken up. This has now just about been taken care of, and he wondered if real growth is better than $2\frac{1}{2}$ per cent, as will appear next year. Barber said, 'I know, but what else could I say?'

Walden said when you see Ministers face to face across the central

316

gangway you have an excellent chance of judging character. He says Whitelaw is easily the best of them. He lives in the real world, unlike Ted. I said he has evidently failed in Ireland and will this not effect his standing. Walden said, no, mainly because there is no one else, except Carrington, whom Walden does not see because he is in the Lords. He was particularly contemptuous of Peyton, whom he described as a fool—with a sense of humour. According to Walden he does not read his papers and appears in the House as a buffoon. This is certainly not my impression.

On Ireland, Walden thought the power-sharing idea was just a gimmick to gain time. With luck they can go on arguing about power-sharing until the election, and then it's another ball-game anyway. He said, in contemporary politics you must never forget how many moves are made to gain time, and how many others are made as diversions to distract attention. No use is made of the time so gained, and people whose foresight is limited to a period of days think only in terms of getting through the next week. He said, when playing bridge you pick up your hand and wonder whether you should lead clubs or spades. If you have any strength of character you sit back and work out which is the wiser lead. But our politicians would not be able to make up their minds, and so would lead (say) diamonds.

Over the Middle East, Walden said our arms embargo and our diplomatic efforts have earned us the hostility of the Israelis and the contempt of the Egyptians. With the Russians we have no influence. They have written us off long since as a third-class power of no account. Walden thought Nixon had his back to the wall, and would use the Middle East crisis ruthlessly to protect his political position at home. His self-esteem has been badly mangled and he might resort under further pressure to anything, including nuclear war.

On the general outlook, Walden assumes inflation would continue to accelerate until a crash came, when the British people would insist on drastic reforms. He thinks such a crash is not imminent and might be eight years away.

Thursday, November 1st, 1973

George Bolton to lunch—in cracking form. He had recently had some talk with Enoch Powell and tried to persuade him to stick to the evils of inflation—he attacks on far too wide a front. Enoch said he saw the point, but regarded coloured immigration as an evil as great as inflation. George had also seen du Cann, chairman of Keyser Ullman which he regards as the up and coming merchant bank. Te thinks Warburg's is at peak. Du Cann said he had lined up fifty Hories who were prepared to tell Ted that the economy is over-heated and must be cooled. But surely Ted will defy him, and at this stage in the life of Parliament there is not much they can do to emphasize their point. If they turned Ted out he would have an election and the Tories would lose.

George said the Jews he knows are very suspicious of Kissinger and think he will let Israel down. He has a reputation for telling everyone what they want to hear. George says the master-plan that is being discussed in diplomatic circles is that Iran should take over the Persian Gulf—they have the third best army in the world; that Russia should assume a protectorate over Syria and Iraq; and that the U.S. should do the same over Libya and Egypt. There would be no protectorate over Israel, but any potential attacker would be looked after by the super-powers. I was not clear what was to be the position of Jordan and Saudi Arabia.

I said I thought the Jews in the United States were too powerful and were asking for trouble. George said he well remembered a conversation in 1934 which two German-Jewish bankers and a German-Jewish lawyer had. They all said the Jews in Germany were far too powerful and would bring dire trouble down on themselves.

George is a director of the Canadian Pacific Railway and Sun Life of Canada. He said Canada is the country of the future, with resources of water, wood, oil, gas and metals that have hardly been scratched. The Americans are looking more and more to the north; bright young Canadians no longer look to the south. The Canadian High Commissioner told George his Government had turned back an estimated 30,000 would-be American immigrants.

As chairman of the Commonwealth Development Finance Corporation George was approached by an American who had made a fortune growing rice in California, beginning during the last war. He came to see George about a loan to develop 30,000 acres he had bought in British Honduras! George asked if he was going to live there with his family. He said, yes. The venture was due to the fact that he found the United States unattractive and California intolerable.

I said that when I saw Gordon Richardson on Saturday he seemed

318

tired, but delighted to be Governor. George said he had been angling for the job for ten years. He wants the prestige and the peerage, but knows nothing of central banking. He asked a personage what should be done about the Bank (I was not clear whether the 'personage' was inside the Bank or not). Anyway, the reply he got was that to restore the morale of the Bank staff it would be necessary to sack the Chief Cashier and all the executive directors! Fforde, for example, is a terribly nice man and highly intelligent, but he is an extreme introvert and terribly shy. Yet his job is as contact man with the City. Is he mis-cast?

In January the sterling area came to an end, but the Government apparently did not realize that almost everyone in this country has relations in the old Empire, and that between this country and the said relatives there is a constant interchange of gifts, legacies, trust funds and so on. So now the Bank gets 6,000 letters per day in the Exchange Control Department. George said that at C.D.F.C. they used to get their foreign exchange requirements as a result of a telephone call. Now an application takes three and a half months.

I said I had met Robert Carr on Saturday—what a nice man, but with nothing to him. George said his relations with the police could not be worse. The police feel that Carr has let them down at every opportunity.

Wednesday, November 7th, 1973

At lunch yesterday, given by Foyles at the Dorchester, I sat next Elizabeth Longford. On her other side was Terence O'Neill, who declined to meet my eye, though we have met. He gave us lunch on his first day as P.M. at Stormont. O'Neill told Elizabeth that he thought there would be an appalling massacre of Catholics if the British Army withdrew. In any case, he rated the chances of civil war pretty high. He deeply distrusted Faulkner, and was almost certain, though not quite, that Paisley was a bad man—a wrecker. Elizabeth said Paisley gave her 'the shivers'.

At 5.20 we met Paisley at the House. He had just come from the P.M. and was off to another meeting, so we had only twenty to twenty-five minutes. He said that the situation in Northern Ireland was getting worse. The picture given in the newspapers and by the Government is quite false. Northern Ireland is not settling down. I said Merlyn Rees had told his Labour friends that Paisley and Craig, in conversation, had expressed a readiness to discuss border changes.

Paisley said he had never mentioned border changes. In any case, this was no moment to talk of such things.

Paisley and James Kilfedder had been with the P.M. for an hour or more. From Paisley's point of view the idea was to extract from Heath a firm statement that integration with England was not on. Heath said this at the meeting, refused to have a referendum on the subject, but declined to make a public statement to that effect. So Paisley will try to put down a question on the subject in a form that will require a clear answer. Paisley does not believe the withdrawal of the British Army would mean a wholesale massacre of Catholics, but any such withdrawal would have to be over a period, carefully thought out and carefully phased.

In the United States Nixon's position gets steadily weaker, but the end is not yet in sight. In the Middle East, it is not clear what is happening. The rumoured terms of a peace settlement involve moving the frontiers of Israel very nearly back to what they were in 1967, with an international force on the Golan Heights and at Sharm el Sheikh on the Red Sea. Israel would keep Jerusalem, but not much else. This would constitute a massive diplomatic defeat for Israel after a military victory. Could this be sold to the American or Israeli public? Meanwhile, the Arab oil boycott should be alarming the great industrial powers, but they are still shrugging it off—perhaps assuming that the Middle-Eastern crisis will soon be over. A cut of more than 25 per cent in the Arab oil supply will bring Japan and Western Europe grinding to a halt. So far, even the mildest measures of conservation have been put off while our Government at any rate makes soothing noises.

Yesterday I had some talk with Manny Shinwell before lunch—he is a grand little man. His theme was that he has known all the political leaders since 1903 (he is now eighty-nine) and what a miserable lot of puppets they were!

Wednesday, November 14th, 1973

Just back from Dublin, doing a television programme in connection with my book.* We had some talk with one Healey, political editor of the *Irish Times* who came out with one bright remark. The Irish, he said, are still peasants. Peasants have got to co-operate with their neighbours to survive. Men in big cities are under no such obligation, but in Ireland the full effect of city life is not yet felt.

* *On Ireland* (London: Cape).

In conversation with Mulcahy, editor of *Hibernia*, I found complete bewilderment over Ted Heath's policy. What is he up to? When he came to Dublin he was confined to the military airfield at Baldoyle, which was surrounded by tanks and several *thousand* police and troops. Mulcahy was very suspicious of Paisley. We tried to persuade him that Paisley is a man of peace and an honest man. I am not sure that we succeeded.

The main news yesterday was that at last the Government has seen a red light. The accumulated effects of the oil embargo, the coal go-slow, the electrical engineers ban on overtime and the disastrous trade figures have together wiped the silly smile off the Government's face. The minimum lending rate which was to have been fixed by the Treasury Bill rate on Friday has now been operated on a Tuesday. So we are back at bank rate under a different name. A short while ago we had the futile gesture of reducing the M.L.R. by $\frac{1}{4}$ per cent (bank rate never moved by less than $\frac{1}{2}$ per cent). Now it has been put up by $1\frac{3}{4}$ per cent. The official statement that petrol rationing is unnecessary seems ill-founded. Is there any other reason for postponing what looks like an inevitable decision? I don't think the Government has yet realized the disastrous results worldwide of the Arab oil embargo. They seem to feel they will somehow be exempt. Meanwhile, after all the fanfare over peace in the Middle East we have yet another breach of the cease-fire by the Israelis, while Mrs Meir told the Israeli Parliament that they would not go back to the October 22nd cease-fire line, still less to the 1967 frontier. American influence on the Israelis seems minimal in spite of all the propaganda. Perhaps they think the American Government is so weak it can be defied. But what will the Russians do? King Faisal says he will keep up the oil embargo until East Jerusalem is restored to Arab hands—even if that means keeping it up till 1980. The Israelis would fight in the last ditch to retain East Jersualem, so we shall continue to have a confrontation that may well end in nuclear war.

Thursday, November 15th, 1973
At Heath's press conference in Dublin he was asked by an I.R.A. representative about the responsibility of the British Secret Service for the Dublin bomb. This question was the only one that roused his anger—though all the Irish journalists present believed it to be true.

Saturday, November 17th, 1973

Lunch yesterday for Bill Barnetson. He says Whitelaw is anxious to be back in London, and Ted is as anxious to have him—and this will be done as soon as there is a break in the clouds over Northern Ireland. I asked what slot can there be for him to occupy? Apparently the only one available is the Ministry of Labour, where Maurice Macmillan is an admitted failure. Poor Willie Whitelaw knows nothing about industrial relations and I doubt whether his charm will avail him. An attempt was made to shift Alec Home to the Scottish Office, on the grounds that the Tory Party in Scotland has done much worse than it should for many years past; Ted has devoted much time to Scotland, but Alec, who was very popular as a Junior Minister in the Scottish Office might really turn the trick as Secretary of State. Alec did not warm to the idea and Mrs Alec turned it down flat. He had made enough sacrifices—he had renounced his earldom and had relinquished the Prime Ministership without making a fuss. He would soldier on until the election. Besides, both of them like it at the Foreign Office—particularly Mrs.

Barnetson was at 10 Downing St on Tuesday when Ministers emerged from the emergency meeting of the Cabinet over the disastrous trade figures. Ted looked buoyant; Barber was worried, biting his nails; John Davies looked very gloomy. Barnetson has been busy trying to get more publicity for Davies, who has recently almost disappeared from sight, but he was advised by some senior Minister to lay off—presumably because Davies is about to be pushed.

Barnetson talked about Fleet Street. United Newspapers are more than 100 per cent up in profits, in spite of dear newsprint and labour troubles—*Punch* is making more than £100,000 a year, and was losing that amount when they took it over. He thinks the *Express* is losing money, the *Standard* and *Glasgow Citizen* are just in the black, and the group is dependent on the *Sunday Express*.

On Thursday night Ted gave an interview on I.T.V. His interviewer was a deplorable little man. Ted's line was one of confidence, and his only worry was the miners' go-slow. They have been told they can have a 16-per-cent increase in pay but are demanding more. Price increases for October alone were 2 per cent, so inflation is gathering momentum. Anyway, the most menacing aspect of the moment is the oil situation, to which Ted hardly alluded. Most other countries are doing something about it, but as usual we have done little more than resort to exhortation.

Wednesday, November 21st, 1973

Hugh Fraser to supper on Sunday; lunch with the Lunch-time Comment Club yesterday; and Ruth had a word with Mrs Peyton. Hugh Fraser sad and diminished—unhappy about the outlook with no good news anywhere. At the Connaught Rooms had a word with Enoch Powell, who had come to the wrong room. He also is much diminished from the last time I saw him. In fact in a crowd you would not see him. Mrs Peyton did not mention her husband's views, but said that their friends in the Cabinet are convinced by Ted's confidence that he really has all the answers. If only we don't lose our nerve, in a year or two we shall be out on the sunny uplands with steady growth, a rising export trade and booming prosperity all round. This seemed to me out of the question before the oil embargo; now it is wishful thinking of a most dangerous order. The Government seems to think that if it does not react to the oil embargo, it will just fade away. It has been pushed by the oil companies into a 10-per-cent cut in deliveries, but there is to be no petrol rationing—it is to be left to exhortation to drive more slowly, and only to make necessary journeys. The Stock Exchanges here and in New York have reacted much more quickly than the various Governments, and have registered quite spectacular falls.

Thursday, November 22nd, 1973

At the Printers' Charitable Corporation dinner last night there were two interesting speeches— by Charles Snow, and by Jim Callaghan. It was a presumably festive occasion, but both men gave a solemn warning of the effects of inflation unless speedily curbed. Snow added a word to the effect that television had down-graded the written word, to our over-all detriment. I spoke to Callaghan and said his Party's policy was surely for further massive inflation. He said he was not dealing at that moment with the Party Conference! Meanwhile Peter Walker last night was speaking to the Society of Actuaries and talking of the glorious future before us all. This is following the P.M.'s line of nonsense with a vengeance.

At Stormont they are said to have arrived at a compromise acceptable to the Alliance Party, the S.D.L.P. and Faulkner.

Craig's comment was that the deal would see Whitelaw through till tomorrow—but no further!

The Government is slowly being pushed by the oil companies into some realization of the troubles facing us owing to the oil embargo.

The Fleet Street people last night were saying that labour relations there are now a perfect nightmare. Drogheda said the compositors on the *Financial Times* now get £180 per week. When last heard of it was only £95.

Friday, November 23rd, 1973

Lunch yesterday for Stonehouse. He was talking of the censure debate on Monday when, he said, the two front benches were locked in a struggle that had little or no relevance for their respective backbenchers, let alone for the voting public. The great feature of the debate was apparently a brilliant speech by Barber. He began with a very ordinary and rather limp defence of Government policy, and then suddenly switched to a devastating attack on Harold Wilson. It was so well done that it reduced the Labour benches to silence and had the Tories in ecstasies. This event has of course no effect outside the House, but did much to raise Tory morale in the House and to boost Barber's standing there.

Whitelaw announced the composition of the power-sharing executive. This has been greeted in the House, and in the papers, as a huge victory. In the debate following Whitelaw's announcement, the plan was damned by most of the Northern Ireland M.P.s stretching from Captain Orr to Bernadette (late) Devlin. Craig has suggested it was a propaganda exercise that will hold up for a day or two. The I.R.A. and the U.V.F. have damned it out of hand. The Government has apparently attached weight to Fitt and Faulkner, two discredited back numbers, and in any case seems mainly concerned to get Whitelaw back to London, presumably to replace Maurice Macmillan.

Monday, November 26th, 1973

Lunch with Edwin Plowden. He had recently entertained a top-level group of European industrialists—three from each of the large countries down to one from Luxembourg. The Shell man, who was one of them, said it had so far proved impossible to convince any Euopean Government of the importance of the oil embargo. They all seemed to suppose that if little was said the whole nightmare would disappear.

Plowden doubted if the Americans would have either the will or the power to force the Israelis back to their 1967 line. In particular Faisal was insisting on East Jerusalem. Could any Israeli Government give this up?

If the embargo dragged on, you would see millions of unemployed in Western Europe and Japan. Under these circumstances would the Russians agree to bring pressure on the Arabs to restore the oil if, in return, we all abrogated our alliance with the U.S.?

Plowden thought the middle and professional classes provided no leadership, and he thought the future was more likely to see a dictatorship of the Left. Clearly nothing serious was likely to be done about inflation.

Of personalities, he said he did not know Walker well but disliked and distrusted him. He knew Robert Carr well and liked him, but said his intellectual level was a Pass degree in (say) geography. He thought Whitelaw's return to London would be a good thing, as he had good judgment and was a good influence on Ted.

Tuesday, November 27th, 1973

General Gale to dine last night. He and the other officers and ex-officers present commented on the fact that in the recent Arab-Israeli war there was no mention of anti-tank mines. Gale commanded the Parachute Division at the Normandy landing, and said if the German artillery had been better handled he and his men would have been thrown back into the Channel.

Thursday, November 29th, 1973

Lunch yesterday at the G.E.C. with Arnold Weinstock. He was out of sorts and had not much to say. They are suffering from an acute shortage of labour which has lead to poaching from one firm to another at rising wages. This is the inevitable result of an insufficiently policed wage control. The price control leads them to purchase abroad British materials, which are not available here because of the price freeze. Arnold did not think the electrical engineers' go-slow or the oil embargo would seriously hurt them. Their factories mostly have their own generating plant. He thought the price of copper, now sky high, would not fall much even if there is a recession due to the oil embargo.

Also at lunch, and sitting next me, was Oliver Poole. He was very friendly and made two interesting comments. (1) Humphrey Trevelyan (also a director of G.E.C. and formerly our Ambassador in Moscow) told them that he does not believe in the Russian détente with America. The Russians have been doing, and continue to do, as much harm to America as they can do without risk to themselves. First they used the Vietnam war, and now that American participation has ended they are using the Middle East. (2) Poole is recently back from the U.S., still immensely impressed with the power and adaptability of the American economy. He thinks anyone today should invest his money in the U.S. rather than here. He regards the Japanese economy as fragile; the German mark as still over-valued; but the future of sterling he can only see on a declining curve against the dollar for the next five years. Though a former chairman of the Tory Party, he can see no effective force operating to pull our economy round. Arnold said that in their field the Americans could take any contract they wanted, but they were not bothered by Japanese competition.

Saturday, December 1st, 1973
The City is increasingly unhappy these days. Commodity prices are soaring, there were two suspensions on the Stock Exchange yesterday, and prices have dropped a long way and are still sagging. The Prime Minister continues to make optimistic statements about everything, including Ireland, but he carries less and less conviction.

We were at the Festival Hall on Thursday night for an E.M.I. concert. Ted was there, but we had no talk with him. At supper I sat next Mrs Alistair Cooke; she's American, and revealed that she was born the same day as President Nixon. She said he has abandoned any hope of rebuilding his prestige or his credibility, and is now merely trying to keep out of jail. Alec Jarratt was there—a big man and highly intelligent.

Monday, December 3rd, 1973
Lunch for Vic Feather—rather lost in his very recent retirement. He is to be chairman of the Human Rights Board for Northern Ireland—a superfluous body if ever there was one. However, he was appointed on the recommendation of Whitelaw, with the approval of Ted and the acquiescence of Faulkner, Fitt and the

C.B.I. He has not been told the salary, but thinks it is about £2,000 per annum.

He does not take inflation seriously and thinks it will soon taper off. He says the miners will not strike and therefore will not be balloted. Daly and his friends are out for a victory over Ted on Phase 3. Even twenty pence above the allowable would gain them their point.

He is convinced—even more than last time—that there will have to be a wages schedule for all employed persons. He thinks Ted's great assets are Wilson, Benn and Powell. He thinks both Benn and Powell are counting on their respective Parties losing the next election, and are fighting the election after that.

Meanwhile the labour market gets tighter, and all sorts of supplies are in very short supply—at the moment bottles of all kinds and petrol.

The Government changes are at last announced. Whitelaw to the Ministry of Labour, Macmillan to the Treasury; both he and Davies are still in the Cabinet. Pym to Northern Ireland. It seems to be a mark of Whitelaw's influence that his Deputy Chief Whip succeeds him in Stormont, and his P.P.S., Raison, becomes a Junior Minister at Education. Eccles goes. He is an older man, but much abler than most of Ted's team.

The papers are even more absurd than usual speaking of Macmillan 'adding strength' to the Treasury team, and of Whitelaw's brilliant success in Ireland.

Wednesday, December 5th, 1973

A friend had two amusing stories. He went to see Ted about a propaganda department, and Ted's reply was that his job was to govern, not to explain. That remark explains a lot of Ted's mistakes. The same friend wrote to Rab Butler to congratulate him on his memoirs. Rab's reply came back 'wondering if he had not found the book too short'.

The impression given by the news is that the commercial world—here and abroad—is really scared by the oil outlook, while this Government anyway is inclined so far to shrug it off.

Whitelaw made an unimpressive performance in an industrial debate yesterday, while Pym did the same in Ireland—a country of which he apparently knows nothing.

Friday, December 7th, 1973

The Stock Exchange had yet another break yesterday, and the Institute of Economic and Social Research came out with a desperately gloomy forecast. This is the opposite of its usual form, as it has normally been quite unrealistically optimistic. Meanwhile, Ted is engaged in Irish negotiations with Pym and Alec Home, neither of whom know anything about Irish affairs. While optimistic statements are being put out in Sunningdale, the dissident Unionists have been strengthening their position in Belfast. Paisley rang up this morning and is confident Faulkner will have been ousted from the leadership of the Unionist Party by the end of next month.

The industrial situation looks bad, both in the mines and on the railways. The Government has put out a statement that they are more worried about coal than about oil. This must give a fillip to the miners!

Had lunch with Tony Bloomfield yesterday. His old mother recently died at a nursing home in Bishop's Avenue, Hampstead. The nursing home has closed down and the premises, which cover three acres, have been bought by the Chinese as a residence for their Ambassador. The price was £350,000 to which is to be added £250,000 for alterations.

Faced by mounting inflation I am surprised that ordinary shares are so weak. Land is expensive and politically very vulnerable; antiques are fetching the wildest prices—a chipped and damaged china ewer fetched £160,000 this week; but ordinary shares, which should be a better hedge than either, are low, and falling.

Tuesday, December 11th, 1973

There was a scene in the House of Commons yesterday that has not been seen for years, in which members of all Parties showered congratulations on the Government for their Sunningdale agreement over Ireland. Only one voice spoke against the agreement and that was the voice of Captain Orr, the only Northern Ireland M.P. who spoke! The partial recognition of Northern Ireland by Cosgrave is a gain; the rest just will not stick.

I had lunch with Robens yesterday. He is in excellent form, but has no idea what the future holds. Employers everywhere, he says, are saying they would give more to their men if the Government would allow them to do so. This weakens the Government's weak hand and encourages inflationary thoughts. On top of the rail chaos from tonight, the miners' go-slow, the ambulance drivers' ditto, and the power engineers, we are shortly to have an A.E.W. ban on overtime. The Communists in the trades union movement are determined to break Phase 3, and hope to break the Government. *The Times* yesterday went so far as to ridicule the *Sunday Telegraph* for drawing attention to Communist influence in the trades unions. Perhaps there is a Communist cell in *The Times*.

When the Industrial Relations Bill was being brought up Robens was consulted by Geoffrey Howe and gave him various points for inclusion—one of which was that the right to picket should be limited to a man's place of work. In the final draft all his points were ignored, and he then realized that he had only been consulted out of courtesy—not with a view to improving the Bill.

Robens held forth on our fuel policy. £400 million were spent switching the home consumer to North Sea gas. This involved closing a number of pits. These should have been kept open, and the North Sea gas should have been kept for special purposes.

The Magnox atomic power stations are crippled by corrosion problems. The engineers were warned that it would probably be wiser to make the pressure vessel of stainless steel, but this was turned down on the ground of expense on the authority of one man. The pressure vessels were made of mild steel and cannot be altered or replaced. It is also not realized that when an atomic station is worn out it cannot be dismantled but must be sheathed in lead and left for all time. This is why Robens wanted them put underground, but this too was vetoed on the ground of expense.

I asked about the coal-field east of Selby. Robens said its existence was known, but it was only recently that its quality was realized. The seam varies from eleven to thirty feet thick. The only trouble is that it runs underneath the Humber, and subsidence would play old Harry with the river levels if all the coal was taken. Under Coventry they have left pillars of excellent coal of enormous value. At Selby they would probably take six feet of coal and leave the rest.

Wednesday, December 12th, 1973

Dinner with Oswald Mosley last night. He spoke as if it were an established fact that at the time of the Israeli war in October, the Americans were ready to move in to the Arab oil-fields, but that the European countries vetoed the idea. There has been no hint of this in the papers I have seen, but Kissinger's anger with Great Britain, which still simmers, might depend on more than our refusal of landing facilities to planes laden with war material for Israel. And, anyway, Nixon made a reference to the Europeans 'freezing' which made no sense in the context in which it was reported.

Thursday, December 13th, 1973

Dinner last night with Nicholas Ridley. There were some young people—one Schreiber had been in the Conservative Party Central Office—but the principal guest was Enoch Powell. He was in good form, and both he and his wife were most friendly. She told Ruth that her daughter, a classics student at Wycombe Abbey, was refused admittance to Cambridge. She supposed left-wing university authorities would not admit Enoch's daughter to any British university.

Ridley had some political comments to make, but the discussion generally was not political. Ridley's idea seemed to be that a return to the free market in wages and everything else, plus a restriction of the money supply, would see us out of all our trouble.

Enoch propounded the view that men's lives make their faces very different from each other, though they dress alike. Women's faces much more resemble each other (in his view they are almost indistinguishable) but they dress as differently as possible. He thought men do not seek to disguise their intelligence, though women do. He had been studying the tombs of the medieval earls of Oxford at Earl's Colney in Essex, and apropos of these tombs, said you never find a woman's effigy on a tomb between her two husbands, but often find a man between his two wives. He had advised his wife, on his death, to go on a cruise and pick up some nice kind widower, but on her death he expected her to be buried by his side. These fragments are just to give an idea of the intelligence and originality of his conversation. He is a great personality, and a highly intelligent and articulate person. Whether he would be a good Prime Minister is a wholly different question. The young people last night very evidently thought him to be in the running, though elsewhere I have got the impression his chances have been waning. The country is so obviously in a mess, and dissatisfaction with the Government is so obviously widespread that anything may happen. The papers now talk of a mid-winter Budget, and an election at latest in March.

Friday, December 14th, 1973

So the balloon has begun to go up. The P.M. announced yesterday that we shall be going on to a three-day industrial week to save electricity during the current trouble with the miners, the train drivers and the power engineers. There is to be a mini-Budget on Monday, despite all the denials. The P.M. put it all down to the miners and hardly mentioned the oil embargo. In fact, as Lord Robbins writes in the *Financial Times* today, this trouble was coming on us anyway, even if there had been no industrial trouble and no oil embargo. I dare say one of the reasons for the three-day week (and how is it to be enforced?) is to cause short-time working and so bring pressure on the miners and railwaymen from their fellow unionists. I doubt if this will work—the resentment is more likely to build up against the Government—and rightly so. Ted's call for national unity on the box last night could not have been flatter or less inspiring.

Sunday, December 15th, 1973

Ruth just back from Belfast. Her visit was a musical one, but she fitted in a debate at Stormont, and some talk with Paisley and Peter McLachlan. Peter has swallowed the official line—hook, line and sinker—and thinks the Sunningdale agreement is the greatest agreement in Irish history for generations. Paisley sees it won't work and thinks Faulkner will be dismissed from the leadership of the Unionist Party at a meeting to be held on the 29th. But this will leave him in his seat as Chief Executive, so events may drag on in an indecisive way for some time. Apparently Faulkner has struck up a warm friendship with Hume of the S.D.L.P. and with Cosgrave. It seems that at Sunningdale Ted was determined to bulldoze through an agreement come what. When the agreement came to be signed he was seen to be in tears, so after all, people thought, he has a heart. As a help to Hume and the S.D.L.P. a number of internees are being let out. This, however, will in practice be a help to the I.R.A. and perhaps, to some extent, the U.V.F.

Tuesday, December 18th, 1973

At a high-level dinner party last night our guests included Plowden and Geoffrey Rippon. Plowden had no news, but was visibly shaken by the turn of events. I said, 'The balloon is now going up.' He said, 'It has already gone up—out of sight.' In conversation with me,

Rippon said he was not near Ted, but had formed the opinion he was quite straight. He might make mistakes but he was devoted to doing his best for the country. He talked a bit about his vast Ministry and said, when asked, that John Peyton is an excellent Minister—a bit temperamental at times but no worse for that. In conversation with Ruth, Rippon made it discreetly plain that he had been alarmed about the economy for some time past, and looked on the future with the utmost misgiving. He thought we were on the same course as the Weimar Government, with runaway inflation and ultra-high unemployment at the end. He said he thought the Government was quite unable to put its case across, though to me he said Ted's style was better appreciated in the North (Rippon sits for Hexham) than in London. Ruth had Rippon on her right, and was very struck by his confidence and ability. To me he said Enoch Powell was in some respects a latter-day Mosley and that he could have no real confidence in a man so consumed with hatred (for Ted) and one who changed his policies so radically.

Elizabeth Longford was very unfavourably impressed by Peter Walker—he made her shudder for some undefined reason.

The big event yesterday was Barber's mini-Budget. Poor man! He has no weight and his speech was greeted with laughter and giggles. The measures proposed are partly cosmetic, partly inadequate and partly will take too long to have a significant effect. The conclusion in *The Times* is that the measures were evolved with an election in view.

Wednesday, December 19th, 1973

I now recall another item from Rippon's conversation with Ruth on Monday. He said that over the years his views on current events had coincided with mine—with one notable exception. He entirely disagreed with my opinion of Alec Home. He said Alec was quite excellent in Cabinet, and as chairman of Cabinet Committees was far better than Harold Macmillan had been in his heyday.

Thursday, December 27th, 1973

The miners' executive is to meet today, and there is talk that Phase 3 can be stretched to give them enough for them to call off their ban on overtime. The same may be possible for the power engineers. The 16 per cent already offered the miners is inflationary and anything more would be even worse. The Arabs say they will release more oil in January, not less, so everyone is delighted and sees the end of the energy crisis. Of course the trouble is much less the quantity than the price—now four times what it was in October. Boardman, Minister for Industry, heaves a sigh of relief and says petrol rationing will not now be necessary, and Tommy Balogh writes to *The Times* that we should just ignore the deficit on our balance of payments which, for the coming year, may easily exceed £2,000 million. There is no sign that the Government realizes what horrible trouble we are all in.

Saturday, December 29th, 1973
Ruth gave the Prime Minister as a Christmas card an old map of the Broadstairs area of Kent. What was our surprise this morning when she received a most friendly letter of thanks written from Chequers in his own hand!

Monday, December 31st, 1973
Yesterday evening Ruth had some talk with Paisley on the telephone. He is hopeful of Faulkner being ousted from the leadership of the Unionist Party on Friday, but that, of course, will not oust him from the Executive or the Assembly. The result will be an unworkable, and unpredictable, mess.

1974

The main events of 1974 in the English-speaking world can be quickly summarized—two general elections in Britain, and the resignation of the United States President in calamitous circumstances.

The deepening industrial crisis, and a critical fuel situation exacerbated by a miners' strike and leading to the 'three-day week', forced the resignation of Edward Heath's Conservative administration. An election on February 28th produced an inconclusive result, with no party gaining an overall majority. Harold Wilson formed a minority Labour Government and went to the country again on October 10th. The result was an overall Labour majority of three, which proved in practice an adequate working majority. The elections did nothing to solve Britain's problems. Labour relations appeared to improve temporarily, but inflation continued unchecked. Violence continued in Northern Ireland; a general strike in May merely added discomfort to disorder. The year's events did, however, weaken Edward Heath's position as Leader of his Party.

The series of startling developments known as the Watergate Affair culminated in the resignation of President Nixon in August. He was succeeded by the Vice-President, Gerald R. Ford.

Coups and wars continued elsewhere. In Portugal during April a new and apparently less dictatorial government seized power, but 'freedom' was found to have its dangers as the threat of Communism loomed. The Turks and the Greeks fought once again in Cyprus during April.

Saturday, January 5th, 1974

The Unionist meeting was held in Belfast yesterday and Faulkner was badly defeated—by 80 votes in a total of 828. It was expected latterly that he would lose the vote, but not that he would lose by such a large total. He says he is going to soldier on, and he has had encouraging noises from London and Dublin—the latter, in particular, I should have thought counter-productive. Nevertheless, the writing is on the wall and the Heath–Whitelaw plan for Northern Ireland is a ruin, as was clearly to be foreseen. Now Irish events will sink into insignificance in the eyes of Westminster politicians who will be preoccupied with the miners' overtime ban, the train drivers' go-slow, and the consequent three-day week.

Thursday, January 10th, 1974

To avoid being deposed Faulkner resigned from the leadership of the Unionist Party, and is now talking of forming a break-away Unionist group. I cannot believe that this will get him anywhere. After the election his group numbered twenty-two, to the dissident Loyalists' twenty-seven. It is now more like nineteen to thirty. Ruth had some talk with Paisley last night on the telephone. He says Harry West will be the new Unionist leader and that they plan to bring the Executive to a full stop.

John Peyton had lunch with me yesterday—such a nice man and (in my opinion) so grossly underestimated in the House (and elsewhere). A friend asked Wilson if there was any member of the Opposition of whom he was afraid when he was Prime Minister. Wilson answered, 'Only one—John Peyton.' Apparently he can be very wounding in debate.

Peyton said he attended the ASLEF annual party, and after greeting his hosts, went round the room talking to everyone and finding out who they were. He thought Mrs Buckton a very nice 'cosy' woman; many of the other guests were East European diplomats—Polish, Czech and Russian attachés. A particularly unpleasant specimen was the president of the N.U.T. It was a very Communist get-together. I asked Peyton if Buckton was a Communist and he said no.

I said I thought the Government mistook the situation over the coal miners, and over Ireland, as a case for give and take, whereas in fact it was a struggle for power. And in my opinion in this struggle for power the miners would win.

Sunday, January 13th, 1974

On Friday after lunch at the Garrick with Melvin Lasky I was introduced to a Professor Vaizey, Professor of Economics at Brunel University. Lasky asked him what he thought of the crisis. Vaisey said, 'What crisis? There is masses of coal at the power stations: coal piled high all round. And the price of oil in December will be half what it is now. The only disturbing area is steel, which is in very short supply—about 50 per cent of demand. Inflation is no worse here than in other similar countries.' I said, 'But the bad effect of inflation is internal, regardless of what is happening elsewhere.' Vaizey said, 'Of course inflation will destroy Western society within three years. We all know that!' How he reconciled this last statement with his first did not appear.

The miners show no sign of calling off their overtime ban, and the Government is standing firm. The three-day working week will cause chaos by next month, and this apart from the train drivers, who are threatening an all-out strike for Tuesday. The expectation is growing that Ted will call a snap election in the course of the coming week. It would take place on February 7th or 14th while the miners' overtime ban is still on. It is risky, but the risk is likely to be greater later. If he wins he has time; while if he soldiers on, he is drawing ever closer to the unavoidable election next year. A Conservative victory will do nothing to make the miners or the railwaymen more flexible, and I should have thought he will have to buy off the miners anyway. But apparently his Party would not let him do it now.

The papers assume that though the price of oil has quadrupled since October, we shall continue to consume the same quantity, and that we shall just borrow the wherewithal. The deficit on our balance of payments will be well over £2,000 million for this year, but we should do nothing to bring it into balance as to do so would bring on a recession!

Tuesday, January 15th, 1974

More talk of an early election, but Harold Lever on the telephone this morning thought probably not. If there is an election now the Labour Party would lose, and the unions would be blamed for the defeat. So they will do everything possible to meet Ted's wishes on Phase 3 and so on, to defer the election until at least April.

Paisley on the telephone too. Another Unionist has defected from Faulkner, who now has one fewer Assemblymen than the S.D.L.P. Meanwhile Paisley's legal adviser, Desmond Boal, has come round to support for a united Ireland. Events are moving fast but I think in a direction that will vindicate Paisley.

Friday, January 18th, 1974

We picked Paisley up at the House and brought him home to supper. Conservative back-benchers were in some disarray as there had been a big build-up to an election announcement, but after a Cabinet meeting in the morning there was no announcement—so February 7th is off. There may be a dissolution next week but the week's delay won't help the Conservatives. The reasons for the change of mind seem to be Ted's inability to make a political decision; Whitelaw's reluctance to have an election, as Paisley would gain four seats or more in Northern Ireland; and, finally, Ted's wish to appear to have explored every avenue for industrial peace with the T.U.C. In this connection the *Financial Times* points out what a much more formidable character Len Murray is than Vic Feather, and how he outmanoeuvred the Government during the past week or more.

Paisley was in boisterous good form. The Loyalists are to have a group leadership—Paisley, Craig and West. He says there has been a big change of heart among the Unionists. They no longer feel their former loyalty to Great Britain, and are becoming as hostile to the British connection as are the Catholics.

Paisley's present plan is to present a petition with 100,000 signatories to the House of Commons next month, with a demand for the abolition of the Executive and fresh elections. If this is refused a general strike will be declared, which will bring the whole of Northern Ireland to a standstill. There was a preliminary run this week and it seems such a demonstration would be effective. In an election Faulkner, he thinks, would be wiped out. He has no opinion of Fitt, but regards Hume as the effective leader of the S.D.L.P. One of the S.D.L.P. Ministers is Devlin, who was concerned in the

Haughey case in Dublin, buying arms for the I.R.A.—hardly an appointment that could be acceptable to any Unionist.

Thursday, January 24th, 1974

Ruth saw Rippon yesterday to talk about the future of Hampton Court Palace. In the course of conversation he said the stage was all set for an election last week, but now the moment had gone and no election was being contemplated. He also said the Government is determined not to give in to the miners.

The ban on overtime having failed to produce results, the executive of the N.U.M. is likely to recommend an all-out strike today. I think the Government has played its hand so badly they are bound to lose to the miners—and the ASLEF go-slow still drags on. The Budget has been announced for early March—before the end of the financial year. It is hard to believe that this could be a prelude to an election, though it is possible the declaration of a miners' strike might do so.

The opinion poll in *The Times* today shows that in the past week a 4-per-cent lead for the Tories has become a 3-per-cent lead for Labour. Those questioned thought this Government is doing a bad job, and also thought Labour would be nearly as bad. Weak ministries are making the country ungovernable.

Monday, January 28th, 1974

Toby Jessel to lunch yesterday. He is not well informed, but often reflects the gossip among back-benchers. He is doubtful whether the miners will be defeated; he thinks Ted missed an important boat when he could have had an election on February 7th; he thinks there may now be an election in March; and he spoke of the possibility of a coalition government under Willie Whitelaw.

I don't see how you can have a coalition government this side of a general election unless an entirely new situation develops over the coming months. The miners are likely to strike on February 10th and the strike might last a long time. Could the Government call for an election in the middle of such a strike? Though the Government is determined not to give in, my money is on the miners. They are far more determined than Ted and his friends. The miners' strike is complicated by the ASLEF go-slow, and the most militant and powerful unions—engineers and transport workers—will doubtless dip their oars in at some moment appropriate to them.

Carrington yesterday said a strike would mean a 2½- or 2-day week with steel supplies, at best, cut to half. This all seems to me much more damaging than a general strike, provoked by the Government, would have been.

It is reported today that advertisements from Aims of Industry attacking the Communists have been turned down or modified by most of the newspapers. We have reached a sorry pass when the Communists in the printing unions can prevent their machinations being shown up.

There is a piece in *The Times* this morning deploring statements in the American newspapers that a revolutionary situation is developing here. It is the bare truth, but people like reading soothing irrelevancies. Revolutions are not confined to banana republics!

Tuesday, January 29th, 1974

Lunch with Hugh Fraser. He had no hard news, but various opinions, which are presumably not confined to him alone in the House of Commons.

He 'feels' that there will be no miners' strike: that either the necessary 55 per cent vote will not be obtained or, when it is obtained and a strike called, the Government will settle. This could only be done at the cost of gravely undermining Ted's position, but the prospect of no coal and very little steel until April or May must be terrifying the employers. Hugh thinks that if there is a strike, Ted will have to call an election. If he buys off the miners there cannot be an election for some months.

Mick McGahey, the miners' vice-president and a Communist, spelled out in unmistakable terms the Communist determination to use the strike to bring down the Government. While we all know that this is the intention, it was foolish to say so—as he now realizes. According to Hugh the Labour Party are in a state of some panic and are doing their best to urge miners not to vote for a strike. They don't want the Labour Party to be associated with Communist union leaders as it would hurt them at the polls. Even if they won, a trades union movement running wild would be enough to scare any P.M.

Hugh was talking to Ted in the House recently and said he shows no sign of anxiety or strain. He seems to have no idea of the mess he is in. After all the euphoria induced by Whitelaw's return from Ireland, Hugh says all Whitelaw's initial bounce has gone—and no wonder. To be thrown into the deep end of grave industrial trouble with no knowledge whatever of industry is enough to take the starch out of anyone.

Sunday, February 3rd, 1974

The miners' ballot will be known tomorrow morning, but it is assumed already that the result will be a big majority for a strike. Ted has offered a Royal Commission, and anyway is having more talks with the T.U.C. and the C.B.I.—whatever they may be worth.

The Eccleses looked in yesterday afternoon. David mentioned in passing that Rippon is not doing well in his Ministry—he is incapable of controlling his civil servants. I know Rippon's reputation in the House is not as high as I should have expected, but I supposed this was due to his political limitations. Perhaps his administrative abilities are not as high as I have thought—or is his department too vast to be managed?

Thursday, February 7th, 1974

The strike has been called for Saturday midnight, and the vote was 81 per cent in favour. It is assumed this morning that Ted will call a general election for February 28th. This will be fought with much bitterness and an entirely uncertain outcome. It will, of course, do nothing to solve trades-union militancy but it would, if successful, give Ted a clear five years to work out some solution. He has entirely misjudged the industrial relations problem, as he has misjudged the Irish situation, and on the economic front seems to have thought that we were coping with a temporary difficulty that would soon resolve itself. This country is in deep, deep trouble; and Wilson is even less able to cope than Heath.

Friday, February 8th, 1974

The election has been called, and so far there has been one complete surprise—Enoch Powell is to stand down. He says the election is a fraud—to confirm a policy that will immediately be abandoned when victory is achieved. The *Financial Times* surmises that he is assuming that Ted will lose, and that he will then stump the country on behalf of the new Conservatism. He must have some objective in abandoning his seat, but I cannot guess what it is. Why not stand as an independent Conservative?

344

Saturday, February 16th, 1974

The election has so far pursued an undramatic course. Ted has been better—much better than in 1970; Wilson has been worse; Callaghan has revived. After skirmishing around, the Labour Party has come to the obvious conclusion that prices are the best target for attack and the latest figures are indeed all alarming. Ted attacks the miners and the trades unions, but with no real edge to his remarks—perhaps because he thinks he will have to deal with them afterwards. There is much talk of the evils of inflation, but no one points out that the programmes of all three Parties are violently inflationary. The Liberals and the Scottish Nationalists are fielding many more candidates and getting much wider publicity, so they should do better.

There is much rejoicing in the papers that our oil supplies are keeping well up, but the questions of the price and how we are to meet it are awkward problems to be swept under the carpet—anyway for the present.

Had lunch with Geoffrey Harmsworth on Thursday. He confirmed the suspicion that Northcliffe bought his peerage from Edward VII for a hundred £1,000 notes. The money was needed for Mrs Keppel. Geoffrey said Stern's barony of Michelham was bought at the same time. What is known is that Northcliffe's peerage was pressed on Balfour by Edward.

Thursday, February 21st, 1974

Dinner last night with Mike, who produced two interesting ideas. He is not an original thinker, so I suppose he picked up the ideas from the people—political and industrial—with whom he mixes. The first idea was that the rising Liberal vote, now about 19–21 per cent, is not so much a protest vote as a sort of neutralist one. Labour and Conservative both have programmes, but no one supposes the Liberals will get a majority so their programme is irrelevant. No one knows of whom the Parliamentary Party will consist until the results are in next week, so a vote for the Liberals can be interpreted as a vote for no action at all. Mike's other idea was that if Labour wins, they will buy off the miners; if Ted wins he will accept the finding of the Relativities Board which will give handsome increases over and above Phase 3 for the face workers, but nothing for the surface workers and others. On this analysis the award will be rejected by the N.U.M., but Ted will stand firm,

345

bringing in legislation depriving miners' families of welfare benefits. This will lead to further ill-feeling and the strike will continue.

The election continues on a very uninspiring course—the far Left is lying very low; Ted is doing much better than in 1970. In Ireland, Faulkner is not standing and there are so many candidates the result is difficult to foretell, but it is assumed that the power-sharers will take a bashing. In this morning's *Times* it is reported that the U.V.F. is meeting the official I.R.A. in Dublin, and even *The Times* comments that opinion in Ireland is moving away from the British connection.

Little is being done to reduce the consumption of oil, and it is reported that the oil deficit on our balance of payments will be borrowed. This is estimated at £2,000 million. Now it is suggested that the non-oil deficit of perhaps another £2,000 million will be borrowed too. It is not clear who will be rash enough to lend the money, or when, or by what means we could ever hope to repay it.

Saturday, February 23rd, 1974

The news throughout the week has been of the growing support for the Liberals—up to 23 per cent this morning. The Tories seem likely to win, but not necessarily with a clear majority. Marjorie Proops has been on a tour round the provinces for the *Mirror*. The politics of the paper are unscrupulously Labour, but she found the working-class women she met were unexpectedly voting Conservative. Whatever the husbands may say, the wives are sick of strikes and all that.

Yesterday Scotty Weston had a piece in *The Times*, buried at the bottom of an inside page. His theme was that the election is being carried on in a world of pure fantasy in which the real problems were hardly alluded to by any speaker. In fact, they do all read as if the problem were the division of an ever-growing cake, while in fact we are broke, but determined neither to face the fact nor to do anything about it.

Monday, February 25th, 1974

The polls now give the Liberals up to 28 per cent, so they may well hold the balance of power. Paisley thinks he may get eight seats in Northern Ireland, but more probably seven; Faulkner may get one (Rafton Pounder); and assorted Catholics, four.

Had lunch with Tony Bloomfield, who is voting Liberal this time! He says Rippon is a complete failure in his department, does no work, and is often to be found of an evening at Annabel's bar and night-club in Berkeley Square. Tony would know about Rippon's department because all planning goes through that office and Tony is a property tycoon. He would know about a club in Berkeley Square because his office is there.

Tuesday, February 26th, 1974

Lunch with Derek Ezra. He is a nice man—intelligent and dedicated to the Coal Board—but he has not enough weight or authority. He finds the Government very 'centralized'. Ministers cannot give decisions without reference to Ted. He thinks Whitelaw was keen on a settlement with the miners but that this was not approved. McGahey, the Communist president of the Scottish mineworkers, is a militant on the national stage but very co-operative and effective locally. It was expected that the original offer would have been balloted on, in which case it would have been accepted. This was no doubt the reason why it was not balloted on. It was conveyed to Ezra that quite a small improvement on the offer would be accepted, if it was clearly a breach of Phase 3. This was what Vic Feather told me. In the outcome Phase 3 will be breached and very much more expensively.

Ezra thinks that it should be possible to negotiate a productivity deal and also an agreement on arbitration. I can see that it is just possible agreement on these points could be reached, but the agreements would not be honoured. It was clear that there has been no talk at the Ezra level of serious confrontation at any time or under any circumstances.

I asked about the new Selby coal-field. He said in the early years of this century the old Yorkshire pits were becoming exhausted, and two holes were put down to test the extension northward. They both struck badly-faulted ground with no show of coal in commercial quantities. The extension southward was much more promising and developed into the Doncaster coal-field. Then there was a long period of decline when no one was interested in coal, and it is only in the last year they have got around to serious testing of the Selby coal-field, which extends as far as York and is the largest area of virgin coal in Europe. Owing to the serious consequences of subsidence, the coal will be cut out so as to leave massive pillars. The first development is to involve a complex yielding five million tons a year; the largest existing pit produces only $1\frac{1}{2}$ million tons.

Saturday, March 2nd, 1974

The figures for the general election are now all in and the result is a complete deadlock. Obviously the great British public thinks nothing of either main Party and the electoral system does not help the other Parties. So there are 297 Tories, 301 Labour, 14 Liberals, 11 Ulster anti-Faulkner Unionists, 7 Scottish Nationalists, 2 Welsh Nationalists, and sundry odds and ends. It was announced last night that Ted is trying to form an anti-Socialist alliance. The Liberals seem willing to play ball but may demand a new P.M. To me the situation demands a change as there will have to be an election before very long, and if the Tories go into another election with Ted in the lead, they will be massacred. It seems that Powell's announcement that he was voting Labour had a considerable effect in the West Midlands to damage the Conservatives. His announced decision seems to me to amount to political suicide. He would have been better advised to stand in his old constituency as an Independent Conservative.

Paisley originally told me he hoped to win four or perhaps six seats when the election came. During the election his housekeeper told Ruth that they were praying for eight. In fact he got eleven—only Fitt kept his place. Paisley rang this morning: he said he had been trying to get through earlier. Would we convey a message to Ted that his eleven did not want a Labour Government and would support a Conservative Government, on condition that there was a fresh election to the Assembly? This was conveyed to the P.M. The *Financial Times* today says that any deal with the Paisley forces is out of the question, but this hostility to Paisley is hard to understand and surely will be impossible to sustain. Paisley said he would welcome Whitelaw as the new P.M. (if it came to that) as he knows Whitelaw well.

Sunday, March 3rd, 1974

Last night I rang up Thorpe and told him about Paisley's message to Ted; Paisley had said he had no objection to this. Thorpe was grateful, and said that Ted had not told him about Paisley's offer at their meeting in the afternoon.

The political situation remains completely confused. Several

Liberals, including Pardoe (one of their M.P.s), have attacked the idea of any deal with the Tories; Wilson is sticking to his determination to have no deal with anyone; some commentators believe (quite wrongly) that three or four of the Paisleyites will vote Conservative; the Welsh and Scottish Nationalists are thought likely to vote Labour rather than Conservative. The commentators assume that the electorate wants no firm action of any kind—certainly none against miners or trades unionists. I should have thought the result reflects contempt for both main Parties and their leaders. Any call for firm government would depend on a far greater degree of realism in political speakers and propaganda generally.

I should have thought the result will either be a minority Labour Government, or a coalition (at least for a few months) between Conservatives, Liberals and Paisleyites. But this would surely have to be under a new P.M.—presumably Whitelaw. It is interesting that in all the comings and goings at No. 10 there is no report of Alec Home. In any question of the leadership he must be the key figure.

Monday, March 4th, 1974

The crisis continues with much to-ing and fro-ing by Ministers and Liberals. There was no response to Paisley's message to 10 Downing St, but there was an absurd reply to West's telegram saying the same. The reply stated that seven of the Ulster eleven would be acceptable as recipients of the Conservative whip! Ted does not seem to have got the idea at all. The Tories surely cannot go into another election, presumably this year, with Ted in the lead. The Liberals are split between those who think some form of coalition will be necessary and those who won't have one at any price. Some Labour leaders are saying they won't deal with any Conservative Government. The Scottish Nationalists are also split between those who look more or less to the Labour Party and those who tend to be Conservatives on non-Scottish issues.

Paisley is to be the Whip of his group, while West is to be the leader. Paisley thinks this is the best arrangement. The *Financial Times* interprets this as by-passing Paisley! It is extraordinary how in this crisis the newspapers, television and radio all conspire to belittle the importance of the eleven Ulster members, and in particular to write as if Paisley is a man of straw. Paisley this morning said he had heard that Heath is furious over the turn of events in Northern Ireland and that while he is P.M. no progress can be made.

Tuesday, March 5th, 1974

Yesterday evening all attempts by Heath to do a deal with the Liberals broke down, so he resigned and Wilson reigns in his stead. It seems Thorpe and Grimond were offered Cabinet posts but the Party was only offered the reference to a Speaker's Conference on the question of proportional representation. This satisfied no one—how could it?

Wilson, as seen on television, has deteriorated sadly since 1964.

The City is pleased and prices are up—as is the pound. It is presumably relief that we now have a Government, even if it is only a Labour one. Wilson's Cabinet is very similar to what it was four years ago—even Ross, a notorious failure at that time, is back in the Scottish Office. Barbara Castle has the Social Services, while the immensely superior Shirley Williams has Consumer Protection. Merlyn Rees, little thought of in the Labour Party or in Northern Ireland, is to be the new Irish Secretary.

The papers seem to assume that new elections for the Assembly are pretty inevitable, but all comments play down the importance of the Ulster eleven. The difference is so striking, contrasted with the importance attached to the Liberal fourteen, though of course the fourteen are supported by a very large popular vote.

If I were a Tory M.P. I couldn't wait to replace Ted as leader. An election may come at any time and to confront Wilson with Ted *again* would surely not be the way to win.

Thursday, March 7th, 1974

At the House yesterday there was a letter from Heath to West, again offering the Whip to seven of the eleven Ulster Unionists. It was of course turned down and was interpreted merely as a mark of personal hostility to Paisley (one of the four excluded). The miners have been bought off with an award of 29 per cent— even more expensive than the Wilberforce bonanza.

Friday, March 8th, 1974

Dinner last night with the Peytons. He is not to be a front-bench spokesman while the Tories are in Opposition as he will have much greater freedom on the back benches. He said he would have resigned his office as Transport Minister if Ted had done a deal with the Liberals. He also said he would not accept support from Craig (one of the Ulster Unionists). He said Conservative Headquarters blames the loss of five seats in the West Midlands on the effect of Enoch Powell's intervention. Peyton thinks Enoch is unbalanced. He said he expected a new election in June, because Wilson will still be able to attribute all the nation's difficulties to the Tories. Later he will be saddled with them himself. I said I thought Wilson's thirst for office would lead him to stay at No. 10 and take no risks. He had a dreadful experience in 1970 which he will not want to repeat.

Michael Foot is said to have given the Coal Board a limit of £100 million to settle the miners' strike. However, the Board had to go to £108 million, which will be a disastrous precedent for other settlements. The list of Government appointments as so far announced covers the Cabinet (which is almost identical with the administration that had failed so lamentably by 1970) and the principal Junior Ministers. The latter include Orme, Heffer, Balogh and Judith Hart. Sending Orme, an extreme left-winger, to Ireland seems quite daft, and these other militants will hardly engender confidence either here or abroad.

Thursday, March 14th, 1974

We met Paisley at the airport and took him to the House of Commons. He is, of course, delighted by the election results in Northern Ireland. If he had known how well they were doing he could probably have ousted Fitt, whose majority fell from 15,000 to 2,000. He says three of Faulkner's men have decided to come over to his side in the Assembly and others will follow. In any case, if the British and Irish Governments continue to back Faulkner, they will have a general strike on their hands. Paisley says that Whitelaw wanted the Loyalists to be at Sunningdale, and it was owing to Ted's refusal to allow this that Whitelaw resigned.

Saturday, March 16th, 1974

Much blather in the papers about a constitutional crisis. If the Government is defeated on Monday, is it entitled to a dissolution? When counting the votes on both sides much play is made with the Liberal vote (14), the Scottish Nationalists (7), and even the Welsh Nationalists (2), but as far as possible the 11 Paisleyites are ignored. Yesterday the *Financial Times* referred to the 'ten Loyalists plus Dr Paisley'. It seems that a number of back-bench M.P.s are dissatisfied with Ted's leadership and want a national government of all Parties. The challenge to Labour on Monday seems to have been more or less forced on Ted by his back benches. So far he has shown no signs of realizing that he was defeated. The *Financial Times* was very critical of Carr's appointment as Shadow Chancellor. He knows nothing about economics and finance, and the *Financial Times* thinks Keith Joseph the obvious man. In the various re-arrangements Rippon is moved down and Whitelaw and Carrington are not promoted or praised. At the final Cabinet meeting of the Tory Government Ted did not thank his colleagues—nor did they thank him!

Tuesday, March 26th, 1974

Just back from Boston, where I have been for the inside of last week. At dinner one night our hosts drank the health of the Queen, but refused to drink the health of the President. They realize what serious harm Watergate is doing the country, both internally and externally, but seem unable to bring the matter to a head. They seem still to regard England as such a stable country—one to be envied!

At dinner last night at the George Earle Memorial Lecture, in the Haberdashers' Hall, I had a word with John Foster, who didn't stand at the recent election. He said he doubted if Ted could be removed as Leader of the Party before the next election. In the meantime, Ted is blaming the voter for not giving him a majority! He does not seem to know the score.

The Budget this afternoon was apparently well put over by Denis Healey. It is a better job than Barber would have done, and perhaps was the best possible under the circumstances. I was interested in a commentator from Wall Street on the six o'clock radio. He said it was the general opinion on Wall St, and in Washington, that this country is bankrupt, and this Budget would obviously not help in that respect. The trade deficit for February is well over £400 million. A loan of $2,500 million has been raised abroad by the big banks to tide the Government over, but with a trade deficit of that order this large loan (for ten years) will be neither here nor there.

Friday, March 29th, 1974

It has been decided by the Tory powers that it would be unkind to deprive Ted of the leadership now. The leadership is evidently thought of in personal and 'club' terms, not in connection with winning the forthcoming election.

Ted is so shaken he has not yet answered any of his letters of sympathy.

Tuesday, April 2nd, 1974

Lunch with Hugh Fraser yesterday. He feels very strongly that the Conservatives cannot win the next election under Ted, but he has no convinced ideas of the identity of Ted's successor. He said Whitelaw was in good heart, but Hugh evidently had reservations about him as P.M. Du Cann was a name he had apparently not thought of. He thought there might be a national government, possibly under Healey, before long, but had no idea how or when this could come about. Hugh had not heard the report that Whitelaw resigned just before Sunningdale because Ted insisted on the exclusion of Paisley and his supporters.

Violence reached a new peak over the weekend in Northern Ireland. Merlyn Rees has made a speech in which he said that the military force would be reduced; that there would be no fresh elections to the Assembly; and that the Government would press ahead with the ratification of Sunningdale. Paisley is in a state of deep depression, and said that this is a formula for civil war. He thought the armed Protestants would vent their sense of frustration on the British troops. One of the curious aspects of British politics is that once a blunder has been made, every effort is made to avoid correcting it—e.g. Concorde, the Industrial Relations Act, and now Sunningdale. The Dublin Government attaches quite illusory value to the Council of Ireland—meaningless unless supported by the Northern Protestants. The Labour Government is pursuing Heath's misguided Irish policies, perhaps with the idea that by pursuing a bi-partisan policy they ensure themselves against attack by the Conservatives. Meanwhile, the Irish situation continues to deteriorate.

Hugh said he rather liked Peter Shore, and that Harold Lever had told him that Shore's bark was worse than his bite.

Saturday, April 6th, 1974

The principal recent events have been Thursday's debate on Ireland and yesterday's meeting between Wilson and Cosgrave. The decision has been made to press on with Sunningdale and ignore the election results. This is coupled with a decision to cut down the strength of the Army in Northern Ireland and step up the role of the police. More detainees are to be released, and the ban on Sinn Fein and the U.V.F. is to be lifted. This policy seems to amount to sops to the Unionists and the Catholics, whilst ignoring Paisley and his friends. Faulkner can hardly be helped by part of the programme, and promises to bear down on terrorists on both sides of the border are hardly likely to be effective. It is hard to see why Cosgrave should lend a hand to an obviously abortive policy. The Labour Party's motive is presumably that by pressing on with Heath's policy they cannot be attacked by the Conservatives over anything that happens in Ireland. Also it is unlikely that they will get much support from the Paisley Unionists—except in return for fresh elections to the Assembly. This would destroy Faulkner and the Heath policy, and would end the possibility of a bi-partisan policy in Ireland. In Irish terms this policy is insane, but taking a purely Westminster view it makes temporary sense. Paisley's fear is that the next development is likely to be Protestant attacks on the Army. He says all feelings of loyalty to, or affection for, England are rapidly fading.

Wednesday, April 10th, 1974

Have just returned from two days' house-hunting in Dublin. I had some talk with the editor of the *Irish Times* and dinner with the editor of the *Irish Independent*. They seemed neither well informed nor to have any worth-while contacts. The *Irish Independent* man was interesting on the lack of curiosity in the South about events in the North. They only lead the paper on events in Northern Ireland if all else fails. Such news does not now sell papers. The *Irish Times*'s line was that Paisley is an evil man—gifted no doubt, but evil. Given time, the Sunningdale agreement would work; Paisley would never be accepted as the Protestant's no. 1 man; the key to the whole situation was the S.D.L.P. and particularly Hume. I said the weakness of the S.D.L.P. was that it had no support from the I.R.A. This was swept aside, and I was told that power-sharing had come to stay because the S.D.L.P. would insist on it.

The *Irish Independent*'s editor, on the other hand, was far less political. His strongest feeling over the whole situation was a hatred of violence. He thought the Provos were now a small number of freelances operating without any central direction, though the papers while we were in Dublin were saying that David O'Connell had returned to the South after a visit to Belfast, which lasted three days. The *Irish Independent*'s editor thought that at some later stage the Official I.R.A. would move in on the Provos and wipe them out. After all, the Officials were Marxists and had powerful friends abroad. He thought Cosgrave, whom his paper supported at the close of the last election, was in control of his Government far more than Lynch ever was. He is very anti-I.R.A.

On other matters, my informant said that if Britain withdrew from the Common Market, Ireland would probably stay in. Their export trade with the Continent was growing, and they were shipping large numbers of sheep and some cattle to North Africa. The *Irish Times* is doing quite well but the *Irish Press* (de Valera's paper) looks to be on its way out.

The recent violence in Northern Ireland, and Merlyn Rees's statement of last week, have seriously weakened Faulkner's position, which was already pretty shaky. He and his principal lieutenant, Roy Bradford, have been issuing flatly contradictory statements about the situation.

Thursday, April 11th, 1974

The Irish picture is darker than ever, with Rees making silly promises to 'stamp out terrorism'.

The French Presidential election is to be held in the middle of next month. The choice seems to be between Chaban-Delmas, Giscard d'Estaing and Mitterand. Any of the three will be a marked change from Pompidou. I suppose Giscard would be the best man, but is least likely to win. Pompidou impressed me very favourably on the two occasions on which I met him. It is hard luck that he should have died at sixty-two.

Mrs Meir has apparently finally resigned, which leaves an additional element of instability in the Middle East. The Italians still await a right-wing coup; the German regime is not too strong; and ours is hamstrung with no majority. Jim Callaghan as Foreign Secretary seems a clumsy disaster. He has antagonized the Europeans and publicly insulted the Greeks, Chileans and South Africans. To make up, he speaks of closer links with the Commonwealth, the United Nations, the U.S.A. and Russia. Closer links with everyone except our neighbours and the right-wing governments of places like Greece is clearly meaningless. If this policy is pursued we shall have no friends at all. Wilson has perked up since what was obviously a very unexpected success in the

355

election, but he is nothing like his old self—which was inadequate anyway.

I am told that a man to watch is Daly, the very new Catholic Bishop of Derry. He distinguished himself as a parish priest in the riots of Bloody Sunday* in Derry, when he went to the comfort of wounded parishioners.

Wednesday, April 17th, 1974

The Loyalist strategy, which seems to me correct, is to demand full integration with England. When this is refused, they can then call for independence as more acceptable than second-class citizenship. It is interesting that Paisley had not seen a piece in the *Observer* of April 7th cautiously advocating independence. From the pen of Terence O'Neill this seemed to me significant.

Thursday, April 18th, 1974

Lunch for A.B. [a senior civil servant] whom I had not seen for months—partly because he has been away ill. I asked why Ted had invited a second beating at the hands of the N.U.M. He said he lost out the first time, but felt he had done well under Phase 2, so he thought he could win on the third occasion. Like other P.M.s, A.B. said, Ted felt he could persuade the miners to be reasonable even if no one else could. A.B. said Ted was not very enamoured of the Industrial Relations Act, but his offer to amend it was nullified by the Labour Party's promise to repeal it. Ted, throughout the negotiations with the T.U.C., was very conscious of Communist influence; but very little of this strong feeling leaked out in public. I said Len Murray seemed a more formidable character than Vic Feather. A.B. agreed he was more intelligent, but pointed out that he had been unable to have his nominee made deputy secretary. The job went to Jack Jones's henchman. This was a serious set-back, and Murray has not ventured since on an independent line.

A.B. said Prior was a good Minister. He had no ideas above his station, but was a good chairman of Cabinet Committees and a good Leader of the House. A.B. said Rippon was out of sympathy with Ted's left-of-centre policy and, whether for this reason or another, spent time elsewhere that he should have spent at work.

* See p. 163.

356

A.B. said there was a great contrast between Wilson now and Wilson in 1964. He had not expected to be back in office, but now that he was he was content to leave a lot to his Ministers. About the Common Market, A.B. thought Callaghan's bluster was to impress his Party, and to provide an opening bargaining position. He doubted whether we would leave the E.E.C.

A.B. said he believed Barber, who did not stand in the election, would have left politics even if the Tories had won the election. Robert Carr he described as a man with a very muddled mind.

In general terms A.B. thought the Budget inflationary, the rate of inflation worse than ever, and no event or personality in sight to mend matters. He doubted whether North Sea oil would be a happy way out of all our afflictions, and expected the next twelve months to be very rough going. He expected an early election—not for the usual reasons, but because Wilson was having great difficulty holding his Party together. But even if he won an election he would gain only a temporary respite on the Party issue—and an election would do nothing to solve inflation or militant trades unionism.

I said the nationalized industries had been so messed about that no industrialist of standing would accept the chairmanship of any of them. A.B. agreed, and said that senior civil servants were about the only group who would welcome such an appointment. They were used to dealing with civil servants and Ministers and would welcome the money. But both this Government and the last would not hear of civil servants being considered for these jobs.

Sunday, April 28th, 1974

The principal news these last few days has been of the coup in Portugal. The regime was becoming fossilized, and the continuing fighting in Africa was expensive, unsuccessful and unpopular. Spinola, a popular general, has been put in power by a number of junior officers. He sounds more realistic than the ousted regime but, as Peregrine Worsthorne points out in the *Sunday Telegraph* today, the rejoicings by liberals in this country may be falsified. It is likely that liberalizing the regime in Lisbon will get out of hand and give the Communists their chance. This, presumably, Spinola would crack down on. But any relaxation in Angola, and particularly in Mozambique—and there must be some—must be most unwelcome in South Africa, and even more so in Rhodesia.

357

Thursday, May 2nd, 1974

The latest outcome of the Poulson affair is the report that Edward Short received £250 from Mr T. Dan Smith, recently jailed. The sum is small and the payment long ago, but Short misrepresented his relationship with Dan Smith, as was shown by the *Express* yesterday which published facsimiles of the letters that passed between the two. It had been reported for some years that there was much corruption among Labour politicians in the North-East but no attempt seems to have been made to show it up or stop it. In fact, Mr Milne, M.P. for Blyth in Northumberland, is being expelled from the Labour Party for harping on the necessity for an inquiry.

Wednesday, May 8th, 1974

The big news today is that all the engineers are on strike over the sequestration of their assets to pay claims for damages awarded by the Industrial Relations Court. It is difficult to see why Scanlon has taken this course. Presumably, the Government will buy the engineers off—but this can only be done at a disastrous cost in prestige and morale. Otherwise the strike would soon bring the whole country to a standstill.

Meanwhile, the Poulson affair rumbles on. Short foolishly keeps his end of the story running by demands for an apology; another Labour M.P. from the North-East has been brought into the picture; and on Tuesday night Granada put on a devastating story of a hospital in Malta, built by Poulson at the expense of H.M.G., opened by the Queen, and unoccupied—a costly white elephant.

Thursday, May 9th, 1974

Later we were at Edwin Plowden's annual party. I had some talk with Keith Joseph, who looked much thinner than when we met last. His theme was that we grievously lacked eloquence in our politics—Macleod is dead, Hailsham enmeshed in the higher ranks of the judiciary, and Enoch Powell batting for the other side. He mentioned no other names. Cyril Kleinwort, just back from the U.S., said that even with all the political scandals American society seemed much more stable than ours. Eric Roll said Henry Grunfeld was just back from the U.S.—his comment was that for the first time 'profit' had become a dirty word in the American vocabulary.

The engineers' strike has been called off by the intervention of an 'anonymous donor', who has paid £65,000 into court and allowed the engineers' sequestrated assets to be restored to them. This is an unqualified victory for the engineers, and a serious blow to the authority and prestige of the law.

Friday, May 17th, 1974

The world continues on the road to chaos. The new Government in Lisbon is very left-wing, with two Communist Ministers. Can the Spaniards and Americans allow this? Schmidt in Bonn may be more effective than Brandt, though not such a personality. In France the election on Sunday might go either way.

In Northern Ireland, the Ulster Workers' Council have staged an intermittent general strike against Sunningdale and all its works. So far the Government is clinging desperately to Faulkner. It is surprising how British Governments persist in misconceived policies—far more than in wise ones.

Saturday, May 18th, 1974

The principal news today is that a number of car bombs went off in Dublin yesterday evening, and one or two more in Monaghan, near the border. There was no warning and twenty-eight people were killed. It is not obvious who might be responsible—clearly not the I.R.A., who accuse the S.A.S. (a semi-secret British military force). Others will accuse Protestant extremists, and at least one car involved *was* stolen in Northern Ireland. However, it is hard to see what the Protestants would gain by such an act, though there is always the possibility of freelance action by some extremist splinter group. Their motive would be revenge for all the I.R.A. bombs.

Merlyn Rees yesterday had a meeting with some of the Loyalists. He refused a fresh election to the Assembly, and said that their present policies would lead to a clash between the Protestants and the Army. I might add that he was warned of this some weeks ago when the new Government decided to ignore the fact that eleven of the twelve Ulster M.P.s are anti-Sunningdale. As the Government persists in its misconceived policies, the danger of chaos and civil war north and south of the border are clearly mounting.

When the news of the car bombs in Dublin reached Paisley & co., he asked Wilson to meet a delegation of his group and others. Wilson said he was 'too busy'.

Monday, May 20th, 1974

Hugh Fraser to dine last night. He had no particular news, except of growing exasperation with Ted in the Conservative Party. He has not seen Enoch very recently, but says his behaviour can only be explained on the assumption that Enoch felt sure Ted would win the election. Now that he has lost, Enoch has made a speech urging reconciliation within the Tory Party. I cannot see how this can be taken up after he had urged his followers to vote Labour in February.

In Northern Ireland a State of Emergency has been declared. This may be to enable troops to be used to man the power stations. Anyway, the Ulster Workers' Council has postponed the complete electricity black-out threatened for midnight last night. *The Times* this morning has a piece on its main inside news page saying the militant Workers' Council has bypassed the Loyalist politicians. This is not so. Paisley told us of plans for a general strike weeks ago. *The Times* leader urges the Government to stand firm and engage in a trial of strength with the militant Protestants. They don't seem to know that this means a clash between the British Army and the various Protestant volunteer forces. It is amazing that the Government should take such appalling risks to prop up Brian Faulkner.

Tuesday, May 21st, 1974

The march back to work in Belfast, led by Len Murray of the T.U.C. has been a flop. Roy Bradford, of the Stormont Executive, shows signs of leaving Faulkner and will be followed by others. The strike will be stepped up. I hope the Government will have the sense to withdraw before there is a clash between the Protestants and the Army.

Mike came to dinner last night and recalled that on one of the long nights at No. 10, when he was at the C.B.I., he had some talk with a senior civil servant. He asked why the Government did nothing to show the influence of the Communist Party on the trades union movement. The civil servant made it plain that he was strongly against doing any such thing. He was influenced by Senator McCarthy's antics in the U.S., and felt that an anti-Communist campaign might get out of control.

Lunch yesterday for Brian Walden. He told me he is making between £25,000 and £30,000 a year. He was offered office by Wilson. Stonehouse was not offered office, nor was David Marquand, whom Walden described as much the ablest man on Labour's back benches. Walden said he had no special information, but had a hunch that the election would be in October, and Labour would have a majority of about fifty. However, Labour has never had a majority in England, and Hugh Fraser the other night prophesied that the Scottish Nationalists would have twenty-five seats in the next Parliament, as against seven in this one.

I asked about Merlyn Rees, whom he knows particularly well. Walden said he is the nicest man in the Parliamentary Party— upright, courageous and terribly nice. But he has little personality and no imagination. He will plod on with the present Irish policy until he is told to stop. And in Walden's opinion it is becoming urgently necessary to get the Army out of Ulster. It is this aspect of Irish affairs that will impress Ministers most.

I asked him what he thought of the trades unions and all that. He said the situation was getting worse day by day. I said the alternatives were to tackle a general strike now, or to let inflation run its course, with the destruction of our society as the result. The bloodshed involved in the second course would be worse than that inevitable in the first, but it would be delayed. Walden said the trades unions would not be tackled by this Government, nor by Labour if it won the next general election.

Walden agreed that all Parties denounced inflation while recommending inflationary policies. He thought that inflation, and the lack of industrial investment, were the two major problems confronting us. He agreed that recent policies of both Heath and Healey were bound to effect a reduction in industrial investment, which had been conspicuously too low for twenty years or more.

Walden said Ted has no idea of public opinion, so Carrington thought it would help if he brought Sir Harmar Nicholls to see him. Nicholls is a man for whom Walden has no respect, but he has been a Conservative M.P. for many years, and according to Walden has a wonderful feel for the opinion of the Conservative voter at any particular time. The meeting was a complete flop. Ted took no interest in what Nicholls had to say and had recourse to polite questions about his family!

Friday, May 24th, 1974
The strike in Northern Ireland continues, and it is surely only a matter of a day or two before the troops are brought in. I am afraid

that if this happens they will be shot by Protestants, and the demand to withdraw from Ireland will become irresistible.

Parliament has risen for a fortnight, but yesterday in the House, Merlyn Rees attacked Paisley for being a 'democrat at Westminster and demagogue in Belfast'.

Wilson has summoned the Assembly leaders to talk things over; part of the Sunningdale agreement has been put in cold storage until 'fresh Assembly elections in 1977 or 1978'! In a situation in which no one knows what will happen from day to day, to talk about plans for 1977 seems quite insane. At the moment it looks as if troops may be withdrawn and money cut off leaving the Six Counties in chaos. The damage done at Sunningdale, by ignoring the result of the Parliamentary elections in February, and by the personal ambitions of Faulkner and Hume, is incalculable.

Wilson announces today his third batch of life peers since he took office: fifteen of them, including Marcia, who is still to remain his confidential secretary. This is an act of defiance hardly helped by a peerage for Ted Castle, the husband of Barbara Castle.

Later. In the course of conversation with the editor of the *Sunday Express*, John Junor, we talked about the revelation in Roskill's book on Hankey that Ramsay Macdonald paid off a blackmailer out of Secret Service funds.

It is announced today that Stanley Orme, the Junior Minister in the Northern Ireland Office, is to be a Privy Councillor—another example of the policy of rewarding failure.

Sunday, May 26th, 1974

The leaders of the three Parties in the Northern Ireland Executive saw Wilson on Friday. This was followed by a Cabinet meeting, and the announcement that Wilson would speak to the nation on television on Saturday night. It was supposed that this could only mean that the troops were to move in to the power-stations and to take over the distribution of petrol. In the outcome the speech was mere verbiage and no grounds for its delivery were revealed. The B.B.C. commentator last night and the papers this morning imply that moving in the troops had been the idea, but the commanding officer, General Sir Francis King, who has taken over from Tuzo, refused. Nevertheless, Wilson and the papers continue to say we must press on with a policy which has never got off the ground.

Monday, May 27th, 1974

At 6.00 a.m. this morning the troops after all did move in—to the oil depots—whereupon all the power workers walked out, and the Province is at a standstill. It appears, from the papers this morning, that Gerry Fitt issued an ultimatum yesterday. If the troops did not move in, he and the other S.D.L.P. members of the Executive would resign, and the whole power-sharing policy would very visibly collapse. Of course, if you are going to send the troops in—and that against the evident advice of the General in charge—to do so as the result of an ultimatum from the Catholics is the worst possible background to a policy which looks disastrous anyway. At this most serious crisis in our affairs, Heath is in China! Pym last night made the Conservative ministerial speech balancing Wilson's the night before. Pym's words were better than Wilson's, but on television he looks like an insignificant clerk, and what he had to say might make some appeal in this country but none at all in Ireland. It is hard to believe, but apparently Wilson still believes that the Sunningdale agreement can be rescued. Whatever may come out of the crisis, it will certainly not be Sunningdale.

Thursday, May 30th, 1974

On Tuesday morning Faulkner asked Rees to negotiate with the Ulster Workers' Council; Rees refused and Faulkner, with his Unionists, resigned. With the collapse of the Executive, the Workers' Council called off their strike. One might have expected Wilson to be in London through all this—or at least that he would return post haste. But not so. He only held a meeting of Ministers yesterday, and afterwards saw the other two Parties at Westminster. The idea is to prorogue the Assembly for four months, during which time Ulster will be run by the Junior Ministers for Northern Ireland—Stanley Orme and Lord Donaldson—under the general supervision of Rees. Parliament is to be recalled, and there will be a two-day debate next week. Rees will not meet the Ulster Workers' Council but is to meet all the elected representatives at Stormont today. I imagine he will have a very rough ride from Paisley and Co. The Dublin Government has been expressing concern—but support for the British Government. They would have done better to be silent.

Wilson appeared on commercial television last night. He did not seem to have any grip on the situation at all. Rees appeared briefly in 'the News', looking haggard and mainly concerned to say he would never negotiate with the Ulster Workers' Council. Rees is an ineffective little man, and neither he nor his Junior Ministers have any experience of running anything. So we can only hope that they will be mere window-dressing, and that the work will be done by the civil servants. There is this to be said about the latest developments: the independence of Northern Ireland and withdrawal of the British troops are now policies that can be mentioned, if not advocated.

The Price sisters are continuing their hunger strike, and are in poor shape. If they die, this will cause serious trouble all over Ireland. I cannot see why H.M.G. takes so many risks to keep them in prison here instead of Northern Ireland.*

Saturday, June 1st, 1974

Dinner last night to pay tribute to Eric Cheadle, who has been deputy managing director of the Thomson Organization since 1959, on his retirement. I had some talk with Alf Robens. He said Wilson was behaving like the non-executive chairman of a company. He presides at meetings, but otherwise lets his Ministers carry on as they think fit. He thought Wilson to be entirely concerned with winning the next election. After five further years of office he would retire. Ruth sat next to Bill Barnetson at dinner. Bill is rather close to Ted Heath. He said the effect of his defeat on Ted was that of severe shell-shock. It took him weeks to recover. It is astonishing to me that he should have taken it so hard. He had seen Harold Wilson and Jack Lynch go down to unexpected defeat, and his standing in the opinion polls was abysmally low.

Merlyn Rees gave a press conference yesterday. One of his more astonishing statements was that Paisley's activities were mainly aimed at securing Harry West's post as leader of the Ulster Loyalists for himself! How does one hope to govern Northern Ireland when the Minister is so hopelessly misinformed? His distaste for the Loyalists was emphasized at the meeting on Thursday when Rees greeted the pro-Sunningdale politicians at the Stormont front door, but sent a civil servant to greet Paisley and co. Discourtesies of this trivial kind are hardly likely to help.

* Dolours and Marion Price were sentenced to life imprisonment in November 1973 for their part in causing car bomb explosions in London. They began a hunger strike shortly after sentence in an effort to persuade the Government to permit them to serve their sentences in Northern Ireland. Artificial feeding of the Price Sisters was stopped on medical advice on May 19th, and at this time their lives were said to be in danger. Eventually the Price Sisters abandoned their hunger strike.

Bill Deedes made a speech last night about Ireland, from which it became clear that bi-partisanship is wearing thin. He also remarked on the fact that Cosgrave in Dublin seemed tone deaf to political opinion in the North.

Further about my conversation with Alf Robens, he said the climate in industry was such that no one was investing in anything. He found among his Conservative friends a strong feeling that Ted must go—but how to get him out? As successors, Carr was too weak, Whitelaw's stock had fallen over Ireland, and the only likely candidate is now seen to be Soames.

Monday, June 3rd, 1974

We met Paisley at the airport and drove him to the House. On the plane with him were Craig, West and two more of his M.P.s that I did not recognize. I had not met Craig or West before. They are no fanatics. According to Paisley the affairs of the last ten days were far more dramatic than has appeared publicly. The Cabinet, ten days ago, decided to move in the Army, arrest Paisley and his group and try them for high treason—hence Wilson's proposed broadcast to the nation. In the outcome the high treason policy had to be called off, and Wilson had to do what he could by way of a broadcast.

Paisley feels that there will now have to be Assembly elections in September or October. He says the S.D.L.P. are split between the Gerry Fitt-John Hume faction and the Paddy Devlin–David Cooper faction. In an election they would do badly. The Alliance Party would disappear, and so would most of Faulkner's men—possibly including Faulkner. In another Westminster election Paisley would expect to hold his eleven seats, and perhaps win Fitt's as well. Paisley says Whitelaw is finished; Rees he thinks a silly little man. The Army's move into the petrol stations was an even feebler gesture than appeared at the time. They took over 21 out of 1,500 places, and got no help from the oil company's staffs at any level.

Paisley is quite certain there will be no blood-bath on the withdrawal of British troops. He is a man of peace and not anti-Catholic. He wants no dialogue with Dublin until it can be between Belfast and Dublin—with no English participation.

In the strike nothing was left to chance—the organizing committee was backed by another one in reserve, and a third in reserve behind that, in case of widespread arrests. Barr, the spokesman for the strikers, is a member of Paisley's Church.

Wednesday, June 5th, 1974
Peter McLachlan, a member of the Assembly, came to see me last night—at his request. He had seen Heath and Pym earlier in the day, but did not say what happened at their meeting. He really wanted to hear my views and was pressed for time. However, he did say that he did not believe a blood-bath would follow the withdrawal of British troops. He wondered if Paisley really had control of the resurgent Protestant working class. He said the S.D.L.P. is an overwhelmingly middle-class party, while the I.R.A. is working class. They don't speak the same language. Peter thinks there will have to be fresh elections to the Assembly. He expects the I.R.A. (under whatever name) to get some seats and provide a channel for communication between them and the Protestants.

The two-day debate on Northern Ireland was undistinguished. Wilson launched a bitter attack on Paisley, who responded in kind. Wilson and Heath both maintained that power-sharing was the only hope. However, independence and the withdrawal of the British troops are now freely spoken about, which is a gain for realism.

Saturday, June 15th, 1974
Lunch yesterday for Carrington. He is the nicest man, and was in crashing form. We talked about Ireland. He is somewhat less antagonistic to Paisley than he was, but described him as the 'bigot. of all bigots'. He thought pulling the troops out was risky—but so was any course. He thought fresh Assembly elections inevitable, and said he thought the Government had no idea what to do.

Carrington thinks our economic situation is deteriorating so fast that Wilson is bound to have an election in the autumn; the result might be something very similar to what we have now. If the Tories were to win, what on earth would they do? If they lost, that would be the end of Heath as leader. He thought a future leader of his Party is Jim Prior. He got a First at Cambridge, and in Cabinet is very sensible, and has come on a lot. I asked why they did not bring back Soames? Carrington said he is really a sixteen-inch gun, but considers it to be his duty to soldier on in Brussels. I asked why they did not use Biffen, who is often spoken of as the best Tory back-bencher. He said Biffen is a Powellite, and has refused to join the front bench. I asked about Powell. He said he thought Powell had still to be reckoned with—particularly after another defeat in October.

Carrington thought there would very possibly be a coalition government. The Tories would not serve under Wilson, Jenkins (too feeble), or Healey (too arrogant), but would accept Callaghan. Because of 1931 and all that, there could only be a coalition if things got *much* worse.

Carrington said he was keen to have the election on February 7th, when they would have won. The reason it was postponed was not mainly Ireland, but the fact that Ted and Whitelaw thought an election such a long time before the end of the Parliamentary span would be regarded as unnecessary and unpopular.

Carrington recently had lunch with the head of Esso, who told him that up to five years ago British labour, in their world of refineries, pipe-lines, etc., was about 80 per cent as efficient as American. This had now sunk to 40 per cent.

I said I thought some government of the future, whether of the Left or the Right, would have to break the political power of the trades unions. He clearly saw nothing but a steep deterioration in our society in the immediate future, followed by some very autocratic regime.

It was interesting after this lunch to watch the 'Money Programme' on B.B.C. 2 in the evening. An American from the Brooking's Institute said our growth rate had been lower than other European countries, and would soon be negative. The only way to avoid bloodshed was through economic growth, as anything else would mean unacceptable transfers of economic power from one group in our society to another. He and his team had no axe to grind, but were deeply pessimistic about our future. To balance the programme we had the Oxford Professor of Economics who waffled, and Kearton, who pooh-poohed almost everything the American had to say.

I asked Carrington if the suggestions in the newspapers that Keith Joseph might lead his Party had any foundation? He said, 'No.' He said Joseph had managed to give a great deal of money to the Social Services without securing any benefit for the Party. I said surely your Party needs a propagandist. He said, what we need more is a politician! The Shadow Cabinet each week discusses what subject should be brought forward for debate. Much time and thought is given to the problem, but Carrington points out to them that these debates are of interest only to M.P.s and leave the voter stone cold.

Monday, June 17th, 1974

The papers are full of a plan by a West Belfast branch of the U.D.A. for a conference with the I.R.A., no elections for two years, and then no politicians at a discussion of the future of the Province. Paisley, on the telephone, said this was a plan unearthed by the Army when they raided an Orange Hall. The publicity has been provided by the Army in an attempt to discredit Paisley and co. According to Paisley, this represents the view of a small group of U.D.A. men and is of no significance. Meanwhile, he is campaigning in Antrim in an Assembly by-election. The dead assemblyman was pro-Faulkner, but the election has been delayed for a year as it was assumed the new man would be pro-Paisley. Paisley is not counting any unhatched chickens but obviously expects to win.

Both *The Times* and the *Financial Times* this morning plump for an election in early October. This is likely on all the obvious grounds, but Wilson may think a year in the hand is worth five years in the bush—and what years they are likely to be!

Saturday, June 22nd, 1974

The Government has been defeated three times this week, and has had to withdraw its proposals for increased charges for electricity for storage heaters. There has been trouble from SOGAT in the printing industry, and we had no *Times* or *Financial Times* for two days. The retail price index shows a strong rise, and there are to be threshold wage increases of 80p following on last month's £1·20. At the time they were introduced the usual optimists forecast that at most there would only be one increase of 40p and there are still several months to run. The Stock Exchange continues to slump, and we are now down to the lowest level for fifteen years—a worse decline than even that of 1929–31, though less dramatic. It shows what confusion we are in that on the front page of the *Financial Times* one piece groans over the inflation while the article next door is relieved to learn that Healey is ready to reflate. As against the reflation hope, *The Times* says both Whitehall and the Bank are becoming seriously worried, or even alarmed, at the accelerating inflation.

In the by-election for the Assembly in North Antrim, caused by the death of a Faulkner supporter, the Paisley candidate got 30,000 votes, the S.D.L.P. candidate 10,000, the Faulkner Unionist 5,000 and the Alliance man 2,000. The Assembly has been prorogued, but the papers imply that the Government tried to avoid an election although they could not legally do so, and that they had put it off for a year already.

Tuesday, June 25th, 1974

Tony Crosland and David Eccles to dine last night. I had a few words with Crosland about Ireland, from which it appeared that elections to the Assembly are now thought unavoidable. He seemed to think the withdrawal of British troops would follow, though not immediately. Eccles said on leaving that the present Government is ruining the country and cannot see that it is doing much worse than its predecessor. Anyway—apropos of Crosland's Ministry of the Environment and its inability to do anything about the state of Hampton Court Palace—he said it was impossible, with present arrangements, for a Minister to do anything. Mrs Crosland said that Crosland had so much on his plate he had to postpone till next year all transport problems.

Peyton, in the *Spectator* last week, said it was possible for any man or group rich enough to hold up a wide range of developments by means of the Public Inquiry. The Inquiries are expensive, and at the least result in long delays—of which the worst current example is that of the proposed third London airport.

Thursday, June 27th, 1974

Mike to dine last night. He was told by a political informant that Wilson's abdication of authority in his Government was not a voluntary one. It was due to illness.

Friday, June 28th, 1974

Lunch yesterday for Nicholas Ridley. He had no particular information, and seems to be much under Powell's influence, whom he had seen on Wednesday evening. He said Powell was in good form and he ridiculed the idea that Powell is a mental case. He said Powell thought the Tories would lose the election, and his action at the time was to make certain of Ted's defeat. He did, however, rather naïvely suppose that a Labour Government would take the country out of the Common Market, while present indications are that Wilson has no such intention. Ridley said Powell is gambling on Ted going after the next election, and the Tory Party turning to him as their leader. In these troubled times anything is possible, but surely such a denouement is wildly improbable.

Ridley sits for Cirencester, and has spent a lot of time there recently. It is an agricultural constituency and farmers are doing exceedingly badly. They are slaughtering their breeding herds of pigs and cattle, and this must mean very high prices later on. Ridley also said we are forcing a shortage of sugar, which will mean rationing or much higher prices in the autumn. He thought Wilson would have done well to have the election about now. Real trouble might hold off till October, but it might not. On the other hand, Wilson rather enjoys a tightrope act and if he goes to the country he might lose. Why not soldier on?

Ridley thought it possible neither to confront the unions nor to be submissive. Powerful unions that demanded more money would get it—and provided that it was recouped out of higher prices or taxation this would not be inflationary. Strikes should only be seriously fought when they are political—and he doubted if union members would have their hearts in a political strike. This is essentially Powell's point of view. It would mean widespread bankruptcies and unemployment instead of—or perhaps even associated with—inflation.

Ridley said he had recently had lunch with a Swiss banker who said no more Swiss money would be available for H.M.G. There were other sources of loans, but they too would be exhausted soon.

The banking community is becoming uneasy. We have had heavy exchange losses by two important Continental banks, one German and one Swiss; an important American bank in New York and a lesser one in California have gone broke; and now a big German bank in Cologne has closed its doors. This is all a bit too reminiscent of the collapse of the Viennese Kredit Anstalt in the early 1930s.

Ridley said anti-Ted feeling had been growing these last few weeks—an unexpected development for midsummer. He also said that in the House Wilson is far better than when he was P.M before—courteous, witty and benign. All this impresses M.P.s though no one else.

Monday, July 1st, 1974

My Son Francis looked in yesterday. He had some talk with Don Ryder last week. Don had been visiting the packaging plants of Reed's and reported that orders—normally for six weeks ahead—are so strong that they are booked up till the end of February. On packaging for Easter eggs, they have firm orders for twice this year's volume. Packaging is always a fair barometer of trading activity, and this story of boom does nothing to bear out official stories of the levelling off of inflationary pressures.

Don is on the Gas Board, and said that in Peter Walker's day they called on the Minister and asked if he had an energy policy. He said he certainly had one. It was—to have no energy policy!

Later. Lunch at Warburg's with Henry Grunfeld and Eric Roll. Grunfeld had met Wilson at lunch a week ago and said he was in good health and excellent form. Last night on television he was puffy and white with a double chin.

Naturally, they are unhappy about the political and economic situation; but they are particularly nervous about the banks. They think the policy of floating exchanges is not working well, and is encouraging irresponsible gambling. When Herstatt, the Cologne bank closed, it appeared that the Chase Manhattan lost $30 million, and the main Seattle Bank $22 million. The trouble is that no one knows how far out these losses extend.

On balance, my hosts thought this Government somewhat better than Heath's. They expect an election in September with the Tories doing a bit worse than last time.

They thought the attacks on Armstrong, for accepting the chairmanship of the Midland Bank, were unjust. They had considerably upset him.

Thursday, July 4th, 1974

Just back from Dublin, where I had an hour with Cosgrave. He is a terribly nice man—small, modest and honest. I went to see him to tell him of my interest in Irish affairs, as I am about to take up my residence in Dublin. He was friendly and polite, listened to all I had to say with a minimum of comment. Judging by the things said in the Irish newspapers, and by the pronouncements of Irish Ministers, they are entirely out of touch with events in Belfast. Perhaps they take their news and views from the S.D.L.P.

I had lunch with some of the directors of Allied Irish Banks. They seemed fairly cheerful about the state of business in the Republic, but had little information of the state of affairs in the City, and were relatively unmoved by the troubles in the international banking world.

Later. Lunch for John Peyton, now pursuing an independent line on the back benches. He said that if the Tories do not win the next election Ted's days as leader are over. I asked who would be the new leader. He said he had no idea. I suggested Jim Prior, but this evoked no response. I asked about Soames. He said Soames, at the right time and with the right inducement, could be lured back into politics at home, but it would be very difficult to find him a seat. He thought Ted Heath had many fine qualities, but alas is no politician and discourages people from 'looking him straight in the eye and telling him something he doesn't want to hear'.

Peyton thought Wilson was not enjoying himself as P.M., and would seek an early opportunity of resigning. He knew nothing of Wilson's health, which is said to be good in a piece in *The Times* today.

There is much talk in the papers and elsewhere of a national government. I have thought for years that this is inevitable at some stage, but is not possibly on the cards till after the election, and then only if things get obviously worse. Peyton thought the coalition P.M. would more probably be Jenkins than Callaghan.

Peyton has refused to speak on Transport as his Bills—including the Channel tunnel—are being taken over by Crosland.

On the state of the country, Peyton takes a very gloomy view but says the public just doesn't want to know—and clutches at any anodyne phrases when bad news has to be announced.

This afternoon the Government issued a White Paper on Northern Ireland. There are to be elections to a constitutional assembly, but not before the end of the year. Any proposals reached by this body will have to include power-sharing and some all-Ireland feature. When the plan has been agreed in Northern Ireland, it will have to be approved by the House of Commons and approved by a referendum. I have only heard this on the radio, but my immediate reactions are: (1) they don't want the Northern Ireland elections until after the general election; (2) they want to give Faulkner time to retrieve his position; (3) the Government can have no idea of the mess we are in, if they think that Irish affairs can be left to simmer for a whole year.

Tuesday, July 9th, 1974

Lunch yesterday for Norman Collins. He has a position in the Tory Party and the Carlton Club, and sometimes knows what is going on. He had lunch with Ted just before Ted went to China and said Ted was in crashing form. He could not have been more euphoric if he had just won a general election in a landslide! If the Tories do no better in the next election than in the last one, Ted, as leader, is out—to be succeeded probably by Whitelaw. If he gets more votes than Labour, but no over-all majority he will be allowed to linger on, with much discontent in the Party. He will be hard to dislodge as one cannot see him in a secondary position. To step down would probably be to step out. Norman thought Soames is the ultimate right-wing leader of the Party, but he is a difficult man. Norman said Soames could have had the Chichester seat, but that went wrong.

The back-benchers would like to see du Cann as leader, but this is even less likely than it was, owing to the difficulties of Keyser Ullman.

Norman was rather sad about A.T.V. shares, which have dropped from 164 to 46 while profits remain the same. The yield is now over 15 per cent.

As we were leaving Claridge's we ran into Jules Thorn. He is a very cheerful little man (and enormously able). He said he didn't at all like the look of things: did we agree? Indeed we both did. He had written to Wilson, and had had two letters from him—very friendly, very polite, and very optimistic. Does he really know what is happening? I said, probably not, but of course what he says and what he thinks in his case are not necessarily identical.

Wednesday, July 10th, 1974

Lunch yesterday for George Bolton. He was in crashing form—the reason, he said, is because our plight is becoming obvious for all to see. Such clarity will make it easier to do something. He had various items of interest to impart. The loans to nationalized industries and municipal corporations in foreign currencies were launched at 8 per cent at 98; they are now 65 and unsaleable. The British Government cannot now borrow from any foreign source.

Bolton thought much of the trouble in the City was due to Peter Walker. Walker had inserted into a Bill for the Department of Trade and Industry a proviso that the Department could license banks. The secondary banks that have got into trouble were banks that were refused licences by the Bank of England but granted them by Walker, who did not fail to point out the dynamic advance of his banks compared with the older ones. This 'dynamism' consisted of borrowing short and lending long in the property market. Hence all the current tears. Bolton thought the secondary banks should have been allowed to go to the wall. However, they were rescued, whereupon the weaker property companies found themselves in trouble, and they were bailed out, too. Bolton said these two salvage operations meant that the banks now had £3,500 million tied up, essentially in loans on property which they couldn't sell. Bolton is a financial adviser to the Kuwait Government, and so has some idea of what the Arabs are up to. He says most of their oil money is on deposit, withdrawable at seven days' notice. It is a bit doubtful how quickly in practice they could in fact withdraw these huge sums of money. But, anyway, they are very suspicious of Western governments, and have no confidence in their currencies. They were very unfavourably impressed by the propaganda here in favour of an exchange floating downwards to help our exports.

Bolton said it was extraordinary how slow Heath and his Government were to take North Sea oil seriously. This is by far the best news for us since the last war. The oil will begin to flow properly in three years time. But how are we going to bridge the three years? Our credit abroad has gone, and we may have trouble in paying for our food. Bolton, like Ridley, thought sugar rationing inevitable later this year. He thought a very evident crisis unlikely to hold off till October. Wilson should have had his election in mid-summer.

As a result of his years at BOLSA Bolton is close to events in Spain and Portugal. He is very unhappy about events in Portugal. He said General Spinola's book was published with Caetano's consent, and Spinola was nominated by Caetano to take over the coup—provided he and Tomas were looked after. (They are both now living in comfort in Brazil.) Spinola is pretty naive, and supposed development in Africa could be spread over twenty years. Bolton thinks Angola will emerge as an independent state; Guinea he didn't mention; in Mozambique, Vorster of South Africa is busy

374

with both whites and blacks—he is trying to set up a semi-independent state in the southern half of the country, with its capital at Lourenço Marques, which would be under South African domination, aided and abetted by the Rhodesians.

Bolton thought Spinola too naive to last. He thought it impossible for the Spaniards to allow a Communist state to be set up in Lisbon, but the Communists seem to be the only disciplined and coherent group to emerge from the coup. In this morning's paper it is reported that four Ministers have resigned, including the Prime Minister. They cannot work with their Reds.

Thursday, July 11th, 1974

Dinner for Hartley Shawcross—such a nice man, as well as brilliant, and heart-broken at the recent death of his wife. The party, *à trois*, was to try and distract his attention from his sorrows. He said his bank, Morgan Guaranty, had lost money as the result of the collapse of the Herstatt Bank in Cologne—but much less than some others. They have a lot of Arab money deposited with them for three months at a time. This is very hard for them to use, and they are persuading the Saudis to invest at longer term. This is of course early days, and the sums involved will soon be much larger. Like others, he thinks Ted's days as Leader are numbered—but none of the successors are convincing. Hartley supposed Willie Whitelaw would get it, but did not think he would shine as P.M. Norman Collins the other day was trying to promote the cause of Selwyn Lloyd.

Monday, July 15th, 1974

We were at dinner with Hugh and Antonia Fraser last night. Frank Longford was there. He had no real news. He got together a conference on Ireland which met at Oxford. It was good publicity for Frank, but what else? He said last night it was clear at the conference that Faulkner had no longer any part to play.

Tuesday, July 16th, 1974

Lunch for Arnold Weinstock, surely the leading industrialist of the day. He has recently withdrawn somewhat from atomic energy matters, as he does not agree with the latest policy statement by the Government. The C.E.G.B. wanted to order several reactors from the United States, but their request has been turned down and a much smaller programme of British reactors has been authorized instead. The American reactors are of a proven type: they will work; the engineering problems have been solved; the time it takes to build them is known. The heavy water reactors we have chosen are prototypes, that may or may not work, and even if they are satisfactory no one knows when they will be operating. However, the programme is a small one and the Government's decision means in effect that we are opting out of atomic power for the next twenty years, relying on coal and oil which will be much more expensive. Weinstock said atomic energy has wasted far more money than Concorde, though it is Concorde that gets all the criticism.

He met Harold Macmillan one evening recently, and said that there were three alternatives before the country: (1) an extreme left-wing government; (2) an extreme right-wing one; or (3) a national government. Macmillan thought the last much the most likely. I said I thought a national government inevitable, and had thought so for a long time. I assume it will be a failure and will be replaced by some autocratic regime of the Right or Left.

I said I thought conditions at Westminster were such that an election was becoming inevitable in October. Weinstock did not think an election mattered much. What went on in the House would not affect the country one way or the other. If there is an election he supposes it will produce a minority government like the present. Any such government will not be able to pay its way by printing money for more than a few months, and a national government under Callaghan would ensue. He did not think Wilson all that keen to stay on as P.M.

He thought Ministers had a nerve to criticize businessmen, who were not as good as they should be but far superior to Ministers.

He thought Healey's Budget wrong in principle. The top tax on income is to be 98 per cent, and there are to be wealth taxes as well. This amounts to confiscation; and if property rights are to be ignored, what safety is there for other rights?

He thought the policy of successive governments for many years had been in effect to discourage industrial investment, and now he thought any young man with confidence and ambition would do well to move to some other country.

Weinstock thought Benn had been a good Minister in the last Labour Government, but had talked a lot of nonsense in Opposition.

Soames, he thought, the only sixpenny article in the Tories' two-penny stall, but he will only come back into politics if he has a good chance of becoming P.M. Mary Soames, according to Weinstock, would prefer retirement.

Thursday, July 18th, 1974

Lunch yesterday for Stonehouse. He said conditions at Westminster are impossible; there will have to be an election, presumably on October 3rd. He assumes the result will be no over-all majority for either Party. He has heard it suggested that more than half the Scottish seats will go to the Scottish Nationalists. This would mean another thirty seats. The result would presumably be a coalition government, with the Conservatives, Liberals and Scottish Nationals in office. This would mean that the new P.M. would be chosen by Thorpe or Mrs Ewing! Under these sort of conditions there is no future for Heath or Wilson.

Stonehouse said Labour would not take part in a coalition government. Over the last fifteen years or so the position of Labour M.P.s has changed. Formerly, an M.P. could not be de-recognized by the local constituency organization, except with the consent of Transport House, which was not given. His own constituency of Wednesbury started a new policy. The local constituency committee dismissed his predecessor, and were allowed to get away with it. Since then, all Labour M.P.s are liable to have the support of the constituency Party withdrawn and, in effect, to be dismissed at the next election. But these constituency organizations are dominated by militants of various kinds, so there is constant pressure on M.P.s to countenance left-wing policies with which they are not in agreement. Of the three hundred Labour M.P.s, two hundred are deeply concerned —for financial, professional or social reasons—to keep their seats, and therefore make no effort to withstand the pressures put upon them—and this pressure would be all against a coalition government with Labour participation.

I asked Stonehouse why he had not been offered high office. He said—only partly in jest—that favourable mention in my diary was no recommendation in Wilson's eyes. Of Wilson, he said that he is not interested in governing the country, or in his standing in the history books, or in the personal respect in which he is held. He wants to be in 10 Downing St; he is *the* complete pragmatist, and his behaviour is shaped to that one end.

Stonehouse said the Labour Party is not keen on governing—only in governing a socialist state. If they cannot have socialism, they would be quite content with Opposition.

Stonehouse thought Ted stupid, and said it was astonishing what few changes he had made after losing the election. Barber and Chataway had moved off, probably of their own accord; and Maurice Macmillan was the only one to be sent to the back benches, which he should never have left. I asked who was likely to succeed Heath if he had to go in October. He said he thought Keith Joseph the most likely. He dismissed out of hand any idea of Jim Prior, and thought Willie Whitelaw had slipped back in the race. I asked about Soames. He said Soames was unknown to the younger Tory M.P.s and his return as Leader would be blocked by the jealousies and ambitions of the older Tories. He did not mention any possible successor to Wilson.

The coup in Cyprus seems to have been a complete success—the island is quiet, and Makarios is on his way to New York. It is a pity he was not killed, as he will keep the crisis going for months. The Turks are breathing fire and slaughter and are preparing to invade the island. We and the Americans are bound to try and calm the Turks down. The Russians will try and use the occasion to damage the Greeks, to get us out of Cyprus, and to get the Americans out of Turkey. Both the Greek and the Turkish Governments are weak, and may seek a military adventure as a means of shoring up the regime.

The Portuguese are finding that 'freedom' has its problems. The new Government contains more of the officers responsible for the coup, but left-wingers are still in place. Can the Americans or the Spanish tolerate a Communist or semi-Communist regime in Lisbon? That is what it is beginning to look like. Franco appears to be dying, which must inhibit the Spanish Government from any decisive action.

Sunday, July 21st, 1974

The Turks have successfully landed a force in Cyprus, and say their troops will remain for a long time. The Cypriot Greeks are naturally killing off any Cypriot Turks that come to hand. The British Government and the U.N. plead for 'talks'. The Americans seem to be cautiously pro-Greek while the Russians are cautiously pro-Turk. The Greek Army is being mobilized and is said to be massing on the frontier opposite Istanbul, but the Greek Army is smaller and inferior in fighting quality to the Turkish. Both Greek and Turkish Governments are insecure, and it is impossible to guess to what extent this episode is due to wobbly governments seeking to strengthen their internal political stability, and to what extent the future of Cyprus is the real issue. Claims to oil-drilling rights in the Aegean loomed large a short while ago. This issue has not been mentioned since the Cyprus coup, but may be important.

Wednesday, July 24th, 1974

Things in Greece and Cyprus took an unexpected turn yesterday. The new 'President' of Cyprus resigned after eight days and was replaced by one Clerides, and the Greek regime announced a return to civilian government. Meanwhile the Turks are well dug in at Kyrenia and on the road from there to Nicosia. The Greek attempt at Enosis was obviously a bad miscalculation, but the Turkish invasion cannot make the position of the Turkish minority any more secure. In Greece the Army took over in 1967 because successive Governments were not a success. It is difficult to believe that reversing the process will help.

I had lunch at the Bank yesterday—Gordon Richardson in good form and everyone very friendly. There was no particular news— Richardson was obviously alarmed at the growing inflation. He thought the Tory policy had been self-contradictory; prices and incomes restraint on the one hand frustrated by a huge increase of the money supply on the other.

Healey's mini-Budget will make inflation slightly worse. The papers say it is an electioneering Budget, but I doubt if it will have any impact on the voter. *The Times* surmises that it is really aimed at the trades-union chiefs to encourage them to press on with the social contract. However the railways' wage award, announced this morning, of 30 per cent shows what a lot of baloney that is.

Tuesday, July 30th, 1974

There have been three-power peace talks in Geneva, but up to last night they have got nowhere, as the Turks are pouring troops and armour into Cyprus. It is difficult to see what the Greeks can do as they have a smaller Army inconveniently far away, but it is sur-prising that the Americans have done so little to help them.

I spent the weekend with the Walstons. Harry is a fairly regular attendant at the House of Lords. I asked him how he viewed the situation. He said he saw growing confusion caused by inflation and strikes but, further off, events disappeared into an impenetrable fog. He thought—but gave no reasons—that we should get through without violence.

I bumped into John Peyton this afternoon in Piccadilly. I asked how things looked to him. He said 'awful'. He thought it likely that neither major Party would have a clear majority; that there would be more Liberals and Scots Nats in the new Parliament; but he regarded this as only one aspect of the general disintegration to be seen on every hand. No strong government could be provided by such a coalition.

I see in the *Guardian* today attention is called to a General Sir Walter Walker, who seems to be active on the Right. I wonder what he amounts to—if anything.

A point made by Harry I thought interesting. He said that by the time a problem gets to ministerial level for decision there are usually no alternative options, because of decisions made long ago and lower down. This is one of the consequences of our Ministers taking only the shortest views, and not realizing the future of decisions left now to middle-rank civil servants.

Friday, August 9th, 1974

So Nixon has at last resigned, having done all possible damage to his own reputation; to that of the United States abroad; and to the mystique of the Presidency within the United States. The decision was forced on him by the Republican leaders, who showed him that he would be impeached by a huge vote in the House of Representatives, and that he would not be supported by more than fifteen Senators, instead of the requisite thirty-four. It is a contemptible end to a shoddy little man. What is surprising is that his lamentable character has been well known for twenty years or more, but in spite of that he went on being elected. Ford, the new man, is reasonably honest, but gives the impression of being stupid. He takes on the biggest administrative job in the world with no experience of administration of any kind.

In Cyprus the negotiations continue while the Turks enlarge their enclave. It is not clear what is their ultimate objective—presumably in the short run to build up a strong bargaining position which can then be used over Cyprus, and over oil rights in the Aegean.

Thursday, August 15th, 1974

The Cyprus fighting continues, and the Turks seem bent on occupying some 30 per cent of the island, though their population constitutes only about 18 per cent. The United Nations peace-keeping forces, and the British forces in the Sovereign bases have displayed their complete futility, and the Americans seem to have abdicated. All-out war between Turkey and Greece seems unlikely, as the Turks have much stronger armed forces. Whatever is the outcome, the outlook for the Cypriots is pretty bleak.

The *Financial Times* index continues its fall and is now down to the level of fifteen years ago when, however, the purchasing power of the pound was twice what it is now. Other stock exchanges are doing badly—notably the American and French. It does not appear that any Western government has any grasp of the situation. Our balance of trade figures for July were catastrophic, but the Government—and most of the country—seems disposed to ignore them.

Monday, August 10th 1974

The Cyprus fighting continues with the Turks occupying nearly 40 per cent of the island, and showing signs of cutting off Nicosia. Apparently they already occupy territory containing 80 per cent of the wealth of the island, and the refugee problem is becoming uncontrollable. The Americans have been making soothing noises but no more, and Wilson, more excusably, the same. It is not clear yet what the Turks intend, nor why the Americans have abdicated.

Meanwhile, at home the Court Line holiday group has collapsed leaving 100,000 holiday-makers stranded. Both Peter Shore and Tony Benn are being attacked for making reassuring statements that are now seen to have been unjustified. I think Benn was over-keen on nationalizing the shipping side of the group, and both Ministers were less cautious in their public statements than they should have been. It obviously does not help the Labour Party with an election coming up. In Scotland the Labour Party has reversed itself, and is now in favour of an assembly for Scotland. I should have thought the change of heart a bit late to ward off the Scots Nats.

Monday, August 26th, 1974

The Peytons came to lunch yesterday. They had no actual news—John was wondering if the election would be September 19th. If so, it would have to be announced this week. The argument in favour of an early election is that the Labour Party Conference would be avoided—left-wing militants at the Conference would be no help in an election. Of course there may be no autumn election. This might suit Wilson, but he will be under great pressure.

In Cyprus the Turks are digging in and showing no signs of giving up any part of the island that they occupy. They are talking of bringing in Turks from the mainland. Meanwhile there are 200,000 Greek-Cypriot refugees with no housing, or work, for them in the unoccupied area. The Americans continue to sit on their hands.

I asked John Peyton what would happen to the leadership of the Conservatives if they did badly in the coming election. He said he supposed Ted would have to go, but he did not feel any enthusiasm for the alternatives. He said he did not think Whitelaw ever saw himself as the no. 1 man. He thought well of Soames, and thought he should be brought back, but this was obviously not possible at the moment. Carrington, he thought, had dropped out.

Friday, September 6th, 1974

The news this week has been the T.U.C. Congress, and its attitude to the Social Compact or Contract. I think it would be fair to say that the speakers showed more awareness of the dangers of inflation than they have before. The engineers, train drivers and one or two smaller unions were against any limitations on their right to free bargaining, but the engineers were persuaded at the last moment to pipe down, and the result was a massive vote for the Contract. I cannot believe it really means anything, even in the short term. The stronger unions will go on pressing for big wage increases, and any Labour Government will do nothing serious about inflation. Jim Callaghan spoke to the T.U.C. on Tuesday and was more realistic about inflation than is usual for Labour Ministers. It is said, too, that now he is better informed at the Foreign Office, he has come to see the advantages of the Common Market.

Yesterday we had Wilson's speech to the T.U.C. It was mainly routine stuff and not particularly well received. The main interest of the speech was his remarks about the election—still expected on October 3rd—to be announced some time next week. I think the Labour leaders expect to win a clear majority, but the latest opinion poll shows the Conservatives in the lead. Among politicians the expectation is that Labour will lose a number of seats in Scotland,

and perhaps a few in the Midlands which were lost by the Tories owing to the defection of Enoch Powell. The Conservatives may lose some to the Liberals, and the final outcome is quite uncertain.

Thursday, September 12th, 1974

It is now assumed that the election will be on October 10th—it is to be announced early next week. The advantage of October 10th over October 3rd is said to be that the Liberal Conference will help the Liberals and damage the Tories. Today was its big day, and I cannot think it will do more than rally the faithful. Labour keeps on pouring out White Papers. I doubt whether they will win votes, and they are certainly inflationary. The Conservative manifesto is better than the recent form of the Conservatives would lead one to expect. It reads as if it owed more to Keith Joseph and Mrs Thatcher than to Ted Heath. Nevertheless, the programme is inflationary. Did not Ted say today that inflation was the enemy and was to be given first priority—but after pensions and housing!

The crises in Cyprus and Portugal have been damped down, but the whole situation in both areas looks very unstable. The South African P.M. says the South Africans are going to do nothing about a black government in Mozambique—in spite of the importance to them of Lourenço Marques, just over the border. The Argentine does not look too steady, either.

Thursday, September 19th, 1974

The election is to be on October 10th. The announcement came yesterday at midday. It is difficult to say what will happen, though a decisive result is not expected: by decisive I mean a substantial over-all majority. Last night on television we heard the three Party leaders: Wilson, with his white puffy face, has now none of his old bounce left; Jeremy was clear, at times witty, but has a far better hand if only he knew how to play it; Ted was the best of the three, though television is not his medium. He carries a certain amount of weight which the others do not.

Friday, September 20th, 1974

Dinner last night at the Institute of Economic Affairs to hear Professor Friedman. However, he did not talk about inflation or the money supply, which is what we had come to hear, but about free enterprise. I sat between Vernon, a flour miller, I think now part of Spillers, and Dobson, chairman of the British American Tobacco Company. Vernon was almost lyrical about Shirley Williams—easily the best Minister he had ever had to deal with. I talked to a number of people, Geoffrey Eley, Gerald Thompson, Reay Geddes and Norman Collins among others. The atmosphere was pretty gloomy as no one now has any confidence in any of the politicians.

Norman Collins is on the board of some educational institution in London. They had to submit their budget for next year to the I.L.E.A.* They were told to estimate that over-all costs would rise by 20 per cent, but that printing costs would go up by 60 per cent. This seemed so large that he inquired of his friends in print, who said 60 per cent was on the low side, and that he had better raise the figure to 75 per cent!

Friday, September 27th, 1974

Lunch yesterday at Putney with Walter Bolton to meet General Sir Walter Walker, who is organizing a nationwide group of people to help the Government in an emergency. Naturally, he is accused of being a fascist assembling an army of strike-breakers. Walker was until two years ago the general commanding the NATO troops in north-west Europe; he then fell into some official unpopularity for pointing out how overwhelmingly strong the Russian forces were in his area. He argued yesterday that the area from Scotland to Greenland, and all points north and east, are dominated by Russian submarines, which are more numerous and far more powerful than the German submarines at the height of the last war. It is natural that he should pass from the military might of the Russians in western Europe to their political activities within Western countries, where they infiltrate their institutions—and notably the trades unions in this country. He wrote a letter to *The Times* which had a big response, and he still gets five hundred letters a day from citizens anxious to help, but wondering what to do.

Walker is a quick, bright little man, obviously intelligent but not, I should judge, any kind of a national leader. He had not, of course, any secrets to tell me but I got the impression that he thought his followers, by sheer weight of numbers, would swamp the subversive Left.

What Walker said about the Russians reminds me of a Norwegian friend, who seemed to have contacts with the higher intelligence

* Inner London Education Authority.

echelons of NATO. He was present on the Austrian border when the Russians moved into Czechoslovakia to dislodge Dubĉek. At that time he thought the Russians had secured ultimate control of western Europe. Dotting i's and crossing t's could come later.

Tuesday, October 1st, 1974

The election campaign is a flaming disgrace. The Labour Party are confident of a majority and are making the wildest claims—all of which will make the job of governing the country, if in fact they do get in, that much more difficult. Heath looks more convincing on television than he did in February, but that is not saying much. He is fielding his old team of Carr and Walker, while Keith Joseph is the only one who has made any impression on the public mind. The three Parties' policies are all inflationary. *The Economist* costs the Liberal policies at £4,000 million; the Labour one at £2,000 million; and the Conservative at a bit less than £1,000 million. No attempt has been made to tell the British public that they can look forward to a lower—perhaps much lower—standard of living.

Ford, the new American President, is making a very shaky start, and is not helped by his wife undergoing extensive surgery for cancer. Franco is a very weak eighty-one, and Ford and Watergate have diverted the attention of the Americans. So events in Lisbon have been allowed to get out of hand. Spinola has resigned, and it looks as if the alternatives are a Communist takeover or civil war. The repercussions of independence for Mozambique have yet to be seen in Rhodesia and South Africa.

Thursday, October 10th, 1974

This is election day and, for the first time, I do not intend to vote. The performance of all three Party Leaders has been disgraceful— falling over each other to dish out benefits to all and sundry, while only making the vaguest references to the crisis we are in. From all the opinion polls it seems that Labour will win an over-all majority, and that the Scottish Nationalists will do well. The Liberals seem likely to match their February performance but no more. Ruth was talking to Mrs Paisley last night. They seem very optimistic. No mention was made of Gerry Fitt's seat, but they thought they would hold Mid-Ulster, and even Harry West's seat in Fermanagh. I cannot help feeling that the winner of this election will have been presented with a poisoned chalice, if ever anyone was!

Saturday, October 12th, 1974

So it is a majority of three for Labour. On the opinion polls it looked a majority of between 100 and 150. On a low poll the Conservatives did badly, so did the Liberals; the Scots Nats picked up four more seats, but made no impression on Labour. In Northern Ireland the Ulster Unionists did even better than before, except in Fermanagh where Harry West is out, and in South Down where Powell stood as a United Ulster Unionist candidate—he got in but his majority was cut in half.*

For all the brave talk, I doubt if Labour can carry out a very radical programme, or moderate the demands of the unions. I suspect Wilson will be crucified in the next year or two and is almost bound to lose his majority in by-elections if he staggers on for any length of time.

Tuesday, October 15th, 1974

The Times this morning has a long and ponderous leader about the Conservative leadership, the conclusion being that Whitelaw, with all his faults, is likely to get it. The Monday Club has declared itself, demanding a new leader. The contestants are reported as Whitelaw, Keith Joseph and Mrs Thatcher in that order, with Soames as an outsider—and he has only surfaced in the papers in the last two days, while Carrington has been running him for years. I should have thought Soames was the best choice. The fact that he has been out of the House since 1966 is mainly an advantage. Dear Whitelaw is so nice, but Ireland dented him badly and he almost proclaims his ignorance of economics. Perhaps he could act as an umbrella under which a wide diversity of able men would be willing to serve. I cannot see him as a national leader in the rough weather ahead.

Wilson made a speech to the nation last night—pure verbiage with no solid content. The fact that we were facing a crisis of unparalleled magnitude was put over in such a soothing way that it would not have alarmed the most windy listeners.

Wednesday, October 16th, 1974

Dinner last night with Mike. Other guests were Lord Greenhill and Jo Grimond. The conversation turned at one point on the further

---

* The Rt Hon. Enoch Powell had not stood for re-election in February; his speeches attacked Common Market entry and by implication urged the voters to vote Labour.

future. I said we were heading for a dictatorship, either of the Right or the Left, and much would turn on the attitude of the Army. Greenhill said the Army could play no part—look at their impotence over the strike in Northern Ireland. I said a sufficiently ruthless man, with all the machine-guns and the power of the Government behind him, could surely be decisive. Greenhill would not agree, but when I said, 'Then you think a Communist takeover inevitable?' he wouldn't answer. He seemed to me quite futile as I had thought when I met him before. Jo Grimond refused to be drawn about the election. He said I had always been right in my gloomy prognostications, what did I think now? I said this Government is bound to collapse in a year or two, and then I think there will be a national government under whatever name. Jo said, 'But Labour won't come in.' I said, 'They are in; they will be begging for help.' He said, 'Under whom?' I said perhaps Callaghan, perhaps Healey. Jo thought anyway not Jenkins, who seems to be losing ground in the eyes of other politicians.

The talk about a successor to Heath goes on. He should, of course have resigned last February, or at latest last week. But he has not done so. Of the alternatives—Whitelaw, Keith Joseph, Mrs Thatcher and Christopher Soames—I should have thought the last the best, but it seems more likely to be the first, who neither wants the job nor feels adequate for it.

Grimond last night thought the political situation had been left to drift too far, and it is now probably too late to do anything to avoid chaos.

Thursday, October 17th, 1974

Lunch yesterday with Tony Bloomfield to meet Davidson, deputy chairman of the National Westminster Bank, Plumridge, deputy chairman of Pearl Assurance, and Fleet, City editor of the *Daily Telegraph*. We talked a lot about the difficulties of Jessel Securities— very little concrete emerged. They seemed to think share prices had grounded, and property was now unduly cheap, and that Healey would have to help the business world in his November Budget. There was little speculation of any kind—economic or political—beyond next month.

Meanwhile, disorder in Northern Ireland continues and grows. As it is now clear what the composition and policy of the Constituent Assembly would be, there is talk of not convening it. The consequences of pursuing a policy that is clearly not viable are appalling, but there is no sign of any one of the three Parties here changing their course.

This morning I ran into Humphrey Trevelyan in Grosvenor Square. He was very friendly. I asked him how things were, and he said, 'Bad.' In further conversation I asked him what he thought of the Conservative leadership—who should succeed Ted? He said Soames. When he was Ambassador in Moscow he said of all the visiting Ministers of both Parties, Soames was outstanding. He was surprisingly good at handling the Russians.

Friday, October 18th, 1974

Lunch at White's with Hugh Fraser. It had seemed to me that Ted should have resigned from the Party leadership in February—or at the latest, last week. When a man's leadership becomes a subject of angry debate he no longer has the authority or goodwill on which he must depend to continue. But not so, Ted is determined to stay. He has mobilized Central Office and the Whips, and threats are being uttered to anti-Ted members of the 1922 Committee. I said Ted cannot win—the best he can hope for is a split Party, in which he leads one wing. In the meantime his friends will have irreparably damaged all possible successors. Hugh did not seem to think Soames would be acceptable at this stage. For him to come in there must be an interim under, presumably, Whitelaw. But Whitelaw is very loyal to Ted and doesn't want the job. What if Ted calls an election? Whitelaw might refuse to stand against him and Ted might be re-elected! This would not alter the fact that the Tory Party cannot win an election under Ted.

Hugh says Wilson is cock-a-hoop, because he now has his left wing under control. I wonder how long he will be left with that illusion.

Tuesday, October 22nd, 1974

The political news is limited to the violent reactions to a speech of Keith Joseph's at Birmingham over the weekend. He is a highly intelligent man and has been in politics a long time, so it is surprising that what was obviously meant to be a major affair was not more carefully considered. The general theme was the need to remoralize Britain which, God knows, needed saying; but the speech covered far too much ground and included some unwisely phrased words about birth control and the low class, low-grade mother. The result is a huge uproar, which can hardly enhance his chances (in any case slim) of succeeding Ted in the leadership.

Saturday, October 26th, 1974

The papers become more and more trivial. Today *The Times* leads the paper on a Government grant to the thalidomide children. A few days ago it was pointed out that tax would have to be paid on the income from the compensation money. So the Government has chipped in with a grant of £5 million, which will give the thalidomide children a total of £32 million! A further grant of £3 million is to go to non-thalidomide children with serious defects at birth. This huge sum is the result of the campaign in the *Sunday Times*. It means that a handful of thalidomide children are to receive benefits altogether unrelated to the relief paid to other children equally disabled, but from other causes.

No wonder, as George Burton (chairman of Fisons) was saying the other day, the pharmaceutical world is turning away from human remedies to animal ones, and to insecticides and herbicides and, in some cases, is by-passing the English market altogether.

Thursday, October 31st, 1974

Paisley looked in for a couple of hours yesterday evening. He was in excellent form. *Hibernia* has a piece in the current issue prophesying that the new Assembly will have 45 Paisleyites and 19 S.D.L.P. out of 78. If this is clear, why bother with an election? Paisley, I think rightly, argues that there must be an election, and he hopes to get 50 seats.

It is hard to make headway in Irish affairs as Rees is exhausted and depressed, and Wilson has on three occasions refused to meet the Ulster M.P.s. Maguire, the new M.P. for Fermanagh, is the nominee of McManus, the former M.P. If not I.R.A., he is very close to them.

On other than Irish politics Paisley was utterly contemptuous of both Wilson's and Heath's speeches on the Queen's Speech. It seems to be thought that Wilson will retire in a year or so. Heath, Paisley said, is as white as a sheet and very badly shaken. Whitelaw clearly thinks he will be the new Leader of his Party. Paisley thinks —in fact is told by Labour friends—that the Labour Party will be split over the Common Market. When Callaghan was speaking about it yesterday, Michael Foot could not conceal his rage. Paisley thought Prior's performance quite pathetic. The Tory Party has no policy, and in the House back-benchers are vocal in their longing for Ted's departure.

Monday, November 4th, 1974

Lunch with Norman Collins and Frank Longford. Collins is in favour of Ted hanging on for a year and being succeeded by Soames. He is not certain that Soames wants the job. He is said to be anxious to be President of the Common Market Commission in two years' time. Frank didn't take his prospects seriously and thought Ted should hang on.

We talked about Ireland, but it is hard to get any sense out of Frank. He is violently opposed to Paisley and the I.R.A., but seemed to me to have no constructive thoughts.

Later I spent some time at the Irish Embassy talking to the First Secretary. They are committed to power-sharing but seem ready to give it a much more flexible interpretation than hitherto. They don't want border modifications, as they think that would worsen the position of those Catholics left in the Six Counties. They want to see an integrated community in the North, where religion is a private matter, and this they regard as more important than unification. I said such policies were long term. What we wanted now was the next step towards peace and I think that that step is independence. I see it as the only way forward. There is a strong feeling in this country that the Government can make nothing of Ireland and should pull out.

Friday, November 15th, 1974

Since my last entry we have had Healey's third Budget, and have had a couple of days to observe the consequences. Healey provided some relief for industry by relaxing the price code and providing cash for those with liquidity problems. It is not enough to be effective but, judging by his left wing's anger, it is all he could have got away with. He has abolished the favourable treatment for death duties for agricultural land and forests. This, I think, is overdue. He has put a 25 per cent V.A.T. on petrol. We are told that the nationalized industries will have to get around to realistic prices, but the first move in that direction is not to be made till the New Year. So far fairly good, but his warning of the very serious crisis facing us was couched in such anodyne terms that it would mean

nothing to the man in the street. The rest of his Budget was inflationary. In March the 'borrowing requirement' was under £3,000
million; it is now over £6,000 million. The social services are to get
more now, and £1,000 million more in April. The total effect of the
Budget can only be to make a very bad situation slightly worse. It
has been a commonplace for twenty years or more that we have been
spending too much on personal consumption and investing too little.
The continued rise in payments for social security must make a bad
situation worse. Old-age pensioners spend their money; they don't
save it.

Meanwhile, on the international front the deficit on our foreign
trade for October was even worse; the pound has suffered on the
exchange market and the price of gold has soared. So far the pound
has not done too badly as the Arabs have been placing some of their
money here. This of course could change overnight as the money is
on very short-term deposits.

Sunday, November 24th, 1974

Am now permanently resident in Dublin. I have written to Garret
Fitzgerald for an interview but have not yet had a reply. In the
meantime, things in Northern Ireland have gone from bad to worse,
and a number of people have been killed by bomb explosions in
Birmingham. The I.R.A. disclaim responsibility for the latter.

Merlyn Rees is coming out with two Government papers: (1)
describing power-sharing in other parts of the world; and (2) stating
the conditions under which the Constituent Assembly, when elected,
will be able to conduct its work. The first is totally irrelevant and the
second will be ignored. The election is presumed to be due early in
March, as the new electoral register does not come into force until
February. The delay is insane as anything may happen in the interim
and the new register will make no difference. But until the new
Assembly meets it will be impossible for Paisley to make any very
definite move. It is difficult to see what the I.R.A. can do either—
other than carry on with their terror campaign to get the British
Army out of Ireland.

It appears that my friend John Stonehouse was drowned while
on a trip to Florida.* He had purposely lain very low lately, but was

---

* It eventually emerged that John Stonehouse had not drowned. He had in fact
engineered his own disappearance, and at the time of going to press is in Australia
facing extradition proceedings.

an able man, and might have come to the fore under altered circumstances in the Labour Party.

There has been another hijacking of a British airliner at Dubai. It has been flown to Tunis. As usual the Arab authorities are weak as water and are releasing some of their few captured terrorists to secure the release of hostages. Surely the proper course would be to announce the death of all terrorist prisoners if any hostages are harmed—as well as, of course, all the hijackers.

I am interested that the Irish Government has put out a White Paper which is virtually a carbon copy of Denis Healey's. There are to be no austerity measures; priority is to be given to full employment and the maintenance of living standards, even though this does not involve borrowing more each month, both internally and externally. Nobody seems to be bothered about the precipice at the end of that road.

Thursday, December 12th, 1974

Had forty minutes this morning with Garret Fitzgerald at Iveagh House. I had not met him before; he is an attractive man and obviously intelligent. I did not know what the policy of the Dublin Government is and I called on Fitzgerald to find out their thoughts on Northern Ireland.

BIOGRAPHICAL NOTES

ADAMSON, Campbell. Born 1922. Director-General, C.B.I., since 1969. Held various managerial appointments in industry 1945–69. Seconded to the Department of Economic Affairs 1967–9 as Deputy Under-Sec. of State. Has been a member of the National Economic Development Council since 1969.

ALDINGTON, Toby (Lord Aldington). Born 1914. Created Baron 1962. Company director and chairman of the Port of London Authority. Barrister-at-law. Conservative M.P. for Blackpool North 1945–62. Min. of State Board of Trade 1954–7. Chairman B.B.C. General Advisory Council.

BALNIEL, Robert (Lord Balniel). Born 1927. Created Life Peer 1974. Conservative M.P. for Hertford 1955–74, Welwyn and Hatfield 1974. Min. of State Ministry of Defence 1970–72, Foreign and Commonwealth Office 1972–4.

BARBER, Anthony (Lord Barber). Born 1920. Created Life Peer 1974. Barrister-at-law. Conservative M.P. for Doncaster 1951–64, Altrincham and Sale 1965–74. Economic Sec. to the Treasury 1959–62, Financial Sec. to the Treasury 1962–3, Min. of Health 1963–4, Chancellor of the Duchy of Lancaster 1970, Chancellor of the Exchequer 1970–74. Has now retired from active politics.

BARNETSON, Sir William (Lord Barnetson). Born 1917. Created Life Peer 1975. Chairman and managing director United Newspapers since 1966, Reuters since 1968. Leader writer, editor and general manager *Edinburgh Evening News*, 1948–61. Member of the Press Council 1958–61 and since 1968. Director Press Association 1963–70.

BENN, Anthony Wedgwood. Born 1925. Sec. of State for Energy since 1975. Labour M.P. for Bristol South-East since 1950. In 1961 was debarred from sitting, having inherited the title of Viscount Stansgate on the death of his father – he succeeded in disclaiming the title and was re-elected to the Commons in 1963. Postmaster-General 1964–6, Min. of Technology 1966–70, Sec. of State for Industry 1974–5. A member of the Labour Party National Executive Committee 1959–60 and since 1962, he was chairman in 1971.

BIFFEN, John. Born 1930. Conservative M.P. for Oswestry since 1961. Previously worked in Economist Intelligence Unit.

BOARDMAN, Tom. Born 1919. Conservative M.P. for Leicester South-West 1967–74, Leicester South 1974. Min. for Industry, Department of Trade and Industry, 1972–4, Chief Sec. to Treasury 1974. Director and vice-chairman of Allied Breweries.

BOLTON, Sir George. Born 1900. Banker and company director. Adviser to the Bank of England 1941–8, director of the Bank of England 1948–68. Alternate governor of International Monetary Fund 1952–7. Deputy chairman of Lonrho since 1973.

BOYD-CARPENTER, John (Lord Boyd-Carpenter). Born 1908. Created Life Peer 1972. Chairman Civil Aviation Authority since 1972. Barrister-at-law. Conservative M.P. for Kingston-upon-Thames 1945–72. Financial Sec. to the

Treasury 1951–4, Min. of Transport and Civil Aviation 1954–5, of Pensions and National Insurance 1955–62, Chief Sec. to Treasury and Paymaster-General 1962–4.

BRIGINSHAW, Richard (Lord Briginshaw). Created Life Peer 1974. General Secretary National Society of Operative Printers, Graphical and Media Personnel since 1951. Member T.U.C. General Council since 1965. Council member Conciliation and Arbitration Service since 1974.

BROWN, George (Lord George-Brown). Born 1914. Created Life Peer 1970. Labour M.P. for Belper 1945–70. Deputy Leader of Labour Party 1960–70, unsuccessfully contesting leadership in 1963. Min. of Works, 1951, Sec. of State for Economic Affairs 1964–6, for Foreign Affairs 1966–8. Productivity counsellor Courtaulds 1968–73, and now company director. In 1971 published a volume of memoirs, *In My Way*.

CALLAGHAN, James. Born 1912. Sec. of State for Foreign Affairs since 1974. Labour M.P. for South Cardiff 1945–50, for South-East Cardiff since 1950. Assistant Sec. Inland Revenue Staff Federation 1936–47. Delegate Council of Europe 1948–50, 1954. Unsuccessfully contested the Labour leadership in 1963. Chancellor of the Exchequer 1964–7, Home Sec. 1967–70. A member of the Labour Party National Executive Committee since 1957, he has been Treasurer since 1967, and was chairman in 1974.

CARR, Robert. Born 1916. Conservative M.P. for Mitcham 1950–74, for Sutton Carshalton since 1974. Has held various managerial appointments in industry since 1938. Sec. of State for Employment 1970–72, Lord President of the Council 1972, Home Sec. 1972–4. Lost his position on the Conservative Party front bench 1975.

CARRINGTON, Peter (6th Baron Carrington). Born 1919. High Commissioner for U.K. in Australia 1956–9. First Lord of the Admiralty 1959–63. Leader of House of Lords 1963–4. Leader of the Opposition, House of Lords, 1964–70. Sec. of State for Defence 1970–74, for Energy 1974.

CASTLE, Barbara. Born 1911. Sec. of State for Social Services, since 1974. Labour M.P. for Blackburn 1945–50 and since 1955, for Blackburn East 1950–55. Local government and Government service 1937–45. Min. of Overseas Development 1964–5, of Transport 1965–8, Sec. of State for Employment and Productivity 1968–70. A member of the Labour Party National Executive Committee since 1950, she was chairman 1957–8.

CHANNON, Paul. Born 1935. Conservative M.P. for Southend West since 1959. Min. of State Northern Ireland Office 1972, Min. for Housing and Construction 1972–4.

CHATAWAY, Christopher. Born 1931. Conservative M.P. for Lewisham North 1959–66, for Chichester 1969–74. Min. of Posts and Telecommunications 1970–72, for Industrial Development 1972–4. Has now retired from active politics. Represented Great Britain at the 1952 and 1956 Olympics. In 1954, held the world 5,000 metres record. Formerly staff reporter for I.T.N. and B.B.C., 1955–9.

CHICHESTER-CLARK, James (Lord Moyola). Born 1923. Created Life Peer 1971. Unionist M.P. for South Derry, Northern Ireland Parliament, 1960–72. Chief Whip 1963–7, Leader of the House 1966–7, Min. of Agriculture 1967–9, Prime Minister 1969–71. Vice-Lieutenant of County Derry since 1972.

COLLINS, Norman. Born 1907. Deputy chairman, Associated Television Corporation. Worked for Oxford University Press, *News Chronicle* and Gollancz 1926–41, and then for B.B.C., where he was Television Controller 1946–50. Helped to establish Independent commercial television, becoming a director of A.T.V. and I.T.N. Has written over 15 books including *London Belongs To Me* (1945).

COSGRAVE, Liam. Born 1920. Taoiseach (Head of Irish Government) since 1973. Leader of Fine Gael Party since 1965. Barrister-at-law. Member of Dail Eireann since 1943. Min. for Industry and Commerce 1948, for External Affairs 1954-7. Led first Irish delegation to the U.N. assembly.

CRAIG, William. Born 1924. Unionist M.P. for Larne, Northern Ireland Parliament, 1960-73, United Ulster Unionist M.P. for Belfast East, House of Commons, since 1974, Vanguard Unionist Progressive Member for North Antrim, Northern Ireland Assembly, since 1973. Chief Whip 1962-3, Min. of Home Affairs 1963-4 and 1966-8, Min. of Health and Local Government 1964, of Development 1965-6. Founder and Leader of Ulster Vanguard since 1972, and of Vanguard Unionist Progressive Party since 1973.

CROSLAND, Anthony. Born 1918. Sec. of State for Environment since 1974. Labour M.P. for South Gloucestershire 1950-55, for Grimsby since 1959. Lecturer in Economics, Trinity College, Oxford, 1947-50. Sec. of State for Education and Science 1965-7, President of the Board of Trade 1967-9, Sec. of State for Local Government 1969-70. His publications include *The Future of Socialism* (1956) and *Socialism Now* (1974).

CROSSMAN, Richard. 1906-1974. Labour M.P. for Coventry East 1945-74. Fellow of New College, Oxford, 1930-37. Assistant Editor *New Statesman* 1938-55, Editor 1970-72. Min. of Housing and Local Government 1964-6, Leader of the House 1966-8, Sec. of State for Social Services 1968-70.

CUDLIPP, Sir Hugh (Lord Cudlipp). Born 1913. Created Life Peer 1974. Chairman International Publishing Corporation 1968-73. Editor *Sunday Pictorial* 1937-40 and 1946-9. Held editorial and managerial positions on *Sunday Express, Daily Mirror* and *Sunday Pictorial* 1950-63. Chairman Daily Mirror Newspapers 1963-8. Director Associated Television since 1956.

DAVIES, John. Born 1916. Conservative M.P. for Knutsford since 1970. Held various senior managerial and directorial posts in Anglo-Iranian Oil and Shell-Mex and B.P. 1946-65. Director-General of the C.B.I. 1965-9. Min. of Technology 1970, Sec. of State for Trade and Industry and President of the Board of Trade 1970-72, Chancellor of the Duchy of Lancaster 1972-4. Member of N.E.D.C. 1964-72.

DEVLIN, Bernadette (Bernadette McAliskey). Born 1947. Independent Unity M.P. for Mid-Ulster 1969-74. Was the youngest M.P. in the House of Commons when elected.

DOUGLAS-HOME, Sir Alec (Lord Home of the Hirsel). Born 1903. Inherited title (14th Earl of Home) in 1951, but in 1963 disclaimed it for life. Created Life Peer 1974. Conservative M.P. for South Lanark 1931-45, for Lanark 1950-51, for Kinross and West Perthshire 1963-74. Min. of State Scottish Office 1951-5, Sec. of State for Commonwealth Relations 1955-60, Leader of the House of Lords 1957-60, Sec. of State for Foreign Affairs 1960-63 and 1970-74, Prime Minister 1963-4. Leader of the Opposition 1964-5.

DU CANN, Edward. Born 1924. Conservative M.P. for Taunton since 1956. Founded Unicorn group of Unit Trusts 1957. Economic Sec. to the Treasury 1962-3, Min. of State Board of Trade 1963-4. Chairman of Conservative Party Organization 1965-7. Now chairman of Keyser Ullman, merchant bankers.

DUNCAN, Sir Val. Born 1913. Chairman of Rio Tinto-Zinc since 1964. Assistant director, Marketing, National Coal Board 1947-8. Joined R.T.Z. in 1948. Director of the Bank of England.

ECCLES, David (1st Viscount Eccles). Born 1904. Conservative M.P. for Chippen-
ham 1943–62. Min. of Works 1951–4, of Education 1954–7 and 1959–62,
President of the Board of Trade 1957–9, Paymaster-General 1970–73. British
Museum Trustee since 1963, chairman 1968–70. Chairman of British Library
Board since 1973.

EDEN, Sir John. Born 1925. Conservative M.P. for Bournemouth West since
1954. Delegate to Council of Europe and Western European Union 1960–62.
Min. for Industry, Department of Trade and Industry, 1970–72, of Posts and
Telecommunications 1972–4.

EZRA, Sir Derek. Born 1919. Chairman National Coal Board since 1971. N.C.B.
representative at Economic Commission for Europe committees 1948–52.
Delegate to European Coal and Steel Community 1952–6. Director-general of
Marketing, N.C.B., 1960–65. Deputy Chairman, N.C.B., 1967–71.

FAULKNER, Brian. Born 1921. Unionist Member for South Down, Northern
Ireland Assembly, since 1973. Chief Executive Member, Northern Ireland
Executive, 1974. Unionist M.P. for East Down, Northern Ireland Parliament,
1949–73. Chief Whip 1956–9, Min. for Home Affairs 1959–63, for Commerce
1963–9, for Development 1969–71, Prime Minister and Minister for Home
Affairs 1971–2.

FEATHER, Victor (Lord Feather). Born 1908. Created Life Peer 1974. General
Sec. T.U.C. 1969–73. Co-operative employee 1923–37. Joined T.U.C. staff
1937. Assistant Sec. 1947–60, Assistant General Sec. 1960–69. Member of
N.E.D.C. President of European Trade Union Federation since 1973.

FFORDE, John. Born 1921. Executive director of the Bank of England since 1970.
Entered Bank of England 1957. Fellow of Nuffield College, Oxford, 1953–6.
Chief Cashier Bank of England 1966–70.

FITT, Gerry. Born 1926. Social Democratic and Labour Party M.P. for Belfast
West since 1966. S.D.L.P. Member for North Belfast, Northern Ireland
Assembly, since 1973. Leader of S.D.L.P. since 1973. Eire Labour M.P. for
Dock Division of Belfast, Northern Ireland Parliament, 1962–72. Deputy
Chief Executive, Northern Ireland Executive, since 1974. Formerly a mer-
chant seaman.

FOOT, Michael. Born 1913. Sec. of State for Employment since 1974. Labour
M.P. for Plymouth Devonport 1945–55, for Ebbw Vale since 1960. Editor,
Evening Standard 1942, *Tribune* 1948–52, 1955–60. Formerly a political
columnist and critic. Has published many books, most recently a two-volume
biography of Aneurin Bevan (1962–73).

FRASER, Hugh. Born 1918. Conservative M.P. for Stone 1945–50, for Stafford
and Stone since 1950. Sec. of State for Air 1962–4. Was a candidate in the
first Conservative leadership election under the Douglas-Home rules, 1975.
Merchant banker.

GARDINER, Gerald (Lord Gardiner). Born 1900. Created Life Peer 1963.
Barrister-at-law; K.C. 1948. Law Reform Committee member 1952–63. Lord
Chancellor 1964–70. Member of the International Committee of Jurists since
1971. Chancellor of the Open University since 1973.

GEDDES, Sir Reay. Born 1912. Leading Industrialist. Member N.E.D.C. 1962–5.
Director of Midland Bank since 1967, of Shell Transport and Trading since
1968, of Pirelli since 1971. Chairman of Dunlop Holdings since 1968.

GRIMOND, Jo. Born 1913. Liberal M.P. for Orkney and Shetland since 1950.
Leader of the Parliamentary Liberal Party 1956–67. Formerly worked with
U.N.R.R.A., 1945–7.

GREENWOOD, Anthony (Lord Greenwood of Rossendale). Born 1911. Created Life Peer 1970. Labour M.P. for Heywood and Radcliffe 1946–50, for Rossendale 1950–70. Sec. of State for Colonial Affairs 1964–5, Min. of Overseas Development 1965–6, of Housing and Local Government 1966–70. A member of the Labour Party National Executive Committee 1954–70, he was chairman 1963–4. Now a member of the Commonwealth Development Corporation and chairman of the Local Government Staff Commission.

GUNTER, Ray. Born 1909. Labour M.P. for South-East Essex 1945–50, for Doncaster 1950–51, for Southwark 1959–72. Formerly in Railway Clerks' association. Min. of Labour 1964–8, and of Power 1968, from which post he resigned. A member of the Labour Party National Executive Committee 1955–66, he was chairman 1965. President of Transport Salaried Staff Association 1956–64.

HAMILTON, Denis. Born 1918. Editor-in-chief Times Newspapers Ltd since 1967, chairman since 1971. Worked on provincial newspapers 1937–9. Editorial director, Kemsley Newspapers 1950–67. Editor *Sunday Times* 1961–7. Member of the Press Council.

HART, Judith. Labour M.P. for Lanark since 1959. Min. of Social Security 1967–8, Paymaster-General 1968–9, Min. of Overseas Development 1969–70 and 1974–5. A member of the Labour Party National Executive Committee since 1969.

HEATH, Edward. Born 1916. Conservative M.P. for Bexley 1950–74, for Bexley Sidcup since 1974. Administrative Civil Service 1946–7. Government Chief Whip 1955–9, Min. of Labour 1959–60, Lord Privy Seal attached to Foreign Office (in which capacity he undertook the 1963 E.E.C. negotiations) 1960–63, President of the Board of Trade 1963–4. Leader of the Opposition 1965–70 and 1974–5, when he was defeated in the first election for the Conservative leadership under the revised rules. Prime Minister 1970–74.

HESELTINE, Michael. Born 1933. Conservative M.P. for Tavistock 1966–74, for Henley since 1974. Min. for Aerospace and Shipping 1972–4.

HOGG, Quintin (Lord Hailsham of St Marylebone). Born 1907. Inherited title (2nd Viscount Hailsham) in 1950, but disclaimed it for life in 1963. Created Life Peer 1970. Fellow of All Souls College, Oxford, 1931–8. Barrister-at-law; Q.C. 1953. Conservative M.P. for Oxford City 1938–50, for St Marylebone 1963–70. First Lord of the Admiralty 1956–7, Min. for Education 1957, Lord President of the Council 1957–9 and 1960–64, Leader of the House of Lords 1960–63, Min. for Science and Technology 1959–64, Sec. of State for Education and Science 1964, Lord Chancellor 1970–74. Numerous political publications.

HOUGHTON, Douglas (Lord Houghton). Born 1898. Created Life Peer 1974. Labour M.P. for Sowerby 1949–74. Chancellor of the Duchy of Lancaster 1964–6, Min. without Portfolio 1966–7. Chairman Parliamentary Labour Party 1967–74. Formerly Sec. of the Inland Revenue Staff Federation 1922–60. Member of the T.U.C. General Council 1952–60.

HOWE, Sir Geoffrey. Born 1926. Barrister; Q.C. 1965. Conservative M.P. for Bebington 1964–6, for Reigate 1970–74, for Surrey East since 1974. Solicitor-General 1970–72, Min. for Trade and Consumer Affairs 1972–4. Member of Council of Justice 1963–71. In 1975 unsuccessfully contested Conservative party leadership, under the revised rules.

HUME, John. Born 1937. S.D.L.P. Member for Londonderry, Northern Ireland Assembly, since 1973. Min. of Commerce, Northern Ireland, 1974. S.D.L.P. M.P. for Foyle, Northern Ireland Parliament, 1969–73.

JARRATT, Alex. Born 1924. Chairman and chief executive Reed International since 1975. Higher Civil Service 1949–70. Sec. to the National Board for Prices and Incomes 1965–8. Deputy Under-Sec. Department of Employment and Productivity 1968–70. Managing director International Publishing Corporation 1970–73.

JAY, Douglas. Born 1907. Labour M.P. for Battersea North 1946–74, for Wandsworth, Battersea North since 1974. Fellow of All Souls College, Oxford, 1930–37. Journalist on staff of *The Times*, *The Economist* and *Daily Herald* 1929–41. Civil Servant during Second World War. Economic Sec. to the Treasury 1947–50, Financial Sec. to the Treasury 1950–51, President of the Board of Trade 1964–7. Author of a number of political publications.

JELLICOE, George (2nd Earl Jellicoe). Born 1918. Foreign Service 1947–61. First Lord of the Admiralty 1963–4, Lord Privy Seal, Min. in Charge of the Civil Service Department and Leader of the House of Lords 1970–73. Resigned from Cabinet 1973.

JENKINS, Roy. Born 1920. Home Sec. since 1974. Labour M.P. for Central Southwark 1948–50, for Birmingham Stechford since 1950. Son of Arthur Jenkins, M.P. from South Wales. Chairman of Fabian Society 1957–8, Executive Committee 1949–61. Min. of Aviation 1964–5, Home Sec. 1965–7, Chancellor of the Exchequer 1967–70. Deputy Leader of the Labour Party 1970–72, from which post he resigned over the issue of holding a referendum on the E.E.C. President of the United Kingdom Council of the European Movement. Author of many historical and political studies, including *Mr Balfour's Poodle* (1954) and *Asquith* (1963).

JONES, Jack. Born 1913. Member of T.U.C. General Council since 1968. Gen. Sec. Transport and General Workers' Union since 1969. Worked in engineering and docks industries 1927–39. Fought in Spanish Civil War. Held various district, regional and executive secretaryships of T.G.W.U. 1939–69. Has also served in local government. Member Labour Party National Executive Committee 1964–7. Member of N.E.D.C. and C.A.S.

JOSEPH, Sir Keith. Born 1918. Conservative M.P. for Leeds North-East since 1956. Fellow of All Souls College, Oxford, 1946–60. Min. for Housing and Local Government and Welsh Affairs 1962–4, Sec. of State for Social Services 1970–74. Now serves as an economic adviser to the Leader of the Opposition.

KEITH, Sir Kenneth. Born 1916. Chairman Rolls Royce (1971) and Hill Samuel Group since 1972. Chartered accountant. Director of many important companies, including Times Newspapers Ltd. Member of N.E.D.C. 1964–71. A member of C.B.I.–N.E.D.C. liaison committee.

LAMBTON, Antony (Viscount Lambton). Born 1922. Inherited title (6th Earl of Durham) in 1970, but disclaimed it, though keeping courtesy title. Conservative M.P. for Berwick-upon-Tweed 1951–73. Parliamentary Under-Sec. of State, Ministry of Defence 1970–73. Resigned in 1973.

LEVER, Harold. Born 1914. Labour M.P. for Manchester since 1945 (Exchange 1945–50, Cheetham 1950–74, Central 1974–). Financial Sec. to the Treasury 1967–9, Paymaster-General 1969–70. Since 1974 has served as Chancellor of the Duchy of Lancaster and economic adviser to the Government.

LYNCH, Jack. Born 1917. Member of Dail Eireann since 1948. Irish Civil Service 1936–45; also practised at Bar. Min. for Education 1957–9, for Industry and Commerce 1959–65, for Finance 1965–6, Taoiseach (Head of Government) 1966–73. Leader of Fianna Fail party since 1966.

MACLEOD, Iain. 1913–1970. Conservative M.P. for Enfield 1950–70. Min. of Health 1952–5, of Labour 1955–9, Sec. of State for the Colonies 1959–61, Chancellor of the Duchy of Lancaster, Leader of the House of Commons and Chairman of the Conservative Party 1961–3. Became Chancellor of the Exchequer in 1970, but died suddenly a month after the formation of the Conservative Government.

MACMILLAN, Harold. Born 1894. Conservative M.P. for Stockton-on-Tees 1924–9, 1931–45, for Bromley 1945–64. Min. of Housing and Local Government 1951–4, of Defence 1954–5, Sec. of State for Foreign Affairs 1955, Chancellor of the Exchequer 1955–7, Prime Minister 1957–63. President of Macmillan Ltd, publishers, previously chairman. Chancellor of Oxford University since 1960.

MACMILLAN, Maurice. Born 1921. Conservative M.P. for Halifax 1955–64, for Farnham since 1966. Economic Sec. to the Treasury 1963–4, Chief Sec. to the Treasury 1970–72, Sec. of State for Employment 1972–73, Paymaster-General 1973–4. Chairman of Macmillan Ltd 1969–70. Son of Harold Macmillan.

MARSH, Richard. Born 1928. Chairman British Railways Board since 1971. National Union of Public Employees official 1951–9. Labour M.P. for Greenwich 1959–71. Min. of Power 1966–8, of Transport 1968–9. Member of N.E.D.C. since 1971.

MASON, Roy. Born 1924. Sec. of State for Defence since 1974. Labour M.P. for Barnsley since 1953. Formerly a miner and National Union of Mineworkers official 1938–53. Min. of Defence (Equipment) 1967–8, Postmaster-General 1968, Min. of Power 1968–9, President of the Board of Trade 1969–70. Member of the Council of Europe and Western European Union.

MAUDLING, Reginald. Born 1917. Conservative M.P. for Barnet 1950–74, for Barnet, Chipping Barnet since 1974. Economic Sec. to the Treasury 1952–5. Min. of Supply 1955–7, Paymaster-General 1957–9, President of the Board of Trade 1959–61, Sec. of State for the Colonies 1961–2, Chancellor of the Exchequer 1962–4. He became Home Secretary in 1970, but resigned in 1972, when an investigation was undertaken into the affairs of Mr John Poulson, because he felt it inappropriate for him, as Police Authority for the Metropolis, to continue to hold office, in view of the fact that his name had been mentioned at the hearing. He rejoined the front bench as Shadow Foreign Sec. in 1975.

MELLISH, Robert. Born 1913. Labour M.P. for Bermondsey since 1946. Formerly a T.G.W.U. official. Min. of Public Buildings and Works 1967–9, Chief Whip in Government and in Opposition since 1969.

MOSLEY, Sir Oswald. Born 1896. Conservative M.P. for Harrow 1918–22, Independent M.P. 1922–4, Labour M.P. 1924, for Smethwick 1926–31. Chancellor of the Duchy of Lancaster 1929–30. Founded British Union of Fascists 1932, and imprisoned under Regulation 18B during Second World War. Has since lived abroad. Published autobiography, *My Life*, in 1968.

MURDOCH, Rupert. Born 1931. Australian newspaper proprietor. Managing director News Ltd, Australia. Director London Weekend Television since 1971. Chairman News International, publishers of *The Sun* and *The Daily Mirror*.

NIXON, Richard. Born 1913. President of the United States of America 1969–74, resigning after the revelation of his involvement in the Watergate bugging scandal. Lawyer by profession. Congressman 1947–50, Republican Senator from California 1950–53, U.S. Vice-President 1953–61. Unsuccessfully contested Presidency 1960, and Governorship of California 1962.

O'BRIEN, Leslie (Lord O'Brien). Born 1908. Created Life Peer 1973. Entered Bank of England 1927. Chief Cashier 1955–62, Governor of the Bank of England 1966–73. President of the British Bankers' Association since 1973. Director of, or consultant to, many important companies.

PAISLEY, Ian. Born 1926. Protestant Unionist M.P. for North Antrim 1970–74, United Ulster Unionist M.P. since 1974. Protestant Unionist M.P. for Bann-side, Northern Ireland Parliament, 1970–72, Democratic Unionist Member for North Antrim, Northern Ireland Assembly, since 1973. Minister in the Free Presbyterian Church since 1946. Moderator, Free Presbyterian Church of Ulster, 1951. Has published several religious works.

PEART, Frederick. Born 1914. Labour M.P. for Workington since 1945. Min. of Agriculture 1964–8 and since 1974, Lord Privy Seal 1968, Lord President of the Council and Leader of the House of Commons 1968–70. Formerly a schoolmaster, and in local government. Delegate to the Council of Europe 1952–5.

PEYTON, John. Born 1919. Conservative M.P. for Yeovil since 1951. Min. for Transport 1970, for Transport Industries 1970–74. Unsuccessfully contested Conservative leadership in 1975.

PLOWDEN, Edwin (Lord Plowden). Born 1907. Created Life Peer 1959. Chairman of Tube Investments since 1963. Higher Civil Service 1939–46. Chairman Atomic Energy Authority 1954–9. Director of several important companies. Member of Civil Service College Advisory Council. His wife, Bridget Plowden, the educationalist, gave her name to the Plowden Report on primary education.

POMPIDOU, Georges. 1908–1974. Began his career as a schoolmaster with brilliant academic record. A member of General de Gaulle's Cabinet 1944–6. Subsequently director-general of Rothschild's Bank. Director-General of General de Gaulle's Cabinet 1958–9, Prime Minister of France 1962–8, President of France 1968–74.

POWELL, Enoch. Born 1912. Conservative M.P. for Wolverhampton South-West 1950–74, United Ulster Unionist M.P. for South Down since 1974. Fellow of Trinity College, Cambridge, 1934–8. Professor of Greek, Sydney University, 1937–9. Financial Sec. to the Treasury 1957–8, Min. of Health 1960–63. Aroused much controversy from 1968 onwards by his speeches on immigration. Author of many scholarly and political works.

PRIOR, James. Born 1927. Conservative M.P. for Lowestoft since 1959. Farmer and land agent. Min. of Agriculture 1970–72, Lord President of the Council and Leader of the House of Commons 1972–4. Unsuccessfully contested Conservative leadership in 1975.

PYM, Francis. Born 1922. Conservative M.P. for Cambridgeshire since 1961. Previously in local government. Government Chief Whip 1970–73, Sec. of State for Northern Ireland 1973–4.

RAWLINSON, Sir Peter. Born 1919. Conservative M.P. for Epsom 1955–74, for Epsom and Ewell since 1974. Barrister-at-law; Q.C. 1959. Solicitor-General 1962–4, Attorney-General 1970–74, Attorney-General for Northern Ireland 1972–4.

REES, Merlyn. Born 1920. Sec. of State for Northern Ireland since 1974. Labour M.P. for South Leeds since 1963. Teacher and lecturer 1949–63.

REES-MOGG, William. Born 1928. Editor of *The Times* since 1967. Formerly a journalist on *Financial Times* 1952–60 and *Sunday Times* 1960–67 (Deputy Editor 1964–7). Director of Times Ltd since 1968.

RICHARDSON, Gordon. Born 1915. Governor of the Bank of England since 1973. Barrister-at-law 1946–55. Director of many important companies, including Lloyds Bank 1960–67, and Rolls-Royce (1971) 1971–3. Member of Court of the Bank of England since 1967, of N.E.D.C. 1971–3.

RIDLEY, Nicholas. Born 1929. Conservative M.P. for Cirencester and Tewkesbury since 1959. Delegate to Council of Europe and W.E.U. 1962–6. Under-Sec. of State Department of Trade and Industry 1970–72. Formerly director of a firm of engineering contractors.

RIPPON, Geoffrey. Born 1924. Conservative M.P. for Norwich South 1955–64, for Hexham since 1966. Barrister; Q.C. 1964. Mayor of Surbiton 1951–2. Member London County Council 1952–61. Leader of Conservative Party on L.C.C. 1957–9. Min. of Public Building and Works 1962–4, of Technology 1970, Chancellor of the Duchy of Lancaster 1970–72, Sec. of State for the Environment 1972–4.

ROBENS, Alfred (Lord Robens of Woldingham). Born 1910. Chairman Vickers Ltd, since 1971. Director of the Bank of England since 1966, of Times Newspapers Ltd since 1967. Union of Distributive and Allied Workers' official 1935–45. Labour M.P. for Wansbeck 1945–50, for Blyth 1950–60. Min. of Labour and National Service 1951. Chairman of the National Coal Board 1961–71, of which he published an autobiographical memoir, *Ten Year Stint*, in 1972. Member of N.E.D.C. since 1962.

ROLL, Sir Eric. Born 1907. Director of the Bank of England since 1968, and chairman of S. G. Warburg and Co. since 1974. Professor of Economics at Hull University 1935–46. Higher Civil Service 1946–66, including delegations to Organization for European Economic Co-operation, NATO, E.E.C. Head of Treasury delegation, Washington, 1963–4. Permanent Under-Sec. Department of Economic Affairs 1964–6. Director of many companies, including Times Newspapers Ltd, since 1967. Member of N.E.D.C. since 1971.

RYDER, Sir Sydney (Sir Don) (Lord Ryder). Born 1916. Created Life Peer 1975. Industrial adviser to the Government since 1974. Chairman National Enterprise Board since 1975. Chairman Reed International 1968–75. Editor *Stock Exchange Gazette* 1950–60. Director International Publishing Corporation 1963–70 and managing director Reed Paper Group 1963–8.

SANDYS, Duncan (Lord Duncan-Sandys). Born 1908. Created Life Peer 1974. Conservative M.P. for Norwood 1935–45, for Streatham 1950–74. Min. of Works 1944–5, of Supply 1951–4, of Housing and Local Government 1954–7, of Defence 1957–9, of Aviation 1959–60, Sec. of State for Commonwealth Relations 1960–64. Founded European Movement 1947, led delegation to European Consultative Assembly 1970–72.

SCANLON, Hugh. Born 1913. President Amalgamated Union of Engineering Workers since 1968. Official of the Amalgamated Engineering Union 1947–67. Member of the T.U.C. General Council since 1968, of N.E.D.C. since 1971.

SHAWCROSS, Hartley (Lord Shawcross). Born 1902. Created Life Peer 1959. Barrister-at-law; K.C. 1939. Chief Prosecutor at Nuremburg Trials 1946. Labour M.P. for St Helens 1945–58. Attorney-General 1945–51, President of the Board of Trade 1951. Delegate to the United Nations 1945–9. Director of many important companies. Chairman of the Press Council since 1974.

SHORE, Peter. Born 1924. Sec. of State for Trade since 1974. Labour M.P. for Stepney 1964–74, for Tower Hamlets since 1974. Political economist. Head of Labour Party Research Department 1959–64. Sec. of State for Economic Affairs 1967–9, Min. without Portfolio 1969–70.

SHORT, Edward. Born 1912. Leader of the House of Commons since 1974.

Deputy Leader of the Labour Party since 1972. Labour M.P. for Newcastle-upon-Tyne Central since 1951. Formerly a schoolmaster and in local government. Government Chief Whip 1964–6, Postmaster-General 1966–8, Sec. of State for Education and Science 1968–70.

SOAMES, Sir Christopher. Born 1920. Vice-President Commission of the European Communities since 1973. Conservative M.P. for Bedford 1950–66. Sec. of State for War 1958–60, Min. of Agriculture 1960–64. Ambassador to France 1968–72.

STEWART, Michael. Born 1906. Labour M.P. for Fulham since 1945. Schoolmaster 1930–42. Sec. of State for Education and Science 1964–5, for Foreign Affairs 1965–6 and 1968–70, for Economic Affairs 1966–7.

STONEHOUSE, John. Born 1925. Labour M.P. for Wednesbury 1957–74, for Walsall North since 1974. Director of London Co-operative Society 1956–62. Delegate to the Council of Europe and W.E.U. 1962–4. Min. of Aviation 1967, Min. of State for Technology 1967–8, Postmaster-General 1968–9, Min. of Posts and Telecommunications 1969–70. Disappeared off Florida in 1974, reappeared a month later in Australia, and has since been extradited in connection with the activities of several companies of which he was director.

THATCHER, Margaret. Born 1925. Leader of the Opposition since 1975. Conservative M.P. for Finchley since 1959. Research chemist 1947–51. Barrister-at-law. Sec. of State for Education and Science 1970–74. Became the first woman to lead any British political party on winning the Conservative leadership in 1975.

THOMPSON, Gerald. Born 1910. Chairman Kleinwort Benson Ltd since 1971; previously vice-chairman and director. Joined Kleinwort Sons and Company in 1933. Director of associate companies.

THOMSON, George. Born 1921. Member Commission of the European Communities since 1973. Labour M.P. for Dundee East 1952–72. Editor *Forward* 1948–53. Chancellor of the Duchy of Lancaster 1966–7 and 1969–70, Sec. of State for Commonwealth Affairs 1967–8, Min. without Portfolio 1968–9.

THOMSON, Roy (Lord Thomson of Fleet). Born 1894. Created 1st Baron 1964. Newspaper proprietor. Chairman The Thomson Organization (subsidiaries include *The Times* and *Sunday Times*). Other interests include package holidays and North Sea Oil. Controls a number of provincial newspapers and has extensive transatlantic newspaper interests. Vice-chairman of Commonwealth Press Union Council 1963–72.

THORN, Sir Jules. Chairman of Thorn Electrical Industries since 1937, and of many other important companies. Chairman of the Radio Industry Council 1966.

THORPE, Jeremy. Born 1929. Liberal M.P. for North Devon since 1959. Leader of the Liberal Party since 1967. Barrister-at-law.

TREVELYAN, Humphrey (Lord Trevelyan). Born 1905. Created Life Peer 1968. Indian Political and Civil Service 1929–47. Entered Diplomatic Service, and pursued a distinguished career. Served in Baghdad and Peking, Ambassador to Egypt 1955–6, Iraq 1958–61, U.S.S.R. 1962–5. Now director of many important companies, including B.P. and General Electric.

TWEEDSMUIR, LADY (Baroness Tweedsmuir of Belhelvie). Born 1915. Married 2nd Baron Tweedsmuir, but created Life Peeress in her own right in 1970. Conservative M.P. for South Aberdeen 1946–66. Delegate to the Council of Europe 1950–53, to U.N. General Assembly 1960–61. Min. of State Scottish Office 1970–72, Foreign and Commonwealth Office 1972–4.

WALDEN, Brian. Born 1932. Labour M.P. for Birmingham since 1964. University lecturer. Member of National Union of General and Municipal Workers. Opposition front-bench spokesman on finance 1971–3.

WALKER, Peter. Born 1932. Conservative M.P. for Worcester since 1961. National chairman of Young Conservatives 1958–60. Chairman Rose, Thomson and Young 1956–70. Deputy Chairman Slater Walker Securities 1964–70. Min. of Housing and Local Government 1970, Sec. of State for the Environment 1970–72, for Trade and Industry 1972–4. Lost his position on Conservative Party front bench 1975.

WEINSTOCK, Sir Arnold. Born 1924. Managing director General Electric since 1963. Junior Administrative Officer Admiralty 1944–7. Engaged in finance and property dealing 1947–54, in Radio and allied industries 1954–61. Director of Rolls-Royce (1971) 1971–3.

WEST, Harry. Born 1917. Leader of Unionist Party since 1974. Unionist Member for Fermanagh and South Tyrone, Northern Ireland Assembly, since 1973. Unionist M.P. for Enniskillen, Northern Ireland Parliament, 1954–72. United Ulster Unionist M.P. for Fermanagh and South Tyrone, 1974. Minister of Agriculture 1960–67 and 1971–2.

WHITELAW, William. Born 1918. Conservative M.P. for Penrith and the Border since 1955. Chief Opposition Whip 1964–70. Lord President of the Council and Leader of the House of Commons 1970–72, Sec. of State for Northern Ireland 1972–3, for Employment 1973–4. Unsuccessfully contested Conservative leadership in 1975.

WILLIAMS, Shirley. Born 1930. Sec. of State for Prices and Consumer Protection since 1974. Labour M.P. for Hitchin 1964–74, for Hertford and Stevenage since 1974. General Sec. Fabian Society 1960–64. Member Labour Party National Executive Committee since 1970. Held various junior ministerial posts in the Labour Government of 1964–70.

WILSON, Harold. Born 1916. Prime Minister and First Lord of the Treasury since 1974, and 1964–70. Labour M.P. for Ormskirk 1945–50, for Huyton since 1950. Lecturer in economics at Oxford 1937–45. Sec. for Overseas Trade 1947, President of the Board of Trade 1947–51. Became Leader of the Labour Party in 1963. Leader of the Opposition 1970–74.

WINDLESHAM, David (Lord Windlesham). Born 1932. Succeeded to title (3rd Baron) in 1962. Managing director of A.T.V. since 1974. Formerly held managerial and directorial positions in Rediffusion and Grampian Television 1965–70. Min. of State Northern Ireland 1972–3, Lord Privy Seal and Leader of the House of Lords 1973–4.

INDEX

Adamson, Campbell, 28, 31, 47, 54–5, 89, 95–6, 132, 186–7, 267
Agnew, Spiro, 148, 253, 311
Aitken, Jonathan, 222–3
Aitken, Sir Max, 82, 115–16, 167
Aldington, 1st Baron (Toby Low), 54, 56, 67, 73, 81, 229
Ali, Reuter man in Teheran, 226
Allen, Sir Douglas, 33, 101, 118, 187
Allen, Maurice, 63, 274
Allende, Señor, 241
Amalgamated Engineering Union, 195, 203
Amalgamated Society of Woodworkers, 194
Amalgamated Union of Engineering and Foundry Workers, 46, 114, 329
Amery, Julian, 16
Amin, General Idi, 163, 275
Anatomy of Britain (Sampson), 166
Anderson, U.D.A. leader, 232
Andrews, Senator John, 188
Annan, Noel (Baron Annan), 16, 200
Anne, Princess, 295
Armstrong, William, 158
Armstrong, Sir William, 371
Asquith, H. H. (Earl of Oxford and Asquith), 236
Association of British Chambers of Commerce, 118–19
Associated Society of Locomotive Engineers and Footplate Men, 241–2, 266, 339, 342
Associated Television Corporation, 27, 45, 272, 373
Astor, Gavin, 15, 72
Attenborough, Richard, 272
Attlee, Clement (Earl Attlee), 210
Avon, Earl of (Sir Anthony Eden), 27, 135

Baden-Powell, 3rd Baron, 304
Baldwin, Stanley (Earl Baldwin of Bewdley), 276
Balfour, A. J., 345
Balniel, Lord, 16, 35, 148–9, 154, 175
Balogh, Thomas (Baron Balogh), 333, 351
Bank of England, 13, 20n, 33–4, 36, 51, 53–4, 72, 81, 108, 116, 155, 201, 206, 234–5, 238, 263, 265, 273, 277, 293, 300, 306–7, 315, 319, 368, 374, 379
Barber, Anthony, 28–9, 52, 53, 56, 82,
106, 126, 142, 148, 153–5, 178, 187, 352; succeeds Macleod, 26–7, 46; ability of, 33, 35, 38, 50, 55, 57, 66, 79, 107–8, 115, 118, 186, 222, 237–8, 247, 264, 276, 291, 300; and mini-budgets, 77, 332; plans for reflation, 122–4; and industrial relations, 195, 213; and tax reforms, 206; appointed chairman Conservative Party Policy Committee, 225; and inflation, 256, 277, 284, 286, 299; and E.E.C., 270; proposed move of, 271, 274, 286; attacks Powell, 311; and 5% growth, 316; and trade figures, 322; attacks Wilson, 324; retirement of, 357, 378
Bareau, Paul, 265
Barnes, Sir Denis, 15
Barnetson, Sir William, 64, 71–2, 84–5, 112–13, 136, 214, 279–80, 322, 364
Barr, spokesman for Irish strikers, 366
Barran, Sir David, 146
Barrios, Brazilian politician, 105
Baylis, Clifford, 59, 201
Beeching, Dr Richard (Lord Beeching), 34, 87, 267, 286
Belfast Telegraph, 196–7
Benn, Anthony Wedgwood, 30, 132, 145, 177, 192, 228–30, 236, 241, 248, 327, 376, 381
Benney, A. G., 285
Bernstein, Sydney, 113, 213
Berry, Michael (Baron Hartwell), 18, 64
Berry, Lady Pamela (Lady Hartwell), 155
Berthoin, Georges, 243
Bessborough, Eric, 47, 46
Bethell, Major-General Donald, 121, 155
Beuve-Méry, M, 182
Bevin, Ernest, 37
Biffen, John, 212, 219, 247, 266, 298, 366
Birch, Reg, 203
Blakely, Stormont Minister, 140
Blakenham, Viscount (John Hare), 123
Bloomfield, Tony, 206, 215, 234, 246–7, 273, 281, 299, 328, 347, 387
Boal, Desmond, 137, 141, 147, 151, 341
Boardman, Tom, 231–2, 282, 284, 333
Bolton, Canon, 285
Bolton, Sir George, 53–5, 67–8, 104, 115, 117, 146, 151, 166, 209, 223, 265, 278–9, 290, 317–19, 373–4
Bolton, Walter, 384

405

Bonfield, John, 83
Borthwick, meat importer, 301
Boyd-Carpenter, John (Baron Boyd-Carpenter), 107, 120
Boyle, of B.B.C., 242
Boyson, Dr Rhodes, 167
Bracken, Brendan, 242–3
Bradford, Roy, 355, 360
Brandt, Willy, 53, 68, 113, 183–4, 359
Brezhnev, Leonid, 240
Briginshaw, Richard, 18, 64, 70–71, 83, 203, 240–41, 288
British Broadcasting Corporation, 20, 32, 47, 102, 183, 229, 242, 248, 270, 305, 309, 362
Brittan, Samuel, 278
Brookeborough, Lady, 207
Brown, Dr, 170 and n
Brown, George (Lord George-Brown), 15, 17, 28, 83, 91
Brown, Sophie (Lady George-Brown), 91
Brunton, Gordon, 58
Buchan-Hepburn, 184
Buckton, Ray, 340
Buckton, Mrs Ray, 339
Burgess, Sir John, 123
Burnet, Alastair, 152
Burnet, of National Westminster Bank, 293
Burroughes, civil servant, Belfast, 57
Burton, George, 389
Butler, R. A. (Lord Butler of Saffron Walden), 83, 158, 327

Caetano, 374
Cahill, Provisional I.R.A. leader, 208
Callaghan, James, 17, 92, 121, 131, 142, 149, 157, 159–60, 172, 177, 186, 323, 345, 355, 357, 367, 372, 376, 382, 387, 389
Cannon, Leslie, 18
Caradon, Lord (Hugh Foot), 214
Carli, of Central Bank of Italy, 68, 104
Carr, Robert, 28, 36, 56, 66, 94, 100, 123, 153, 156, 175, 180, 187, 193, 195, 198, 204, 272, 315; at Ministry of Labour, 15, 22; ability of, 25–6, 31, 41, 43, 46, 54, 78, 95, 107, 222, 238, 299, 325, 357; and wages, 29, 34–5, 37, 58, 77, 91; addresses industrialists at C.B.I., 44; and power go-slow, 71; bombs at house of, 79; and Industrial Relations Bill, 92, 177; becomes Home Secretary, 217, 220; and industrial relations, 219, 224, 244; and Ugandan Asians, 225; and relations with police, 319; appointed Shadow Chancellor, 352; as possible successor to Heath, 365; and Oct. 1974 election, 385

Carrington, Lord (Peter Carrington), 15, 69–70, 100, 120, 130, 135, 148, 175, 196, 202, 267–8, 271, 368; at Ministry of Defence, 22, 34; and Northern Ireland, 35, 129, 154, 214, 221, 308, 366; and 1970 election, 36; ability of, 39, 46, 55, 79, 101–2, 115–17, 119, 121, 317; and industrial relations, 98–9, 343; and economic prospects, 215, 367; and formation of March 1974 Shadow Cabinet, 352; and party relations, 361; and possibility of succeeding Heath, 382, 386
Carroll, chairman of BOLSA, 146
Castle, Barbara, 18, 25, 57, 88–90, 132, 153, 157, 203, 350, 362
Castle, Ted (Lord Castle), 362
Castro, Fidel, 62
Cecil King Diary 1965–1970, The, 238n
Chaban-Delmas, Jacques, 182, 355
Channon, Paul, 188, 232
Chapple, Frank, 83
Chataway, Christopher, 206, 282, 378
Cheadle, Eric, 364
Chenevix-Trench, Anthony, 35–6
Chichester-Clark, Major James (Baron Moyola), 17 and n, 18, 57, 80, 93, 99
Churchill, Randolph, 243
Churchill, Sir Winston, 65, 182–4, 242
Clapham, Sir Michael, 236
Clerides, of Cyprus, 379
Cole, Baron (George Cole), 58, 103, 119
Collins, Canon, 41
Collins, Norman, 28, 45–6, 98, 111, 152, 158, 199, 271–2, 373, 375, 384, 390
Confederation of British Industry (C.B.I.), 28 and n, 44, 47, 54, 82, 89, 118–19, 122, 123, 125, 127, 132, 146, 177, 180, 208, 219, 228–30, 234–7, 245, 267, 273, 286, 305, 327, 344, 360
Connally, John, 148, 179
Conway, Cardinal, 97, 215
Cooke, Mrs Alastair, 326
Cooper, David, 365
Cooper, John (Baron Cooper of Stockton Heath), 114
Cooper-Key, Neill, 79
Corfield, Sir Frederick, 90, 106
Corriere della Sera, 65
Cosgrave, Liam, 269, 308, 313, 328, 331, 353–4, 355, 365, 371
Court, Charles, 53
Couve de Murville, Maurice, 85–6, 104–5
Cowles, Mike, 85–6
Craig, William, 93, 202, 205, 207, 214, 272, 296, 319, 324, 341, 350, 365
Creswell, Sir Michael, 17
Critchley, Julian, 304
Cromer, 3rd Earl of, 51, 56, 68, 81, 300
Crosfield, Hermione, 268